"This is an outstanding volume with a star-studded lineup of editors and authors, with strong credibility in behavioral science and its progression. The editors mount a compelling case for the merits of behavioral science as an academic and applied field, and one in which these integrate coherently. For authors or students wishing to update on what behavior analysis has done since Skinner, this volume is a must. While it is dense and accurate, it is readable and digestible. An excellent addition to a complex area of psychology, but one which the editors and authors convince us is worth grappling with."

> —**Yvonne Barnes-Holmes, PhD**, associate professor in behavior analysis, and senior research fellow at Ghent University

"A truly remarkably and needed book that provides a comprehensive analysis of fundamental behavioral processes and contemporary theory, research, and practice published in the areas of language and cognition. It synthesizes Skinner's analysis of verbal behavior with contemporary relational frame theory (RFT), and progressively introduces important core concepts such as stimulus equivalence classes, response generalization, referencing, perspective taking, problem-solving, and rule-governed behavior. Acceptance and commitment therapy (ACT) is presented as a contemporary behavior analytic therapy that addresses the implications of the science of language and cognition for practice and instruction of applied behavior analysis. This book should be required reading in every graduate program in psychology and behavior analysis."

> —**Martha Pelaez, PhD**, professor in the department of educational psychology at Florida International University

"I highly recommend this book to academicians, researchers, and scientific practitioners who are interested in the advancement and application of behavior science. Central threads in behavioral accounts of sociocultural phenomena highlight communication, and ways language plays a fundamental role in human behavior. The selection of chapters coedited by Fryling, Rehfeldt, Tarbox, and Hayes illustrate the power of behavior science and collective abilities of our scientific group to respond to the emerging opportunities for scientific impact. In that regard, the authors lay substantial groundwork for the advanced analyses of language and cognition with workable implications for development and dissemination of associated technologies."

> —**Ramona A. Houmanfar, PhD**, professor in the department of psychology, and director of the behavior analysis program at the University of Nevada, Reno

Applied Behavior Analysis of Language & Cognition

CORE CONCEPTS & PRINCIPLES FOR PRACTITIONERS

Edited by
MITCH FRYLING, PhD
RUTH ANNE REHFELDT, PhD
JONATHAN TARBOX, PhD
LINDA J. HAYES, PhD

CONTEXT PRESS
An Imprint of New Harbinger Publications, Inc.

Distributed in Canada by Raincoast Books

Copyright © 2020 by Mitch Fryling, Ruth Anne Rehfeldt, Jonathan Tarbox,
and Linda J. Hayes
Context Press
An imprint of New Harbinger Publications, Inc.
5674 Shattuck Avenue
Oakland, CA 94609
www.newharbinger.com

Cover design by Amy Shoup

Acquired by Ryan Buresh

Edited by Rona Bernstein

Indexed by James Minkin

Figure 16.1. is used by permission from Springer Nature. Adaptation of "Derived Stimulus Relations and Their Role in a Behavior Analytic Account of Human Language and Cognition"; Barnes-Holmes, Finn, McEnteggart et al; *Perspectives on Behavior Science.* Copyright January 1, 2017.

Library of Congress Cataloging-in-Publication Data on file

Printed in the United States of America

22   21   20

10   9   8   7   6   5   4   3   2   1   First Printing

Contents

CHAPTER 1

An Introduction to Applied Behavior Analysis of Language and Cognition

Linda J. Hayes
University of Nevada, Reno

Progress toward a natural science of behavior has been delayed by a number of difficulties. The first of these—the attribution of causal status to nonmaterial entities—has been overcome by the exclusion of hypothetical, nonnatural elements and their powers from the events making up the subject matter of a science of behavior (Kantor, 1924). While not all behavior scientists have forfeited the right to postulate unobserved entities for purposes of explanation, the need for such entities and their forces is proportional to the absence of information derived from observational sources. Hence, advances in observational methods and technologies may be expected to make such distractions increasingly unnecessary.

A second difficulty pertains to the definition of a unit behavioral event. The units of analysis problem has been resolved, for the most part, by sacrificing the uniqueness of individual responses for the affordances of response class constructions. More than one such unit has been proposed, though Skinner's (1938) concept of the operant has proven particularly valuable. The criteria proposed by Skinner for the membership of responses in operant classes included their conditions of occurrence, a provision enabling not merely prediction but also control over class member occurrences. Further, because prediction and control of class member occurrences are more readily demonstrated when such occurrences are taking place at high frequencies, Skinner (1953) proposed that preliminary investigations focus on simple responses of arbitrary form that could occur at high frequencies without significant fatigue for extended periods of time. The notion was that this preparation would permit for the development of laws and principles of behavior that, subsequently, would be applicable to more complex, nonarbitrary forms of responding. With this aim and upon this premise, the science of behavior proceeded.

The absence of sophisticated observational technologies at the time of these developments placed severe limitations on the automated detection of even simple responses, however, representing a third factor delaying progress of the natural science of behavior.

Automated detection of responses demanded that they be localized on particular mechanical operanda (e.g., levers, keys), the operations of which were substituted for measures of responding. As a result, the nuances of individual responses fell below the threshold of instrumental precision. Still, Skinner's experimental preparations (e.g., Skinner, 1938; Ferster & Skinner, 1957) resulted in a corpus of principles (e.g., stimulus control, reinforcement, extinction) that proved applicable to the behavior of a wide variety of species and led to the development of a powerful technology of behavior change presently being employed in many domains of human activity. All the research presented in this volume, with the exception of that in chapter 7 by Emilio Ribes, rests on a foundation of the principles of behavior as construed by Skinner.

Challenges Related to the Subject of Behavior

The promise of an experimental analysis of unrestricted, nonarbitrary forms of responding, and their elaboration into more complex forms, has not been fully realized. For the most part, this circumstance is owing to the subject matter of behavior science. Behavior has a number of features that complicate its scientific investigation. In the first place, behavior is not a thing localizable in an organism, but is rather a function resulting from responding and stimulating, taking place in a field of many other factors. As such it is not possible to identify or classify behavior in the absence of information about the setting in which it is occurring. Measurement practices thereby must be capable of capturing functional relations between behavior and environmental variables, not merely the occurrence of responses with particular formal properties.

Secondly, behavior does not come in discrete units, but rather occurs as a continuous stream of activity. Hence, where one event ends and another begins must be determined on the basis of arbitrary criteria, presenting significant difficulties for the replication of findings. While substituting switch closures for responses solves this problem of measurement, it also distorts the character of the events measured. More worrisome is that the prediction and control of behavior—operations achieved by way of a frequency-based interpretation of probability—*require* that the character of behavior be distorted in this way. Practices capable of depicting behavior as a continuous stream of activity are needed to solve this problem.

Added to this, behavior is the action of the whole organism, and in this regard, it is always a complex phenomenon involving the simultaneous participation of multiple response systems (e.g., muscular, neurological, sensory, glandular). Complete descriptions of behavior thereby entail consideration of its relevant organismic components, implying the need for measurement in real time.

Finally, behavior is corrigible. This is to say it is a continuously changing repertoire, becoming more elaborate and more varied with respect to contextual circumstances over the course of its development. As such, response events initially selected for measurement are likely to have evolved into different forms and to have developed different relations with environing events over the course of their investigation. This circumstance is of particular concern when the behavior at issue is verbal in kind. Verbal behavior is especially difficult to investigate due to its substitutive character (Kantor, 1936, 1977), conventionality—and thereby arbitrariness—of response forms (Kantor, 1982), and enormous topographical variation. Perhaps it is for this reason that more than one conceptualization of the verbal repertoire, as revealed in the chapters of this book, have been developed in the science of behavior over the last half century.

Most behavior analysts are familiar with at least some aspects of B. F. Skinner's (1957) analysis of this repertoire. More specifically, most are familiar with the elementary verbal operants, particularly those in which the stimulus products of verbal responding show formal similarity with prior verbal stimuli (i.e., echoic, copying text), those in which the stimulus products of responding share point-to-point correspondence with prior stimuli (i.e., taking dictation, textual) and those occurring under the control of conditions other than prior verbal stimuli (i.e., tact and mand). Less familiar, and less often investigated and validated in application, are the elementary operants characterized by more complex contingencies (i.e., intraverbal and autoclitic). The elementary verbal operants were differentiated by the unique contingencies into which response instances could be organized as members. These classes have enormous numbers of members, and their identification was not Skinner's primary aim in writing the book *Verbal Behavior*. Rather, his primary aim was to consider the contributions of historical conditions and current stimuli such as to foretell the topographical and dynamic features of a "single forthcoming instance of verbal behavior" (1957, p. 28). How he proposed to pursue this aim is not obvious until after the eighth chapter of *Verbal Behavior* where he discusses multiple causation and supplementary stimulation. With respect to *this* aim, and in the present author's perspective, Skinner comes closer to its achievement than any other theorist.

Criticisms of B. F. Skinner's Position

As is evident in some of the criticisms of Skinner's position, not everyone working on this topic has shared Skinner's aim. Critiques of Skinner's position (from within the behavioral community at least) have focused on two aspects of his work. First, it has been argued (e.g., Hayes, 1996) that Skinner focused exclusively on the occurrence and characteristics of the *speaker's* behavior, neglecting the same of the listener save the latter's role in the mediation of consequences for the speaker's behavior—much of which had to be assumed as opposed to directly observed. While Skinner did not in fact ignore the verbal aspects of the listener's behavior entirely (e.g., see Skinner, 1957, pp. 357–367), he did argue that the behavior of the speaker could be analyzed without considering the behavior of the listener (1957, p. 2).

Interestingly, it might be argued that **relational fame theory** (RFT) has focused almost exclusively on the behavior of the listener, to the neglect of the speaker. In much of the early RFT research, in which a match-to-sample procedure was employed, the responses measured were acts of selecting a particular stimulus from an array of stimuli. Acts of this sort demonstrate a "knowing" of relations among stimuli—which is an act of listening, perhaps, or understanding, but not an act of speaking. For example, when a child points to stimulus X upon being asked to "show me X" in the presence of an array of stimuli in which X is included, the response of pointing to X is not an instance of speaking. By contrast, upon being presented with stimulus X and being asked to say what it is, the response of naming the object is one of listening and understanding *as well as speaking*.

The same is true of the early work on **stimulus equivalence**. In this case, though, some attempts to evoke topographically distinct response forms were made or were at least imagined to be ongoing (Horne & Lowe, 1996). Added to these is Kantor's (1936, 1977) interpretation of psychological linguistics, which is not a critique of Skinner's position per se but rather an independently developed alternative to it. From Kantor's perspective, as exemplified in chapter 6 by Patrick Ghezzi, linguistic acts of the referential type were held to involve simultaneous stimulation from two sources, one of which was always the listener. Accordingly, it was not possible to focus on either the speaker's or the listener's behavior in isolation.

The other major criticism of Skinner's analysis of verbal behavior has had to do with his conceptualization of stimulus events. Stimulus events have come to be understood as having both functional and object properties (e.g., see Hayes, Barnes-Holmes, & Roche, 2001). While Skinner (1957) did distinguish the function of a stimulus from its status as a physical object, and he did make use of this distinction in addressing particularly complex episodes of verbal behavior involving autoclitics, he did not do so consistently. For the most part, stimuli were conceptualized as objects, which were or were not present in a given circumstance, giving rise to such claims as "Apart from an occasional relevant audience, verbal behavior requires no environmental support (Skinner, 1974a, p. 100), and such analyses as "seeing in the absence of the thing seen" (Skinner, 1957, p. 363). It was this issue that prompted Skinner to propose a category of operant behavior that, unlike all other categories of operant behavior, was not contingency shaped, namely rule-governed behavior. Rule governance was a less-than-convincing solution to the problem, however (see Parrott, 1987). The problem was accounting for the control exerted by stimuli in their absence, and the solution was to promote the distinction between the functional and object properties of stimuli. It was this issue that gave rise to an important body of research, generally referred to as **stimulus equivalence**. And it was this distinction and its implications, in turn, that gave rise to RFT. Interestingly, the distinction between stimuli as objects and stimuli as functions is one of the hallmarks of Kantor's analysis of behavior (1924, 1958), including behavior of the linguistic type (1936, 1977).

The implications of making this distinction are profound. The distinction makes it possible to assume that the functional properties of a stimulus are possible in the absence of its physical object properties. This is to say the functional properties of stimuli may operate from nonoriginal sources which, according to Kantor, is an outcome of historical relations between original and nonoriginal sources. Kantor (1936, 1977) refers to this phenomenon as **substitute stimulation**. Other theorists, as is apparent in most of the remaining chapters of this volume, account for this phenomenon in different ways and refer to it with different terms. Nonetheless, all are pointing to the same phenomenon and all are recognizing its implications for the understanding of exceedingly complex forms of human behavior.

The development of a natural science of behavior has been impeded by several factors, including the attribution of causal properties to hypothetical entities, the definition of the unit of a behavioral event, and the lack of sophisticated observational technologies. B. F. Skinner's radical behaviorism, including its analysis of verbal behavior, resolved many of these challenges. Conceptual difficulties remained with Skinner's analysis, however, including an understanding of the behavior of the listener and referential behavior. The conceptualization of **rule-governed behavior** and the study of **derived stimulus relations** (and later RFT) permitted for an analysis of the behavior of both the speaker and listener. J. R. Kantor's analysis of substitute stimulation made it possible to assume that the functional properties of a stimulus are possible in the absence of its physical object properties. These developments, including the notion of substitute stimulation, permitted for the understanding of complex human behavior.

About This Book

The aims of the present book flow from this general understanding of the corrigibility of behavior science. Essential to this evolution is the incorporation of new materials into our educational curricula. *Applied Behavior Analysis of Language and Cognition* provides an analysis of the most innovative and contemporary research published in the area of language and cognition to date. Authors share important perspectives that will guide the reader in their own research or clinical work in the areas subsumed under each chapter. The book is designed to maximize readers' grasp of the complex issues involved in this subject. At the beginning of each chapter is a "Link and Preview" box, in which the editors provide a brief overview of the topic at hand and its link to previous chapters. Each chapter—written by experts in their respective areas—contains an in-depth discussion of the topic, a consideration of implications and future directions, a summary of the chapter's key points, and a list of study questions to facilitate mastery of the concepts presented in the chapter. Finally, as our field is teeming with terminology and acronyms, a glossary of acronyms is included at the back of the book for readers' reference.

It is the editors' belief that the most important new materials for practitioners of behavior science pertain to matters of language and cognition. This book reflects our best efforts to make these materials available and accessible.

CHAPTER 2

Basic Concepts

Linda J. Hayes
University of Nevada, Reno

Kenneth W. Jacobs
University of Nevada, Reno

Matthew Lewon
University of Nevada, Reno

Link and Preview

While the majority of this text is devoted to specific topics related to language and cognition in **applied behavior analysis** (ABA), as described in the introduction, the present chapter describes the basic concepts and principles involved in ABA. We believe it is important to provide an overview of these concepts and principles at the beginning of the text given their foundational role in understanding behavior.

Basic concepts seem to be involved in everything in behavior analysis, from the simple to the complex. We begin our overview with brief comments on the historical context of behavior analysis, followed by a description of respondent and operant processes. The chapter also provides an overview of select advanced topics related to stimulus control and motivation.

Historical Context

In the one hundred plus years since John B. Watson (1913) regarded psychology as a science of behavior, and the over fifty years since Skinner's (1963) restatement in terms of radical behaviorism, there have been two enduring conditioning paradigms within the science of behavior: **respondent conditioning** and **operant conditioning**. Ivan Pavlov

(1927) established the former, and B. F. Skinner (1938) the latter. The operant conditioning paradigm directly spawned the development of ABA (Baer, Wolf, & Risley, 1968), whereas both respondent and operant conditioning informed behavior therapy (Wolpe, 1976a, 1976b). Barring some overlap, these learning processes and their associated applications remained relatively independent of one another (Williams, 1987). The supposed distinction between respondent and operant conditioning, for instance, was "shrouded with ambiguity" (Kazdin, 1979, p. 632). More recently, there has been a convergence of thought, where respondent and operant conditioning have been conceptualized as complementary rather than distinct (e.g., Delgado & Hayes, 2013, 2014; Domjan, 2016; Rehfeldt & Hayes, 1998).

In addition to the classical and operant paradigms, J. R. Kantor (1924) developed the field-theoretical position known as **interbehavioral psychology**. A similarity fundamental to both operant and interbehavioral psychology is their adherence to *behavior* as the proper subject matter of a natural science of psychology (Morris, 1984). Kantor's lifelong pursuit was to construct a natural science of psychology impervious to the mentalistic vernacular of nonscientific institutions (Clayton, Hayes, & Swain, 2005). Although it had few followers to begin, the explicit and thoroughgoing explication of interbehavioral psychology's philosophical assumptions has guided theoretical developments in behavior science to this day (Fryling & Hayes, 2015; Hayes & Fryling, 2009, 2014, 2015; Smith, 2016).

An even more recent addition to the ABA, behavior therapy, and interbehavioral movements is **contextual behavioral science**. The philosophy of contextual behavioral science, **functional contextualism**, is aligned with and also extends Skinner's (1945) radical behaviorism (Hayes, Barnes-Holmes, & Wilson, 2012; Hayes, Hayes, & Reese, 1988). The contextual behavioral science approach to clinical application (Hayes, Levin, Plumb-Vilardaga, Villatte, & Pistorello, 2013) and language and cognition (Hayes, Barnes-Holmes, & Roche, 2001) is unique, but most importantly, is consistent with and committed to a natural science of behavior. The assumption that a natural science of behavior is possible is a thread that unifies each of behavior science's respective movements. We mention these theoretical foundations because they are a part of the larger context from which the basic concepts reviewed in this chapter are derived.

Respondent Conditioning

Respondent behavior describes responses (**unconditioned responses**; URs) that occur in the presence of particular environmental events (**unconditioned stimuli**; USs) without a history of learning. While the relationship between the US and UR is relatively constant (i.e., given the US, the UR will always occur), the UR may in some cases be modified by consequences (Domjan, 2005). In other cases, the repeated and consistent presentation of the US may gradually reduce the magnitude of the UR to the US, a process called **habituation**. For example, you may notice the loud sounds of airplanes coming and going every time you visit your friend who lives near the airport. Your friend, however, may hardly notice those sounds, if they notice them at all. You might say that habituation has occurred in this case (your friend no longer responds to the loud sound of planes, the US, or at least not as strongly as they used to). The inverse, **dishabituation**, is when the magnitude of the habituated UR recovers due to the subsequent presentation of the US following exposure to a different stimulus (Groves & Thompson, 1970). In other words, if your friend was not exposed to the sounds of the airplanes for a while, and was then exposed to them again, your friend might again respond to the sound and find it disruptive.

Respondent conditioning, also known as Pavlovian or classical conditioning, is when one stimulus acquires the functional properties of another. This occurs when two stimuli consistently occur together, either in space (i.e., near each other) or time (i.e., during or right before or after each other). The most reliable conditioning is obtained when two stimuli frequently occur together and infrequently occur independent of one another (Rescorla, 1967, 1988). A prototypical example is the acquisition of the eliciting function of a US by a stimulus that previously did not elicit that response (we often call this stimulus, prior to conditioning, a **neutral stimulus**). When the previously neutral stimulus elicits a response similar to the UR elicited by the US, we call it a **conditioned stimulus** (CS), which elicits the response now called a **conditioned response** (CR). Fears and phobias are examples of the outcomes of respondent conditioning, where an initial experience with a US (e.g., a prick from a needle) causes a previously neutral stimulus (e.g., the doctor's office or the sight of a needle) to become a CS. It is important to note that stimuli may also acquire other functions via respondent conditioning, including reinforcing (conditioned reinforcers; Williams, 1994), aversive (conditioned aversive stimuli; Azrin & Holz, 1966), discriminative (Hayes, 1992), and motivational functions (conditioned motivating operations; Michael, 1993).

Operant Conditioning

Antecedent, behavior, and consequence constitute the **three-term contingency**. **Antecedent** refers to an event or condition that precedes a **behavior**, and **consequence** refers to an event or condition that happens after a behavior. Each component of the contingency is defined in terms of the other (Timberlake, 2004). This is to say that where there is behavior there are consequences, and those consequences coordinate behavior with stimuli (Skinner, 1974a). While consequences increase or decrease the probability of a behavior occurring, antecedents regulate the probability of that behavior occurring in a given setting or situation.

Antecedent, behavior, and consequence are open-ended terms in the sense that no stimulus is guaranteed to function as an antecedent or consequence and no behavior is guaranteed to function strictly as a respondent or operant (Domjan, 2016; Timberlake, 1988). Antecedent, behavior, and consequence represent **candidate elements**: stimuli and responses that may or may not function as conditioned stimuli, discriminative stimuli, reinforcers, or punishers (more on these terms below). Determining what does or will function as an antecedent or consequence is a matter of observation and experimentation.

In the sections that follow we describe the processes and outcomes of antecedents and consequences as they relate to operant behavior. We will elucidate the conditions under which candidate antecedents and consequences have discriminative or reinforcing functions. Furthermore, we will describe the conditions under which motivation and emotion influence the three-term contingency as a unit of analysis.

Consequential Control

Consequential control refers to changes in behavior due to reinforcement or punishment. Below is a thumbnail take on how behavior analysts speak of reinforcement and punishment, then and now (cf. Killeen & Jacobs, 2017a, 2017b). Afterward, we describe the particulars of reinforcement and punishment procedures and the process of extinction.

STRENGTHENING

Early in his career, Skinner (1938) described reinforcement as the process by which behavior is *strengthened.* The converse, punishment, was described as the process by which behavior is *weakened* (Skinner, 1953). "Reinforcement builds up these tendencies; punishment is designed to tear them down" (Skinner, 1953, p. 182). The "tendencies" Skinner referred to arc behavior: the acts of whole organisms in context. Those acts are "strengthened" or "weakened" in the sense that there is an observed change in their probability of occurrence. In lay terms, behavior that occurs a lot, or intensely, might be said to be strong, and that which occurs infrequently, or at a very low magnitude, might be said to be weak.

The notions of response strengthening and weakening are metaphors. They are figures of speech that represent an assumption fundamental to any experimental or applied behavior analysis (i.e., behavior is probabilistic). The occurrence or nonoccurrence of a response is indicative of its probability, its likelihood of occurrence on any given occasion. **Rate of responding** is a measure of response probability that has been deemed the basic datum of the science of behavior (Skinner, 1956, 1966b). Other measures such as count, percent, duration, and latency can be indicative of response probability as well, so our applied analyses of behavior are not limited to rate of responding alone. This means behavior change can be measured in a variety of ways.

The probability that a response will or will not occur depends on its consequences within a given setting. We can predict the likelihood that a response will occur, and can even control its occurrence, but we do so in terms of **response classes**. This is to say that behavior analysts do not predict the occurrence of particular response forms on any given occasion. Instead, behavior analysts predict whether or not a particular **class** of behavior will occur.

Within any given class of behavior are many variations of response form. For instance, one might request water when thirsty in various ways: "Water, please?" "Can I have water?" "I want water," and so on. Regardless of how they request that water, the consequence is the same: access to water. When the consequence for a variety of response forms is the same, behavior analysts *functionally class* those responses; they group those responses into classes on the basis of their consequences. In addition to the water-related response class there are food-related response classes, attention-related response classes, escape-related response classes, and so on.

In the case of a thirsty client, the applied behavior analyst can make a class-based prediction: When in the presence of listeners who may have water, a water-deprived client will engage in one or more various forms of verbal behavior that have produced access to water in the past. We cannot predict with certainty that the individual will ask, "Water, please?" versus "Can I have water?" but we can predict that the individual will request water in some form.

SELECTION

Later in his career Skinner (1981) dropped the notions of strengthening and weakening in favor of selection. In a masterstroke, Skinner (1981) described genetic, behavioral, and cultural processes in terms of **selection by consequences**. Consequences are responsible for the traits of a species, the behavioral repertoires of a species' members, and the cultural practices of a group. Variation at all three levels is key, as it makes the selection of an adaptive trait, behavior, or practice possible (Hayes, Sanford, & Chin, 2017). At the behavioral level, consequences are reinforcers and punishers that differentially select responses, which constitute the functionally defined classes of behavior already described. When a response class is stereotypic, and therefore restricted in terms of variation, applied behavior analysts are tasked with expanding that response class or shaping and maintaining new ones (Hayes & Sanford, 2015).

In keeping with Skinner (1981), we will describe the processes and outcomes of consequential control in terms of selection. Evolutionary science is a natural ally to the behavioral sciences (Wilson, Hayes, Biglan, & Embry, 2014), as consequential control is a product of our "evolved susceptibility to reinforcement" (Skinner, 1981, p. 501).

Reinforcement

The outcome of **reinforcement** is an increase in the probability of a response on future occasions. There are two sorts of reinforcement: **positive reinforcement** and **negative reinforcement**. Positive reinforcement entails the presentation or addition of a stimulus, whereas negative reinforcement entails the removal or subtraction of a stimulus. Both positive and negative reinforcement increase behavior based on the contingent presentation or removal of a stimulus, respectively. Reinforcers, however, are not exclusively stimuli. Events or activities may also function as reinforcers (Jacobs, Morford, King, & Hayes, 2017; Premack, 1959; Timberlake & Allison, 1974). For the sake of brevity we will speak in terms of stimuli, but we will indicate which candidate reinforcers are stimuli, events, or activities when those designations are applicable.

POSITIVE REINFORCEMENT

If contingent access to a stimulus follows a target response and increases that target response, then positive reinforcement is observed. An example of positive reinforcement is the case in which a parent provides a child with access to a preferred toy (stimulus) as long as the child says "please" (target response). We say the toy functioned as a reinforcer if and only if its contingent presentation was observed to increase the rate of the target response (i.e., saying please).

NEGATIVE REINFORCEMENT

If the contingent removal of a stimulus follows a target response and increases that target response, then negative reinforcement is observed. An example of negative reinforcement is if a teacher removes an academic demand (activity) on the condition that the child appropriately requests a break (target response). The academic demand is said to have functioned as a negative reinforcer if and only if its contingent removal was observed to increase the rate of the target response (i.e., requesting a break). Another example is the case in which the removal of a headache (event) is contingent upon your taking medicine (response). If the probability of taking medicine increases on future occasions, then the removal of that headache is said to have functioned as a negative reinforcer.

Punishment

The outcome of **punishment** is a decrease in the probability of a response on future occasions. There are two sorts of punishment: **positive punishment** and **negative punishment**. As is the case with reinforcement, positive and negative refer to the presentation or removal of a stimulus, event, or activity contingent upon a particular behavior.

POSITIVE PUNISHMENT

If the contingent presentation of a stimulus follows a target response and decreases that target response, then positive punishment is observed. An example of positive punishment is if a parent requires a child to excessively clean up a room (activity) on every occasion the child engages in property destruction (target response). We say that excessive cleaning functioned as a positive punisher if and only if its contingent presentation was observed to decrease the rate of the target response (i.e., property destruction). This procedure is also known as **overcorrection** (see Timberlake & Farmer-Dougan, 1991).

NEGATIVE PUNISHMENT

If the contingent removal of a stimulus follows a target response and decreases that target response, then negative punishment is observed. Negative punishment is the case in which a teacher, for example, removes access to playtime (activity) on every occasion the child hits another individual (target response). Playtime is said to have functioned as a negative punisher if and only if its contingent removal was observed to decrease the rate of the target response (i.e., hitting). This procedure is also known as time-out. Additionally, and critically, negative punishment requires the removal of a positive reinforcer for its procedures to be effective in decreasing behavior.

Extinction

Up until this juncture we have described what happens to behavior when natural or scheduled events follow behavior on particular occasions. We have described the processes and outcomes of reinforcement and punishment. The question before us now is: What happens to behavior when previously obtained consequences are lacking or withheld?

Extinction is a reduction in responding that no longer produces reinforcing consequences. In procedural terms, a reduction in responding is observed when reinforcement for a particular response is lacking or withheld. For the effects of extinction to be observed, reinforcement must be lacking or withheld for responses that have produced reinforcing consequences in the past. Like punishment, a reduction in behavior occurs, but not because of the contingent removal of a reinforcing stimulus (negative punishment). Whereas negative punishment *is* a contingency, extinction is the decoupling of contingencies. In other words, extinction involves the discontinuation of the relationship between responses and their reinforcers.

Importantly, we can only say that extinction has occurred when there is an observed decrease in a previously reinforced behavior. Here the word "extinction" may be used to refer to a procedure (i.e., no longer providing the reinforcer) and an outcome (i.e., the reduction in behavior). Besides its primary effect of reducing behavior, the process of extinction has at least three additional effects: an initial burst in responding, variability in responding (operant variability), and variants of response recovery.

EXTINCTION BURST

When reinforcement for a previously reinforced response is withheld, a rapid increase in responding may be observed initially. An **extinction burst** refers to that initial rapid increase in responding. If reinforcement for socially appropriate requests is withheld, then a burst in socially appropriate requests is likely to ensue. For example, if a child has learned to say "Mom" to get his mother's attention, he may say "Mom" repeatedly, and perhaps more loudly, when attention is no longer forthcoming. As extinction proceeds, those requests for attention may also vary in form, which brings us to the next effect of extinction.

OPERANT VARIABILITY

A client may not emit the same socially appropriate request when reinforcement for that request is withheld. For example, the child may say, "Look at me," "Pay attention," or other responses after the response "Mom" is no longer followed by attention. Extinction is said to induce **operant variability** in such a way that new response forms, and variations of old response forms, can be selected by their consequences.

RESPONSE RECOVERY

Subsequent to an extinction burst or operant variability, the response form for which reinforcement is withheld will eventually subside. A particular request, after extinction, may now have a zero probability of occurrence within a particular setting. With the passage of time or change in context, however, the previously extinguished response may recur at or near its original baseline level of occurrence. After a period of rest between extinction sessions, for example, extinguished responding might recover due to extraneous sources of control within the setting where extinction took place (Pierce & Cheney, 2013). Continuing with our previous example, it is possible that the child will resume yelling "Mom" in a few days. This effect, known as **spontaneous recovery**, is only one of the many different forms of **response recovery** after extinction. We briefly describe those other forms of recovery, but encourage readers to see Bouton, Winterbauer, and Todd (2012) for references and review.

Renewal, resurgence, and reinstatement are terms that describe the recurrence of responses previously extinguished. Bouton et al. (2012) describe these types of response recovery as **relapse effects**. In the case of **renewal**, extinguished responding recurs due to changes in context. If a response was selected by its reinforcing consequences in context A, but extinguished in context B, the extinguished response will renew (i.e., recur) if the individual returns to context A. This is known as the **ABA renewal effect**. **Resurgence** occurs when an initially reinforced response is put on extinction while an alternative response is now reinforced. If you then extinguish the alternative response, the previously extinguished initial response will resurge (i.e., recur; see Lattal et al., 2017, for a review of the definition of resurgence). Lastly, **reinstatement** is the case in which a response recurs because the previously extinguished response is reinforced on a later occasion, which reinstates its occurrence.

Antecedent Control

Antecedent control is a general term used to describe a change in the probability of a particular response when in the presence of certain stimuli. Whereas consequential control refers to changes in the probability of behavior due to events that follow it, antecedent control refers to changes in the probability of behavior due to several classes of events that precede it. Antecedent control includes both stimulus control and motivating operations, on which we elaborate below.

STIMULUS CONTROL

Stimulus control is a continuum on which stimulus discrimination and stimulus generalization are opposite endpoints (Dinsmoor, 1995a; Rilling, 1977). On one end of this continuum, stimulus discrimination occurs when measures of behavior vary systematically across two or more different settings. On the other end, stimulus generalization occurs when consequences for behavior in one setting affect measures of behavior in another setting. In applied situations, either can be desirable or problematic depending on the nature of the performance. The processes and outcomes of each, as well as the factors that affect them, are described below.

Stimulus discrimination. **Stimulus discrimination** refers to a change in the probability of an operant response in one setting versus another. That change in the probability of a response is due to discrimination training, which entails a history of differential reinforcement, punishment, or extinction across settings. In procedural terms, **discrimination training** is when a given response is consistently followed by one outcome, on a particular schedule in one setting, while that same response is followed by either a different outcome or the same outcome, on a different schedule in another setting (Dinsmoor, 1995a; Terrace, 1966). Such training may be arranged intentionally or occur adventitiously.

SD & S-delta. The most common discrimination training procedure involves reinforcing a response in one setting and extinguishing it in another. Other combinations of reinforcement, punishment, extinction, or different schedules of reinforcement/punishment for a single response—across different settings—may also bring about stimulus discrimination. In the prototypical procedure, the stimulus in the presence of which a response is reinforced is referred to as the **discriminative stimulus** (abbreviated S^D or S+). Due to a history of reinforcement in its presence, the presence of the S^D increases the probability of the response. The stimulus in the presence of which the response is extinguished is typically referred to as **S-delta** (S^Δ or S-), and its presence serves to decrease the probability of the response. While the term "discriminative stimulus" implies that only the S^D exerts discriminative control, both S^D and S^Δ may be considered discriminative in the sense that both affect the probability of a response: the former increases it while the latter decreases it. Stated generally, the probability of a given response in a particular setting is related to that response's history of reinforcement/punishment/extinction in that setting.

Stimulus classes. In addition to the stimulus control exerted by a particular setting, specific properties of stimulus objects or events may come to acquire discriminative functions under the relevant contingencies. A **stimulus class**, or **concept**, is defined as a group of stimuli that share a specific property and that are functionally related to responding in the same way (Chase & Danforth, 1991; Herrnstein, Loveland, & Cable, 1976; Zentall, Galizio, & Critchfield, 2002). The property shared by all members of a given stimulus class may be established as an S^D via **concept training**: a given response is followed by a particular consequence in the presence of members of one stimulus class, and is followed by a different consequence in the presence of members of another stimulus class. The outcome is that the response will become more or less probable in the presence of the property that is shared among all members of the given stimulus class, even if various members of the class differ in other regards. An example of this is reinforcing the verbal response "red" in the presence of many different red objects, while extinguishing the same response in the presence of objects of other colors. Subsequent to this training, the response "red" will be more likely in the presence of all red objects and less likely in the presence of non-red objects.

Stimulus control factors.
Practical applications are often concerned with establishing specific stimuli or stimulus properties as discriminative (i.e., we want behavior to occur in the presence of certain stimuli but not in the presence of other stimuli). A number of factors affect the extent to which this is achieved. The first is **stimulus salience**, which pertains to the magnitude of the difference between an intended S^D and other stimuli present during training (Dinsmoor, 1995b). Stimuli that are more distinguishable from background stimulation are more likely to acquire discriminative functions under the appropriate contingencies. Salience is related to many factors, including but not limited to the intensity of a stimulus relative to the setting in which it occurs (Mackintosh, 1976), sensory capacity (i.e., what an individual is capable of detecting; Heffner & Heffner, 2007; Horowitz, 1987), and the biological relevance of stimuli (Domjan, 1983).

Another factor affecting discrimination training is **stimulus disparity**, which is the extent to which an intended S^D for a given response differs along some physical dimension from $S^\Delta(s)$ during training (Dinsmoor, 1995b). The greater the difference between an S^D for a given response and various $S^\Delta s$ present during training (i.e., $S^D s$ for other responses, often called "distractors"), the more readily the former will acquire the appropriate discriminative function.

Stimulus generalization.
Stimuli that are similar in certain ways tend to evoke similar patterns of responding, or **stimulus generalization**. This term refers to circumstances in which the consequences of a given response in one setting affect its probability in another similar setting. The conditions under which stimulus generalization occurs have been studied extensively in the laboratory (Honig & Urcuioli, 1981; Rilling, 1977). In applied

settings it is often important to explicitly program for generalization such that performances established in treatment occur in the appropriate circumstances outside of treatment (Stokes & Baer, 1977). In some situations, though, generalization may be undesirable
(e.g., it may be important that a given response occur in only one of two similar settings),
and appropriate discrimination may require further training. Terrace (1966) described
how this may be expedited by beginning training with S^Ds and S^Δs that are dissimilar and
gradually making them more similar across training, that is, until the response is only
occurring in the appropriate setting. This process is known as **fading** or **errorless learning** and is the basis for various prompting and transfer of stimulus control technologies
(Green, 2001).

Overshadowing. When a response is reinforced, punished, and/or extinguished, a
plethora of environmental stimuli are present, but not all stimuli will necessarily acquire
discriminative functions. Only those stimuli that are consistently correlated with a particular consequence, for a particular response, will acquire such functions (Mackintosh,
1977). Furthermore, if two equally relevant stimuli are present when a response produces
a particular consequence, one of them may acquire discriminative functions while the
other does not (e.g., Reynolds, 1961). This is known as **overshadowing**. Overshadowing
may also occur when an already-established S^D (S1) and another stimulus (S2) are both
present when a response is reinforced or punished. Under these conditions, S1 may
prevent S2 from acquiring discriminative functions unless the consequences or schedule
of reinforcement for the response change with the introduction of S2 (Kamin, 1969;
Rescorla & Wagner, 1972).

In light of the above, it is important to recognize that a variety of stimuli are present
during discrimination training and that any of these may adventitiously acquire some
discriminative functions in the course of training. The delivery of reinforcers (Bouton &
Trask, 2016; Franks & Lattal, 1976) or aversive stimuli (Ayllon & Azrin, 1966; Holz &
Azrin, 1961), states produced by drugs or other motivating operations (Lubinski &
Thompson, 1987; Overton, 1984), and the stimulation provided by an individual's own
behavior (Killeen & Fetterman, 1988) are all capable of acquiring and exerting discriminative control over behavior. In some cases, it is even possible for these events to interfere
with the discriminative control established by a practitioner.

MOTIVATING OPERATIONS

The study of motivation in behavior analysis pertains to changes in the probability
of behavior that occur due to the influence of environmental events functioning as motivating operations. **Motivating operations** (MOs) are antecedent events that have two
functions. First, they alter the value of reinforcers and aversive stimuli, increasing or
decreasing their reinforcing/punishing efficacy. Second, they alter the probability of
behavior relevant to those events/activities as consequences. The former has been
referred to as the **value-altering effect** and the latter as the **behavior-altering effect**
(Laraway, Snycerski, Michael, & Poling, 2003).

There are two subclasses of MOs: **establishing operations** (EOs) and **abolishing operations** (AOs; Laraway et al., 2003). We take each in turn.

Establishing operations. EOs are events that increase the efficacy of reinforcers or aversive stimuli and increase the probability of behavior. If an individual is exposed to an EO for a reinforcer, the probability of all responses that have produced that reinforcer in the past increases. If an individual is exposed to an EO that increases the extent to which an event functions as aversive, the probability of behavior that has produced the reduction or removal of that aversive stimulus in the past increases.

Abolishing operations. AOs have the opposite effect: they reduce the efficacy of reinforcers or aversive stimuli and decrease the probability of behavior. An AO for a particular reinforcer will decrease the probability of responses that have produced that reinforcer in the past, and an AO for an aversive stimulus will decrease the probability of responses that have resulted in the removal/reduction of that stimulus in the past.

Note that EO and AO are relative terms. Whether a particular event functions as an EO or AO depends on the motivational condition(s) to which it is compared. For example, six hours of food deprivation is an EO relative to no food deprivation, but is an AO relative to twelve hours of food deprivation.

Types of motivating operations. A wide variety of events function as MOs, and various MOs for different reinforcers/aversive stimuli may operate concurrently (Sundberg, 2013). **Unconditioned MOs** function as MOs without a prior history with those events, and **conditioned MOs** are events that acquire motivational functions through correlation with other events (Michael, 1993). The types of events that function as MOs include various deprivation operations (e.g., food, water, sex, or sleep deprivation), aversive stimulation (a given aversive stimulus can serve to punish the response that precedes it and also function as an MO for its reduction/removal; Michael, 1993), drug or alcohol intake (Valdovinos & Kennedy, 2004), pain or illness (O'Reilly, 1997; O'Reilly, Lacey, & Lancioni, 2000), verbal stimuli (sometimes referred to as augmentals; Hayes, Barnes-Holmes, & Roche, 2001), events associated with emotions (Lewon & Hayes, 2014), and the repeated presentation of reinforcers or aversive stimuli (known as habituation, described earlier in this chapter; Azrin & Holz, 1966; McSweeney & Murphy, 2009).

TERMINOLOGICAL DISTINCTIONS

Since the terms MO and S^D both fall under the umbrella that is antecedent control, it is worth emphasizing their distinctive functions for technical as well as practical purposes. Michael (1982, 1993) distinguished between the effects of S^D and MO on the basis that the former relates to the differential *availability* of reinforcement for a given response while the latter relates to the differential *effectiveness* of a particular reinforcer. This is often a useful distinction in practical applications, as behavioral excesses or deficits related to the presence or absence of S^{D}s will require different intervention strategies from those related to MOs.

Despite their technical differences, a variety of S^Ds and MOs are always present and interact in the evocation of behavior. Research has shown that EOs increase the probability of a given response in the presence of an S^D, but to a lesser extent they also increase the probability of the response in the presence of other stimuli not explicitly established as S^Ds (Edrisinha, O'Reilly, Sigafoos, Lancioni, & Choi, 2011; Lotfizadeh, Edwards, Redner, & Poling, 2012). This is to say that a particular response is most likely when both the S^D and an EO for the relevant reinforcer are present, and least likely when both are absent.

Implications and Future Directions

The principles of classical (i.e., respondent) and operant conditioning are the theoretical foundations of behavior science movements both new and old. No matter how foundational, though, those principles are verbal constructions. Even though they are the products of meticulous observations, they remain susceptible to misinterpretation in the form of mentalisms and dualisms. This is to say that the principles of behavior are not static, as they evolve in accordance with the behavior of scientists, practitioners, and the cultural milieu within which they operate. Testaments to such evolution are Skinner's (1963) take on the law of effect, Rescorla's (1988) take on classical conditioning, Premack's (1959) probability-differential hypothesis, Timberlake and Allison's (1974) response-deprivation hypothesis, and Baum's (2012) rethinking of reinforcement. While the principles of behavior are fundamental, they are subject to refinement and evolution over time.

Conclusion

While behavior science is diverse in its research and application of the principles of behavior, there is a common thread that unites such diversity: the pursuit of a natural science of psychology, or more specifically, a natural science of behavior. The aim of this chapter was to provide an overview of fundamental behavioral processes, including some relatively advanced topics. These processes serve both as a foundation for the remaining chapters and as a starting point for the behavior analysis of language and cognition pursued in this text.

Study Questions

1. Provide an example of habituation.

2. What is dishabituation? Elaborate on your example from question 1 and explain how dishabituation may occur.

3. Give an example of respondent conditioning, being sure to describe a previously neutral stimulus, a US and UR, and how the neutral stimulus became a CS eliciting a CR.

4. What are the differences between positive and negative reinforcement and punishment?

5. How is extinction different from punishment? Explain with an example.

6. What are the effects of extinction as reviewed in the chapter?

7. Distinguish between S^D and S^Δ. Provide an example of each.

8. How might overshadowing interfere with the establishment of stimulus control during discrimination training?

9. What are the two effects of MOs?

10. How are MOs distinguished from S^Ds?

11. Provide an example of both an EO and an AO.

CHAPTER 3

Basic Verbal Operants

Rocío Rosales

University of Massachusetts Lowell

Yors A. Garcia

The Chicago School of Professional Psychology

Sebastian Garcia

Southern Illinois University, Carbondale

Ruth Anne Rehfeldt

Southern Illinois University, Carbondale

Link and Preview

While chapter 2 focused on general behavioral processes, this chapter begins to consider language from the perspective of behavior analysis. Specifically, the authors focus on the basics of B. F. Skinner's (1957) approach to verbal behavior, including an overview of fundamental concepts, research, and implications for practice. These principles are important in their own right, and also set the stage for more complex topics to be addressed later in the book.

Behavior analysis is a science dedicated to identifying functional relations between behavior and environmental variables (Delprato & Midgley, 1992). A behavioral account of language (Skinner, 1957) places special emphasis on the conditions that affect the occurrence of verbal behavior: motivation, discriminative stimuli, and reinforcement. The focus on the pragmatic function of language distinguishes Skinner's approach from more traditional accounts of language that focus on the topography or structure of language (i.e., Chomsky, 1966).

Verbal Operants as Defined by Skinner

Skinner (1957) defined verbal behavior as "behavior reinforced through the mediation of other persons [who] must be responding in ways which have been conditioned precisely in order to reinforce the behavior of the speaker" (p. 2, p. 225). He accordingly described a taxonomy of several elementary verbal operants:

1. The **mand** is "a verbal operant in which the response is reinforced by a characteristic consequence and is therefore under the functional control of relevant conditions of deprivation or aversive stimulation" (pp. 35–36). That is, the mand (a sign or gesture, selection of a picture or activation of a vocal-output device, or a vocalization) specifies its reinforcer and is influenced by relevant establishing or motivating operations (Laraway, Snycerski, Michael, & Poling, 2003; Michael, 1988).

2. The **tact** is a response (i.e., vocalization or sign) evoked by a particular nonverbal discriminative stimulus (object, event, or property of an object or event) and is maintained by generalized conditioned reinforcement such as praise or attention from a listener (pp. 81–82).

3. The **intraverbal** is a verbal response (i.e., written or vocal) under the control of a verbal stimulus with no point-to-point correspondence or formal similarity to the response, and is maintained by generalized conditioned reinforcement (p. 71).

4. The **echoic** is a response (i.e., imitation or vocalization) under the functional control of a verbal stimulus with point-to-point correspondence and formal similarity to the response, and is maintained by generalized conditioned reinforcement.

5. **Textual** behavior is a response (i.e., overt or covert vocalization) evoked by a verbal stimulus (i.e., written text) with point-to-point correspondence but no formal similarity (p. 65).

Michael (1982) further expanded upon the last two operants proposed by Skinner, echoic and textual responding, by describing the **codic** and **duplic**. He suggested that we adopt the term "codic" for relations preceded by a verbal stimulus with point-to-point correspondence but no formal similarity (i.e., textual and taking dictation) and the term "duplic" for relations preceded by a verbal stimulus with both point-to-point correspondence and formal similarity (i.e., echoics, imitation, and copying a text). For example, if a learner is presented with the auditory stimulus "D-I-N-O-S-A-U-R" and accurately writes each corresponding letter on a whiteboard, this is an example of a codic. If the same learner is presented with the visual stimulus *DINOSAUR* in a book and proceeds to write each corresponding letter on a whiteboard, this is an example of a duplic.

According to Michael, this arrangement resulted in useful categories and prevented confusing extensions such as referring to Braille as textual behavior and imitation of signs as echoic behavior.

Importantly, the **topography**, or form, of verbal behavior is not limited to vocalizations. Rather, all of the verbal operants may be emitted as a gestural sign, a picture exchange, or a touch or point to activate a speech-generating device. The topography is not relevant because it does not provide us with information about the function of the response. According to Michael (1985), verbal behavior can be either selection based or topography based. **Selection-based** verbal behavior (and selection-based communication systems) requires the same response topography across many responses (i.e., a point, a touch, a press of a button, or a picture exchange). **Topography-based** verbal behavior (and topography-based communication systems) requires a unique response form that has point-to-point correspondence with the relevant response product (i.e., a vocalization, a written response, or a manual sign). Skinner's analysis was primarily focused on the function of a verbal response because the topography of a response does not help to inform us about the functional relationships that exist between antecedent and consequent stimuli that evoke a specific response. In other words, Skinner's analysis of verbal behavior was a **functional analysis**, which has important implications for intervention development.

In the last several decades, a large and growing body of empirical support has emerged for Skinner's analysis of verbal behavior as a framework for teaching language to individuals with developmental delays (Aguirre, Valentino, & Leblanc, 2016; Carr & Miguel, 2012; Dixon, Small, & Rosales, 2007; Sautter & LeBlanc, 2006). Continued study of verbal behavior is important for advancing the analysis of language and cognition from a behavioral perspective. Skinner's interpretation of language also has copious practical value for the clinical services provided to individuals with autism spectrum disorder (ASD) and other related disorders (Sundberg & Michael, 2001). For example, traditional approaches to language assessment do not fully capture the function of the learner's repertoire. This may be due in part to the lack of consideration of motivating operations and automatic reinforcement, and the overemphasis on words and their meanings (Sundberg & Michael, 2001). Collectively, these factors can lead practitioners to underestimate the complexity of verbal relations and make inaccurate assumptions about a learner's existing repertoire. Inaccurate assumptions can include attributing the learner's failure to acquire skills to a diagnosis rather than to an incomplete analysis of the environmental variables that may contribute to such failure (Sundberg & Michael, 2001).

Verbal Behavior Research

In this section we turn our attention to the empirical support for and clinical implications of three of the elementary verbal operants: echoics, mands, and tacts.

Echoics Defined

The echoic is one of the earliest verbal operants observed in young children and is said to be dependent on the exposure to speech sounds produced by the verbal community (Horne & Lowe, 1996). When a child readily imitates novel verbal behavior in the absence of contingent social reinforcers, they are emitting **generalized echoic responding**. Generalized echoic responding is fundamental to the development of more complex behaviors such as self-instructions, listener behavior, and naming (Horne & Lowe, 1996), and it is considered a behavioral cusp because it facilitates many new interactions (Rosales-Ruiz & Baer, 1997). In behavioral interventions for children with language delays, an echoic repertoire is useful for teaching other verbal operants (Barbera & Kubina, 2005; Kodak, Clements, & Ninness, 2009). Thus, a generalized echoic repertoire is fundamental for the development of more complex verbal behavior.

Skinner (1957) asserted that echoic behavior should not be confused with self-reinforcing responses that are not socially mediated. For example, an infant's babbling is automatically reinforcing if it persists in the absence of feedback from parents (p. 58). Automatic reinforcement occurs when reinforcement is the product of a response and is not socially mediated (Vaughan & Michael, 1982). From the time of an infant's birth, parents' sounds and words that are paired with reinforcing activities (i.e., feeding) become conditioned reinforcers for the infant. These sounds, when produced by the child, will help strengthen the muscle movements that are necessary to produce babbling. As a result, infants will babble the sounds that are paired with socially mediated reinforcement more frequently.

The process of automatic reinforcement helps strengthen a child's vocal verbal repertoire and prepare them for speaking in words and eventually full sentences (Sundberg, Michael, Partington, & Sundberg, 1996). The process of automatic reinforcement involves two steps: (1) sounds and words heard by a young child become conditioned reinforcers when paired with the parent's positive feedback and interactions (e.g., as mother talks to her infant while she feeds her); and (2) production of the sounds by the child is strengthened by the product of her verbal behavior in the form of auditory stimuli (e.g., the infant makes vocalizations that begin to sound like her mother's voice, and these auditory stimuli serve as reinforcers for more vocalizations). The closer the sound production (e.g., the infant's vocalization) is to the sound conditioned as a reinforcer (e.g., the mother's voice), the higher the value of that reinforcer (Sundberg et al., 1996).

ECHOIC INSTRUCTION

When children with language delays fail to develop an echoic repertoire, vocal models help to prompt simple vocalizations (Barbera & Kubina, 2005; Bourret, Vollmer, & Rapp, 2004). If the child does not emit any vocalizations, echoic instruction may involve a shaping procedure whereby the instructor provides a vocal prompt and differential reinforcement for successive approximations to each target sound (Cook & Adams, 1966; Harris, 1975). For example, when teaching a child to say "mama," the mother may initially place emphasis on the beginning sound of the word ("mmmm") and initially reinforce any approximation to this sound with enthusiasm. The shaping procedure would require the mother to fade out this enthusiastic reinforcement over time and as additional opportunities to echo the sound were made available. After a few instances of the child reliably saying "mmmm," the mother may change her reaction to this vocalization and provide enthusiastic praise for a closer approximation (e.g., child says "mmmma"). This process may be difficult and slow if vocalizations of any topography occur at very low rates. An alternative procedure with moderate empirical support is the **stimulus-stimulus pairing** (SSP) procedure (Petursdottir, Carp, Mathies, & Esch, 2011; Shillingsburg, Hollander, Yosick, Bowen, & Muskat, 2015).

STIMULUS-STIMULUS PAIRING

Stimulus-stimulus pairing is designed to increase vocalizations using the same process that is thought to result in increased infant babbling (Yoon & Bennett, 2000). Many variations of SSP have been reported to date. The essential feature of SSP is an adult presenting a vocal sound paired with delivery of highly preferred tangible or social stimuli. No overt response is required by the child in this procedure. Through the repetition of sounds paired with preferred stimuli, as emitted by the therapist, the goal of SSP is to establish unique and specific vocal sounds as conditioned reinforcers (as described above). Following repeated presentations, the child may produce sounds that are the same or very similar to what they hear (Sundberg et al., 1996). The increase in any vocalization has important clinical implications because these behaviors provide an opportunity for reinforcement, shaping, and mand instruction. In other words, once the child is producing initial vocalizations through the use of SSP, those vocalizations may then be expanded upon using additional interventions.

To date, the empirical support for the efficacy of SSP is mixed. A recent literature review by Shillingsburg and colleagues (2015) suggests that conclusions are difficult to draw from the evidence base because of varied participant characteristics, information reported on participants' verbal repertoires, and reported procedural differences (e.g., number of pairing trials, number of experimenter-emitted sounds, and type of preferred items used during instruction). As such, clinical recommendations for the specific use of SSP are difficult to establish. In general, the results of the literature review show higher success with SSP when participants were younger (i.e., under age five), with use of a delayed pairing procedure (i.e., delivery of the preferred item overlapped with presentation of the target sound), and when there was control for adventitious reinforcement (i.e., the experimenter withheld access to preferred items for a specified time if the participant emitted a sound immediately following presentation of the vocal model). As noted by the authors of the review, although this last finding is surprising, it could be partially accounted for by the fact that the majority of studies that controlled for adventitious reinforcement also happened to be conducted with younger participants. Additional research is needed to control for these variables. Applied researchers are encouraged to continue working on this important line of work, especially in identifying specific participant characteristics that can predict success with this procedure (Shillingsburg et al., 2015). One important avenue for future research may be to establish initial vocalizations with SSP and then implement more traditional echoic and manding teaching procedures.

Mands Defined

In nontechnical terms, a **mand** is a request that occurs under specific motivation and specifies the reinforcer to be delivered. As discussed in chapter 2, a **motivating operation** (MO; Laraway et al., 2003) is defined as a change in the environment that momentarily increases (**establishing operation** [EO]) or decreases (**abolishing operation** [AO]) the value of a reinforcer and evokes behavior that has previously resulted in access to the reinforcer (Michael, 1982). For example, if a child has been denied access to their favorite toy dinosaur, the reinforcing value of the dinosaur is temporarily increased, and behaviors that have produced access to the dinosaur are evoked (i.e., the child says, "Give me the dinosaur" or simply "dinosaur").

Selection of **mand modality** is an important component of clinical assessment and intervention for learners with language delays. Several studies have systematically evaluated outcomes for topography- versus selection-based mand forms in learners with **autism spectrum disorder** (ASD) and related disorders. In aggregate, the results of these studies provide support for the use of selection-based communication systems (Adkins & Axelrod, 2001; Barlow, Tiger, Slocum, & Miller, 2013; Chambers & Rehfeldt, 2003; Gregory, DeLeon, & Richman, 2009; Lorah, Parnell, Whitby, & Hantula, 2015; Tincani, 2004; Ziomek & Rehfeldt, 2008), but there are idiosyncrasies across findings and the number of participants included is generally small. Therefore, further research is needed to draw firm conclusions. Shafer (1993) outlined considerations for selection- and topography-based systems (described above in the chapter introduction). We offer some clinical recommendations for the selection of a mand modality based on the information discussed by Shafer and the empirical evidence to date.

SELECTION-BASED MAND SYSTEMS

First, a widely used selection-based system with ample empirical support is the **Picture Exchange Communication System** (PECS; Frost & Bondy, 2002). A meta-analysis conducted by Tincani and Devis (2011) revealed that PECS has been moderately effective in establishing mands up to the fourth phase (of six total phases) and that PECS has been shown to facilitate vocalizations in some participants. A second form of selection-based verbal behavior is the use of **speech-generating devices**, which now encompass the use of more accessible high-tech devices such as the iPad, but results from studies investigating the efficacy of this modality relative to others are mixed (see Lorah et al., 2015; Still, Rehfeldt, Whelan, May, & Dymond, 2014).

Potential disadvantages for the use of selection-based responding systems include prerequisite skills that may be required for successful implementation (i.e., scanning and making conditional discriminations). Gregory et al. (2009) evaluated the relationship between matching and motor imitation skills with regard to the acquisition of both manual sign and exchange-based systems for six children with developmental disabilities. Following an assessment to determine if motor imitation and matching were already in each participant's repertoire, participants were taught to mand for the same preferred items using both systems. The results showed strong correspondence between motor imitation and manual sign acquisition, but also between matching and manual sign. In addition, the correspondence between both assessments and exchange-based communication was almost as strong. However, three of the six participants did not learn either communication system. These results support the claim that these skills may expedite the acquisition of these communication forms.

A second noted disadvantage of selection-based responding systems is that the learner must have the pictures or device available at all times, which may limit its use in natural settings (Sundberg & Partington, 2013). This second disadvantage is at least partially addressed by the use of high-tech portable devices that are more readily available and commonly used by neurotypical peers for other purposes (i.e., iPhone or mini iPad). In this regard, the use of high-tech devices may be more socially acceptable because virtually everyone in today's society makes frequent use of such devices and therefore their use may "stand out" less than manual sign (Lorah et al., 2015).

TOPOGRAPHY-BASED MAND SYSTEMS

Topography-based responses such as manual sign have been described as conceptually similar to speech (Sundberg & Partington, 2013) because there is point-to-point correspondence for each response with its relevant response product. The use of manual sign has demonstrated efficacy as a viable communication system for learners with language delays, with some studies showing increased vocalizations following instruction that is paired with tacts of the requested items (i.e., "total communication"; Barrera, Lobato-Barrera, & Sulzer-Azaroff, 1980; Barrera & Sulzer-Azaroff, 1983; Brady & Smouse, 1978; Carbone et al., 2006; Carbone, Sweeney-Kerwin, Attanasio, & Kasper, 2010). A commonly noted disadvantage for the use of manual sign is that the verbal community that can interact with the individual leaner will be limited. In addition, manual sign may not be a good fit for learners with ASD who also often present with motor impairments (Green et al., 2009). Manual sign has the advantage of requiring only simple discrimination repertoires, and the response topography is easily identified across different individuals, so long as the individual is capable of executing the standard sign (as opposed to a unique modified version of the sign).

Studies that have evaluated *preference* for a mand topography demonstrate mixed results, with some showing a clear preference for speech-generated devices (Lorah et al., 2015; McClay et al., 2016) and others indicating that some learners prefer a picture exchange system (van der Meer, Sutherland, O'Reilly, Lancioni, & Sigafoos, 2012).

Recent studies have demonstrated that although learners may show a preference for specific mand topographies, this preference does not always impact the success of interventions designed to decrease challenging behavior (Winborn-Kemmerer, Ringdahl, Wacker, & Kitsukawa, 2009). Other considerations that should be made in mand modality selection include the response effort required by the learner (Horner & Day, 1991; Torelli et al., 2016), proficiency in use of the mand topography (Ringdahl et al., 2009), and the history of reinforcement for use of a specific modality (Matter & Zarcone, 2017).

The collective results from studies that have evaluated preference for mand modality indicate that a mand topography assessment should be conducted with all learners using augmentative communication systems. A mand topography assessment is conducted with procedures similar to typical preference assessments with actual objects or pictures. Guidelines for implementation of this type of assessment are beyond the scope of this chapter; interested readers should reference studies that have outlined the steps to perform this type of assessment (see LaRue et al., 2016; van der Meer et al., 2012). Future research on mand modality selection should consider the skills that learners must present with in order to benefit from multimodal communication systems (Shafer, 1993) and how teaching multimodal systems may help to facilitate vocalizations and emergent verbal relations, a topic we will discuss later in this chapter.

MAND INSTRUCTION

Mand instruction should be an essential component of any early intervention curriculum because it increases the child's control over their environment (Sundberg & Michael, 2001). In addition, if therapists begin treatment planning with mand instruction, it provides them with an opportunity to pair themselves with unconditioned and previously established conditioned reinforcers. Through mand instruction and the pairing that occurs, therapists are likely to become conditioned reinforcers themselves. The goal of mand instruction is to teach independent requests that are under the control of relevant MOs. Therefore, ensuring the relevant MOs are present during mand instruction is of paramount importance.

Two common strategies designed to ensure relevant MOs are present during instruction include capturing learning opportunities as they occur in the natural environment (Fenske, Krantz, & McClannahan, 2001) and contriving or creating an opportunity by manipulating other relevant stimuli in the environment (Hall & Sundberg, 1987). For example, incidental teaching requires caregivers to identify MOs that occur naturally in the child's environment, such as when a child shows interest in a toy, and then use a series of prompts to encourage manding (Fenske et al., 2001). A common strategy used to contrive MOs during incidental teaching includes withholding reinforcers for specified periods before a mand instruction session begins (to create sufficient levels of deprivation, an EO). O'Reilly, Aguilar, et al. (2012) evaluated levels of deprivation for preferred items prior to mand instruction sessions. Results confirmed that limiting access to the preferred item prior to the teaching session produced evocative and reinforcing-establishing effects (an EO), whereas having access to the reinforcer immediately before the start of the teaching session produced an abating and reinforcer-abolishing effect (an AO; Michael, 1988; O'Reilly, Aguilar, et al., 2012).

A second evidence-based approach for contriving MOs is the **interrupted behavior chains procedure** (Carter & Grunsell, 2001; Duker, Kraaykamp, & Visser, 1994; Rosales & Rehfeldt, 2007; Sigafoos, Kerr, Roberts, & Couzens, 1994). This procedure involves contriving **transitive conditioned establishing operations** (CMO-T). Michael (1993) defined CMO-Ts as previously neutral conditions whose occurrences alter the effectiveness of another stimulus and evoke responses that produce or suppress that stimulus. The procedure begins with the therapist teaching a sequence of steps (e.g., getting dressed to go outside). Once the child learns the sequence of steps, the therapist interrupts the sequence by removing a needed item to complete the behavior chain (e.g., moving the shoes out of sight). Following a brief pause to allow the child an opportunity to respond independently (e.g., "Shoes please"), the therapist provides a response prompt (e.g., "Say…"). Following the missed step, the child completes the remaining steps and the therapist delivers the reinforcer (i.e., going outside). A major strength of the interrupted chains procedure is that it can momentarily transform a previously neutral stimulus (e.g., shoes) into a reinforcer, because it is necessary to continue the chain and access the larger reinforcer at the end, thereby providing the opportunity to teach a learner to mand for the item that they normally would not be motivated to mand for.

Transfer of stimulus control (ToSC) procedures are also effective for establishing a mand repertoire. These procedures can be used in combination with those outlined above (Thomas, Lafasakis, & Sturmey, 2010). ToSC requires the teacher or therapist to introduce and then gradually fade prompts in one of several ways (i.e., time delay, fading the stimulus prompts gradually over time, use of a less intrusive prompt, or changing the topography of the prompt). In this manner, a stimulus that already exerts control over the target behavior is systematically faded until the child produces the target response independently.

Teaching simple mands (e.g., single words) is a prerequisite for teaching more advanced language skills such as mands for information (e.g., "Where is the milk?" or "When is my birthday?"; Lechago & Low, 2015). Previous studies on this topic have combined CMO-T with an interrupted behavior chain to produce mands for information. For example, Landa, Hansen, and Shillingsburg (2017) taught the mand for information "When" (e.g., "When can I have…") to three children with ASD. They alternated two conditions: presence of EO (e.g., therapist denied access to items or activities) and absence of EO (e.g., therapist denied access to reinforcers and requested completing an additional activity). When the therapist withheld relevant information from the learner, the learner produced mands for information exclusively.

Other researchers have examined the effects of procedures to establish variability in manding. This is important because individuals with ASD often engage in repetitive and restrictive language. For example, a child with ASD may emit the same mand form (e.g., "I want…") without engaging in an alternative mand form (e.g., "I would like…") to gain access to preferred items. One strategy with empirical support for teaching mand variability is the use of a **lag schedule of reinforcement**, in which the wording of a mand cannot be identical twice in a row, in order for the learner to receive reinforcement (Lee & Sturmey, 2006). A second strategy with empirical support is **script-fading procedures**. Scripts are visual or auditory supports that serve as discriminative stimuli for the student to emit a response. Brodhead, Higbee, Gerencser, and Akers (2016) investigated the effects of a script-fading and discrimination-teaching procedure on mand variability in individuals with ASD. Scripts were faded progressively (e.g., "I would like_____", "I would_____", "I_____") in the presence of a discriminative stimulus using lag schedules of reinforcement. Sellers, Kelley, Higbee, and Wolfe (2016) also evaluated script training and fading for the acquisition and maintenance of varied mand frames (i.e., "May I have_____", "Please give me_____") for preschool children with ASD. If participants did not demonstrate increases in their mand variability following a continuous schedule of reinforcement, the researchers implemented post script-fading extinction to induce variability. This procedure was effective for all but one of the participants in the study. These results demonstrate that this is an effective procedure that should continue to be evaluated.

In summary, mand instruction is an essential component of early intensive intervention for young children with language delays, but it should also be prominent when intervening on problem behavior for learners of any age. Several studies support the use of assessment-based intervention for skill acquisition, but there is a paucity of research to identify the most effective intervention to establish verbal operants for a given individual. Future research should evaluate how such an assessment may be conducted.

Tacts Defined

In nontechnical terms, tacts are labels or descriptions of the world around us, and "tacting" refers to this behavior of labeling and describing.

BENEFITS OF A TACT REPERTOIRE

Tacts are of primary benefit to the listener because they convey information on environmental stimuli. Stimuli that evoke tacting can include all of the senses (visual, auditory, olfactory, sensory, and gustatory). Tacts may serve as the basic building blocks for conversation. For this reason, they are often targeted in early curricula for learners with ASD and related disorders (Partington, 2008; Sundberg, 2008). Additionally, the development of a tact repertoire may help reduce the frequency of nonfunctional language emitted by children with ASD (Karmali, Greer, Nuzzolo-Gomez, Ross, & Rivera-Valdes, 2005). Initial targets for tact instruction may consist of learning tacts for objects and persons, followed by representative pictures of these items. Mastery of these initial targets is typically followed by tacts of feature, function, and class of common items; prepositions and actions; and relational descriptors (e.g., soft/rough, more/less, hot/cold, wet/dry; Partington, 2008; Sundberg, 2008).

TACT INSTRUCTION

When echoic and mand repertoires are well established, these verbal operants can be used as prompts in ToSC procedures (Barbera & Kubina, 2005). For example, in the echoic-to-tact transfer, a stimulus is presented and the instructor presents an echoic prompt (i.e., tacts the stimulus and waits for the learner to respond). If the learner does not tact the stimulus independently following the initial echoic prompt, a second prompt may be added (i.e., "Say_____") followed immediately by the discriminative stimulus once more (i.e., "What is it?"). Barbera and Kubina (2005) successfully demonstrated this prompting sequence as an effective method to establish stimulus control for their selected targets.

It is important to note that the supplemental question "What is it?" is not part of Skinner's (1957) definition of a tact, and this additional discriminative stimulus may sometimes interfere with the teaching procedure (Marchese, Carr, LeBlanc, Rosati, & Conroy, 2012). The introduction of a supplemental question in tact instruction can be problematic because the learner may not respond appropriately to stimuli in their environment (considered a "pure" tact form). That is, the learner may not emit a response until a question is posed (Marchese et al., 2012). A related problem with presenting supplemental questions during tact instruction is that the question may acquire intraverbal control over early responses and lead to interference with the acquisition of new responses (Partington, Sundberg, Newhouse, & Spengler, 1994). One other potential problem with inclusion of a supplemental question during tact instruction is that learners may begin to imitate part of the question. This is especially likely if the learner engages in echolalia under other conditions. While additional intervention can remediate this problem (McMorrow, Foxx, Faw, & Bittle, 1987), it could lead to unnecessary delays in targeting other important treatment goals. Sundberg, Endicott, and Eigenheer (2000) targeted signed tacts for two young children with ASD who presented with previous difficulty acquiring tacts. They compared two conditions: object with supplemental question versus object with a prompt to "sign [object name]." Results of this study demonstrated superior performance in the sign-prompt tact acquisition condition.

The instructional procedures outlined above for mands and tacts may be best suited for learners with an established or emerging speaker repertoire. An alternative procedure that has received attention in recent years is **listener training** (Fiorile & Greer, 2007). Listener training involves teaching conditional discriminations to a learner via match-to-sample procedures and then testing for the emergence of speaker responses (i.e., mands and tacts). A related procedure that has received empirical support is **multiple exemplar instruction** (MEI). We will discuss both of these topics below.

Functional Independence of Verbal Operants

The notion of **functional independence** of verbal operants has been presented as a major tenet of Skinner's analysis of verbal behavior (Lamarre & Holland, 1985). The concept of functional independence suggests that establishing one verbal operant within the repertoire of a learner will not necessarily lead to emission of any other verbal operant for that learner. For instance, a child who reliably emits a mand "chocolate" under the pure control of MOs would not be expected to say "chocolate" in the sole presence of a nonverbal stimulus (i.e., they would not necessarily be expected to tact just because they mand). The same is true with the opposite relation, acquiring the mand response "chocolate" after learning to tact for the same item. Whether verbal operants are functionally independent has been a matter of debate in recent years. Some empirical support exists for functional independence across verbal operants (Hall & Sundberg, 1987; Lamarre & Holland, 1985; Partington et al., 1994; Simic & Bucher, 1980; Twyman, 1996), while other studies demonstrate *interdependence* of mands and tacts (Finn, Miguel, & Ahearn, 2012; Gilliam, Weil, & Miltenberger, 2013; Kooistra, Buchmeier, & Klatt, 2012; Wallace, Iwata, & Hanley, 2006) and other elementary verbal operants (Grow & Kodak, 2010).

Fryling (2017) recently suggested that Skinner neither called for research to confirm the functional independence of verbal operants nor openly declared that the verbal operants were functionally independent. In fact, Skinner included a full chapter on multiple causation (Michael, Palmer, & Sundberg, 2011), which can be interpreted as an implication that verbal behavior is controlled by different antecedent variables. Regardless of whether Skinner urged for clarifying the role of functional independence across verbal operants, the data so far are equivocal (Gamba, Goyos, & Petursdottir, 2015). In their review of the literature on functional independence of mands and tacts, Gamba and colleagues (2015) reported procedural differences in training and testing probes that were employed in the published studies on this topic. For this reason, they conclude that the reported lack of transfer between mands and tacts in the published literature (and vice versa) could be attributed to alternative explanations, such as problems in capturing the relevant controlling variables to evoke the mand or tact response (i.e., contriving or capturing MOs) or establishing trained responses that do not function as mand or tacts, but are instead controlled by other variables present in the training situation (i.e., presence of an item during mand probes). Thus, Gamba and colleagues suggested that the existing support for functional independence presents problems related to issues of construct validity, and as such, no single published study has reported exceptionally strong evidence for mand-tact independence.

Gamba and colleagues (2015) suggest that unless future research on this topic controls for critical variables (e.g., appropriate participants, use of standardized language assessments, separate antecedent and consequential control for mands and tacts), more research seems unnecessary. These authors suggest designing alternative strategies that do not involve teaching one operant and then testing for the other, as it may be extremely difficult to design such a study that does not leave room for alternative interpretations, regardless of the outcome. Instead, future research may evaluate existing verbal repertoires in a functional analysis to determine how each operant is used (Lerman et al., 2005). Alternatives are to evaluate the emergence of both mands and tacts following listener training (Ribeiro, Elias, Goyos, & Miguel, 2010) or to test for the functional independence of verbal operants by manipulating schedules of reinforcement for each verbal operant that is assessed.

The goal of identifying functional independence or interdependence in applied research and in practice is to establish effective and efficient communication for learners with language delays. Research in this area has been primarily focused on establishing emergent verbal relations. **Emergent relations** are defined as responses that are acquired under the controlling conditions for one verbal operant (i.e., a tact) that transfer to conditions of another verbal operant (i.e., a mand) with no further teaching or direct instruction (Finn et al., 2012; Gilliam et al., 2013; Kooistra et al., 2012; Wallace et al., 2006). Practitioners who are well informed on the definition and importance of functional independence and interdependence (i.e., the conditions under which functional interdependence has been observed) will be better equipped to develop and implement treatment plans that will establish emergent relations (Egan & Barnes-Holmes, 2010). This translates into better, more efficient intervention, potentially enabling teaching more skills in the same amount of time.

To this end, we offer some clinical recommendations: First, practitioners should conduct frequent assessment and probes to evaluate the functional independence or interdependence of verbal operants. Clinicians are cautioned against *assuming* functional interdependence as this may lead to failures in curriculum development and disproportionately increase one verbal repertoire over the other (Carr & Miguel, 2012; Sautter & LeBlanc, 2006). Second, practitioners should consider teaching mands first under pure MO control, and if tacts do not emerge, then incorporate ToSC procedures. It would be wise to use visual, vocal, or textual stimuli, along with the presentation of the manded item, to bring the response under nonverbal discriminative stimulus, and then deliver generalized conditioned reinforcement instead of the preferred item (Lechago & Low, 2015). Third, practitioners should use mixed operant training, that is, combine mands and tact trials in one single teaching block (e.g., say "dinosaur" under S^D and MO control), then test for the emergence of either verbal operant (Arntzen & Almås, 2002).

Fourth, clinicians are advised to use MEI. For example, Nuzzolo-Gomez and Greer (2004) evaluated the effects of MEI on the emergence of untaught mands or tacts of novel adjective-object pairs in four children with ASD or other developmental disabilities. The experimenter provided initial probes for mands under appropriate levels of deprivation (i.e., the participants had access to the stimuli used in the study only during the experimental conditions, and if a child did not make a selection during an initial probe, the experimenter terminated the session until a state of deprivation could be established). Once the child made an initial selection, the experimenter placed the item out of view in a cup, bowl, or box as the child observed. They then placed the item in an array in front of the child with two other containers of the same type but a different size (i.e., small, medium, and large cup). Tacts consisted of the experimenter's placing the three items in front of the child and pointing to the object to be tacted with no further verbal antecedents. The experimenter explicitly taught the participants to mand and tact using up to three different adjective-object response forms that were different from the original set used during baseline probes. MEI included learning opportunities for mands and tacts. Participants received instruction for the mand with one adjective-object pair followed by instruction for the tact response with the same adjective-object pair. This instruction was followed by probes for the original untaught responses. If the participant did not meet the mastery criterion, they were exposed to a second and then a third adjective-object pair for both mand and tact response forms. Results of the study showed that MEI produced high levels of correct responding on the untrained operant.

Most of the published research on functional independence has been conducted with mands and tacts. More work is needed to assess functional independence across other verbal operants (Aguirre et al., 2016; Carr & Miguel, 2012). There may be prerequisite skills that facilitate the emergence of verbal operants, but those data are not yet available. Future research should focus on targeting prerequisite skills before assessing for functional interdependence of verbal operants (Aguirre et al., 2016).

Synthesizing Skinner's Analysis of Verbal Behavior with Relational Frame Theory

As we have discussed thus far, Skinner's (1957) account of verbal behavior advanced the field of behavior analysis by incorporating a topic that had not previously been discussed from a behavioral perspective. Since the publication of Skinner's book, other behavior analysts have expanded upon his analysis (Greer & Speckman, 2009; Hayes, Barnes-Holmes, & Roche, 2001; Horne & Lowe, 1996; Sidman, 1994). Barnes-Holmes, Barnes-Holmes and Cullinan (2000) proposed a synthesis of Skinner's work with **relational fame theory** (RFT) that has led to applied research with significant clinical implications for learners with autism and related disabilities (Rehfeldt & Barnes-Holmes, 2009; see chapters 11 and 12 in this volume for more elaborate overviews of RFT). The main benefit of combining these two approaches is the development of teaching applications that are focused not only on contingency-based learning, but on derived or emergent (not directly taught) skills (Murphy, Barnes-Holmes, & Barnes-Holmes, 2005). In addition, the nature of derived or emergent relations can help account for the generativity of human language (Murphy & Barnes-Holmes, 2009a).

Rehfeldt and Root (2005) evaluated a procedure to establish **derived mands**, defined as mands not directly taught but that emerged from a history of conditional discrimination instruction. Specifically, Rehfeldt and Root first taught three adults with developmental disabilities to mand for preferred items using pictures. This was followed by conditional discrimination instruction to establish two relations: dictated name to picture and dictated name to corresponding text. Next, the experimenters conducted probes for derived mands (i.e., mands for preferred items using text instead of pictures). All participants demonstrated derived manding following this procedure. Rosales and Rehfeldt (2007) also evaluated derived manding for adults with moderate developmental disabilities. This study extended the previous findings by evaluating "pure" mands, where the reinforcer was not in view of the participant during the derived mand probes. This was accomplished through the utilization of the **interrupted chained task procedure** (Hall & Sundberg, 1987). Results showed that all participants were successful in the derived mands probes although performance declined at follow-up.

A series of studies by Murphy et al. (2005) and Murphy and Barnes-Holmes (2009a, 2009b, 2010) also demonstrated derived manding skills in typically developing children and children with ASD. The focus of these studies was on mands for "more" or "less" tokens of various amounts. For example, Murphy et al. (2005) taught children with ASD derived mands for single tokens in the context of a game. They first taught participants to mand for a specific number of tokens (X1 and X2) by presenting a corresponding card to the experimenter. Importantly, the stimuli were arbitrary symbols and nonsense syllables printed on cards. They then implemented a conditional discrimination procedure to establish stimulus classes with three nonsense syllables (i.e., A1-B1/A2-B2 and B1-C1/B2-C2) and directly taught participants to mand for tokens using only the original stimuli (X1 and X2). On subsequent test probes, participants demonstrated derived mands using the stimuli that were conditionally related during training (i.e., C1 and C2).

A follow-up study by Murphy and Barnes-Holmes (2009a) included derived mands for the addition or removal of a single token, and a third study showed derived manding skills for more or fewer tokens of specific amounts (Murphy & Barnes-Holmes, 2009b). Collectively, these results support the synthesis of Skinner's analysis with RFT to establish derived manding skills in children with and without ASD and in adult learners with moderate developmental disabilities.

The teaching approach employed in this series of studies should be further explored in verbal behavior programming for children with ASD in applied settings. The evidence from applied studies indicates these teaching procedures are likely to prove effective and efficient for teaching multiple mand responses. However, absent the data to support these procedures in applied settings, this remains an empirical question. Future studies should also evaluate the effectiveness of the procedures with individuals with less sophisticated verbal and cognitive repertoires. Another suggestion for practitioners working with this population is to establish flexible responding from the beginning of instruction by teaching multiple mand targets that lead to the same outcome simultaneously (i.e., water, drink, and juice) instead of teaching one at a time to criterion (Murphy & Barnes-Holmes, 2009b).

Implications and Future Directions

Understanding Skinner's analysis of verbal behavior is important for practitioners tasked with the development of appropriate treatment planning for individuals with language delays. For this reason, practitioners should be familiar with the variety of topographies and teaching techniques available for alternative communication. Selecting appropriate targets and learning to manipulate variables to evoke vocalizations and other topographies of verbal behavior are skills that practitioners should develop in order to provide the most enriching learning environment for their clients.

Skill-acquisition programming should include a goal for functional communication that begins with teaching a learner how to mand for preferred and needed items. Starting with an assessment of the existing verbal behavior repertoire, capitalizing on the use of MEI, and testing for emergent relations are all of utmost importance in order to make the most impact with limited instructional time. We also recommend that practitioners familiarize themselves with the different strategies for contriving and capturing MOs and automatic reinforcement, two variables that will have an impact on the development of early verbal repertoires (Sundberg & Michael, 2001).

The issue of functional independence and interdependence should be explored with procedures different from those of past studies (Gamba et al., 2015). Another area with a dearth of empirical support is language intervention for individuals exposed to and/or learning multiple languages (Lang et al., 2011). The U.S. Department of Education, National Center for Education Statistics (2017) estimates that 13.8% of the total English language learner (ELL) population enrolled in US public elementary and secondary schools are students with disabilities. Given these statistics, it is evident that teachers and practitioners will be required to develop intervention plans for learners who are bilingual or multilingual. Practitioners and researchers alike should aim for cultural competency when working with families from diverse backgrounds and develop a better understanding of when the learner will benefit from one language versus the other. For example, some researchers have recently started to evaluate whether ELLs have a preference for the home language (Aguilar, Chan, White, & Fragale, 2017), the impact of the language of instruction on rates of challenging behavior (Padilla Dalmau et al., 2011), and rates of acquisition for new skills when instruction is presented in a bilingual format (Leon & Rosales, 2017).

Leon and Rosales (2017) evaluated the effects of tact training when instruction was presented only in English and compared this training to instruction presented in a bilingual format with both English and the participant's home language. This study was the first to directly compare rates of acquisition in the context of bilingual training. The results showed faster acquisition when instruction was in English, but better generalization and maintenance for stimuli trained in the bilingual instruction condition. The results should be evaluated with caution given the participant's age (six years, eight months) and history of reinforcement for listening to and speaking in English only in his school environment. Applied researchers should continue researching bilingual modifications to verbal behavior instruction as it is an area ripe for investigation. For example, it would be interesting to continue to evaluate rates of acquisition for mands and tacts when instruction is presented in one or multiple languages, and also to evaluate the learner's preference for monolingual or bilingual instruction.

Skinner (1957) described his analysis of verbal behavior as an "exercise in interpretation rather than a quantitative extrapolation of rigorous experimental results" (p. 11). While only a handful of researchers applied his interpretation to working with individuals with ASD and related disabilities early on, there is now a robust body of evidence to support Skinner's analysis of verbal behavior (Aguirre et al., 2016; Dixon et al., 2007). Basic and applied research in behavior analysis has been focused on designing procedures that incorporate Skinner's analysis to teach relevant language skills to learners with and without disabilities, although arguably the focus has been on young children with disabilities. Stewart, McElwee, and Ming (2013b) pointed out that despite the upsurge of research on the basic verbal operants, the generativity of language has been addressed far less. They described language generativity as the "ability to produce sentences never before said, and to understand sentences never before heard" (p. 137). While the research that has been described in this chapter has been largely focused on elementary verbal operants with some discussion on how procedures can be designed to promote the emergence of untaught verbal operants, the research agenda established by Stewart et al. (2013b) will only further enhance the utility of a behavior analytic interpretation of language.

Conclusion

This chapter provided a synopsis of Skinner's conceptualization of verbal behavior, including an overview of his taxonomy of verbal operants, which is based upon a functional analysis. A distinction was made between selection-based and topography-based verbal behavior. Three elementary verbal operants were defined according to Skinner's taxonomy—echoics, mands, and tacts—along with research in support of Skinner's conceptualization of each operant. Research by applied behavior analysts has focused on identifying best practices in teaching manding, tacting, and echoic behavior, and recent research has bridged Skinner's analysis of verbal behavior with relational frame theory.

Study Questions

1. Provide an example of an echoic.

2. What is the difference between a codic and a duplic?

3. Briefly outline two procedures to teach echoic responding.

4. What is a mand? Distinguish between a selection-based and topography-based mand.

5. Describe two strategies to teach mands.

6. What is a tact? How is a tact distinguished from a mand?

7. How is an echoic-to-tact transfer procedure used to teach tacts?

8. Provide an example of the functional independence of mands and tacts.

9. Use the same example to describe the functional interdependence of mands and tacts.

10. What is a derived mand? Give an example.

11. What does it mean to establish flexible responding?

CHAPTER 4

Complex Verbal Behavior

Yors Garcia

The Chicago School of Professional Psychology

Rocío Rosales

University of Massachusetts Lowell

Sebastian Garcia-Zambrano

Southern Illinois University

Ruth Anne Rehfeldt

Southern Illinois University

Link and Preview

The previous chapter provided an overview of the conceptual importance and empirical support for three of the elementary verbal operants defined by Skinner: echoics, mands, and tacts. Beyond those elementary verbal operants, Skinner defined more complex forms of verbal behavior, including, for example, the intraverbal, various extensions of the tact, the speaker serving as his or her own listener, and autoclitics, to which he devoted a full-length chapter. These complex forms of verbal behavior will be the focus of the current chapter.

Skinner's *Verbal Behavior* (1957) was a theoretically rich and comprehensive account of language from a behavioral perspective. It is evident that Skinner's analysis was not limited to the elementary verbal operants, yet much of the empirical work on verbal behavior has been largely focused on these operants (de Souza, Akers, & Fisher, 2017; Dixon, Small, & Rosales, 2007; Dymond, O'Hara, Whelan, & O'Donovan, 2006; Petursdottir & Devine, 2017). Two recent literature reviews specifically focused on the simple intraverbal (Aguirre, Valentino, & LeBlanc, 2016) and multiply controlled intra-verbals (Stauch, LaLonde, Plavnick, Bak, & Gatewood, 2017), showing a steady increase in research on this particular verbal operant.

One possible explanation for the dearth of applied research on the more complex verbal operants is that these operants typically involve multiple sources of control and therefore cannot be addressed until the relevant prerequisite skills are established (Eikeseth & Smith, 2013; Michael, Palmer, & Sundberg, 2011; Sundberg, 2016). In addi-tion, language assessments that help guide treatment planning have not always been helpful in guiding language intervention on more complex repertoires (Gould, Dixon, Nadjowski, Smith, & Tarbox, 2011), although a more recently developed behavioral lan-guage assessment has begun to address this gap (Dixon, 2014a, 2014b, 2015). Applied researchers and practitioners alike must not lose sight of the importance of programming for more complex forms of verbal behavior. Learners with autism spectrum disorder (ASD) and related disabilities require individually tailored and comprehensive treatment programming to meet their unique needs. Complex forms of verbal behavior are related to important skills such as academic performance (Greer, Yaun, & Gautreaux, 2005), problem solving, (Sautter, LeBlanc, Jay, Goldsmith, & Carr, 2011), conversation, (Beaulieu, Hanley, & Santiago, 2014), and obtaining employment (O'Neill & Rehfeldt, 2017).

In this chapter, we will define and review the empirical literature on more complex forms of verbal behavior, beginning with the intraverbal and ending with dictation taking, copying text, and speaker-as-own-listener behavior (chapter 5 focuses on the speaker-as-own-listener). There is ample empirical support for a variety of **transfer of stimulus control** (ToSC) procedures that result in the acquisition of intraverbals, and research is emerging on techniques that result in derived or untaught intraverbal behav-ior for learners with and without developmental disabilities (Aguirre et al., 2016; de Souza et al., 2017; Grannan & Rehfeldt, 2012; May, Hawkins, & Dymond, 2013). Fewer studies, however, have evaluated methods to improve intraverbal behavior related to the conversational speech of typically developing adults (de Souza et al., 2017; Petursdottir & Devine, 2017). Likewise, research on intraverbal behavior has expanded into areas such as simple and conditional discrimination processes, compound stimulus control, diver-gent and convergent stimulus control, and reverse and derived intraverbals. In the next section we will review some of this research and provide recommendations for clinicians.

Research on Complex Verbal Operants

A number of conceptually interesting and clinically important areas of research may fall within the purview of "complex verbal operants," including the intraverbal, dictation taking and copying text, and speaker-as-own-listener. We begin with the intraverbal.

Intraverbal

Skinner (1957) defined the **intraverbal** as a verbal operant that is under the stimulus control of a preceding verbal stimulus, without point-to-point correspondence, and is maintained by generalized conditioned reinforcement. For instance, a child says "Alex" when asked, "What is your name?" and this response is followed by praise or acknowledgment by an adult or peer. In this example, there is no topographical point-to-point correspondence between the S^D "What is your name?" and the response product "Alex." Intraverbals range from simple chains of verbal stimuli (e.g., 1, 2..., A, B...) to fill-in-the-blank responses (e.g., "You buy things with _____?"), answering questions (e.g., "How old are you?"), and categorization (e.g., "Tell me some mammals?").

Palmer (2016) called attention to two different types of intraverbals, **intraverbal control** and **intraverbal operant**. In the case of the intraverbal operant, a single verbal stimulus (written, spoken, gesture) evokes an intraverbal response "as the result of a history of reinforcement for emitting that response in the presence of that stimulus" (p. 97). We observe multiple examples of intraverbal operants when we respond to specific questions presented to us (e.g., "What's your phone number?" "Where do you live?"). Nevertheless, as Palmer (2016) remarks, intraverbal responses are sometimes under multiple sources of stimulus control (i.e., intraverbal control), for example, when verbal stimuli interact with supplemental stimuli to facilitate problem solving (e.g., self-prompts, auditory imaging; Aguirre & Rehfeldt, 2015; Kisamore, Carr, & LeBlanc, 2011; Mellor, Barnes, & Rehfeldt, 2015).

A number of instructional methods for teaching intraverbal responses have been empirically validated. One of the most widely used procedures is ToSC. In this procedure, the instructor concurrently presents a stimulus (prompt) that already exerts some control over the target behavior along with the target verbal stimulus and then systematically removes (fades) the stimulus until the learner produces the target response independently. Multiple studies have used echoic (e.g., saying the correct response vocally and providing an opportunity for the participant to repeat the correct response; Watkins, Pack-Teixeira, & Howard, 1989), textual (e.g., showing the correct response as a written word; Krantz & McClannahan, 1993), tact (e.g., showing the correct response as a visual or auditory stimulus; Goldsmith, LeBlanc, & Sautter, 2007), and echoic prompts combined with error correction (Kodak, Fuchtman, & Paden, 2012) to increase precise stimulus control over intraverbal responses.

Other teaching methods have also demonstrated efficacy for establishing intraverbal repertoires. These include **instructive feedback** (IF; Carroll & Kodak, 2015), **multiple exemplar instruction** (MEI; Lechago, Carr, Kisamore, & Grow, 2015), **peer-mediated interventions** (PMIs; Beaulieu et al., 2014), **compound tact instruction** (Devine, Carp, Hiett, & Petursdottir, 2016), **stimulus pairing** (Byrne, Rehfeldt, & Aguirre, 2014; Vallinger-Brown & Rosales, 2014), **lag schedules of reinforcement** (Contreras & Betz, 2016), **chaining procedures** (Valentino, Conine, Delfs, & Furlow, 2015), **differential observing responses** (DORs; Kisamore, Karsten, & Mann, 2016), **distributed trials** (Haq & Kodak, 2015), and **precision teaching** (Cihon et al., 2017). Furthermore, Aguirre and colleagues (2016) reported that research has expanded into derived intraverbals that are the product of a different operant or conditional discrimination instruction (e.g., Grannan & Rehfeldt, 2012; May et al., 2013) and from the instruction of other intraverbals (e.g., Dickes & Kodak, 2015). Research has shown that intraverbal responses may be under **simple stimulus control** ("jump," "1, 2,…"), **conditional discrimination** ("If your name is Charlie, say your ABCs!"), and **compound stimulus control** ("get up" and "jump"; Axe, 2008; Eikeseth & Smith, 2013; Sundberg, 2016). In the coming sections we will review some of the conceptual and empirical work that has been recently conducted on simple and multiple controlled verbal operants. In addition, we will present some of the procedures that have been more effective in teaching direct and derived intraverbals in individuals with ASD and related disabilities, and offer some clinical recommendations.

SIMPLE VERBAL DISCRIMINATION

Skinner (1957) defined a verbal stimulus as a product of prior verbal behavior. For example, when an individual sends a text message to someone else saying, "How are you?" this stimulus product may evoke in the listener either a written verbal response product (e.g., typing "good") or a vocal response product (leaving a voicemail message; Sundberg, 2016). Verbal stimuli may also control private verbal responses, as when the speaker-as-own-listener engages in thinking (e.g., *I have to pay my bills*). Verbal stimuli may control simple discriminations; for example, the written word "STOP" on a traffic sign evokes an observing response (looking to both sides of the street before crossing it). In the case of learners with ASD, lacking simple verbal discrimination skills will impede the acquisition of more advanced intraverbals. For instance, intraverbal questions such filling in the blank (e.g., "A, B…," "1, 2…") or animal sounds (e.g., "A dog says _____?") require learners to discriminate between "C" and "D" or "ruff-ruff" and "meow," respectively. In particular, "A, B" is the S^D and "C" the intraverbal response. If a participant fails to respond "C," one potential solution would be to teach both "C" and "D" under simple discrimination format until the learner is responding reliably (Eikeseth & Smith, 2013; Sundberg, 2016).

ToSC is one of the most effective procedures for teaching simple verbal discriminations in children with ASD (e.g., Finkel & Williams, 2001; Ingvarsson & Hollobaugh, 2011). For instance, Watkins et al. (1989) taught simple intraverbal responses to three individuals with intellectual disabilities using echoic prompts and a simple verbal stimulus (e.g., "name a color," "name a size," or "name a texture"). Similarly, Finkel and Williams (2001) used textual and echoic prompts to facilitate intraverbal responses in a child with ASD. In this study, the child's stimulus control was enhanced through echoic prompts (e.g., "I like to eat muffins"). Results regarding the efficiency of each prompting strategy are mixed. Some studies report that a history of reinforcement (Coon & Miguel, 2012), visual imaging occasioned by the presence of pictures (Ingvarsson & Hollobaugh, 2011), and preexisting repertoires and individual preferences (Vedora & Conant, 2015) may impact the effectiveness of each form of instruction.

Sundberg and Sundberg (2011) noted that some of the problems related to the acquisition of intraverbals stem from the complexity of the verbal discriminative stimuli and the lack of generalized tact, mand, and listener skills established in the learner's repertoire. Although the research on intraverbal prerequisite skills is lacking (Axe, 2008), some studies suggest that simple discrimination skills may facilitate the acquisition of simple and complex intraverbals (Guerrero, Alós, & Moriana, 2015; Stauch et al., 2017). In this case, starting with simple nonverbal discrimination and instruction following, for example, might involve the clinician's presenting two blocks together, where one stimulus, "green," is correlated with reinforcement (S^{R+}), and the other stimulus, "red," is placed under extinction (i.e., S-delta, or S^{Δ}). The clinician repeats the same procedure with spoken instructions (e.g., to clap hands upon hearing the instruction "clap your hands"). Once these skills are in the participant's repertoire, simple intraverbals may be taught (e.g., "A kitty says _____," "One, two...", "How old are you?"; Sundberg, 2016). We recommend that clinicians assess prerequisite skills such as simple visual discriminations, echoic responses, and learning history prior to conducting intraverbal instruction.

VERBAL CONDITIONAL DISCRIMINATION AND COMPOUND STIMULUS CONTROL

Advanced intraverbal responses are under conditional discrimination and compound stimulus control (Eikeseth & Smith, 2013; Sundberg, 2016). This type of antecedent control may further be subsumed into what has been named divergent and convergent control (see Michael et al., 2011). In **divergent control**, a single **discriminative stimulus** (S^D) controls different response topographies (e.g., hearing "car" may evoke different responses, such as "drive," "wheels," "vehicle," or "auto"; see Feng, Chou, & Lee, 2017; Lee, Chou, & Feng, 2017). The opposite occurs in **convergent control**; that is, multiple discriminative stimuli contribute to the strength of a single response topography (e.g., "the person who does your nails is a _____"). In this last example, the response "manicurist" is under the control of two stimuli: "person" and "nails" (see Devine et al., 2016; Haggar, Ingvarsson, & Braun, 2018). Two specific verbal stimuli are under convergent control, **verbal conditional discrimination** (VC^D) and a **compound stimulus**.

These stimulus control procedures have one significant difference. In VC^D, one verbal stimulus affects the evocative function of another verbal stimulus (e.g., "What do you wear that is brown?"). In this example, the verbal stimulus "wear" alters the function of "brown"; that is, saying "shoes" is under the control of two different verbal stimuli. On the contrary, under compound stimulus control, two independent verbal stimuli are combined to evoke a particular response, for instance, "talk slow" and "talk fast," "eat slow" and "eat fast" (see Eikeseth & Smith, 2013). Although a compound stimulus can occur during conditional discrimination instruction, in compound stimuli one stimulus does not determine the function of the other stimulus.

Prior to teaching complex intraverbals, practitioners should assess appropriate conditional stimulus control. This means that a correct vocal response (e.g., "shoes") must be evoked by the presence of the verbal stimulus (e.g., "brown"). If other responses are evoked (e.g., "sweater," "watch"), further simple verbal discrimination teaching may be needed to bring both verbal stimuli under conditional control (Eikeseth & Smith, 2013; Kisamore et al., 2016; Sundberg & Sundberg, 2011).

PREREQUISITES AND INTRAVERBAL ASSESSMENT

Little research has been conducted on the identification of the specific prerequisite skills learners must acquire prior to intraverbal instruction. Nonetheless, Axe (2008) and Sundberg and Sundberg (2011) provide some general guidelines. First, one should ensure that the learner has reliable mand, echoic, tact, and listener repertoires prior to beginning intraverbal instruction (e.g., Vedora & Conant, 2015). Second, the instructor should be sure that simple discrimination skills are in the child's repertoire before teaching basic intraverbal questions such as fill in the blank and animal sounds. Third, teaching advanced intraverbal questions (e.g., "What do you wear that is green?") requires conditional discrimination and compound stimulus control; therefore, one should teach these skills first in case the repertoire is absent. Prerequisite skills that facilitate conditional discriminations are simple and compound tacting and sorting pictures (Axe, 2008; Devine et al., 2016; Ribeiro, Miguel, & Goyos, 2015). Fourth, a practitioner should ensure that the learner has a basic listener repertoire of responding by feature (i.e., parts of items, descriptions), function (i.e., use or purpose), or class (i.e., category). For instance, the learner will point to a picture of a cookie when asked to identify it by its features ("round," "crunchy"), function ("you eat it"), and class ("food" or "snack"). Fifth, one should use available verbal behavior curricula to assess current verbal skills (Dixon, 2014a, 2014b, 2015; Partington, 2008; Sundberg, 2008). With these guidelines in mind, we now turn to intraverbal instruction.

INSTRUCTIONAL PROCEDURES

In this section, we describe the different instructional procedures to teach intraverbals under divergent and convergent control. We also present current research on establishing derived intraverbals along with some applications for teaching more advanced social skills.

Divergent control and intraverbals. In divergent control, as noted earlier, a single verbal S^D occasions diverse intraverbal responses (e.g., intraverbal categorization). Some of the most effective procedures to promote intraverbals under simple verbal control are IF, lag schedules of reinforcement, and ToSC. Instructive feedback typically involves adding additional nontarget stimuli to the antecedent or consequence events of direct instructional trials (Carroll & Kodak, 2015). In each trial, the instructor presents a target instruction, provides an opportunity to respond, delivers the appropriate consequence, and presents an additional nontargeted IF stimulus. The learner is not required to respond to the IF stimulus, and if they do, the instructor does not deliver consequences. For example, the instructor may present an intraverbal question "What are some fruits?" When the learner says, "apple," the instructor delivers praise and an IF stimulus such as

"Right! Banana is a fruit too." In this case, banana is the IF stimulus. Multiple responses may be added to the IF so that divergent control may be established.

Several studies have demonstrated the effect of IF in the establishment of intraverbal responses. For example, Carroll and Kodak (2015) found that using prompt delay with IF increased response variability when intraverbal categories were taught. Tullis, Frampton, Delfs, and Shillingsburg (2017) found similar effects when IF was implemented to teach problem-solving skills. In this study, the instructor presented a verbal question to the participant ("What is the problem?"), provided reinforcement for correct problem selection (e.g., "shoe with no laces"), and added IF in the form of problem explanation to the consequence (i.e., "That's right. This is a problem because the laces are missing so you cannot tie the shoe"). One participant acquired the secondary target without explicit teaching, whereas the other two participants required additional instruction for the problem explanation section. Haq, Zemantic, Kodak, LeBlanc, and Ruppert (2017) reported that the efficacy of IF may depend on the learner's repertoire before instruction begins, such as attending and echoic behavior. Thus, during instruction, prompting attention to the target stimulus and using vocal prompts may facilitate the acquisition of novel intraverbal responses (Carroll & Kodak, 2015; Haq et al., 2017).

Implementing lag schedules of reinforcement is a second alternative for fostering divergent intraverbals. Lag schedules differentially reinforce intraverbal variability by making reinforcement available for responses that differ from preceding responses based on the value of the lag. For example, on a Lag 2 schedule, a response is reinforced if it differs from the immediately preceding two responses (e.g., saying, "I like apple" and "I like ice cream" when asked, "What do you like to eat?"). In a recent study by Contreras and Betz (2016), individuals with ASD were taught to provide variable responses to questions using a lag schedule of reinforcement. For example, participants were exposed to Lag 1 and Lag 3 (e.g., "Tell me things that fly" with potential responses under Lag 3 being "flies," "birds," and "eagles"). The results showed an increase in varied responding in two participants, while the other participants required additional variability instruction. The results are promising in terms of increasing varied vocal responding using different lag schedules of reinforcement (Lee & Sturmey, 2014; O'Neill & Rehfeldt, 2017; Wiskow, Matter, & Donaldson, 2018).

Lastly, ToSC procedures have also facilitated the acquisition of divergent intraverbals. Diverse procedures such as **tact prompts, errorless learning, schedule thinning, prompt delay,** and **intraverbal prompting** have yielded positive results (Feng et al., 2017; Goldsmith et al., 2007; Lee et al., 2017).

In sum, to increase intraverbal variability (i.e., divergent control), start with simple verbal discrimination instruction using ToSC procedures. If prompt dependency is a problem during instruction, use an alternative prompt method (e.g., Ingvarsson & Hollobaugh, 2011; Mueller, Palkovic, & Maynard, 2007) while also implementing more efficient error-correction procedures (Kodak et al., 2016). We also recommend inserting IF trials early during the instruction and probing for novel intraverbals. Finally, including lag schedules of reinforcement during instruction to maximize intraverbal categorization and beginning with a simple Lag 1 prior to requiring more response variability (e.g., Lag 3) may also be effective.

Convergent control and intraverbals. In convergent control, multiple antecedent variables influence the strength of a single response (Michael et al., 2011). For instance, if a learner says "parrot" in response to "Tell me a green animal," in this case, the response "parrot" is under the control of two stimuli, "green" and "animal" (i.e., conditional discrimination). Several studies have used methods such as conditional discrimination instruction (e.g., Guerrero et al., 2015; Kisamore et al., 2016; Pérez-González & Alonso-Álvarez, 2008), multiple tact instruction (Belloso-Díaz & Pérez-González, 2015; Devine et al., 2016; Mellor et al., 2015), and intraverbal chains (Valentino et al., 2015) to teach complex intraverbal responses to individuals with developmental disabilities; we discuss these below.

Conditional discrimination. The purpose of this strategy is to establish discriminative control under additional stimuli. Take for example two complex questions that, though relatively similar, are difficult to discriminate for some learners with ASD: "What do you eat?" and "What do you eat with?" In this case, each question leads to a different accurate response, "chicken" and "fork," respectively. However, for learners with ASD who may lack complex conditional discrimination skills, these answers will take numerous trials to master, unless they are taught under specific stimulus control. In this case, the correct response would have to come under differential stimulus control of the words "eat" and "with." Similarly, asking participants to repeat the words before providing the intraverbal response may facilitate auditory discrimination in multiple controlled intraverbals.

Kisamore et al. (2016) used conditional discrimination teaching procedures and the requirement of a DOR to teach multiply controlled intraverbals to individuals with ASD. For instance, when the experimenter asked "What's a fruit that's green?" the participant was required to repeat part of the question "fruit green." If the participant did not repeat the verbal stimulus, the experimenter presented a vocal prompt (e.g., "Say, fruit green"). Results showed that conditional discrimination instruction with the DOR was more effective than the prompt-delay procedure with error correction in establishing convergent intraverbals in four of the seven participants.

Blocked-trial procedures have also been effective in establishing intraverbal relations to promote complex intraverbal relations under conditional discrimination control (Haggar et al., 2018; Ingvarsson, Kramer, Carp, Pétursdóttir, & Macias, 2016). In this procedure, the number of trials is gradually reduced contingent upon specific criteria, and the procedure ends with sample stimuli randomly interspersed. Ingvarsson et al. (2016) used constant prompt delay and error correction to teach responses to intraverbal questions through a blocked-trial procedure. Question pairs were selected that took the form "What do you _____?" versus "What do you _____ with?" A total of eight question pairs were included for each participant. Presentation of each question was randomly alternated until ten consecutive answers occurred. Contingent on meeting mastery criterion (i.e., four consecutive trial blocks with no more than two errors), participants proceeded to the next phase. In the subsequent phases, the number of correct consecutive answers and accuracy criterion were lowered. In the last two phases of the teaching procedure, questions were counterbalanced until fifteen consecutive correct answers occurred. In the last step, two questions were presented in a quasi-random fashion. This procedure was effective in establishing novel intraverbal responses under conditional discrimination control, although two participants required additional error correction to acquire the first discrimination. Additional studies found that adding criterion-level probes after each step of the blocked-trial procedure increased accurate responding (Haggar et al., 2018).

Practically speaking, these studies show that teaching learners to discriminate components of the intraverbal questions using DOR and blocked-trial procedures increases the occurrence of intraverbal responses. Further research is warranted to study some of the behavioral mechanisms (e.g., blocking effect, salience of S^D, density of reinforcement, auditory stimulus control, visual imaging) that could explain the effectiveness of these procedures (Haggar et al., 2018; Ingvarsson et al., 2016; Kisamore et al., 2016). Future studies should also compare the blocked-trial procedure to other potentially more efficient teaching procedures (e.g., varied-trial instruction; Cariveau, Kodak, & Campbell, 2016).

Multiple tact instruction. In this procedure participants are required to tact the name of the stimulus while providing the category of the item (e.g., Belloso-Díaz & Pérez-González, 2015; Devine et al., 2016; Grannan & Rehfeldt, 2012). For instance, the instructor presents a target stimulus (e.g., picture of dog) to the participant and asks, "What is this?" Then, after the participant emits a correct response, the instructor asks, "What else is it?" The instructor then conducts intraverbal probes (e.g., "Tell me some animals"). Most of the empirical literature shows that intraverbals do not emerge after multiple tact instruction, though performance improves upon implementing ToSC procedures (Aguirre et al., 2016). On the contrary, recent studies report that using compound tact instruction—that is, presenting two stimuli simultaneously (e.g., "dog" and "cat")—enhances the emission of intraverbal responses (Belloso-Díaz & Pérez-González, 2015; Devine et al., 2016). Although results are positive, further research needs to clarify the different variables that affect the emergence of complex intraverbals under the control of nonverbal stimuli.

An additional strategy that has shown effective results in acquiring multiple controlled intraverbals is using mediating responses (e.g., visual imaging instruction; Aguirre & Rehfeldt, 2015; Kisamore et al., 2011; Mellor et al., 2015; Sautter et al., 2011). Such responses also allow the individual to manipulate variables covertly and to "prompt and probe his own behavior" (Skinner, 1957, p. 442) to increase the probability of a solution. For example, when someone asks, "What does your school look like?" the response is partially prompted by precurrent responses that involve private visual stimuli (e.g., imagining classrooms and buildings) and the question asked. In particular, Mellor et al. (2015) reported that intraverbals (e.g., saying "camera" when asked, "What makes the sound of a click?") and categorization intraverbals (e.g., "What are some sounds that you know? Tell me as many as you can") emerged after multiple tact instruction (e.g., saying "camera" when presented with the recording of a camera clicking) and auditory imagining (e.g., "I know that a camera goes [camera clicking]; oh right, a camera goes click"). Results showed that multiple tacts and imagining were sufficient to yield criterion-level intraverbals in three and two of four participants, respectively. However, two of four participants needed additional ToSC instruction. Although these studies have demonstrated effective results in neurotypical individuals, further research needs to be conducted in individuals with ASD and related disabilities.

Reverse intraverbals. Intraverbals can be derived from other intraverbals, as is the case with **reverse intraverbals**. For example, teaching an intraverbal response "What is the opposite of tall?" ("short") may also promote the reverse intraverbal ("What is the opposite of short?" "tall"). A number of studies have failed to produce the emergence of reverse intraverbals in neurotypical individuals and individuals with developmental disabilities (Pérez-González, Garcia-Asenjo, Williams, & Carnerero, 2007; Petursdottir, Carr, Lechago, & Almason, 2008). Positive outcomes were obtained only after participants were exposed to MEI (Pérez-González et al., 2007).

One recent study found that teaching original intraverbals produced the emergence of reverse intraverbals in some participants (Dickes & Kodak, 2015). In this study, the researchers taught compound stimuli across categories (e.g., object/function relations, opposites, and animal sounds) using a multiple baseline design across categories (e.g., saying "ooo-aaahh" when asked, "A monkey says?"). In the probe sessions, the researchers assessed directly taught and reverse intraverbals (e.g., "Ooo-aaahh says the _____?"). Teaching direct intraverbals produced emergence of reverse intraverbals in two out of three participants; however, results were variable when reverse intraverbals were taught directly. In other words, direct intraverbal instruction was sufficient to produce emergence of reverse intraverbals. As the authors noted, results should be interpreted with caution due to problems with experimental control; the researchers did not introduce the independent variable in all categories. Future research should explore the role of prior histories with verbal conditional discrimination in establishing reverse intraverbals.

Derived intraverbals. Recent studies have demonstrated that intraverbal responding may also emerge from other basic verbal operants in the absence of direct instruction (Allan, Vladescu, Kisamore, Reeve, & Sidener, 2015; Daar, Negrelli, & Dixon, 2015; Dixon, Belisle, Munoz, Stanley, & Rowsey, 2017; Dixon, Belisle, Stanley, Speelman, et al., 2017; Grannan & Rehfeldt, 2012; May et al., 2013; Shillingsburg, Frampton, Cleveland, & Cariveau, 2018). For instance, a child may be taught a tact relation (e.g., "What is the name of this animal?" [dog]), followed by derived intraverbal probes (e.g., "What is a dog?"). Unlike the other instructional protocols discussed previously, generalized contextually controlled patterns of responding mediate the emergence of derived intraverbals (see Stewart, McElwee, & Ming, 2013a, for further details). This is worth mentioning because the behavioral mechanisms responsible for derived intraverbals may increase the likelihood of novel verbal operants emerging in the absence of direct instruction. Due to limited space, we describe only some of the most relevant findings.

In one study, Grannan and Rehfeldt (2012) demonstrated the emergence of intraverbal categorization through direct tact instruction. Specifically, participants were taught to tact categories when presented with a picture (e.g., the instructor presented a picture of vehicles and asked, "What are some things that take you places?" [cars, planes]), followed by visual-visual conditional discrimination (e.g., matching pictures of vehicles). Results showed that derived intraverbal responses emerged in all participants (e.g., saying "car" when asked, "What are four things that take you places?"). In a similar study, May et al. (2013) also found that derived intraverbals emerge after tacts are directly taught. When derived intraverbals do not emerge, adding listener instruction (Smith et al., 2016), MEI (e.g., Greer, Yaun, & Gautreaux, 2005; Pérez-González et al., 2007) or **stimulus-pairing procedures** (Byrne et al., 2014; Vallinger-Brown & Rosales, 2014), or overlapping S^Ds between directly taught and emergent relations (e.g., Shillingsburg et al., 2018), may facilitate further emergence of untaught intraverbals.

Additional studies have shown that conditional discrimination procedures may be used to establish derived intraverbals such as novel wh- questions (e.g., who, where, what; Daar et al., 2015), metaphorical intraverbal responses about feelings (Dixon, Belisle, Munoz, et al., 2017), and derived intraverbal categorization (Dixon, Belisle, Stanley, Steelman, et al., 2017). For instance, Dixon, Belisle, Munoz, and colleagues (2017) showed that teaching metaphorical tacts (e.g., "If you felt like this [picture of a tornado], how would you feel?" [sad, mad, or upset]) promoted the emergence of metaphorical intraverbals (e.g., the instructor asked, "[Name] was told to clean up his/her toys and feels like a tornado. How might [name] feel?"). In this example, the correct response would be "mad." Results of the study showed that all three children answered metaphorical questions during the first instructional phase; however, during the second phase when novel stimulus sets were presented, one participant required a modification (i.e., reduced stimulus array). Taken together, these studies show that advanced intraverbals may emerge from tact instruction under conditional control (i.e., picture plus auditory stimulus). Although most of the studies on this topic have reported positive results, some have shown that it is important to include alternative procedures to enhance derived responding in children with ASD (see Shillingsburg et al., 2018). In the next section, we will explore one additional procedure that may facilitate more advanced intraverbal repertoires such as that involved in social communication.

Peer-mediated interventions. PMIs consist of teaching typically developing peers how to model and prompt targeted social behaviors for their peers with a diagnosis of ASD or related disabilities. Research on the evaluation of social skills intervention has highlighted PMIs as one of the most promising methods to improve this target behavior in this population (Chang & Lock, 2016). Krantz, Land, and McClannahan (1989) demonstrated the efficacy of PMIs with three adolescents diagnosed with ASD serving as peer prompters for three other peers with ASD. The procedure consisted of a peer's delivering a prompt to talk about a topic of interest (e.g., sports). Generalization probes showed similar levels of performance with peers not involved in the study and in settings outside of the teaching environment, and also showed maintenance of the behavior once the peer prompter was withdrawn.

More recently, Beaulieu et al. (2014) evaluated a PMI **behavioral skills training** (BST) procedure to improve the conversational skills of a college student with a learning disability. The focus of the study was not isolated to intraverbal responding, but rather included several additional indicators of advanced conversation skills, including time spent as listener versus speaker and number of interruptions. Peers were taught to provide instructions, modeling, role-play, and feedback to the participant during all teaching sessions. For interruptions, they delivered feedback visually at first, and then vocally, if necessary. Following the introduction of BST, the participant emitted fewer interruptions, increased the time spent as a listener during the sessions, and showed a decrease in the duration of high-specificity content (defined as an excess of details provided on a topic). The effects of the intervention were maintained with naïve peers and compared favorably with normative data on the conversational skills of three undergraduates without disabilities.

Dictation Taking, Textual Behavior, and Copying Text

Three additional complex verbal operants were described in *Verbal Behavior* (Skinner, 1957), including dictation taking, textual behavior, and copying text. Dictation taking corresponds to what is known as writing; Skinner defined dictation taking as a written response controlled by a vocal verbal stimulus (e.g., writing a sentence as someone says it). Textual behavior is vocal responding controlled by a visual verbal stimulus (e.g., reading the newspaper). Both dictation taking and textual behavior involve point-to-point correspondence and no formal similarity between the verbal S^D and the response product. In point-to-point correspondence, all components of the response match the components of the S^D, for instance, writing "apple" upon hearing the word "apple," or saying "apple" when seeing the written word "apple." In both cases each letter of the S^D matches each letter of the verbal response "apple," and there is no formal similarity between the S^D and response product; both are in a different modality (e.g., S^D is a written stimulus and the response is vocal). These operants are among some of the most advanced verbal skills and are underresearched topics in verbal behavior (Dymond et al., 2006). In this section, we will briefly review some of the procedures to promote the development of these complex verbal operants and provide some clinical recommendations for practitioners.

Some studies have used simple stimulus-control procedures (Asaro-Saddler, 2016; Pennington, 2016; Pennington & Delano, 2012) and derived relational responding technology (de Souza, de Rose, & Domeniconi, 2009; de Souza & Rehfeldt, 2013; Greer, Yaun, & Gautreaux, 2005) to teach written (i.e., dictation-taking) and spoken spelling skills in individuals with ASD (Aguirre & Rehfeldt, 2015). For example, de Souza et al.

(2009) developed a research program that starts with teaching simple words with consonant-vowel sequences (e.g., "bad," "fan," "nap"), followed by teaching complex sequences of words (e.g., "bread, chair, snake") and then integrating reading (textual behavior) and writing skills in a network of derived relations to assess reading comprehension. Additional studies have found that teaching dictation (de Souza & Rehfeldt, 2013), teaching written and spoken spelling skills (Greer, Yaun, & Gautreaux, 2005), and promoting collateral responses (Aguirre & Rehfeldt, 2015) enhance the occurrence of untaught spoken and written skills in individuals with intellectual disabilities. In addition, de Souza and Rehfeldt (2013) evaluated the effect of conditional discrimination instruction (i.e., matching printed words to their printed synonym) on the emergence of untaught vocal spelling. Aguirre and Rehfeldt (2015) examined the effects of visual imaging and instruction on correct written spelling responses in three adolescents with learning disabilities. In the instructional phase, the examiners presented participants with a flash card (i.e., "The word is _____"), which they then removed. They instructed participants to imagine the word for three seconds and later asked them to write the word. An error correction plus reinforcement procedure was added in case participants did not meet mastery criterion of written spelling. Only one participant met the mastery criterion during the visual imaging only condition, and the other two participants required error correction plus reinforcement.

Miguel, Yang, Finn, and Ahearn (2009) taught children with ASD to select pictures and printed words when given their dictated name via match-to-sample. Then, without further instruction, all participants demonstrated emergent textual behavior (i.e., reading aloud written words). Sprinkle and Miguel (2013) obtained similar results. These studies show that textual behavior may be established indirectly through instructional procedures that promote derived stimulus relations between printed words, pictures, and dictated names. These findings are particularly relevant for practitioners who wish to minimize instructional time. Likewise, constructed-response match-to-sample tasks have been implemented to teach vocal and copying skills to students with intellectual disabilities (Hanna, de Souza, Rose, & Fonseca, 2004). In this procedure, an instructor presents a pool of letters (e.g., "C," "B," "A," D," "R") simultaneously with the sample stimulus (e.g., written word "CAR") to the participant, and then asks the participant to construct a word identical to the sample. If the sample stimulus is a printed word, the task is essentially one of copying. In contrast, if the sample is a spoken word, then the participant is required to construct and spell the correct word. Additional procedures such as BST (Pennington, Foreman, & Gurney, 2018), video modeling (Marcus & Wilder, 2009), praising qualifying autoclitics (Hübner, Austin, & Miguel, 2008), and ToSC (Fabrizio & Pahl, 2007; Haq & Kodak, 2015) have also been implemented to teach textual responses.

Taken together, these studies show that arranging for derived stimulus relations, using MEI, and establishing mediating behavior such as visual imaging may increase the emergence of untaught textual (Miguel et al., 2009), dictation-taking (de Souza & Rehfeldt, 2013), and written and spoken spelling skills (Aguirre & Rehfeldt, 2015; Greer, Yaun, & Gautreaux, 2005).

The Speaker-as-Own-Listener

Thus far, we have reviewed how separate speaker (e.g., mand, tact, intraverbal) and listener (pointing, attending, following instructions) repertoires may be established. Skinner (1957) described several repertoires, including thinking, problem solving, self-editing, and self-awareness, that emerge when the speaker mediates their own responding as a listener. Speaker-as-own-listener is an advanced repertoire that allows an individual to achieve significant independence and engage in complex social skills (e.g., writing, reading, perspective taking; Greer & Speckman, 2009; Spradlin & Brady, 2008). For example, when someone is reading a text, they not only read the written words but also listen to what is read. Reading consists of a speaker-listener relationship under the control of print stimuli or pictures. Similarly, when an individual is writing, the speaker and listener within the same skin are under the control of the auditory and textual stimuli. Taking perspective also requires that the individual discriminate their own point of view where events take place and respond to them from the same perspective (e.g., when asked, "How do you feel?"). We only mention this topic briefly here as it is the focus of the next chapter.

Implications and Future Directions

The material presented here on complex verbal behavior has a number of important implications for practitioners and researchers. First, it is not clear what preexisting repertoires must be intact prior to initiating intraverbal instruction, though some efforts have been made in this regard (Partington, 2008; Sundberg, 2008; Sundberg & Sundberg, 2011). More research is warranted to determine the minimal number of tacts, echoics, and listener skills necessary before introducing intraverbal instruction. One interesting research line explored the use of psychometrically sound assessments to evaluate verbal deficits in individuals with ASD (Dixon, 2014a, 2014b, 2015). In the meantime, we recommend that practitioners follow best practice—that is, teach tacts, mands, and listener skills before proceeding to intraverbal teaching (see Sundberg & Sundberg, 2011).

Second, results are mixed regarding the best prompting strategy to teach intraverbals (e.g., Coon & Miguel, 2012; Ingvarsson & Hollobaugh, 2011; Vedora & Conant, 2015). Therefore, we encourage practitioners to assess the type of prompting method that is most suitable for the learner prior to intraverbal instruction (see Seaver & Bourret, 2014, for an example of a prompt assessment). Future studies might also include error analyses (see Devine et al., 2016; Kisamore et al., 2016) and compare echoic and tact prompts with and without error correction during intraverbal training (see de Souza et al., 2017).

Third, research on multiply controlled intraverbals has been conducted in recent years (e.g., Stauch et al., 2017). This area offers important opportunities and challenges for practitioners and researchers alike. Palmer (2016) made an important conceptual distinction between the traditional definition of intraverbal (i.e., intraverbal operant) and a multiply controlled intraverbal (i.e., intraverbal control). In the former case, studies have focused on teaching simple intraverbals such as question answering, fill-in-the-blank responding, and categorization skills using ToSC procedures (see de Souza et al., 2017; Petursdottir & Devine, 2017). In these studies, a single verbal stimulus was established as discriminative for the intraverbal response (e.g., "What is your name?"). Other studies have explored the role of collateral stimuli and verbal conditional discriminations to teach intraverbal responses, primarily in neurotypical individuals (e.g., Aguirre et al., 2016; Kisamore et al., 2011; Mellor et al., 2015; Valentino et al., 2015). For instance, some studies have demonstrated that using visual imaging may enhance problem-solving (Kisamore et al., 2011) and written spelling skills (Aguirre & Rehfeldt, 2015).

Similarly, other studies have used conditional discrimination procedures to teach intraverbal responses, for instance, block-trial procedures (i.e., the same sample stimulus is presented repeatedly across trials instead of alternating each trial; Ingvarsson et al., 2016) and DOR (e.g., naming or touching the sample stimulus before selecting the comparison stimulus; Kisamore et al., 2011). Practically speaking, this means that practitioners must teach simple discrimination repertoires prior to teaching basic (e.g., A, B...) and complex (e.g., "What are some red fruits?") intraverbal responses. Then, they can teach advanced repertoires such as problem solving or covert intraverbal behavior using supplementary stimuli such as visual imaging. Although more research is needed in this area, currently available results are promising.

Fourth, once simple and multiply controlled intraverbals are in the participant's repertoire, it is important to target intraverbal variability (de Souza et al., 2017; Haq et al., 2017; Lee & Sturmey, 2014) and derived intraverbals (Grannan & Rehfeldt, 2012; May et al., 2013). Although the results have been very consistent showing that lag schedules and IF increase intraverbal variability, there is still room for additional research in assessing the controlling variables in these procedures. Similarly, research in derived relational responding has demonstrated that more efficient protocols can be implemented to teach derived intraverbals (Daar et al., 2015; Shillingsburg et al., 2018).

Lastly, data on more elaborate repertoires such as dictation taking, textual behavior, copying text, and speaker-as-own-listener are emerging in the field. We recommend that clinicians assess some prerequisites (e.g., listener skills, fine-motor coordination, and self-regulatory skills such as self-control) prior to teaching dictation-taking skills. Similarly, evidence-based practices such as using speech-generating devices, self-management, visual support (e.g., scripts, pictures), and peer-mediated instruction have been found to be effective in facilitating the acquisition of writing skills in learners with ASD (Asaro-Saddler, 2016; Pennington et al., 2018). Results of other studies promote the use of derived relational responding protocols in teaching written and spoken spelling repertoires (de Souza & Rehfeldt, 2013; Greer, Yaun, & Gautreaux, 2005). Finally, teaching naming and say-do correspondence repertoires facilitates the achievement of important independent skills. Research in this area is well developed (see Greer & Ross, 2008, and the following chapter for more details).

We conclude this chapter with some recommendations for future research in complex verbal behavior. Research is lacking on intraverbal responses focused upon social questions (e.g., "Who is your best friend?"); most research has concentrated on teaching categorization, feature, function, and class responses (de Souza et al., 2017; Stauch et al., 2017). Similarly, there is limited research exploring intraverbals focused upon emotions (Dixon, Beslise, Munoz, et al., 2017) and using peer-mediated interventions with middle and high school students with ASD. Research should also incorporate generalization and treatment fidelity measures (Chang & Locke, 2016). Furthermore, future research should investigate the role of different problem-solving strategies (e.g., organizing and grouping stimuli, visual imagery, observing one's own environment, and covert intraverbal behavior) on the acquisition of complex intraverbal categorization in individuals with developmental disabilities (e.g., Aguirre et al., 2016; Mellor et al., 2015; Petursdottir & Devine, 2017).

Likewise, future research should compare whether instructive feedback or lag schedules of reinforcement is more effective in establishing response variability for children with ASD (Carroll & Kodak, 2015; de Souza et al., 2017). Also, evaluating the role of different types of lag schedules of reinforcement (e.g., Lag 3) in intraverbal instruction (Lee & Sturmey, 2014) and investigating the effects of different reinforcers on intraverbal variability is in order.

Divergent and convergent control is another area that requires further exploration. For instance, research on divergent control is needed to evaluate the efficiency of different instructional methods (e.g., formal prompts, instructional feedback; Feng et al., 2017; Lee et al., 2017). In convergent control (e.g., conditional discrimination and compound stimulus control), a need exists for further evaluation of the effectiveness of blocked-trial procedures and DORs in establishing intraverbal responses. This might involve evaluating generalization across people, environment, and different responses using blocked-trial procedures and whether DOR alone or combined with a blocked trial-procedure is more effective in establishing convergent intraverbals (Haggar et al., 2018; Kisamore et al., 2016). Likewise, future research should extend the use of derived relational responding technology in establishing more complex intraverbal responses, the role of covert verbal responses on overt responses such as academic tasks, and the establishment of vocal spelling with different verbal repertoires (de Souza & Rehfeldt, 2013; Grannan & Rehfeldt, 2012).

What started as a friendly challenge introduced to Skinner by the philosopher Alfred North Whitehead, who said, "Let me see you account for my behavior as I sit here saying 'No black scorpion is falling upon this table'" (Skinner, 1957, pp. 456–457), has turned into a vibrant research program with effective applications, mostly in the area of developmental disabilities (de Souza et al., 2017; Petursdottir & Devine, 2017). Sixty years have passed since Skinner published his most important work. However, buried in his book still lie many areas awaiting empirical testing, for instance, the role of echoic behavior and supplementary stimulation in remembering, metaphorical extensions of the tact, tacting private behavior, and multiple causation (Schlinger, 2017). More research is still needed, particularly with typically developing individuals. Skinner (1969) once mentioned, "Behaviorism, as we know it, will eventually die—not because it is a failure, but because it is a success. As a critical philosophy of science, it will necessarily change as a science of behavior changes" (p. 267). The field of verbal behavior will only prosper and survive by standing on the shoulder of the giants, as was the quest of this chapter.

Conclusion

Skinner's taxonomy of verbal behavior includes several operants that are the foundation of a number of complex skills. Unlike the operants described in the preceding chapter, many such operants are multiply controlled, and for this reason a number of prerequisite skills may be established before such operants are acquired. This chapter explored the processes involved in intraverbal, dictation taking, textual, and copying text repertoires and discussed research on strategies for teaching such repertoires in individuals who may lack such skills.

Study Questions

1. What is an intraverbal? Explain by distinguishing it from one of the other verbal operants reviewed in this text so far.

2. Describe how the same word could be an echoic, mand, tact, or intraverbal.

3. How have transfer of stimulus control procedures been used in intraverbal instruction?

4. Give an example of both divergent and convergent control.

5. What are three prerequisites described in the section titled "Prerequisites and Intraverbal Assessment"?

6. Describe the differential observing response procedure and how it is used in intraverbal instruction.

7. What is multiple tact instruction?

8. Distinguish between dictation taking and copying text.

9. Describe one procedure that has been explored to promote dictation taking or copying text.

10. Comment on two of the implications for practice as described at the end of the chapter.

CHAPTER 5

Identification and Establishment of Bidirectional Verbal Operants

R. Douglas Greer

*Columbia University Graduate School of Arts and Sciences and
Teachers College, New York, NY*

Peter Pohl

Child Psychology Practice, Garmisch-Partenkirchen, Germany

Lin Du

*Columbia University Graduate School of Arts and Sciences and
Teachers College, New York, NY*

Jennifer Lee Moschella

*Columbia University Graduate School of Arts and Sciences and
Teachers College, New York, NY*

Link and Preview

Up to this point the text has provided an overview of fundamental behavioral processes (chapter 2), basic verbal operants (chapter 3), and complex verbal operants (chapter 4). The present chapter goes a step further in the area of complex verbal operants, and in particular focuses on bidirectional verbal operants, including the speaker's functioning as their own listener. Importantly, the chapter is written from the perspective of behavioral development and pertains to the building blocks for some of the most complex forms of verbal behavior.

We now understand a great deal more about the developmental sequence needed for children to become fully verbal. Research from our laboratory and schools (http://www.

cabasschools.org) has resulted in the **verbal behavior developmental theory** (VBDT; Greer & Ross, 2008; Greer & Speckman, 2009). VBDT builds on Skinner's (1957) theory of verbal behavior, as well as relational fame theory (Hayes, Barnes-Holmes, & Roche, 2001), research on derived relations, and other research in verbal behavior. Central to all of this research is Skinner's idea that in the development of verbal behavior in children, the listener (observing or "perceptual" responses) and speaker (speaking or producing responses) are initially independent. There is growing agreement on this point across disciplines. Developmental research in neuroscience has identified correlates in brain physiology that shows that responding as a listener precedes speaking (Imada et al., 2006). Both behavior science and neuroscience now concur that experience is key. In fact, the Imada et al. study provides snapshots of brain changes as a function of experience.

What verbal behavior development contributes to thcsc disciplines is *the identification of the kinds of experiences that make the development possible, the relation of these experiences to the fundamental principles of behavior, and how children come to have the wherewithal to contact or benefit from those experiences.* Verbal behavior development findings have led to increased numbers and sophistication of tools available to professionals to establish components of development children might be missing. These components of development are called **behavioral developmental cusps** (Rosales-Ruiz & Baer, 1997). The onset of cusps allows children to (a) learn what they could not learn before, (b) learn faster, or (c) learn in new ways (i.e., cusps that are new learning capabilities such as the stimuli controlling learning from observation or exposure).

Bidirectional Operants

The focus of this chapter encompasses some of the cusps that are the **bidirectional operants** that mark the particular *intercept of the listener and speaker.* These can be separated into three different categories: (a) verbal episodes between persons, (b) the speaker-as-own-listener (Donley & Greer, 1993; Greer & Speckman, 2009; Skinner, 1957), and (c) the learning of word-object relations as speaker and listener incidentally. All of these are examples of the *joining of the speaker and listener.* Some even argue that we are only fully verbal at the point where the speaker and listener are joined (Barnes-Holmes, Barnes-Holmes, & Cullinan, 2000; Greer & Du, 2015a). Bidirectional verbal operants are involved in talking with others, talking to oneself, and listening to oneself. Social reinforcers are involved in all three types, but they are only conspicuous in the verbal episodes between persons.

Skinner (1957), in his seminal work, stated that *verbal behavior is social behavior.* He and others (e.g., Tomasello, 2008) have theorized that verbal behavior evolved because of the need for the human species to collaborate in order to hunt and gather and later cultivate and harvest. In a review of a body of research, Greer and Du (2015b) argued that behavioral developmental cusps emerge in many cases with the onset of newly learned social reinforcers (i.e., conditioned social reinforcers). Verbal behavior differs from language in that the former pertains to the *function* of communicating, while the latter pertains to the *structure*, or the lexicon, of communication. This does not mean that the two disciplines are necessarily adversarial; rather, they should be complementary. Verbal behavior also differs from the structural aspect of language in that it includes social interactions such as frowns, smiles, grimaces, and gestures. In essence, verbal behavior encompasses the range of interactions in which individuals seek to affect—or be affected by or benefit from—the behavior of others.

What may have initially begun with a need to collaborate for mutual primary reinforcement (i.e., to emit and respond to mands) may have eventually evolved to direct reinforcement of communicative exchanges by the behaviors of the parties involved (i.e., conversational units or tacts as contact reinforcement). One research endeavor focuses on verbal episodes involving communicative exchanges between children or children and adults. This consists of analyses of bidirectional verbal operants involving exchanges between two or more individuals, where an individual is reinforced both as speaker and listener in one exchange. This is referred to in the literature as a **conversational unit** (Baker, 2014; Donley & Greer, 1993; Greer & Ross, 2008; Lodhi & Greer, 1989; Schmelzkopf, Greer, Singer-Dudek, & Du, 2017; Sterkin, 2012). More frequent conversational units speak to the magnitude of the social repertoire of the individual. Still another social reinforcement dimension of the conversational unit is the *initiation* of episodes. Initiating an interaction and responding to an episode initiated by others are each measures of social reinforcement. The complementary phenomenon in linguistics is "turn taking." What verbal behavior adds to the concept of turn taking is that the conversational unit doesn't necessarily require that exchanges "make sense" to an observer; semantics and syntax are irrelevant to these bidirectional operants. Moreover, a *verbal* listener or a *verbal* speaker response need not involve a lexicon. Evidence of reinforcement is the continuation of exchanges and few or no lulls in conversation. The conversational unit includes within it other verbal operants.

In our laboratory and practice we use the presence or absence of conversational units as the essential measure of social behavior in children. This measure is used in interventions that have proved successful in establishing, or enhancing, conversational exchanges by children with adults and with children. These appear to result in establishing the natural *but learned reinforcement* that is characteristic of social verbal behavior. The use of traditional behavior analytic interventions to increase socially appropriate speech in children with autism—scripts or videos, for example—have a long track record (e.g., Charlop & Milstein, 1989; Taylor, Levin, & Jasper, 1999). In these cases, the focus has been on behavior as the target. While these interventions are successful in many cases, there have been problems with maintenance. Our research program has shown that targeting specific behavioral cusps may lead to more expansive verbal behavioral development.

Methods to Identify and Establish Bidirectional Verbal Operants

For each bidirectional operant—verbal episodes between persons, verbal behavior within the skin (also referred to as speaker-as-own-listener or talking to oneself), and incidental learning (i.e., bidirectional naming)—we will describe the cusp and give a general description of how to identify and establish bidirectional verbal operants.

Verbal Episodes Between Persons

Lawson and Walsh (2007) developed a protocol to establish social reinforcement for talking to others, seeking them out, and being sought; we term this **social listener reinforcement** (SLR; Baker, 2014; Greer & Ross, 2008; Lawson & Walsh, 2007; Sterkin, 2012). This protocol is used specifically when children, who have characteristics like those described in the studies, emit tacts and mands but do not initiate conversational units or tacts with adults or other children. However, when a child demonstrates that social reinforcement is present but lacks the behaviors (i.e., does not initiate conversational units), then the use of scripts, videos, and other similar interventions to establish language repertoires is needed. But, if the behaviors are not directly reinforced by communicating with others and being communicated with by others, then establishing the cusp that results in new social reinforcement for bidirectional operants, the SLR protocol, is suggested. When maintenance does not result because reinforcers other than social reinforcers have been used, the establishment of the relevant social reinforcers also may be needed. In some cases, after the cusp is established, scripts and videos can be used to expand the variety of verbal behavior.

Below we describe three procedures that have been shown to be effective in increasing verbal episodes with other individuals: (a) social listener reinforcement involving collaboration contingencies, (b) the intensive tact protocol, and (c) observational conditioning. Each appears to act to condition reinforcers for bidirectional operants between children and adults or between children, but different presenting repertoires of children determine which are appropriate for any given child.

SOCIAL LISTENER REINFORCEMENT

The SLR protocol involves a sequence of increasingly complex games, ending with an empathy phase, that use a yoked contingency game board to establish social listener reinforcement. A game board is designed with two paths (Greer & Ross, 2008; Stolfi, 2005), one for the students and one for the teacher/experimenter. Children must follow the rules of the game and collaborate with a partner in order to "move up" the path toward an agreed-upon prize and avoid the teacher's beating them to the prize. The pair must ask each other questions and listen to each other in order to "move up." For example, the peer confederate holds an unknown item while the target child is blindfolded, and the target child must ask the peer questions (speaker behavior). If the target child emits a correct response by telling the experimenter or teacher exactly what the peer confederate said, the team "moves up" the game board (first listener behavior and then speaker behavior). The procedure is designed to build reinforcement for speaking and listening to peers and to increase the child's conversational units with others. The ages and repertoires of the children determine which games are selected. The types of interactions involving the game board include peer tutoring, video monitoring, and board games to increase verbal operants emitted by participants with a wide range of prerequisite verbal skills (Baker, 2014; Sterkin, 2012). Baker found that the SLR procedure led to more increases in conversational units when compared with traditional video modeling, supporting the notion that the SLR procedure established reinforcement for verbal exchanges, a critical component of truly social behavior and audience control. As the sequence and sophistication of the games progress, the reinforcement should come to incorporate "winning" together as a new reinforcement effect in itself.

INTENSIVE TACT PROTOCOL

The emission of tacts appears to be preliminary to, or a building block for, conversational units. There is growing evidence that the tact is under the control of social reinforcement and not just any type of generalized reinforcers (Eby & Greer, 2017; Schmelzkopf et al., 2017). An intervention that we call the **intensive tact protocol** (Greer & Du, 2010) has proved successful in increasing the initiation of tacts and conversational units. It appears that the procedure has different effects for different children depending on their initial repertoire. For children who initiate few mands and tacts, the procedure increases mands and to a lesser degree tacts, but does not establish conversational units (Baker, 2014; Schmelzkopf et al., 2017). For children with more tacts in their repertoire, the initiated mands decrease and the tacts and conversational units increase, demonstrating the shift toward more social reinforcement (Eby & Greer, 2017). The decrease in mands and a corresponding increase in tacts indicates a shift in reinforcement control to social contact and is a sought after and desirable outcome (Costa & Pelaez, 2014).

The intensive tact intervention builds social listener reinforcement (Delgado & Oblak, 2007; Greer & Du, 2010; Pistoljevic & Greer, 2006; Schauffler & Greer, 2006; Schmelzkopf et al., 2017) and consists of daily presentation of 100 learn units of *pure tact* opportunities, where the participant receives social praise as reinforcement for emitting tacts *without* a vocal-verbal antecedent. That is, a stimulus is presented *without the use of vocal instructions* such as "What is it?" Target stimuli can consist of social studies content (e.g., national monuments) and can be determined by participants' age, grade-level curricular requirements, and grade-level achievement. The procedure can also incorporate autoclitic functions.

OBSERVATIONAL CONDITIONING

An observational conditioning intervention (i.e., Singer-Dudek, Oblak, & Greer, 2011) is another effective protocol to condition social attention and praise as a reinforcer.

Greer, Singer-Dudek, Longano, and Zrinzo (2008) conditioned adult praise as a rein-forcer by presenting a simple task to target participants and peer confederates, while delivering praise *only to the peer confederate* (the target participant was denied praise for completing the task). Schmelzkopf and colleagues (2017) also found increases in conver-sational units with peers as a function of this protocol. (See chapter 8 on observational learning for more on interventions that capitalize on the repertoire of learning by observation.)

The three behaviors discussed above—social listener reinforcement, the intensive tact protocol, and observational conditioning—establish or enhance adult attention as a reinforcer which, in turn, results in more tacts and, more significantly, more conversa-tional units. Once the speaker and listener are joined, the repertoires for listening to others (being "communicated to" as a function of reinforcement stimuli) and speaking to others (communicating to as a function of reinforcement stimuli) are embedded in the stimuli in the interaction. Of course, the onset of the cusp is the very beginning of this repertoire. But, once it is present, the experiences in communicating with others lead to a more sophisticated repertoire because the reinforcers are present.

Children also take on the roles of speaker and listener when they talk aloud as they are alone and engaged in fantasy play. Skinner (1957) argued that this overt behavior, speaker and listener roles, becomes covert as children are made "self-conscious" as a result of certain audiences. We also argue that it is a critical speaker-as-own-listener cusp leading to more complex behavior, which we discuss below.

Verbal Behavior Within the Skin (Talking to Oneself)

While it is empirically difficult to test whether one talks to oneself covertly, it is apparent and observable in young children when they engage in fantasy play, where they talk aloud to themselves. The phenomenon is described as a critical stage by many devel-opmental psychologists who study play and language development (Vygotsky, 1967). Behavior analysts have investigated this phenomenon in children demonstrating the alternation of speaking and listening, where the roles of listener and speaker can be directly observed. Lodhi and Greer (1989) demonstrated that typically developing five-year-old girls engaged in self-talk conversational units (i.e., alternated roles as speaker and listener), providing evidence for Skinner's (1957) "speaker and listener within the skin." Many of the self-talk exchanges in Lodhi and Greer's study also included the **say-do correspondence** repertoire that Paniagua and Baer (1982) identified early on. A child may act as a speaker in saying that they, or an object of play, will engage in an action, and then the child may act as a listener by doing what they said they would do. This demonstrates that the listener and speaker repertoires are joined in the child's verbal behavior development. Say-do correspondence and self-talk signal that bidirec-tional verbal operants are present in the child's verbal repertoire. These functions appear to lay the foundation for more complex listener/speaker interactions within the skin, such as thinking verbally. Then, by extension, once print control becomes part of the relations, one functions as writer and own reader, or self-editor.

Incidental Learning (Bidirectional Naming)

The third bidirectional operant and developmental cusp is what Horne and Lowe (1996) called naming. We concur with Miguel (2016) that the term **bidirectional naming**, and the abbreviation BiN, is less confusing. By extension, we suggest that the term **unidirectional naming** (UiN) refer to the demonstration of the listener component. While it is possible, and even probable, that one can be taught to emit speech sounds (parroting or canonical babbling) before responding as a listener, we argue that this is not really verbal from a developmental and a verbal behavior perspective. For example, one can shape speech such that a child says the name of an item and receives the item; however, if the child did not first acquire the listener relation, it is not truly verbal. When the speech sound is taught or learned first, it may function as a duplicative response, as in singing or parroting under the control of the correspondence rather than the verbal function (see Gladstone and Cooley, 1975, for the seminal study). There are numerous examples of individuals with autism who are not verbal but can sing the lyrics of an entire song. They are presumably under the control of the correspondence between their responses and what they heard before, yet none of the responses are verbal in the sense that they affect the behavior of others in verbal functions. However, if the speech sounds are in repertoire, interventions may join the listener to the speaker.

The specific aspect of BiN that we focus on is how this developmental cusp (i.e., a cusp that is also a new learning capability that changes how children can learn) results in children's learning language and verbal behavior functions without direct instruction (i.e., incidental learning). We believe that the body of existing research suggests that BiN, together with the two other cusps associated with the joining of the listener and speaker within the skin, represents the point at which the child becomes *fully verbal*. The subsequent complex behaviors associated with reading and writing, using the methods of science, authority, and logic, are built on the emergence of these cusps.

We now know that some children who did not demonstrate BiN can do so after they undergo environmental interventions, including **multiple exemplar instruction** (MEI) across listener and speaker responses with training sets of stimuli. After receiving MEI, children from eighteen months to six years of age (neurotypical children and children with language delays) demonstrated BiN with novel stimuli (Corwin & Greer, 2017; Fiorile & Greer, 2007; Gilic & Greer, 2009; Greer, Corwin, & Buttigieg, 2011; Greer, Stolfi, Chavez-Brown, & Rivera-Valdez, 2005). Children who demonstrate or have BiN (i.e., learn words for things incidentally) for novel but familiar types of stimuli (i.e., novel animals, cartoon characters, vegetation) may not demonstrate BiN with unfamiliar stimuli (e.g., constructed symbols such as chemical symbols). However, they can develop BiN for these unfamiliar stimuli after contact with exemplar experiences involving those types of stimuli (Lo, 2016). Children with basic BiN require additional experiences to simultaneously learn the names of the stimuli and at the same time the actions paired with the stimuli (Cahill & Greer, 2014). Similarly, simultaneously learning additional auditory, tactile, and olfactory relations requires additional experiences consisting of pairings with these senses. However, *once basic BiN is present, the additional relations appear to accrue simply by an automatic reinforcement conditioning process.*

It has been more than fifteen years since we first identified how to establish BiN. Our understanding of the cumulative research, in the years since, is that the initial accrual of reinforcement for observing the visual stimuli along with the words (Longano & Greer, 2014) allows those stimuli, in turn, to condition the new actions, scents, tactile stimuli, and sounds as reinforcing stimuli for observing responses, and the new stimuli join with those already in repertoire with repeated experience (Frias, 2017; Kleinert, 2018; Lo, 2016). No instruction or additional reinforcement is needed; simple exposure alone appears to result in the accrual of the new relations. From the perspective of the principles of behavior, this appears to explain the rapid growth of language observed in young children. The stimuli are now clear for "spontaneous" language development (Chomsky & Place, 2000). It is not spontaneous; rather it is under the control of learned reinforcers.

Understanding the developmental phenomenon of BiN has significant applied utility, in addition to the obvious contribution to basic science. Once BiN is present, children can learn in typical education settings, while without it they struggle or cannot (Corwin & Greer, 2017; Greer et al., 2011). In our laboratory and inclusion classrooms, we identified that BiN is an essential cusp needed for children to be successful in general education. Once BiN is present, the expansion of verbal repertoires is no longer dependent on direct instruction. That is, children's responding no longer needs to be directly reinforced or corrected for each skill. Instead, children can observe and learn a response to stimuli as a listener and speaker simultaneously.

Below, we discuss the identification and establishment of bidirectional operants involved in appropriate self-talk, and then we examine different types of BiN.

BIDIRECTIONAL OPERANTS INVOLVED IN APPROPRIATE SELF-TALK

Skinner (1957) described the phenomenon of individuals' talking to themselves as a rotation of speaker and listener responses. He proposed that children speak to themselves aloud until the behavior is punished by the audience (parents or peers), at which point the behavior goes beneath the skin, not unlike going from reading aloud to reading silently. The rotation of listener and speaker roles within the skin is, from a radical behaviorist perspective, "thinking." The indications of a child's being truly verbal and rotating the listener and speaker roles within the skin are (a) say-do correspondence (Farrell, 2017; Paniagua & Baer, 1982) and (b) self-talk in fantasy play (Lodhi & Greer, 1989). These verbal cusps, or components of the speaker-as-own-listener cusp, may be prerequisites or co-requisites to BiN and SLR (Greer & Ross, 2008). The research on these relations remains to be done. Self-talk refers to the emission of conversational units by one individual, where each of the roles of speaker and listener intersect in a conversational unit. Each behavior function, listener and speaker, is reinforced in an exchange. These are bidirectional operants between listener and speaker roles. These responses are distinguished from vocal stereotypy and palilalia because the function of self-talk is the conditioned reinforcement for exchanging of behaving as a speaker and listener and usually involves young children's fantasy play with toys that have anthropomorphic characteristics (e.g., animals, dolls, puppets; see Lodhi & Greer, 1989).

In a recent dissertation, Farrell (2017) told two- and three-year-olds, "Say what I say" (echoic) and "Do what I do" (imitation). The experimenter modeled one action figure saying, "Let's go save the world!" and the other figure saying, "Okay, let's go!" followed by the experimenter's moving the figure. The experimenter then gave the participant an opportunity to do the same and reinforced their echoic and imitating responses. Participants demonstrated first instances of say-do and self-talk conversational units during free-play settings. Intraverbal mutual entailment emerged as a function of the intervention (i.e., untaught responses of example to category or category to example). Say-do correspondence is usually implicit in self-talk and conversational units.

When an individual has say-do correspondence, they can state what they will do (Paniagua, 1990; Paniagua & Baer, 1982), as when a child tells a caregiver, "I'm going to go so high on the swings!" and runs over to do so. Similarly, Farrell (2017) reported that **do-say correspondence** is the same cusp, when children say what they did (i.e., "I went on the slide!"). In essence, the individual behaves as a listener in response to their own speech. Say-do correspondence and self-talk are the prerequisites for more complex repertoires such as problem solving and self-awareness (Greer & Du, 2015b). Say-do correspondence, self-talk conversational units, conversational units with others, and BiN are all examples of bidirectional operants. Say-do, self-talk in fantasy play, and BiN are developmental cusps that are components of the joining of the speaker and listener within the skin.

TYPES OF BIN

BiN is of utmost importance for one's educational and social development. It is one of the cusps demonstrating the joining of the speaker and listener that is necessary to become fully verbal. BiN allows the *learning of word-object relations incidentally* and allows children to learn from demonstration and observation. Typically developing children generally acquire BiN without direct instruction as a result of experiential contact with thousands of verbal interactions. However, if children cannot contact those experiences, even though the experiences are present, they are missing the BiN cusp.

Research suggests there are several effective interventions that can lead to the establishment of full naming or the listener half of naming. One protocol, but not the only, is MEI across speaker and listener responses (i.e., Corwin & Greer, 2017; Feliciano, 2006; Fiorile & Greer, 2007; Greer, Stolfi, et al., 2005; Rosales, Rehfeldt, & Lovett, 2011). MEI involves the rotation of presentations of stimuli across the four response topographies: (1) visual match-to-sample while hearing the tact of object/picture (observing), (2) point to (observation response), (3) tact (production response), and (4) intraverbal tact responses (producing) to the same set of stimuli. This exposure can result in the child's responding as both speaker and listener to untaught responses to novel stimuli. The rotation component between listener and speaker for the same stimuli in MEI was shown to be both sufficient and necessary for the acquisition of BiN for children who lacked this capability. The QR code below is a link to a video that provides a sample of two MEI interventions to induce BiN.

However, those who have acquired basic BiN under observational conditions cannot necessarily learn the names of things by exclusion (Greer & Du, 2015b). Therefore, the participant is asked to discriminate the unknown stimulus (i.e., Chinese logograph) against four other known ones (i.e., common home or school items), as well as point to, tact, and intraverbal tact the novel stimuli. In Greer and Du (2015a), instruction was structured in the same rotated fashion as in traditional MEI; the participant was reinforced sequentially first by observing the stimulus and simultaneously attending as a listener to the word for the object, and emitting listener and speaker responses to the object. This exemplar experience was shown to be effective in the establishment of BiN by exclusion.

Recent research shows that this kind of **transformation of stimulus function** across listener and speaker responding could also occur without direct instruction (Lo, 2016; Longano & Greer, 2014). Longano and Greer (2014) tested the effects of stimulated natural conditions on the emergence of BiN with preschoolers with disabilities. The experimenters presented the novel stimulus to the participant and tacted the stimulus while holding or pointing to it. The participant was not required to emit any responses, and thus no consequence was delivered. They found that exposure to this type of tact word-object relation experience led to increases in the children's echoics and in turn resulted in the emergence of BiN. In a recent dissertation, Lo (2016) presented repeated unconsequated probes to young preschoolers with disabilities until they demonstrated mastery (90% accuracy or above) for each of the four responses, including listener responses to visual stimuli, speaker responses to visual stimuli, listener responses to auditory stimuli associated with the visual stimuli, and speaker responses to the additional auditory stimuli. Lo found that the exemplar experiences with the repeated pairings of visual and auditory stimuli functioned to establish conditioned reinforcement for spoken and nonspoken auditory stimuli. Lo's study suggested that the increases in stimulus control may be responsible for the onset of traditional BiN as well as BiN to auditory nonspeech stimuli.

Additional stimulus control accrues from further experience once an individual demonstrates basic BiN as a result of pairings. Recent verbal behavior development research suggested that such multisensory experience may be responsible for the establishment of other forms of BiN (Cahill & Greer, 2014; Frias, 2017). Cahill and Greer (2014) found that simultaneously presenting actions and names hindered participants' learning of names, but pairing reinforcement with multiple responses across imitation actions, responses to "Find _____," intraverbals, and tacts induced this type of BiN. Another study investigated the relation between naming and additional auditory stimuli, olfactory stimuli, and tactile stimuli entering the naming "frame" (Frias, 2017). The experimenter provided the participant with naming experience of stimulus-stimulus pairing by presenting a stimulus for the participant to observe by seeing (visual), hearing (auditory), touching (tactile), and smelling (olfactory) together with the name of the stimulus (Pérez-González & Carnerero, 2014). Stimulus relations accrue for the names of stimulus modalities after such experience (Frias, 2017).

These studies provide support for the differential development of BiN across varied stimulus modalities. What is especially interesting and important about the expansion of the stimuli accrued from BiN experiences is that once the basic BiN repertoire is established, the additional stimuli are learned without direct instruction. This finding suggests the source of BiN resides in the pairing of existing reinforcers for observing responses with the new stimuli, consistent with research by Longano and Greer (2014) and others showing the strong association between the onset of new conditioned reinforcers and demonstrations of several cusps (Greer & Du, 2015a).

The identification of verbal developmental cusps was driven by seemingly unsolvable learning problems presented by children with language and social deficits and guided by the basic science of behavior. The findings are inherently translational in that applied investigations promote basic findings. The theory and findings of verbal behavior development also suggest relations with biology, a type of relation that has a long history in behavior analysis. We conclude the chapter with a consideration of the potential relevance of operant bidirectionality as a behavioral phenotype in the evolution of verbal behavior.

The Bidirectional Operant as Behavioral Metamorphosis

Together with the foundational cusps of observing and producing as part of the child's preverbal cusps, we have regularly established incidental learning of verbal bidirectional operants in typically developing children earlier than expected (Gilic & Greer, 2009). At the same time, in many other children with language delays, we have induced bidirectional verbal operants experimentally. In both cases, the resulting emission of bidirectional operants was striking and seemed to indicate a fundamental transformation of the child's subsequent development. We felt that this remarkable emergence of operant bidirectionality in the child's behavioral development merited special consideration (Greer, Pohl, Du, & Moschella, 2017; Pohl, Greer, Du, & Moschella, 2018): Accordingly, we report on comparative evidence that suggests that the bidirectional operant may be functionally homologous to the biological phenomenon of metamorphosis and a behavioral phenotype in the evolution of verbal behavior.

In pursuing this hypothesis, we follow Skinner (1966a) and Donahoe (1996), both of whom have provided strong arguments for the functional similarities between natural selection in phylogeny and selection by reinforcement during ontogeny. Donahoe's (2012) review of a collection of papers concerned with developments in evolutionary biology during the 150 years since publication of Darwin's (1859/2013) *On the Origin of Species* concludes that "our understanding of the details of selection by reinforcement is arguably at least as complete as was Darwin's understanding of natural selection" (Donahoe, 2012, p. 256).

Metamorphosis (meta, meaning "change" + morphe, meaning "form") as a biological process is extreme life-stage modularity and means that a single genome produces at least two highly distinctive morphological and behavioral phenotypes, which occupy very different habitats. It is ubiquitous throughout nature, repeatedly evolving in the history of multicellular life, and many species—butterflies, bees, beetles, ants, moths, flies, and wasps, as well as many marine invertebrates (amphibians and fish)—undergo dramatic phenotypic remodeling during development. In a symposium of fourteen comparative biologists primarily concerned with metamorphosis across a number of taxa in the animal kingdom, Bishop et al. (2006) loosely conceived metamorphosis as a component of organismic ontogeny. However, despite considerable differences in the definition of the term, no distinctive life-cycle transitions comparable to metamorphosis in insects (e.g., caterpillar to butterfly) have been documented for mammals.

In her groundbreaking treatise, *Developmental Plasticity and Evolution*, developmental evolutionary biologist and insect social behavior expert Mary Jane West-Eberhard (2003) devotes a chapter to "phenotypic recombination due to learning" (pp. 337–352), wherein she focuses on the importance of learning for the origin of novel adaptive phenotypes. West-Eberhard (2003) notes, "Most people, including most biologists, probably underestimate the importance of learning in the biology of nonhuman animals… So learning itself has not always received the attention it deserves as a phenomenon of general evolutionary interest" (p. 337). Recent evidence supports her insight at the cellular level (Robinson & Barron, 2017). And at the level of behavior, a study on behavioral development in dogs explicitly referred to "behavioral metamorphosis" (Scott & Nagy, 1980), and an editorial by Oppenheim (1980) considered metamorphosis more generally from the perspective of the phenomenon's adaptive advantage.

In his *Biographical Sketch of an Infant*, Darwin (1877) observed that his son, at exactly twelve months of age, began to vocalize for food in a prosodic manner employing the consonant-vowel "mum," with "a most strongly marked interrogatory sound at the end"

(p. 293). Darwin related that observation with farsightedness to a view he had entertained six years earlier in *The Decent of Man* (Darwin, 1871), namely that before any prehuman hominid species began to use articulate language, it uttered notes in a true musical scale similar to the vocalizations of a number of nonhuman primates including gibbons. That the nonhuman primate vocal tract can produce and use sounds to communicate involving both speaker and listener functions, such as in male-female duets, has been well documented by a gibbon vocalization field study carried out by Geissmann (2002).

A recent observational study with baboons (*Papio papio*) suggests that this species of nonhuman primates produces vocalizations comparable to human vowels (Boë et al., 2017). The researchers employed acoustic analyses of vocalizations coupled with an anatomical study of the tongue muscles and dynamic modeling of the acoustic potential of the vocal tract. The data suggest that baboons are capable of producing at least five vocalizations with the properties of vowels, in spite of their high larynx, and that they can combine them when they communicate with members of the same troop. The finding suggests that the last common ancestor of humans and baboons may have possessed the anatomical prerequisites for speech—hinting at a much earlier origin of language than heretofore believed. Could it be that correspondence is also an embedded reinforcement effect at play here as it is with children (Gladstone & Cooley, 1975)?

Regarding speech perception from a comparative perspective, valuable support would be given to the hypothesis developed here if, for example, functional ear asymmetries like those typically found in humans were established experimentally in nonhuman primates. In the first study to document ear advantages for acoustic stimuli in a nonhuman primate species, employing an operant conditioning, same-different auditory discrimination task, Pohl (1983) found in four baboons (*Papio cynocephalus*) highly significant and reproducible ear advantages in the monaural discrimination of pure tones, three-tone musical chords, synthetically constructed consonant-vowels (CVs), and vowels in each of the animals with marked individual differences in the direction of ear asymmetry. The ear advantages found in these baboons under monaural conditions resembled those obtained with dichotic presentation in human subjects (Pohl, Grubmüller, & Grubmüller, 1984) and thus suggest, especially when considered together with the recent Boë et al. (2017) findings on the vowel-like quality of baboon vocalizations mentioned above, that the baboon may provide a valuable nonhuman primate model of functional asymmetry in the central auditory system.

In a subsequent study on ear advantages for temporal resolution in the same four animals, Pohl (1984) hypothesized that the temporal resolution, which underlies an individual's ear advantage for speech perception, would predict an ear advantage for a temporal resolution task to correlate precisely with an ear advantage for the discrimination of CVs that differ in their temporal features. Using the same methodology as in the previous study to test the hypothesis in all four baboons, Pohl employed a gap-detection task that required the resolution of brief intervals of no noise (between seven and twenty milliseconds, depending on the animal) in bursts of random noise. The finding clearly confirmed the hypothesis in that the probability of obtaining by chance the same direction of ear advantage in four animals under two quite different task conditions is <.01. The results suggest that a single perceptual mechanism based on fine temporal analysis underlies the CV discrimination and gap detection tasks in both humans and baboons and that this mechanism may be asymmetrically organized within the central auditory system of primates.

Any attempt to understand behavioral metamorphosis during speech development from a biological perspective must incorporate a set of established facts from studies of birdsong development. The late ethologist Peter Marler seems to have left the science of biology with an unusual legacy. In an early comparison of the ontogeny of birdsong and speech, Marler (1970a) stated, "There may be basic rules governing vocal learning to which many species conform, including man" (p. 669). Soha and Peters (2015) list six basic rules, elaborated on the basis of Marler's extensive research in songbirds, which underlie the ontogeny of vocal behavior in both humans and white-crowned sparrows (*Zonotrichia leucophrys*). We cite these rules here as they are consistent with what has been discovered about verbal behavior development (see Soha & Peters, 2015):

1. Exposure to certain sounds (normally, the vocalizations of adult conspecifics) during development has a crucial impact on the adult repertoire.

2. This exposure has the greatest effect during a certain developmental time range, that is, learning proceeds most readily during an early critical period.

3. Vocal learning is guided by predispositions to proceed in a certain way. In particular, human babies preferentially attend to speech sounds and young songbirds are predisposed to pay particular attention to the vocalizations of their own species.

4. *Individuals must hear their own output during vocal development, as auditory feedback guides the matching of this output to what was heard and memorized previously* (italics ours). Auditory feedback is then less important; in Marler's words, it "becomes redundant" (Marler, 1970b, p. 23) after vocal development is complete.

5. At least some vocal learning apparently proceeds without external reinforcement, suggesting that internal reward reinforces the process of matching vocal output to memorized models. [It should be mentioned here that this is consistent with the Horne & Lowe (1996, p. 207) theory and research findings from Longano and Greer (2014; insertion in brackets ours)].

6. Vocal motor development proceeds in stages. *Young individuals begin by making vocal sounds that do not resemble those of adults* (italics ours), and even deafened individuals produce the earliest versions of these sounds (babbling or early subsong). In normal individuals, the effects of auditory experience then become apparent at the next stage. (Soha and Peters, 2015, p. 934)

In the interim, Patricia Kuhl (2004) and her associates have amply filled this empirical gap between birds and infants with their multidisciplinary research on social and speech development in early childhood. Pertinent to the argument developed here, Kuhl (2003) notes that "Both babies and birds must…rehearse and refine their communicative repertoires, *actively comparing and gradually matching (through auditory feedback) their productions to the sound patterns stored in auditory memory*" (p. 9645, italics ours).

What, then, is Marler's legacy? It hinges on the empirically grounded fact that songbirds need to hear their own auditory output during vocal development as a necessary precondition to the production of typical species-specific singing as juveniles and adults. As we have seen, this fundamental fact of vocal learning during development also holds for the human infant. For babies, the task involves learning the phonemic units and prosodic characteristics (rhythm, stress patterns, and intonation) of their mother tongue. For songbirds, the developmental requirement is to learn the specific notes, syllables, and prosodic characteristics typical of their species' song repertoire. Taken together and combined with the primate data cited previously, these findings suggest that a class of operant behavior underwent selection by reinforcement, enabling the modular design of a bidirectional behavioral phenotype as a necessary precondition for the evolution of human speech development.

We hypothesize that in joining the listener and speaker together in the same skin, the bidirectional operant would seem to represent complete behavioral metamorphosis. To use the classic example from insect ontogeny, if the caterpillar's habitat is the ground, branches, and leaves, and the preverbal child's niche is the immediate physical and social environment, then the butterfly's new habitat is the air and plants, and the verbal child's novel environment is the symbolic universe of a verbal community. Whereas the pre-BiN child behaves more like a nonhuman primate in a proximate physical and social environment, the child who has acquired the bidirectional operants becomes a member of a verbal community, which is the equivalent of a novel environment of symbolic relationships.

The evolutionary prerequisite of that profound behavioral transformation is the ontogenetic selection of separate observing and producing phenotypes and their modular integration into the bidirectional operant through social learning. In this context and with a view toward "a more comprehensive understanding of language," Greer (2008) mentions music and dance in addition to verbal behavior and the visual arts as evolutionary outcomes of the ontogenetic selection of separate observing and producing responses and the cultural joining of them (p. 370). This sets the stage for the hypothesis proposed here concerning the evolutionary origins of the bidirectional operant as an instance of behavioral metamorphosis in *Homo sapiens*. Based on the recent discovery of the bidirectional operant through behavioral research, Marler's legacy is that through his comparative studies of birdsong development, he has enabled our understanding of the bidirectional operant as an exemplar of complete behavioral metamorphosis during human verbal development. It is conceivable that in the years to come this insight could enable the approximation of two subdisciplines of biology, *developmental evolutionary biology* and *developmental verbal behavior analysis*, and spawn future interdisciplinary research on behavioral metamorphosis.

Implications and Future Directions

The present chapter has important implications for research and practice. In taking a verbal behavior developmental theory approach, the chapter draws attention to the concept of behavioral developmental cusps, which expand an individual's behavioral repertoire in meaningful ways. This chapter provides an overview of several instructional protocols that have been developed and researched in efforts to understand how to best promote the emergence of behavioral developmental cusps. More research is needed on the procedures described, including replications as well as studies with individuals with different prerequisite skills, in different settings, with respect to different topographies of behavior, and more. This research program has substantial implications for clinicians, especially considering assessment and intervention efforts in the area of language development. Effective practice is guided by knowledge of not just how to teach various skills, but also *when* to teach them with particular learners, what to do next, and so on. Given this, the behavioral sequence needed to establish fully verbal behavior, as described in this chapter, has remarkable clinical value.

Conclusion

Verbal behavior development builds on a variety of theoretical frameworks, all of which can be used to identify the kinds of experiences, or cusps, that make verbal development possible. This chapter discussed behavioral cusps known as bidirectional operants, which include verbal episodes between persons, speakers-as-own-listeners, and the learning of word-object relations. The joining of speaker and listener repertoires is critical for verbal behavior development. This chapter disseminated research on assessment and instructional methods for identifying and establishing such behavioral cusps.

Study Questions

1. What three things do behavioral developmental cusps allow children to do?

2. Provide two examples of bidirectional verbal operants as mentioned in the text.

3. What is the premise of the social listener reinforcement protocol? When is it most likely to be helpful?

4. Describe the intensive tact intervention and the type of generalized reinforcer that is to be used.

5. What does it mean for an individual to function as both a speaker and a listener?

6. What is say-do correspondence? How does say-do correspondence relate to the speaker's functioning as a listener?

7. What is self-talk? How does self-talk relate to the integration of the speaker and listener repertoires?

8. How do the chapter authors explain "spontaneous" language development?

9. What does it mean to become *fully verbal* from the perspective of the chapter authors?

10. What is the difference between unidirectional and bidirectional naming?

11. How is multiple exemplar instruction used to establish BiN?

12. Is there an animal model of an individual's functioning both as a "speaker" and a "listener"? In which species?

13. Describe bidirectional operants between individuals and bidirectional operants within individuals.

14. Define the conversational unit. How does it serve as a measure of social behavior?

CHAPTER 6

The Scope and Significance of Referential Behavior

Patrick M. Ghezzi[1]

University of Nevada, Reno

Link and Preview

Thus far we have covered basic processes, Skinner's analysis of verbal behavior, including both fundamental and more complex aspects of it, and the analysis of bidirectional operants. This chapter and the next pertain to a relatively less well-known approach to language within behavior analysis, specifically **referential behavior**. The analysis is derived from interbehavioral foundations and is ripe with theoretical, investigative, and practical implications.

"What precisely happens when one speaks?" J. R. Kantor (1936) answered his question in this way: "In effect, the speaker refers, and the hearer is referred to some thing, person, or event" (p. 75). Kantor offered the example of one person, A, saying to a second person, B, "The car is wrecked." Person A is the speaker in this case who refers person B, the listener, to the wrecked car. "It's ruined," replies B, thereby completing the interaction initiated by A, the speaker.

What is plain to see in Kantor's example is that the two people are talking to each other about something. A layperson calls it the "topic of conversation," and Kantor calls it the referent, that is, "some thing, person, or event" to which a speaker refers a listener. The speaker who refers the listener to the wrecked car is stimulated in the moment to say something about it, and the listener, in turn, is stimulated to respond to what the speaker

---

1   Author's Note: The author would like to acknowledge Ainsley Lewon and Vanessa Willmoth for their assistance in the preparation of this chapter.

said about it. A layperson would say the two people are "having a conversation." Technically, the episode is termed a **referential interaction**.

A distinguishing feature of referential behavior is how pervasive it is. The same can be said about other complex human behaviors—thinking and imagining come to mind—yet what further distinguishes referential behavior is how conspicuous it is. It is almost always public in the overt, psychological sense of the term and in the sense that it so often takes place openly for all to see and hear. Individual instances are sufficiently distinct to observe and record, and measures of count and time, long favored in the natural sciences, apply seamlessly to it.

Referential behavior is further distinguished by how early it develops and expands throughout the life span. By two to three years of age, noted Bijou (1989), a young child is fully capable of engaging in it. The expansion of referential behavior is explosive, actually, eventually becoming the cynosure of a person's personal and professional life. It is no overstatement to say that referential behavior is a cornerstone of society, and further, that it constitutes a remarkable adaptation by the human species.

An additional feature of referential behavior is how understudied it is in behavior science. How could something so common, so conspicuous, and so fundamentally human fly so far under the proverbial radar? What is it about an ordinary, everyday, directly observable and objectively measurable behavior that seems so easy to ignore?

The antilogy is even harder to fathom when it comes to young children who experience difficulties engaging in referential behavior and suffer a lifetime because of it. The behavior develops quickly for most youngsters and flourishes naturally throughout adolescence, adulthood, and well into old age. This trajectory is impeded early in life for some children, notably young children with intellectual and developmental disabilities. A common treatment objective for these youngsters, indeed, is to learn how, when, where, and with whom to engage in referential behavior.

The aim of the present chapter is to elaborate upon these features of referential behavior. We begin with a brief survey of J. R. Kantor's writings on language and linguistics to reveal the origins of the analysis of referential behavior, and move from there to discuss referential behavior in detail. Three advancements in the analysis of referential behavior since Kantor's death in 1984 are highlighted next, followed finally by suggestions for future research and development in the field.

Origins of the Analysis

Judging from the chronology of his publications, Kantor took an early interest in language. In a series of articles published in the 1920s (1921, 1922, 1928, 1929), he argued for an objective analysis of meaning and language, and in 1926 devoted a lengthy chapter to language in the second volume of his *Principles of Psychology*. Here, he (1) differentiated psychological data from other language-related things and activates, (2) categorized and analyzed language behavior situations, and (3) speculated on the development of language in relation to cultural and social conditions. Several years later, in another textbook on general psychology (1933), he presented a brief account of his approach to language. Three years after that, in 1936, the breadth and depth of Kantor's views were developed fully in his first volume on language, *An Objective Psychology of Grammar*. In it he emphasized the crucial difference between speaking and listening and the products of these behaviors, namely, words and sentences. The former was taken to be the proper domain for a functional psychology of language, and the latter, the focus of structural linguistics.

After *An Objective Psychology of Grammar*, Kantor published another article on language, this on the role of language in logic and science (1938). He returned to the study of language some thirty years later, when in the 1970s he published four papers under the authorship "Observer" (1970, 1971a, 1971b, 1976). In those articles he reiterated that authentic psychological language, consisting of referential and symbolizing behavior, should be distinguished from the products of these behaviors. His position was subsequently outlined in a chapter of his second textbook of general psychology (Kantor & Smith, 1975). In the same year in an article published in the first issue of the *Mexican Journal of Behavior Analysis*, Kantor (1975) labeled his position "psychological linguistics." The fact that "linguistics" was then, as now, synonymous with the study of words and sentences did not deter Kantor, nor did the fact that the hybrid term "psycholinguistics" was and still is infused with doctrine antithetical to his approach. Regardless, Kantor (1977) published his second and final book on language, *Psychological Linguistics*.

Shortly before his death, Kantor published another series of articles on language. In them he argued that (1) the confusion between speaking and listening and the products of these behaviors was due to the disunity in psychology regarding the basic premises of a natural science of psychology (Kantor, 1981), (2) the use of metaphors in psychology and language (e.g., the brain conceptualized as a computer) has had a regressive effect on both disciplines (Observer, 1983a), and (3) the concept of meaning in psychology and linguistics is misunderstood due to the longstanding confusion between events and constructs (Observer, 1983b).

It is clear that Kantor had much to say about language. Over some sixty years he wrote on every conceivable topic in psychology, maintaining throughout that all psychological activity can be construed as the observable activities of organisms interacting with the things, objects, people, and events collectively called the environment. As a specialized area of study within the field of scientific psychology, language was for Kantor distinguished only by its complexity and preponderance among human beings.

One of the great ironies in the history of behavior science is that to this day, Kantor's writings on language are neither widely acknowledged nor appreciated. There is a notable exception to this, a review by the esteemed behavior scientist Nate Shoenfeld in 1969 of Kantor's (1936) *An Objective Psychology of Grammar*. Shoenfeld proclaimed the volume a "stunning" and "historic" book and urged his colleagues and students to study it. Shoenfeld's advice went unheeded, yet neither Kantor nor Skinner seemed to mind. Kantor did not refer to Skinner's (1957) *Verbal Behavior* in any of his writings, and

Skinner, who died in 1990, never referred to Kantor's (1977) *Psychological Linguistics* in any of his writings. It is common knowledge that Skinner's approach ascended during his lifetime, while Kantor's approach languished during his life in relative obscurity (Ghezzi & Lyons, 1997).

The two approaches to language have since been compared and contrasted in detail by several accomplished behavior scientists, notably Parrott (1984a, 1987) and Morris (1982, 1984). This is not the place, however, to repeat or expand on the issues. Suffice it to say that the similarities between the two approaches are greater than the differences, and that a synthesis of the two, as the present chapter will show, is both possible and desirable. We turn now to referential behavior, our main focus.

Referential Behavior in Detail

What laypeople call the topic of conversation, or what is known technically as the **referent**, is not the only stimulus to which a speaker (and listener) responds. "At the basis of referential behavior," wrote Kantor (1977), "is the psychological process of bistimulation" (p. 62). The concept of **bistimulation** recognizes that, in addition to the referent, individual speakers and listeners themselves are a source of stimulation for referential behavior. In Kantor's (1936) example of the wrecked car, imagine a scenario in which a teenage driver is sobbing and apologizing profusely to his father about what happened to the car, and the father, in turn, is loudly chastising his son for careless driving. When the boy speaks to his mother about the accident, in sharp contrast, he is defiant and his mother, demure.

It is clear to see in ourselves and other people that whom we talk to influences what we talk about and how, when, where, and why we talk about it. Determining the direction and magnitude of the change in referential behavior as a function of the characteristics of individual speakers and listeners is a fertile area for research, one that we will have more to say about later in the chapter.

In addition to bistimulation, Kantor recognized a third factor, **setting conditions**, which Bijou (1996) defined as "the general surrounding circumstances that operate as inhibiting or facilitating conditions in a behavioral unit" (p. 149). Bijou and Baer (1978) and Bijou (1996) have compiled a fairly comprehensive list of biological, physical, and sociocultural setting conditions that can influence operant and respondent behavior. Referential behavior, likewise, can be affected by the biological status of a speaker and listener (e.g., ill, tired, hungry), the physical environment in which a speaker and listener interact (e.g., a stadium, church, bedroom), and the sociocultural practices of the group to which a speaker and listener adhere. As to the latter type of setting event, the imaginary interaction between the teenager and his father involving the car wreck would be more civilized, presumably, if the two were at a busy restaurant. This type of sociocultural setting condition would have an inhibiting effect on the interactions between father and son; after all, it is unacceptable in polite society for a parent to chastise their child in public.

The diagram in figure 6.1 depicts a single episode or unit of referential behavior and interaction with all four factors: speaker, listener, referent, and setting conditions. Note that the speaker, in Phase 1, initiates an interaction by responding simultaneously to a listener and a referent. In Phase 2, the listener responds, in turn, to the speaker and to the speaker's referent, thereby completing the interaction initiated by the speaker. Note, too, that the interaction between the speaker and listener occurs under the influence of setting conditions.

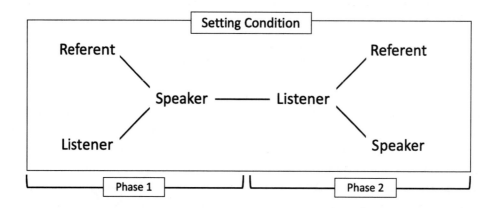

Figure 6.1. A single episode of referential behavior and interaction.

In this figure, the speaker is one person, the listener another. Speakers and listeners can differ along countless dimensions such as age, gender, race, education, occupation, avocation, social status, and level of development. The referent may involve all manner of things, objects, people, pets, relationships, places, events, and activities. It may be real or imaginary, fact or fiction, present or absent, concrete or abstract, timeless, timeful, or ephemeral.

Referential interactions may be narrative, mediative, or both. In **narrative referential interactions**, one person's referential behavior is coordinated with another person's referential behavior, as in casual conversation, the prototype referential interaction. The content and manner of narrative interactions range widely, to say the least, from the simple, everyday exchanges between two coworkers over the weather to two heads of state talking about the growing threat of nuclear annihilation. The sheer volume and breadth of narrative interactions over a person's lifetime, in a word, is astounding. It is hard to imagine a life devoid of narrative interactions. It would be hard to differentiate *Homo sapiens* from other species without this fundamentally human proclivity, and harder still to envision a society in which people never talk and listen to one another about the things and events that matter to them.

A **mediative referential interaction**, in contrast to a narrative interaction, occurs when a speaker's referential behavior is coordinated with a listener's *nonreferential* behavior. There are two major types of mediative interactions, each distinguished by whether a speaker's referential behavior *precedes* or *accompanies* a listener's nonreferential behavior. When a speaker asks or tells a listener to do something such as open a door or pass the salt and the listener complies, a **preceding mediative interaction** is identified.[2] An **accompanying mediative interaction**, by comparison, commonly involves a speaker and a listener who are each engaged in a nonreferential activity that stimulates one or the other person to comment on it. Consider the mother who says to her daughter as they garden together, "You're doing great!" and the child continues to garden without speaking or gesturing. In addition to identifying this as an accompanying mediative interaction, it may be important, for example, to determine whether or not the mother's referential behavior functioned to reinforce more frequent or longer bouts of gardening with her daughter in the future.

A speaker's (and listener's) referential behavior, whether mediative, narrative, or both, varies in content and style according to each person's history of learning and present circumstances. Encompassed in this history and circumstance is the role that society plays in developing a speaker and a manner of speaking that is at once both conventional and idiolectical. As a matter of living in a group, a person learns, along with other members, the customs, norms, traditions, values, beliefs, and manners of the group and, along with other members, learns to speak a common language and to talk to certain people in certain situations according to convention. It is **cultural behavior**, in Kantor's view (1936, 1982), a mode of action that prominently includes referential behavior between the members of the group on a regular basis and with respect to a common set of customs, values, and the like. At the same time and also as a matter of living under conventional circumstances, a person learns to speak in a style or manner that is instantly recognized by family, friends, associates, and admirers as *that* person. Speaking is much like a person's fingerprints in this regard, absolutely unique, utterly distinctive, and seldom mistaken for someone else's.

Before turning to what qualifies as language behavior but not as referential behavior—namely, **symbolizing behavior**—it will be helpful to take a closer look at the distinction Kantor drew between the actual behaviors of speaking and listening, on the one hand, and the products of these behaviors, on the other hand. Understanding Kantor on this point is vital to understanding his approach to language in general and referential behavior in particular.

The Trouble with Words

It is customary for psychologists and linguists, in the ancient tradition of philology, to study language behavior and its development in terms of written words and sentences and their syntactic and semantic properties. The approach is unproductive, in Kantor's view, because it confuses the products of behavior with the behavior itself. Consider the

---

2   Readers familiar with Skinner's (1957) *Verbal Behavior* will recognize the parallel between "manding" and mediative interactions.

following chain of events: (1) a language sample of two people talking to each other is taken, (2) the sample is either transcribed into ordinary words and sentences or transformed into a notational system (e.g., International Phonetic Alphabet; Bloom, 1993), (3) various counts and calculations are performed on the reconstituted sample, and then, once the results are in, (4) an account is given as to how and why the two people in the sample were able to speak and understand what was on each other's mind. Subjecting the behavior of two people talking to each other to this type of analysis and then calling it a psychological analysis is the problem, according to Kantor, and the only way around it is to replace words and sentences as the unit of analysis with referential behavior and interaction.

We turn next to a distinction Kantor drew between referential behavior and symbolizing behavior. The symbolic type of language behavior, as with the referential type, is inherently interactive and fundamentally communicative. However, while the referential type normally involves verbal-vocal behavior and/or gestures, as in casual conversation, the symbolic type centers on creating and using symbols. A distinction is therefore made between two types of language interactions, referential and symbolic, each of which requires a separate analysis.

Symbolizing Behavior

The symbolizing type of behavior involves a person responding to a stimulus that has been designed or created to substitute, stand for, or point to something else, either by that person or by some other person. The behavior of a person with respect to a thing that denotes some other thing or event, in short, is called **symbolizing**. Symbols take many forms—pictures, diagrams, figures, words—and serve many functions—identify, inform, remind, direct, warn, and so on. The property common to all symbolizing is that there is a stimulus that, ideally, corresponds unambiguously to a given circumstance and regularly produces the correct or appropriate response(s) to it. Said another way, there is ordinarily a firm relationship, first, between the symbol and the thing symbolized, and second, between the symbol and the behavior for which the symbol was created. Consider the road sign that reads, DANGEROUS CURVE AHEAD. The sign has a fixed relationship to the condition of the road ahead and, assuming a driver attends to the sign and is oriented to what it signifies, the behavior of slowing down is virtually guaranteed.

A second example of symbolizing behavior involves the exit sign above a door at a movie theater. The sign is placed above the door to show people where to leave from once the show is over and where to go in case of an emergency. A person's response to this type of stimulus may be simply orientational, such as noticing the sign upon entering the theater and taking a seat, or it may entail a more extended response such as noticing the sign and then leaving the theater through the door under the sign after the movie is over. Speculating on the origins of this type of symbol, it is conceivable that someone actually stood guard at the door to a theater in an earlier era, say, in Shakespeare's time, greeting patrons when they arrive to the performance, showing them where to leave from when they depart and where to go in case of an emergency. The exit sign in a modern movie theater serves essentially the same function, now unaccompanied by the referential behavior on which these types of sign are based.

The symbolizing type of language behavior is at least as prevalent, public, conspicuous, and central to life in society as the referential type. The similarity between the two types ends there, however. With symbolizing behavior, the stimulus-response relation is linear in operation and rigid in its function; only a narrow range of responses and stimuli are tolerated by virtue of the function for which they are designed. This differs greatly from referential behavior, where multiple sources of stimulation arising from speakers, listeners, referents, and setting conditions do not symbolize, substitute, or stand for anything, and where considerable variation in conventional and idiolectical behavior especially is allowed and even nurtured.

We turn now to the last section of the chapter on selected advancements in research on referential behavior. The advancements include (1) the codevelopment of a method for analyzing referential behavior and a procedure for conducting descriptive and experimental research, (2) research on interventions for remediating deficits in the referential behavior of young children with intellectual and developmental disabilities, and (3) the results of a longitudinal study on the development of referential behavior in a young child with autism over the course twenty-five months of intensive behavioral treatment.

Selected Advancements in the Analysis of Referential Behavior

The development of a method for analyzing referential behavior and interaction, together with the development of a procedure for conducting research that complimented the method of analysis, is significant for this one reason: Kantor's approach to referential behavior, until then, was long on conceptual analysis and short on research. With a method of analysis and a procedure for conducting research available for the first time, the path was clear, as we shall see, to investigate a variety of topics.

Analyzing Referential Behavior and Interaction

Shortly after Kantor's death, Bijou and his colleagues published two articles describing a method for analyzing referential behavior (Bijou, Chao, & Ghezzi, 1988; Bijou, Umbreit, Ghezzi, & Chao, 1986). A third article served as a manual for teaching people how to code videotapes of research sessions based on the method (Ghezzi, Bijou, & Chao, 1991).

The method was designed as a direct observation system, suitable for descriptive and experimental research in any setting involving two people, a speaker and a listener, who talk to each other while being filmed for later analysis. The analysis entails two phases. In the first, trained raters identify, in successive one-minute intervals, (a) the interactions initiated by the speaker and responded to by the listener, termed "complete interactions," and (b) the interactions initiated by the speaker to which the listener did not respond or responded irrelevantly, termed "incomplete interactions." This first phase distinguishes between referential and nonreferential behaviors and interactions, provides details on the number of complete and incomplete referential interactions initiated by each person in the dyad, and tracks the continuation or change in the referent(s) over the entire course of the conversation.

In the second phase of analysis, the experimenter records the duration and modality (verbal-vocal and/or gestural) of a speaker's initiation, identifying any accompanying concurrent and repetitive behaviors, such as "fidgeting," and determining the referential content of the initiation. This includes time frame (past, present, future, or no time frame), actuality (real, imaginary, or a combination of both), and references to persons (self, listener, others), animals, objects, places, activities, and the like.

The experimenter also identifies the prevailing setting conditions during the second phase. Three categories—physical, social, and interactional—are used. Research conducted in a small room at an elementary school, for example, would constitute one set of physical (room) and social (school) setting conditions, while research conducted in a room of a child's home would constitute a different set of conditions. The interactional setting, which refers to situations wherein two people agree to communicate according to some set format, as in taking turns telling knock-knock jokes or reciting movie lines, may vary over the course of a conversation, in which case the initiation is classified accordingly.

For each interaction initiated by a speaker, there is a corresponding response by the listener; thus the listener's response is also analyzed. The analysis is nearly identical to the analysis performed on the speaker: the experimenter records the duration of the listener's response and classifies it according to modality; notes any concurrent behavior that may have accompanied the listener's response to the speaker's initiation; documents the referential content of the listener's response to each initiation; and records whether the interaction was narrative, mediative, or a combination of the two.

The experimenter also determines whether or not the interaction that immediately follows the interaction under study was initiated by the same person—the speaker—and if so, whether it was a continuation of the referent in the preceding interaction (the speaker stayed on a topic), or whether the referent was changed (the speaker changed the topic). Alternatively, the listener may change the referent, thereby becoming the speaker, provided the other person in the dyad responds relevantly to the new referent, in which case he or she now becomes the listener. The value of these designations is that they show a person's tendency to sustain interactions on the same referent, as opposed to either changing referents frequently or letting the other person in the dyad initiate interactions by introducing their own referents. These designations, incidentally, are aspects of referential behavior that figure prominently in the section below on teaching referential behavior.

The first experimental test of the method (Ghezzi, Bijou, Umbreit, & Chao, 1987) centered on the well-established finding that a child's language is altered in response to the age of the person they are addressing (e.g., Shatz & Gelman, 1973). Ghezzi, Bijou, Umbreit, and Chao (1987) developed a procedure whereby a preadolescent spoke to either a six-year-old child, an age-peer, or an adult for ten minutes a day over several successive days. The dyad met at the same time each day in a small room with decorated walls and some furnishings at the elementary school the children attended. A session began with a brief familiarization period conducted separately for each dyad in which the individuals were allowed "to look at the camera and television" before taking their seat on a bean bag chair in front of a video recorder and TV. Once seated, the dyad was told that they would be watching a short segment of a popular television show and that after it was over, they could "talk about the segment or anything else." The experimenter left the room and returned ten minutes later to end the session.

Both the procedure and the method of analysis exceeded our expectations. The results confirmed and elaborated on the finding that a child's language—what is technically referential behavior—is altered in the presence of people who differ in age. The preadolescents in the Ghezzi, Bijou, Umbreit, and Chao (1987) study talked for a short time to a six-year-old child about a large number of referents, yet spoke at length about a comparatively smaller number of referents to a thirty-year-old adult. As to the referents, the preadolescents talked mostly about themselves or their family and friends when speaking to the adult, yet talked most often about the child or the child's family and friends with the six-year-old.

The combination of (1) creating a method for analyzing referential behavior and interaction, (2) developing a procedure that fit the method, and (3) using the method and procedure to confirm a well-established finding in traditional child language research was significant. Notable, too, was that it stimulated additional research on the effects of varying the composition of speakers and listeners in a dyad.

Lyons and Williamson (1988), in a study involving dyads of adults with schizophrenia and typical adults talking to one another in a lounge-like room, found that the average duration of interactions initiated by both typical speakers and those with schizophrenia was longer when the listener had schizophrenia. Speakers with schizophrenia, compared to typical speakers, initiated interactions of the longest duration regardless of the listener. Lyons and Williamson also found that typical speakers talked much less about themselves than the speakers with schizophrenia did, who talked about themselves almost exclusively and in equal measure with both typical listeners and those with schizophrenia.

Chiasson and Hayes (1993) formed dyads of undergraduate first-year students, undergraduate seniors, and graduate students to investigate how the "social status" of a member affects one another's referential behavior and interaction. The first-year students initiated roughly twice as many interactions when the listener was a fellow first-year student compared to when the listener was a senior or a graduate student. Chiasson and Hayes also reported that the average duration of each interaction was longest when the first-year students spoke to one another, intermediate when they spoke to a senior, and shortest when they spoke to a graduate student.

This collection of findings by Ghezzi, Bijou, Umbreit, and Chao (1987), Lyons and Williamson (1988), and Chiasson and Hayes (1993) shows clearly that a speaker's referential behavior is altered by the characteristics of the listener with whom the speaker is interacting. That this conclusion is drawn from results based on a method and procedure founded on Kantor's analysis of referential behavior is sufficient reason to take the method and procedure in a different direction. The direction Bijou and his colleagues took was teaching referential behavior to young children with intellectual and developmental disabilities.

Teaching Referential Behavior

In a paper on the development of referential behavior, Bijou (1989) described an experiment on social skills training by Ghezzi, Bijou, and Chao (1987; Ghezzi & Bijou, 1994). The study involved three elementary school-aged children (ages six to nine) with mild intellectual delays whom school officials described as unable to carry on a conversation with their typically developing classmates and who were suffering socially because of it. The experimenters tested and developed two interventions. One intervention (A) involved showing a child selected excerpts of videotapes that depicted exemplary and nonexemplary instances of the child initiating a referential interaction or sustaining a series of referential interactions while talking to a typical classmate. An adult trainer taught the target child to eventually identify, without assistance, the exemplary and nonexemplary instances and to practice socially desirable alternatives.

The second intervention (B) involved teaching a child to initiate and sustain a series of referential interactions on referents either supplied by an adult trainer (e.g., plan a party, build a clubhouse) or offered by the child (e.g., favorite sports personalities, toys). The adult, through role-playing exercises, taught the child to talk about, and elaborate on, the adult-supplied or child-offered referents. Toward the end of a session, the adult gave the target child two assignments: (1) to have a conversation with the typically developing member of the dyad (an age-peer) about the same referent(s) introduced and discussed during role-playing, and then, right after the upcoming conversation with the typically developing child was over, (2) to report to the adult on the details of what they had just talked about.

The effects of both interventions were evaluated during five-minute probe sessions in which the dyad (the target child and the typically developing peer) was asked to "have a conversation about anything you like." For the A intervention, both children in the dyad were escorted back to their classroom at the end of the session. For the B intervention, the target child stayed with the adult for about fifteen minutes to report the details of the conversation the child just had with the typically developing member of the dyad.

Intervention A produced three main outcomes: (1) an increase in the number of referential interactions initiated by a target child (i.e., the child started more conversations with the typically developing peer in the dyad), (2) an increase in the proportion of the interactions initiated by a target child that either related to or differed from the referent(s) the child first introduced (i.e., the child either continued talking about a topic or changed the topic altogether), and (3) an increase in the number of relevant responses by a target child to the referential interactions initiated by a typically developing peer (i.e., the child responded relevantly to more of the typically developing child's initiations, thereby completing more interactions). In contrast to the first two increases, the third increase occurred without specific instruction.

Intervention B produced two main outcomes: (1) an increase in the average duration of a referential interaction initiated by a target child (i.e., the child spoke longer while starting a conversation, and (2) an increase in the average duration of a target child's responses to interactions initiated by the typically developing child in the dyad (i.e., the child spoke longer in response to the typically developing child's initiation). This second outcome occurred without teaching.

The analysis of the details of the referential behavior and interactions within and across dyads revealed no large or consistent differences between the two interventions. The children spent roughly half the time talking about each other's interests, relatives, friends, and pets, and spent the remaining time talking about themselves, other people, places, and activities.

The results of this study were significant for several reasons. The two interventions improved a target child's referential behavior as a speaker in three ways: the child introduced more referents, talked more about them, and talked about them for longer periods of time. The interventions also produced two uninstructed improvements in a target child's behavior as a listener: the child responded more often, and for longer periods of time, to the interactions initiated by the typically developing member of a dyad.

That the method for analyzing referential behavior and interaction yielded measures that were highly sensitive to the effects of the interventions paled in comparison to the revelation that referential behavior is exceptionally meaningful to the social development of a child. It is widely acknowledged that a great many children with (and without) disabilities have a problem interacting with their age-peers and are socially disadvantaged because of it (Guralnick, 2001). It so happens that many of these children differ from their age-peers in their preference for solitude over companionship (Wang, 2015). Under prolonged circumstances, a minimal repertoire of desirable social behavior would develop, as friendships and personal relationships would be difficult to acquire and maintain, leading eventually to isolation, loneliness, depression, and, according to some experts, self-harm and suicidal thoughts (Endo et al., 2017).

More often than not, according to Ghezzi (1999), modifying the social behavior of a child is a matter of (1) assessing how the child interacts referentially with other children and adults, (2) intervening on those aspects of the child's referential behavior that are deemed deficient, and (3) evaluating the effects of the intervention on the child's referential behavior and interactions with adults and age-peers. It is a familiar process, one that applied researchers and practitioners alike follow assiduously. What is unfamiliar about the process as it pertains to referential behavior is the most important part: how to measure referential behavior and interaction for purposes of its ongoing assessment, intervention, and evaluation.

A study by Willmoth, Lewon, Taylor, and Ghezzi (2017) is a recent development in the analysis of referential behavior that illustrates the process. A five-year-old boy with autism was nearing the end of nearly two years of early intensive behavioral intervention (EIBI; Klintwall & Eikeseth, 2014). Informal observations of his referential behavior with his home-based adult tutor revealed that while he initiated now and then, he seldom continued to keep initiating on the same referent(s). He would say that he was looking forward to going to the park this afternoon, for instance, and then, after the adult completed the interaction (e.g., "That will be fun!"), he would either say nothing more about the park or would initiate the very next interaction by introducing an entirely new referent (e.g., "Hot dogs are my favorite food").

Willmoth et al.'s (2017) study began with the assumption that a "good speaker" continues to initiate interactions on a referent at a frequency appropriate to the listener, setting, and circumstance. Following a series of baselines sessions, described below, the researchers decided that the frequency at which the child continued to initiate interactions on a referent(s) he himself introduced while talking to his tutor was low. The researchers developed a referential teaching procedure to improve his behavior as a speaker by increasing the number of times he continued to initiate an interaction with his tutor on a referent he himself introduced. Recall that the same aim was set for the young children with intellectual disabilities in the study reported by Ghezzi, Bijou, and Chao (1987; Ghezzi & Bijou, 1994) and discussed by Bijou (1989), the details of which we discuss and interpret below as meaningful to the social development of a child. The route taken with the young child with autism differed from the route taken by the children with intellectual disabilities, however.

Willmoth et al. (2017) conducted baseline sessions over eleven days for five minutes each day in a small room in the child's home. The tutor told the child that they would be "having a conversation" and that they could "talk about whatever they liked." The tutor refrained from taking on the role of speaker by initiating interactions of her own during baseline, and instead replied to the child's initiations without elaboration and without regard to whether or not he continued to talk about the referent(s) he introduced. If the child remained silent, so, too, did the tutor, until either the child initiated a referential interaction or the five-minute session timed out.

The procedure followed a changing criterion protocol whereby social praise was contingent on the child's initiating a series of interactions on a referent he introduced. If the child started talking about a video game, for example, the tutor would (1) reply to his initiation (e.g., "Video games are amazing!") and (2) provide praise (e.g., "What you told me about playing those games is awesome!"), at first contingent on a relatively smaller number of continuations and later, on a comparatively larger number, depending on the number of continuations recorded the last time he had a conversation with his tutor.

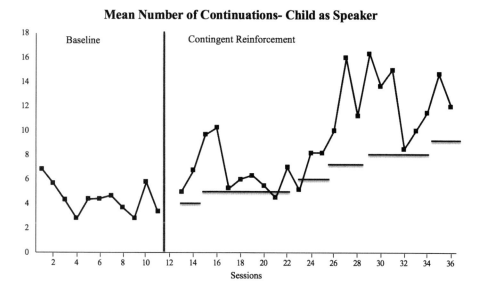

Figure 6.2 Mean number of continued referential interactions by the child as speaker.

The mean numbers of referential interactions continued by the young child per five-minute session throughout baseline and over twenty-three days of the referential behavior training are shown in figure 6.2. The average remained low during baseline at roughly four per session, meaning that, on average, the boy continued to initiate about four consecutive interactions on a referent he introduced. He exceeded that average across the first criterion and, for the most part, across each and every one of the five subsequent increases in the criterion for contingent praise. Near the end of intervention, the child was initiating roughly eight interactions per session with his tutor on referents he introduced, twice as many as in baseline.

It became apparent that while the child was improving as a speaker, his behavior as a listener was "poor" in the sense that he seldom continued to talk about a referent introduced by his tutor. The tutor would start talking, for example, about her dog ("My dog loves to play"), and the child's typical response was to make a simple statement (e.g., "Dogs bark") or to ask a simple question ("Does your dog bark?") and leave it at that without additional follow-up or continued referential behavior relevant to his tutor's dog and what she said about it. It was also apparent that the procedure developed to improve his behavior as a speaker—sustaining a series of interactions on the referent(s) that he introduced—had no discernable effects on his behavior as a "good listener," someone who, presumably, continues to talk about a referent introduced by a speaker at a rate appropriate to the speaker, setting, and circumstance. The baseline rate of this behavior was considered low for this child, which stimulated a procedure designed to increase the number of times he continued to talk about a referent(s) his tutor introduced.

Baseline sessions were conducted over eight days for five minutes each day in the same small room in the child's home. The adult tutor told the child that they would be having a conversation and that he could talk to her about whatever he liked. The tutor assumed the role of speaker by initiating interactions with the child on referents that she selected from a list generated from an informal assessment of his most preferred things and activities (e.g., games, toys, movie characters, bike riding, baseball). The tutor refrained from encouraging the boy to continue interacting about her referent(s), and instead simply introduced a referent (e.g., "Your bike must be fun to ride!"), waited for a response (e.g., "It is!") to complete the interaction, and then proceeded either (1) to initiate another interaction on the same referent (in which case the boy continued to talk about the tutor's referent), or (2) to initiate a new interaction on a different referent (in which case the boy did not continue to talk about the tutor's referent). If the child initiated an interaction by introducing his own referent (e.g., "Do you eat spaghetti?"), the tutor, now listener, would complete the interaction (e.g., "Yes") but without encouragement to the child to continue interacting with her on his referent.

The procedure followed a changing criterion protocol, as before, but this time with praise contingent on the child's continuing to respond to a referent introduced by his tutor in her role as speaker. For example, if the tutor started talking about Spiderman (e.g., "Spiderman is awesome!"), she would continue to initiate interactions about the character so long as the child continued to give a response that was relevant to the referent (e.g., "He's the best!"). When the child met or exceeded the criterion number of continuations set for the day, the tutor would praise the child and then continue to initiate another interaction on the same referent (e.g., "Thanks, buddy, for talking more to me about Spiderman! I wonder if his mom and dad know he's Spiderman."). This cycle of events continued throughout each session, provided the child kept giving a response that was relevant to his tutor's referent. If his response was irrelevant, if he made no response at all, or if he responded to his tutor's referent by introducing a referent of his own (e.g., "It's cold outside"), the tutor would look away from him and wait for a period of roughly ten seconds of silence to elapse before initiating an interaction on a referent from her list of his favorite things to talk about.

The mean number of continuations by the young child as a listener throughout baseline and intervention are shown in figure 6.3. The average decreased from nearly eight continuations per five-minute session at the start of baseline to about four per session thereafter. He exceeded that average once intervention began at the first criterion (four continuations) and, with one exception (Session 25), kept meeting or exceeding the criterion that was set each day for continuing to talk about his tutor's referent. Near the end of the intervention, the boy continued to interact with his tutor on her referent about fourteen times on average, roughly a three-fold increase above baseline.

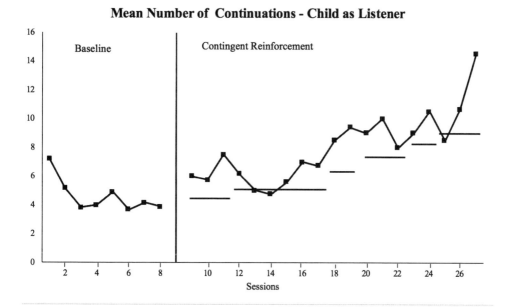

Figure 6.3 Mean number of continued referential interactions by the child as listener.

How the combination of initiating interactions on the child's favorite referents, not responding to initiations on referents that he himself introduced, and changing the criterion for contingent praise contributed to the results of the Willmoth et al. (2017) study are questions for further study. The main point is that as far as referential behavior is concerned, it is entirely possible, and desirable, to assess, teach, and evaluate the effects of teaching referential behavior as a speaker, a listener, or both.

We turn now to a third and final area of advancement in referential behavior research involving the development of referential behavior in a young child with autism over the course of twenty-five months of EIBI.

The Development of Referential Behavior

Bijou (1983, 1989) published two papers on the development of referential behavior from infancy through the preschool years. He described the typically developing child as progressing through four stages from infancy to roughly four years of age: (1) preverbal-vocal communication, (2) primitive referential verbal-vocal interactions, (3) first-approximation referential interactions, and (4) second-approximation referential interactions and the beginning of symbolizing behavior. The mayor types of behaviors and interactions taking place during these periods would populate each stage, according to Bijou, and each stage, in turn, would be further marked by its own transition from the previous stage to the next stage. Later stages of referential behavior would extend through the early elementary school years and beyond into adulthood and eventually old age.

The process of developing a repertoire of referential behavior unfolds naturally and without delay for most young children. For a significant minority of children, however, the process can be slow or even stopped in its tracks. When it is, parents worry about delays and deficiencies in the development of their child's language, communication, and social behavior. Chronic impairments in these three domains in particular can lead to a diagnosis of autism and, in turn, to treatments designed to address a child's deficits in these same three domains.

Because referential behavior entails all three domains, a child's social behavior and functional speech, and perhaps his or her grammatical behavior as well, should develop markedly as the deficits in the child's referential behavior are replaced with more appropriate or desirable referential interactions with age-peers and adults. It is a working hypothesis, one that gains support by the results of the studies on teaching referential behavior reviewed above. It is also a hypothesis that acknowledges the simple yet powerful truth that at the end of the day, what a parent of a young child with autism wants most is to have a conversation with their child (Pituch et al., 2011; Richards, Mossey, & Robins, 2016).

A. Lewon (2019), in an ongoing longitudinal dissertation study, asked these three questions: How does a young boy with autism speak to his mother? How does the mother speak to her son? How do these referential interactions develop over the course of an EIBI program? Lewon posed these questions at the start of a young boy's program, which began shortly after his third birthday and ended just after his fifth birthday, two years later. The child's mother, also a wife and homemaker, reported at intake that her and her husband's first priority was to communicate and be more socially engaged with their son.

Once a month for twenty-five consecutive months, an adult assistant arrived at the family home to videotape a five-minute conversation between the mother and her son while they were seated on a couch in the family living room. The assistant instructed the child and his mother "to stay seated for the next five minutes and have a conversation about anything you like." The assistant left the room and returned five minutes later to end the session.

There were no formal contingencies in effect at any time during the videotaped sessions that related either to the mother or her son, nor were there ever any procedures in place over the course of the child's EIBI program that isolated referential behavior as a treatment target. The videotape sessions, then, were probes designed to track the development of the child's referential behavior for the duration of his intensive intervention program for autism.

The top panel in figure 6.4 displays two data streams, one representing the frequency of *complete* referential interactions initiated by the child's mother (open squares) and the second, the frequency of *complete* referential interactions initiated by the child (closed squares). What constitutes a complete interaction, to reiterate, is a relevant response by a listener to a referent introduced by a speaker, and what constitutes a speaker is the one who initiates, or continues to initiate, an interaction on a referent that they introduced.

During the early months of intervention, as the top panel in figure 6.4 shows, the mother was far more likely to initiate a referential interaction with her son than her son was to initiate an interaction with her. Said another way, the mother had plenty to say to her son, but he had nothing to say to her as a speaker. This imbalance changed gradually but steadily over the course of treatment, culminating at eighteen months in a fairly even mix of interactions initiated by the child and his mother. Proportionately, the child initiated about 52% of the interactions with his mother during the last three months of intervention, compared to roughly 26% during the first three months of intervention.

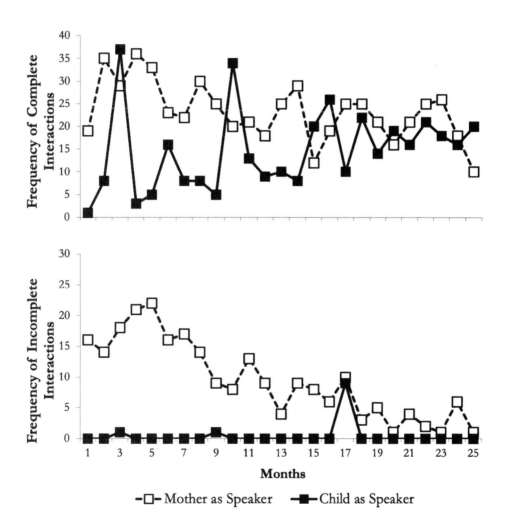

Figure 6.4 Frequency of complete interactions (top panel) and incomplete interactions (bottom panel) initiated by the mother and child as speakers in each monthly sample.

The bottom panel in figure 6.4 contains two data streams spanning the same twenty-five consecutive months of the mother and child's interactions. One data stream shows the frequency of *incomplete* referential interactions initiated by the mother (open squares), and the second stream shows the frequency of *incomplete* interactions initiated by her son (closed squares). The mother's data show that over the first seven months of treatment, she initiated between fourteen and twenty-four referential interactions each monthly session to which her son either did not respond or responded irrelevantly. The mother, in other words, had plenty to say to her son, yet he had nothing to say back to her as a listener. The number of these incomplete interactions fell steadily over the course of intervention to near-zero levels by the end of intervention.

The child's data in the bottom panel of figure 6.4 show that the number of referential interactions he initiated that his mother failed to complete, either by not responding or by responding irrelevantly to her son's referent(s), remained at near-zero levels throughout the study. The mother completed all but a few interactions initiated by her son over the entire course of treatment, as might be expected of any parent who wants their child to talk to them. The contrast between the child and his mother on this measure is striking at first, given how many more interactions she initiated that he failed to complete compared to the number he initiated that she failed to complete. The child improved greatly in this regard such that by eighteen months into intervention and for the final seven months of intervention, he completed most if not all of the referential interactions initiated by his mother.

These positive developments in the child's referential behavior occurred without any direct or specific instruction. They were emergent effects, in other words, clearly the result of the cumulative effects of over two years of EIBI, and yet just as clearly a result that is impossible to attribute to any one aspect of the intervention. The child with autism in the Willmoth et al. (2017) study, on the other hand, also received over two years of EIBI and yet his referential behavior was poor by comparison and did not "emerge" for the better until a program was implemented near the end of intervention to improve his performance as a speaker and a listener. Accounting for differences of this sort in the context of the aims and values of EIBI constitutes a potentially lively area for research.

Implications and Future Directions

At the start of this chapter I made the claim that referential behavior is understudied. It is, in fact, woefully understudied in comparison with the scope and significance attached to it. One speculation is that the analysis of referential behavior in Kantor's time was entirely conceptual and that a clearly identified unit of behavior and the numerical measures pertaining to it was unavailable (Ghezzi, 1999). That has changed, and now there is a functional unit of analysis for referential behavior with standard measures of count and time attached to it. The frequency with which a speaker initiates a complete referential interaction, and the time the listener spends responding to the speaker's initiation, is one example of two metrics available to researchers within a *single* referential interaction.

In a nutshell, the methods and measures described here open a door to countless experimental and descriptive studies on the development of referential behavior from infancy to old age.

In keeping with the theme of this book and the need, in my view, to introduce new and alternative procedures for enhancing the social competence of young children with developmental disabilities, we shall keep mostly to applied matters of this sort.

How the analysis of referential behavior might inform the techniques of contingency management, and vice versa, is an area that deserves close attention. The use of contingent praise enabled the young child with autism in the Willmoth et al. (2017) study both to initiate a greater number of complete interactions as a speaker and to continue interacting with his tutor as a listener. It is a fine example of what is possible when episodes of referential behavior and interaction are treated as units to which contingent consequences can be applied as a means to develop or refine a repertoire as a speaker, a listener, or both.

The tradition in applied behavior analysis is not just to demonstrate a reliable change in behavior but to show a socially relevant and personally meaningful change as well. Social validity, in other words, is a value to which behavior analysts have long adhered (Wolf, 1978). As this pertains to modifying referential behavior, it is presently unknown whether or not a change in a child's referential behavior is related to a change in that child's status as a friend or playmate, for instance, or whether or not the child or the child's parent would regard the change in referential behavior as socially significant or personally desirable. Improvements in a child's social competence may be assessed by means of peer nomination and rating scales (e.g., Ghezzi, Robles, & Bijou, 1992), by asking a child's parent or the child themself to rate their level of satisfaction with the change in behavior (e.g., Hood, Luczynski, & Mitteer, 2017), or by asking total strangers to judge the social appropriateness of a child's behavior (e.g., Peters & Thompson, 2015).

One possible variable in this regard centers on the two cases of teaching referential behavior described above. The instructors decided to increase the number of interactions the child initiated to his tutor as a speaker in the Willmoth et al. (2017) study, and once that was achieved, the instructors increased the frequency of his continuations as a listener to his tutor's initiations. It seems self-evident that a person who strikes an even balance between initiating referential interactions and responding to the initiations of the other person in a dyad would be judged as a "good speaker" and a "good listener," respectively. This may near the mark, or not, but in any case it seems to be a fruitful area for research, one that could provide practitioners with guidelines on the characteristics of referential behavior and interaction that facilitate making and maintaining friendships, for instance, or that foster a child's popularity among age-peers.

How referential behavior develops over the lifespan is another area ripe for research and full of applied significance. Bijou (1983; 1989) provides the framework for exploring the conditions under which an infant moves from gestures and babbling to holophrastic speech and the beginnings of referential behavior. The stages Bijou outlines may be useful guideposts for a young child's social development especially, and may be useful as well to people in the field of early intervention who work closely with parents to identify and ameliorate deficits in the initial development of a child's language behavior before problems arise at later stages.

One last direction for the future pertains to the aims and values of EIBI. Most young children develop an adequate repertoire of referential behavior and enjoy interacting with their peers, siblings, parents, and other adults throughout childhood, adolescence, and adulthood. Other young children fall below this trajectory, but the child with autism falls farther below most. For this child, as well as for the child's parents, referential behavior can be considered the applied endpoint (Pituch et al., 2011). If this is anywhere near the mark, then establishing a treatment environment that effectively teaches the referential behaviors necessary for a child to become a competent speaker and listener at home, in school, and out in the community could be the key to a successful outcome.

Conclusion

The study of referential behavior was inspired by the many writings of J. R. Kantor, the founder of interbehaviorism. In lay terms, referential behavior refers to two people talking to each other about something. Research has shown that referential behavior is established at a very young age in children, and then expands greatly over the course of an individual's interaction with their verbal community. In fact, the repertoire is at the heart of many aspects of personal and professional life. This chapter identified the different types of referential interaction, including mediative and narrative, and provided examples of each. A number of studies have analyzed children's referential interactions, results of which demonstrate the important role of referential behavior in social competence.

Study Questions

1. Describe referential behavior.

2. Distinguish between the referor and the referee with an example.

3. What is "bistimulation"? Explain with an example.

4. Describe two setting conditions that could influence the occurrence of referential behavior.

5. What is a narrative referential interaction?

6. What is a mediative referential interaction?

7. What is the problem with studying sentences and words as a means of understanding language in behavioral perspective?

8. What is symbolizing behavior?

9. What is the main difference between referential and symbolic behavior?

10. What is the general finding of the series of studies by Ghezzi, Bijou, Umbreit, and Chao (1987), Lyons and Williamson (1988), and Chiasson and Hayes (1993)?

11. Why is referential behavior a socially significant target behavior?

12. What are the results of the longitudinal study by Lewon described in the chapter?

CHAPTER 7

Human Behavior Is Referential Behavior

Emilio Ribes-Iñesta
University of Veracruz

Link and Preview

The previous chapter provided an overview of both referential behavior and symbolic behavior, and in particular described the clinical implications of work in this area. The current chapter continues with the very general topic of referential behavior but addresses the topic of language in science more generally. This includes a discussion of terms within psychology and applied behavior analysis specifically. This chapter will be of particular interest to those who are interested in delving further into theoretical issues pertaining to the topic of language in science.

"Language" and "behavior" are not technical terms, although they may be used technically for given purposes. This is one of the reasons why confusion often arises in psychology. Indeed, when people talk about "psychological" terms, they often think they are talking about the same things because they are using the same words, but this is often not the case. Words in ordinary language are multisensical; that is, they are used in different senses in different situations and contexts. Ryle (1949; 1962) pointed out that oftentimes people suppose that they are sustaining a dialogue about a common issue when, actually, two simultaneous monologues about different issues are taking place. In ordinary language words do not have a specific and constant referent or correspondence with things. However, in technical languages some words have specific uses regarding only some things. Clearly that is an important distinction between ordinary language and the technical language of the sciences.

"Language" and "behavior" are also not univocal terms, even in the scientific domains of linguistics and psychology. I will try to delimit the ways in which these terms will be used from now on. "Language," as a term, always has to do, directly or indirectly, with the social practice of human beings. In fact, "language" is the only term inherently reflexive; we can talk about language in language or through language. Language originated with human society, that is, with the organized division of labor and appropriation of goods and mutual services between individuals (Ribes, 2001). This explains why communication in some animal species does not constitute true language, and why it is absurd to postulate "private" languages of different sorts. Language emerged as *conventional practice* and cannot be conceived as an individual product or process. On the contrary, as I shall argue later, human individuals become differentiated from one another, not by language, but *in* language. Language is not external to human life and practice; it is not a means for relations among individuals, but the medium itself in which human practice and social relations take place and, therefore, are sensical or meaningful.

Language and social human practice are one and the same thing and are intrinsically interlocked. No human society without language is known. In this sense, language is not only talking and so forth, but as Ludwig Wittgenstein (1953, p. 19) pointed out, "to imagine a language means to imagine a form of life." Any social form of life as language embraces a diversity of activities, relations, products, and dispositions. It would be impossible to set a single frame to classify them. Nevertheless, following J. R. Kantor (1936, 1977), a useful first step may consist of distinguishing "alive" from "dead" language, that is, distinguishing between language taking place as acts from the vestiges of those acts.

On Human Behavior as "Language"

"Dead" language is related to the vestiges and products from actual practice, as are recordings of all sorts: marks, drawings and pictures, inscriptions, writings, books, codex, tapes, and so forth. Dead language products are not equivalent to the practices from which they resulted, nor are they an outcome of these practices, although sometimes dead language products may provide clues from which to infer part of the conditions prevailing when actual practices took place. Nevertheless, in the same manner by which words and expressions do not correspond to things or events, linguistic vestiges should never be confounded with the actual practices that gave rise to them. By contrast, "alive" language always consists in part of a social practice involving more than one individual—a practice articulated with the multiplicity of interindividual relations occurring in society. The relations so involved do not necessarily have to be simultaneous in time and place, especially when some type of graphing or writing is involved.

In behavioral psychology, language has been considered a special type of operant behavior (Skinner, 1938, 1957) and has been equated with so-called verbal behavior (also see chapters 3 and 4). However, this is a conceptual mistake and leads to confusion. Verbal behavior deals with speech—that is, with orally emitted language—and, although it is in some sense the dominant modality of language practices, it is not the only one nor the most important in all occasions. Because of this, the term "linguistic behavior" will be used to refer to any kind of individual language activity, and "verbal" will be restricted to speech. Alive language is the underlying practice of social relations between individuals and involves different modes or modalities of occurrence as behavior. These modes can be identified as **active modes** or **reactive modes**, although they usually take place simultaneously, not only between individuals but also with a single person. Some active and reactive modes involve inseparable pairs, whereas some active modes usually occur together as functional patterns.

The active modes are gesturing, speaking, and writing, while the reactive modes are observing (not looking), listening (not hearing), and reading (not texting). It is obvious that gesturing-observing, speaking-listening, and writing-reading are complementary pairs, and that normally they occur at the same time with a single individual and in other individuals in relation: gestures are observed (sometimes as proprioceptive observation), speech is listened to, and writing is read. These relations are synchronic and most of the time we are not aware of them, but as developmental studies show (King & Quigley, 1985; Marschark, 1993; Marschark, Mourandian, & Halas, 1994), children with impaired vision and/or hearing are seriously affected in learning to speak and in conventional social gesturing (and reading). Individuals who do not read are unable to write, even if they copy letters or words. On the other hand, when individuals interact with others, active modes of linguistic behavior do not occur in isolation of each other. While speaking and reading we gesture, and while writing we speak "silently" or loudly in the form of reading. Not only do linguistic modes not occur in isolation, but they are always part of an act or activity by the individual in a given circumstance, in such a way that they are patterned as components of situational interactions.

Linguistic behavior, in this perspective, includes aggregate behavior patterns of the individual as part of a social practice, even though some components of the patterns do not *look* linguistic given their morphology. Behavioral response systems include biological, natural reactions and actions that are common to all individuals as members of the human species. In fact, psychological behavior consists of the development of new functions and organization of biological response systems (Kuo, 1967) as a result of the interaction of the individual with different kinds of environmental contingencies related to objects, events, and other individuals. But human beings, in addition to their biological responses systems, develop novel kinds of responding derived from them, arbitrary in their morphology. These novel response systems are, precisely, **linguistic response systems**. Arbitrariness in morphology means that, from a biological point of view, there is no necessary relation between the form of the responses and the physical and chemical circumstances in which they occur. However, the arbitrariness in *form* does not mean arbitrariness in *function*. On the contrary, to the extent that linguistic response systems are conventional and shared in nature, their functions are delimited and established by social practice. Social practices constitute the rules "governing" language functions. Grammar came after writing as a formal description of language uses and functions. These functions always involve and entail necessarily social relations with other individuals articulated with objects and events in the environment.

Given their conventional nature and arbitrariness in form, linguistic response systems, in contrast to purely biological ones, are detachable from the original conditions in which they are (were) first emitted or "learned." This feature of linguistic response systems allows individuals not only to act in similar ways in different situations, but also to respond "in the absence" of the circumstances (individuals, objects, and events included) in which linguistic behavior once took place. Given this detachability of linguistic behavior systems, human beings may relate to past and future times, different places, absent persons or objects, and "constructed" conventional objects (concepts, myths, nonexistent beings, and so forth). It is also possible to relate to the linguistic behavior of absent individuals, both as alive and as dead language.

In the history of humankind, and in individual human development, the first modes of language were (are) gesturing and speaking, with writing being the last one to appear (6,500 years ago and when children are taught to read and write). With the advent of writing, words were created as transcriptions of the articulated sounds when speaking. Words do not represent objects or events. Words represent articulated speech sounds, and words, as grammatical units, did not exist before writing. Like speech itself, words, as graphic representation of speech, are a human construction. Because of this, the advent of writing also represented the existence of linguistic (conventional) objects in the form of words, pictograms, hieroglyphics, and so forth. These linguistic objects coexist with "natural" objects and with artifacts constructed by means of crafts and technology. Writing, as patterning of stimulus objects and conditions, fills spatial and temporal gaps in the relations between individuals under common circumstances (personal interactions). Writing also consists of complex linguistic stimulus objects in different modes of knowing (ordinary, scientific, artistic, formal, religious, technological, and others), with which individuals may interact in different places and time (impersonal interactions).

Understanding

Although what we have identified as reactive modes of language (observing, listening, and reading) have been usually related to *understanding*, this is not an accurate interpretation. Understanding is not a different "process" or moment from speaking and writing. The separation of understanding from the active modes of language is a mistake that leads, most of the time, to the assumption that understanding is a special kind of covert (not implicit) behavior, usually consisting of some sort of self-speaking or self-observing, as in introspection (e.g., Schlinger, 2008). Actually, understanding always involves "overt" behavior, both linguistic and nonlinguistic in form. Understanding entails completing an episode, in concordance with a social convention. Understanding is nothing other than a shared social practice by at least two individuals. Linguistic behavior always occurs in episodic situations, involving at least two individuals, although on occasion an individual may perform two different functional roles, as in a soliloquy. In this last case, it would be absurd to predicate some sort of "self-understanding."

Language, given its inseparability of social practice, wraps all human relations and interactions. It is the *medium* in which all human behavior takes place. Extending Kantor's (1924, 1926) concept of contact medium, we could say that language, articulating social institutional practices as interindividual relations, is the contact medium exclusive of human behavior, a *conventional* contact medium. Wittgenstein (1980, p. 678) emphasized this binding between language and human life when saying "We're used to a particular classification of things. With language, or languages, it has become second nature to us."

Linguistic behavior (as equivalent to human behavior) is conventional in nature (Ribes, 1993, 2006a) and, to that extent, always takes place in concordance with those participating in any interaction or relation. Concordance, inherent to convention, presupposes understanding. Nobody speaks, gesticulates, or writes attempting to be understood, but actually does so because they are always understood. When a person speaks, gestures, or writes to another person, they are sure, beforehand, that it is being understood. Otherwise, people would probe all the time before contacting others. In fact, "understanding" is used in ordinary language practices only when, by special reasons, individuals show inappropriate behavior in relation to what is being indicated, spoken, or written to or for them. Philosophers and psychologists, who have created or followed the myth of the "cognitive" individual as the origin of knowledge and language, are responsible for raising the false problem of understanding.

Behavior and Conduct

In addition to understanding, a second important concept to be examined is that related to behavior. "Behavior" and "conduct" are neither technical terms nor exclusive of psychological descriptions or attributions. These terms are used in everyday language, and in Romance languages, these words (e.g., *comportamiento* and *conducta* in Spanish) derive from the Latin words *comportare* and *conducere*, meaning "what is brought with," and "to lead together," respectively). These terms are ordinary terms, employed not only in reference to the doings of people, but also to changes related to direction in inanimate objects or events. Disciplines other than psychology also employ the term "behavior" to describe changes in conditions of particles, physical bodies, electricity, molecules, cells, groups, institutions, markets, polls, movement, temperature, pressure, direction, and many others depending on the subject matter under scrutiny. "Behavior" and "conduct" are generic terms that apply not only to movements of organisms, but to changes in the activity or conditions of a diversity of "entities" or things. In the case of psychology, behaviorism (Watson, 1913) naturalized the term to define its subject matter (or at least an index of it). Nevertheless, "behavior" has no single meaning within behaviorism.

Kitchener (1977) identified a diversity of definitions of behavior among the various behavioristic formulations, pointing to different conceptual subject matters despite using the same term. This is not a surprising situation, since words and concepts are not the same. Words are the morphological units composing the lexicon of a natural language, while concepts are the functions that exert words. The same word may have different conceptual meanings, that is, pertain to different conceptual frames, and at the same time different words may be conceptually similar. Ribes (2004a) stressed that the term "behavior" is not a neutral, descriptive, or ostensive term corresponding to or denoting "psychological" events or phenomena. Rather, as used in psychology, the term is an abstraction related to different ordinary uses of the word and other akin terms that show

"family resemblance" (Wittgenstein, 1953) according to some explicit or implicit crite‐
rion. Although, as noted above, other disciplines use the term "behavior" in their descrip‐
tions, only in psychology is "behavior" considered a term indigenous to its subject matter,
without the necessary conceptual awareness that this is not the case.

Kantor (1963) called attention to the fact that "behavior" is a term used by different
disciplines, and that psychology adopted it from biology through the conceptual tradition
of reflex physiology. Kantor was especially critical about the organocentric conception of
behavior, as an activity flowing from the organism, either as reaction (provoked or "elic‐
ited") or as action (emitted). To get away from this reductionist conception, he proposed
to distinguish between biological and psychological behaviors, and afterward, these two
from cultural or institutional behavior. Psychological behavior consists of functional con‐
tacts involving an acting/reacting individual and the stimulus properties of objects and
events in the environment, including other individuals and, in some cases, the same
individual interacting with their own linguistic behavior. Psychological behavior is not
movement, or actions, but functional relations between individuals and particular objects
(sometimes other individuals).

Nevertheless, psychological behavior is always to be viewed from the standpoint of
the individual and not from the stimulus object or event, especially when this is another
individual also behaving. The analysis of relations between individuals, as a functional
unit, pertains to the domain of social science. Interindividual relations constitute insti‐
tutional behavior and may be approached as a multidisciplinary enterprise between social
science and psychology (Ribes, Pulido, Rangel, & Sánchez-Gatell, 2016). Psychological
behavior takes place only as individually framed or oriented episodic components forming
part of ecological (survival) or social (living together, coexistence) relations. There are
no autonomous psychological contacts, foreign to ecological and conventional media.
Psychological contacts constitute a special set of relations between individuals showing
differentiated reactional systems and particular stimulus objects and/or other individuals.
However, only some of these relations between individuals and stimulus objects and
other individuals qualify as psychological, always being components of ecological or
social relations. Psychological behavior is concerned only with those relations that can
be identified from the perspective of the individual, and not from the stimulus objects or
as a two-component indivisible relation.

Psychological relations, not surprisingly, usually correspond to those ordinary lan‐
guage practices including or consisting of "mental" terms and expressions. "Mental"
terms and expressions do not occur in isolation. They are always part of social episodes,
in which terms characterize the circumstances of the individual acts in reference to other
individuals, objects, and events. "Mental" terms do not describe, denote, or refer to
special activities taking place "inside" the individual. The so-called mental terms and
expressions are constitutive of the social practice and are part of the circumstances that
constitute the episode in which they take place. Psychological behavior always consists of
an episodic relation *in* ordinary language (Ryle, 1949); it involves episodes in which an
individual may be characterized, by himself and others, as remembering, learning, feeling,

perceiving, and so on. These references are relative not to something happening in the individual, but to something taking place between the individual and other individuals, objects, or events as the circumstances of the relation. This is why psychological behavior may be considered as a collection of episodic segments of ordinary language practices (Wittgenstein, 1969). These segments are part of the referential nature of ordinary language. Reference means that when talking we always talk *about* something (i.e., the talk is referring to a thing but is distinct from that thing itself) *to* somebody (and in special circumstances to ourselves). Speaking (and obviously gesturing and writing) is not a mere denotative or descriptive accompaniment to the reactions and actions taking place when individuals behave. As an accompaniment, language would be dispensable or redundant.

Human behavior is functional because it is integrated with language, even in its reactive modes. Because of this, psychological "language" should be understood as language about the individual circumstances involved in social episodes, and nothing else, irrespective of the fact that this talking about the individual-in-relation is in singular first, second, or third person (I, you, or they). For example, when "remembering" talk occurs, remembering consists of the relations taking place in the episode. Remembering talk is not an index, description, or "reference" of something taking place in the individual. Remembering talk is what remembering is about. The same can be said of any "mental" term or expression corresponding to psychological phenomena in ordinary language practices.

However, if psychological behavior is inherent in social relations between individuals taking place in ordinary language practices, does this mean that psychological behavior is exclusive of human behavior and cannot be attributed to certain animal species? Usually, in daily life, we speak about psychological reactions or acts in those animals that are domesticated or deprived of their natural environment (e.g., zoos, circuses), animals with which we have continuous or intermittent contact under socially established circumstances. We attribute emotions and intentions to our pets, but we do not do so with unknown, unfamiliar animals or with those pertaining to invertebrate phyla, such as insects, arthropods, and echinoderms. Regardless of the daily life extension of psychological attributes to animals, it is only recently that the terms "mental" and "psychological" became part of ordinary language practices, mostly as an effect of the social influence of the psychiatric and psychological professions. In past centuries, "mind" and "mental" were not ordinary terms. Even more, psychology, as a discipline born at the beginning of the last century, became concerned with animal "mind" processes, as an influence of the concepts advanced by Charles Darwin (1974) and John Romanes (1888), in tracing back the conduct of mankind to the evolution of species. Something similar occurred with the incorporation of terms such as "physical," "chemical," and "biological" by ordinary language practices. These terms label special technical languages that are based on the referential functions of ordinary language but have different purposes. The distinct domains of science do not deal with concrete objects and situations but with general properties abstracted from them. Scientific terms and concepts are concerned with properties and relations, not with things and particular events.

Nevertheless, the case of psychology is distinct. Wittgenstein (1953) commented that psychology involved experimental methods and conceptual confusion, pointing to the fact that psychologists have incorrectly identified ordinary "psychological" terms with alleged univocal references, in the form of reports and descriptions of events or experiences supposed to occur within individuals. In contrast to other sciences, psychology has assumed that terms used in ordinary language, such as "perception," "feeling," "sensation," "memory," "thinking," "imagination," and similar ones, constitute reliable references to actual *kinds* of experiences, activities, or events taking place "in" or "by" the individual. As a sequel to this historical condition, psychology borrowed technical terms from other disciplines to become "scientific," while attempting, without fortune, to provide a technical status to ordinary language terms by means of operational definitions and constructed validity tactics. Conditioning theory, theories of cognition based on information and computer models, and psychometric theories are prominent examples of this historical tendency.

Although J. R. Kantor (1924, 1926) formulated a logical model specific for psychological phenomena, he did not advance any theoretical concepts to construct a technical language beyond the terms of ordinary language. In order to construct a scientific theory, it is not sufficient to provide functional interpretations of ordinary language terms. Functional analysis of language is not equivalent to an abstract theory of the psychological phenomena inherent in ordinary "mental" terms and expressions. A scientific theory requires a technical language, denotative in nature, in which terms and expressions have univocal meanings and correspond to abstracted properties, dimensions, and relations of concrete objects and events. Nevertheless, such abstract terms do not refer to particular concrete instances. Facts and events (Hanson, 1958) are always "constructed" by abstraction of those events, objects, and conditions dealt with in the daily practice of ordinary language. To the extent that abstract technical concepts do not refer to particular events or objects, they cannot be used as ostensive or descriptive terms in natural sceneries in daily life. The functional grammar of abstract theoretical concepts is not the same as the diverse grammars framing the sense of terms in ordinary language, and it would be a serious logical mistake to establish or assume direct correspondences between them. Scientific language is denotative, whereas ordinary language is referential. It is hard to imagine a language in which talking consists of naming and describing objects or events. Paradoxically, in spite of its denotative function, nothing socially meaningful for living together would be said to others. Naming and describing are not essential dimensions in social communication.

Field Theory and Interdisciplinary Extensions

J. R. Kantor (1924, 1926) formulated a field model for the scientific analysis of psychological behavior. His fundamental conception of the field construct involved the identification of functional contacts between the individual and particular stimulus objects or events, made possible by a contact medium and promoted by setting factors in the situation and the individual interactive history. Explanation of psychological behavior was conceived as the description and systematic analysis of the interdependent relations established between the components of the psychological field. Nevertheless, the field system was not developed in order to abstract and identify different classes or types of functional contacts (Ribes, 2018), probably because Kantor's efforts were devoted to a theory *about* psychology and not to a theory *in* psychology.

Rather, the conceptual frame was used to examine ordinary psychological terms as if they corresponded univocally to different classes of psychological fields. In the best of cases, such analysis provided a functional interpretation of ordinary language terms, but it fell short of satisfying the requirements of a theoretical technical language. Ordinary terms may be incorporated by the technical language of an abstract theory, but only when they are provided with a univocal sense, under the logical frame of the theory. Otherwise, the use of ordinary terms leads to misunderstandings and confusion. As mentioned earlier, psychological terms are not "references" to anything else. They are part of the individual episodes that constitute psychological phenomena, and, therefore, it is absurd to consider them as a special sort of self-denotative terms with "explanatory" functions. In the same way, these terms, by themselves, isolated from the circumstances in which they occur as part of ordinary language practices, do not represent legitimate problems to be addressed by a scientific theory. Ordinary terms and expressions are multisensical, depending on their meaning or sense from the context in which they take place or are "used." This is why they cannot be directly translated to or from denotative abstract terms. Abstract denotative terms may show a logical coverage including a diversity of ordinary terms, and conversely, a single ordinary term may be analyzed from the perspective of different denotative terms.

Logical Functions of a Psychological Theory

I have proposed that a balanced theory in psychology should include four types of logical categories (Ribes, 2003): taxonomic, operational, measurement, and representational. **Taxonomic categories** cover the abstracted empirical domain to be considered as facts and their properties. **Operational categories** are related to the observational and experimental preparations, methods, procedures, and techniques through which facts and their properties are set to occur, be manipulated, and be recorded, among other operations. **Measurement categories** deal with the way in which recorded facts, as events and properties meaningful for the theory, are transformed into data, and therefore—in evidence of the functional relations—implicitly assumed by taxonomic categories. Finally, **representational categories** consist of the more or less formal schemas in which general functional relations are "pictured" and structurally organized. Below I will elaborate on taxonomic categories specifically.

Taxonomic categories, to the extent that they delimit the empirical domain to be studied, are the first step in the development of a scientific theory. Taxonomic categories frame the facts to be accounted for in terms of processes and states. Kantor (1958) formulated a subject matter for psychology and the logical model to address its study. This logical model consists of a field analysis of functional contacts, made possible by a contact medium and facilitated or interfered with by situational and historic setting factors. However, Kantor did not take further steps to formulate a theory of psychological behavior. To fill this initial conceptual gap, I have proposed a taxonomy consisting of five different functional contacts in a field involving interdependent contingencies between the individual's behavior patterns and the properties and dimensions of stimulus objects (Ribes, 1997, 2018). This functional classification is based upon two central concepts: **mediation**, in terms of the component articulating the field organization, and **detachment**, referring to the progressive functional independence of properties present in the situation in which the contact takes place. The taxonomy covers five types of functional contact, two of which are exclusive to human beings but at the same time build upon the rest of the contacts that are shared with other animal species. The five types of contacts are **coupling**, **alteration**, **comparison**, **extension**, and **transformation of contingencies** (see Ribes, 2018) and are analyzed in terms of molar measures describing directionality, variation, preference, vigor, and persistence. Special operations and experimental preparations have been gradually developed for their experimental study.

Dealing with Natural and Social Settings

In the same way that ordinary psychological terms and concepts cannot be directly related to abstract denotative terms, the latter cannot be directly applied to describe psychological behavior in natural and social settings, or to the complementary analysis required by multidisciplinary intersections, especially with biology and social science. The "application" of scientific findings demands an adaptation of the theoretical knowledge describing abstracted conditions in the form of a technical language formulated to cope with particular conditions characterizing specific situations in natural and social settings. The application of scientific knowledge always entails the empirical findings framed under the concepts and categories of a theory.

Theories in science do not deal with particular situations or concrete events. In contrast, application of scientific knowledge has to do with particular situations, actual individuals, and specific social criteria about the goals, effects, or outcomes of such application. Applications of science always deal with interdisciplinary fields, which consist of special professional domains designed to solve socially important problems and promote the achievement of institutional goals. Examples of interdisciplinary fields are medicine and other health professions, administration and finance, education-related professions, and a wide variety of engineering fields. Interdisciplinary fields delimit the boundaries and characteristics of the contributions to be made by different sciences, technologies, artistic disciplines, and traditional practices. All those contributions must touch upon the different dimensions of the problems to be solved or the goals to be achieved. Contributing disciplines must adapt their knowledge to the demands, requirements, and criteria of the interdisciplinary fields, or, in exceptional cases, provide arguments and procedures to modify the ways in which they are conceived. Consequently, scientific disciplines do not "apply" straightforward knowledge and techniques when participating in an interdisciplinary field or enterprise.

So-called applied behavior analysis (ABA; Baer, Wolf, & Risley, 1968) arose as a direct application of the principles of operant conditioning (equated with the experimental analysis of behavior) to social problems in natural settings. The field of ABA included, in its beginnings, the behavior of patients with mental illness (Ayllon & Azrin, 1968; Lindsley, 1960), children with developmental disabilities (Azrin & Foxx, 1971), physical rehabilitation (Parker et al., 1984), juvenile delinquency (Cohen, 1972; Hobbs & Holt, 1976; Wolf et al., 1976), elementary education settings (Barrish, Saunders, & Wolf, 1969; Burchard & Barrera, 1972; Cossairt, Hall, & Hopkins, 1973; Glynn, Thomas, & Shee, 1973, Holt, 1971; McDowell, 1968; Schutte & Hopkins, 1970), the personalized instruction system, programmed instruction, and precision teaching (Keller, 1968; Lindsley, 1992), psychotherapy (Kohlenberg & Tsai, 1995), industrial and labor settings (Hermann, Montes, Domínguez, Montes, & Hopkins, 1973) and some extensions to community problems (Fawcett, Mathews, & Fletcher, 1980).

ABA was conceived as a direct application of principles identified in the experimental laboratory, mostly with animal subjects, and afterward with the replication of procedures from the animal laboratory with human subjects. Principles consisted of operational categories relating procedures with effects or outcomes, namely reinforcement, extinction, punishment, discrimination, generalization, conditioned reinforcement, and so on (see chapter 2). Experimental operations were transferred to natural settings under controlled situations to assess effects on the frequency of different behaviors, either to establish new behavior or to increase or decrease target behavior. Nevertheless, the effectiveness of such procedures was limited to relatively simple behaviors or interactions, in which the (high or low) frequency of behavior was the relevant issue, not the behavior itself. Moreover, procedures were used mainly under conditions in which it was possible to control the interactions and outcomes of those behaviors. Thus, ABA procedures were more akin to limited demonstrations than to a true technology for behavior change, as it was assumed.

With the passage of time, it became obvious not only that the use of a jargon based on operant conditioning operations had little to do with actual procedures employed in human situations, but also that this jargon became progressively mixed with nontechnical terms or terms borrowed from different professions, disciplines, and even religious practices. The so-called applied behavior analysis procedures required of simplified environments, and their implementation, were not in correspondence with the original definitions supporting them (Ribes, 1977, 2004b). This is to say that operant principles, at least as they have been formulated for the experimental (and theoretical) analysis of behavior, seem to apply to a rather limited set of circumstances (e.g., those involving discrete repetitive responses and stimulus changes related to deprivation or intensity parameters). Indeed, it may be considered somewhat naïve to assume that individuals' daily life is "controlled" by "reinforcers," which are to be identified as any condition or event following behaviors varying in complexity, and which are difficult to compare with each other (e.g., crying, reading letters or books, writing novels, solving problems, consuming drugs). The world and daily life of individuals is not arranged by discriminative stimuli and reinforcers. It is difficult to attempt to conceive human behavior in natural settings in terms of "response classes" being continuously affected, in discrete linear chunks, by *ad hoc* "natural" discriminative and reinforcing stimuli. Skinner's (1957) analysis of language as verbal behavior clearly showed that interpreting human behavior in terms of operant principles is, at best, a hermeneutic exercise, full of contradictions and imprecisions (Ribes, 1999).

Scientific disciplines, in contrast to interdisciplinary fields, are able to take distance from prevailing social ideologies and correlated dominant practices. This does not mean that science is a neutral, pure, human enterprise (see Kantor, 1953). Nevertheless, analytic thinking and empirical criteria for confirmation of knowledge widens the horizons of sciences' perspectives about the determinants and solutions for problems arising in the context of human social organization and activity. Therefore, the participation of science within interdisciplinary fields is not a simple matter of adaptation and application of available knowledge. It implies also a critical appraisal of the social problems involved and challenging traditional views about their nature and solution. In the case of education, unfortunately, the contributions of psychology (and of the other participating disciplines), without any critical perspective, have been assimilated by dominant social criteria to prolongate the conservative nature of the "school."

Competence: The Integration of Intelligence, Learning, and Knowing

The final section of this chapter focuses on an example of an interdisciplinary effort. Specifically, I will focus on the field of education to examine the ways in which psychological theory may participate in an interdisciplinary endeavor. Not only is education a relevant social field to which psychology may contribute, but it also allows us to compare the ways in which applied psychology in general, and ABA in particular, have conceived their role. Education, as a general endeavor, mostly rests on the "school"—the institution devoted to instructing individuals for the social division of labor and for the reproduction of values inherent in a given social formation. Education involves the documentation of the information, abilities, and skills acquired by individuals. Since the French Revolution, education has been designed to be offered in the school to individuals grouped together according to different criteria: age, sex, type of instruction, previous knowledge and abilities, and so forth. Individualized instruction is an exception, even though this may sometimes take place in a home or small work setting. The availability of electronic devices has promoted impersonal educational environments, which, nevertheless, should be conceived to be complementary but not equivalent to those that require the explicit interaction of the learner with the teacher. In any case, there are hierarchical social institutions prescribing, designing, and regulating the educational programs offered in the school. These institutional bodies make the decisions about what, how, where, and to whom the varied contents of educational programs are to be taught. In spite of the fact that teachers are only a part of the operation of the institutional mechanism, they bear the responsibility of educational effectiveness, conceived as the fulfillment of the outcomes demanded by the social formation as a whole.

Two concepts are outstanding in reference to the psychological dimensions involved in education, namely, *intelligence* and *learning*. These two concepts emerged from the natural history of education and point to aspects related to the individual being instructed, trained, or taught—the so-called apprentice, pupil, or student. Whereas instruction depends on the teacher, who is assumed to be knowledgeable about what is being taught and the adequate procedures to teach it, the success of such effort depends in turn on the capacities and abilities of the apprentice. Learning is the concept that describes the final outcome of instruction. Psychology, from different perspectives, has approached the teaching-learning process by focusing on the construct of intelligence, its measurement, and its development, or, on the other hand, by focusing on the design of the teaching procedures that promote effective and fast learning. Psychologists construct intelligence and learning tests and scales and devote themselves to the design of learning environments and procedures, participating in the teaching of teachers. Teachers are, thus, instructed to teach, to assess the intelligence and learning of students, and to plan and administrate educational settings with these purposes. Educational failure is attributed to teaching procedures and to the inadequacy of students in showing basic skills or abilities. Nevertheless, it is unusual to find explicit rationales of the educational process justifying *what* is to be learned by apprentices and how this learning is to be incorporated in the various functional domains of daily life. Learning is often conceived in terms of "knowledge" about something or as basic skills related to reading, writing, and calculating. The school curriculum, from the elementary school to the university, is grounded on the assumption that learning consists of knowledge acquisition and that the "mechanics" of reading, writing, and calculating are mere instrumental devices for the acquisition or application of knowledge. Psychology in general, and ABA in particular, have oriented their contributions to *improve* the efficiency of the school system, without questioning its adequacy, values, and implicit goals.

Intelligence, learning, and knowing (or cognition) are not technical psychological concepts. These terms are part of ordinary language practices and are used in a diversity of contexts. Nevertheless, in all cases, we can identify a common functional sense that in no way makes them adequate for theoretical purposes. "Intelligence" is a term with a long history (since Aristotle) and is especially used in the context of evolutionary thinking as equivalent to species-adaptive capacities. The measurement of intelligence, as a measure of individual differences, emerged with two different purposes: (1) with Galton (1899), to justify racial and class differences in humans, and (2) with Binet and Simon (1916/1973), to measure differences in school performance, initially to provide compensatory teaching, and later to select individuals for different activities according to their capacities and abilities, that is, to classify the affordances of social opportunities.

On the other hand, the term "learning" was seen as the process responsible for behavioral changes and adaptation, in both animals and humans, in such a way that learning almost became synonymous to behavior (Bower & Hilgard, 1981; Thorndike, 1911), contrasting acquired performance with so-called instinctive, inherited action patterns (Lorenz, 1965).

Finally, "knowing" is another ordinary term with a multiplicity of explicit and implicit meanings or uses (Malcolm, 1963). Psychology (and philosophy) incorporated knowing as the common function of other nontechnical terms, namely, "perception," "memory," "thinking," and "consciousness," all related to the subjective capture of the world by a contemplative individual.

An Analysis of Terms

A conceptual analysis of the terms "intelligence," "learning," and "knowing" helps to identify their functional uses, in order to formulate interfacing concepts between them and those describing functional contacts in **interbehavioral theory**. Ryle (1949) and Ribes (1981, 1989, 2007) provided detailed analyses of the three aforementioned terms, so I will only briefly review how they are used in ordinary language practices.

Intelligence is always predicated on doings and outcomes of individuals. Strictly speaking, intelligence is always referred to as intelligent behavior or performance. Intelligent behavior always consists of actions that are effective in the context of their occurrence, usually solving a problem or formulating its correct solution. Nevertheless, intelligence is never predicated on a single occurrence of an effective performance by an individual, but rather to a collection of occurrences by the same individual in a variety of situations. A single effective behavior may be due to chance or fortune, and the repetitive occurrence of the same performance in the same situation, although showing effectiveness, does not show that with a change in the situation the individual could be equally successful. Thus, an individual's behavior is described as intelligent only when the behavior is effective more than once and in varied forms or situations.

Ryle (1949) described intelligent behavior, emphasizing the variety of possible effective performances, by saying that the crucial feature is knowing the final destination and not a particular route to be taken. Contrary to traditional views in psychology and education, intelligence should not be conceived as something that is possessed in larger or smaller amounts, but rather as a characteristic of performance when a problem must be formulated and solved. Figure 7.1 shows a table with two axes: effectiveness of performance and variety of behavior. Only the cell in which varied and effective performance coincide corresponds to intelligent behavior. The other cells show different types of behavior: creative behavior when performance is varied but not effective, operative behavior (i.e., behavior that results from training) when performance is effective but not varied, and "fool" behavior when performance is neither effective nor varied. Not being intelligent does not necessarily mean being a fool.

	VARIED	STEREOTYPED
EFFECTIVE	INTELLIGENT	OPERATIVE
INEFFECTIVE	CREATIVE	FOOL

Figure 7.1 Different types of behavior according to the intersection
of variation and effectiveness continua.

Learning has been conceived by psychologists and neurobiologists as a central process explaining the workings of behavior in animals and humans. In the last century, learning theory became equivalent to behavior theory, and the concept of learning supported the metaphor of the *acquisition* of behavior. This metaphor allowed for the distinction between so-called innate (or instinctive) behaviors and learned behaviors, a questionable and misleading dichotomy. Writings about classical, instrumental, or operant conditioning (among other procedural domains) commonly refer to the salivary conditional response or to the key-pecking or bar-pressing responses as *acquired* or *learned* responses. But it is well known that dogs normally salivate, that pigeons peck on surfaces and objects, and that even rats, left by themselves, press the bar in the operant chamber. In fact, those responses are "available" before any conditioning procedure is developed and occur without explicit elicitation. It is incorrect to speak about the emergence of "new" responses, since what is taking place is the emergence of new *functions* for response patterns already available. The dog salivates to the signal of food, and the pigeon and rat extend the response patterns to food seeking and consumption. The tone has become a component of a stimulus segment determined by food delivery, while pecking and pressing have become components of a behavior segment related to eating. Even in those cases in which the specific response patterns do not seem to be available—as in language learning or some motor skills, including walking—the potential of such patterns is part of the reactional systems of the individual.

Kuo (1967) described development in terms of behavior gradients and potentials. A good example of this is speaking, in that articulated language involves a reduction or restriction of the sound frequencies originally emitted by the newborn, and not new sound frequencies. Differences in phonetics between the different natural languages is an outcome of this process. Based on the acquisition metaphor, psychology has postulated learning to be an underlying process taking place every time a new behavior function emerges. Additionally, the consolidation of what is learned is attributed to a complementary process: memory. However, this is an inaccurate description of what actually happens when it is said that an individual is learning or has learned. When learning is said to have happened, typically only one thing occurs—the performance in a situation—as opposed to two things, the performance *and* its learning and consolidation.

Learning is not identified by means of special activities, except for the case in which the activities themselves are what is being learned. Learning is said to occur when the performance of an individual fulfills a predetermined criterion of mastery of an activity, or a criterion related to the results or outcomes of a set of activities. When no criterion is prescribed or established, it is nonsensical to talk about learning or nonlearning. The appeal to "implicit" learning always consists of a *post-hoc* recognition of a prior nonprescribed criterion. Therefore, it is safe to assert that the same behavioral processes take place when individuals learn and when they do not learn. The prescription of an activity/outcome criterion is the crucial difference between both situations. Learning and not learning can only be identified in reference to a criterion. The postulated stability or permanence of learned behavior is the result of the stability and permanence of the contingencies required and established by the corresponding ecological or social criteria.

Knowing is the third ordinary term dealing directly with the means and goals of education as a social institution. It is assumed that the ultimate end of schooling is to promote the "acquisition" and "use" of knowledge. The terms "to know" and "knowledge" are used in a multiplicity of ways in ordinary language, not only in reference to the mastery of a practice, situation, or domain, but also in relation to doubt, estimation, and certainty, among other uses. Knowledge usually applies to intellectual products as well as to procedures and techniques. Knowing entails an episodic relation of an individual with something or someone, in terms of exposure, information, or mastery in practice, involving a great diversity of linguistic practices. Knowing is not a special kind of activity but rather an outcome of direct and indirect contact with entities (things, persons, living beings, institutions), events, and doings, sometimes under specifically arranged learning situations. Although knowing something is tantamount to being informed about "that," information implies only the availability of potential stimulus conditions. Being informed is not the same as knowing what to do or knowing how something or someone will behave, operate, or work.

Borrowing Austin's (1955/1962) characterization of language expressions, we may speak of constative and performative knowing (Ribes, 2007). **Constative knowing** consists of recognizing, pointing to, informing about, describing, and confirming events, states of things, and previous acts. Constative knowing may be an outcome of direct (e.g., talking, writing) or indirect (e.g., observing, listening, and reading) contacts with what is known. On the other hand, **performative knowing** consists of doing something, and these doings may involve pure linguistic acts, as in theoretical practice (reflexive language), or integrated patterns involving linguistic and effective motor acts. Talking and writing, as Austin emphasized, are sometimes the effective components of behavior. Performative knowing involves mastering how to do things, including ways of talking and writing as acting.

Given that learning is learning of knowing how and knowing about, four general types of learning may be identified (in this case, I take "saying" as representative of the three active modes of language behavior: speech, signaling/gesturing, and writing): (1) learning how to do and to say, (2) learning how to say as a doing, (3) learning how to say about doing, and (4) learning how to do as a saying.

These general types of learning may take place either as intelligent behavior or as operative behavior, with the aim of schooling being to provide the necessary conditions of these behaviors and learnings to occur in different domains of social life. In the case of operative behavior, traditional wisdom prescribes that practice, repetition, supervision, and appropriate feedback are sufficient for its establishment and endurance. By contrast, these *training* conditions, although necessary in certain occasions, are not sufficient for the establishment and development of intelligent behavior. Indeed, even when some intelligent behavior has developed, it is still important to diversify its organization in accordance with different criteria of **functional aptitude**. Functional aptitudes deal with different types of functional contacts of the individual with the stimulus conditions involved in a problem. Different aptitudes involve different skills, techniques, routines, and procedures, or a different organization of the available skills, even when the "formal" situation seems to be the same.

I have formulated the concept of **functional competence** (Ribes, 2006b, 2008) in order to deal with the learning of intelligent behavior in educational settings. A **competence** is the functional organization of skills, techniques, routines, and procedures in order to satisfy a functional aptitude criterion (see figure 7.2). Aptitude criteria correspond to the five types of interbehavioral contacts identified in the field theory: coupling, alteration, comparison, extension, and transformation of contingencies (Ribes, 2018). Thus, a competence is a relation between functional aptness or capacity, in reference to a type of field contact, and intelligent behavior in the form of varied and effective behavior. Competence is the interphase concept that "connects" theory with practice. Through the analysis of competencies, it is possible to look into intelligent behavior, learning, and knowledge a nonlinear way.

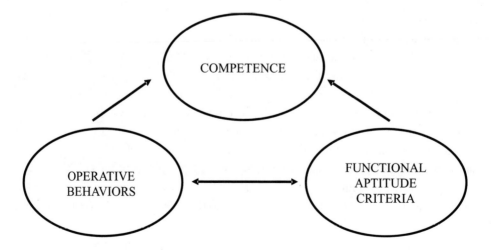

Figure 7.2 Competence as the conjugation of operative behaviors and functional aptitude criteria.

From this perspective, interdisciplinary intervention by psychologists and educators is concerned with designing the conditions in which, for any domain of knowing or life, individuals can deal with problems in any of the five types of aptitude corresponding to interbehavioral functional contacts. The "domain" in which individuals interact may be always the same (for instance, learning about kinetics in physics), but the quality and functional characteristics of those interactions may be completely different depending on the type of interbehavioral contact involved. To diversify functional aptitude in any domain, however, demands a profound change in the structure of the schooling situation. It is not simply a matter of adapting teaching procedures or introducing supplementary media. These are relevant only for providing information or for training techniques and skills, as has been traditional in media-concerned education or in ABA. The "contents" of education must be replaced by competencies pertinent to specific domains of life and knowledge. Competencies must be shown as actual behaviors that are relevant for the mastery of a given domain— that is, doing something (and this always includes linguistic interactions) that is a functional activity in the situation. It is not behavior "external" to the situation involved, but behavior "internal," intrinsic to the usual practices involved in a given domain.

Competencies can only be learned from those who master them in a given situation. One cannot simply be informed about competencies. Rather, competencies have to be taught through example. To teach a competency entails demonstrating it and guiding, prompting, and correcting the apprentice with respect to the different criteria, prescribing the ways in which to interact with the circumstances in a situation. Teaching a competency goes beyond showing constative knowledge. Competencies always involve some form of varied performative knowing, even in cases that are completely linguistic in nature, as in theoretical practice. To the extent that learning a competency always involves some kind of doing or activity, when teaching competencies, no additional evaluation regarding its learning is needed after it is demonstrated by the apprentice. Unlike traditional teaching, in which knowledge is transmitted through textual or spoken language, the use of media, or even demonstrations, competencies cannot be transmitted. The teaching of competencies requires that both teacher and apprentice participate in the actual activities involved in the exercise of performative knowing in a given situation or domain. Competencies consist of episodic interactions and not of specific, pinpointed behaviors or responses. In fact, competencies may be exercised through very different activities, events, and stimulus conditions. The domain and the aptitude criteria in a situation are the factors that identify a competence as being the same, in spite of the diversity of activities and elements involved in any episodic interaction.

I have previously discussed (Ribes, 2006b, 2011) why traditional schooling does not allow or promote the establishment and development of competencies and intelligent behavior by apprentices. Below, I will elaborate on the reasons.

Flaws Inherent in Traditional Education Models

Formal education is most often based on the assumption that apprentices learn "knowledge" as information, not as practical interactions within the boundaries of disciplinary domains and life contingencies. The traditional conception of teaching and learning, as transmission-contemplation, has to be replaced by one in which to learn means to master the competencies involved in the practice of any domain of life and knowledge. This entails replacing the conception of having learned in terms of being informed about something and being able to recognize, repeat, or reproduce it, by one in which learning corresponds to effective interactions in practical circumstances involving new knowing or new ways of showing such knowing. Learning has to be approached in terms of what the apprentice must master as a practice, instead of emphasizing what teachers have to inform students about. This is why present schooling is, at least, deficient. Most learning is planned to take place in a classroom, and sometimes in demonstration laboratories, where apprentices observe and listen to the teacher. The teacher exposes students to what is written in manuals and books and informs them about the actual doings and learning of others. Leaning is evaluated through exams and tests, in which apprentices have to recognize, repeat, or reproduce the information received or the procedures involved in demonstrations.

Psychology and ABA have focused their efforts on improving the "efficiency" of this model of schooling, emphasizing teaching and instructional techniques, as well as assessment methods to evaluate "how much" apprentices have "learned" to duplicate the information and demonstrations provided to them. However, as previously mentioned, the interdisciplinary intervention of scientific disciplines in education, at least, should not be without criticism and provided on an "on demand" basis. Aside from other arguments concerned with the social orientation of the present universal model of schooling, an analysis—based on the nature of learning from the perspective of interbehavioral field theory—leads to the formulation of an alternative model centered on the apprentice and to design situations promoting the development of functional competencies in the diverse domains of knowledge and daily life. This alternative model should also question the ultimate social goals of education and schooling. Following this argument, I proposed an alternative model for preschool and elementary education that can be extended to the complete schooling process (Ribes, 2008). This model involves the development of five kinds of competencies for every segment of disciplinary knowledge in empirical sciences, sequencing their organization in terms of increasing complexity of phenomena (from physics and chemistry, to geology and biology, and finally to social science).

In this new educational model, alive language (Kantor, 1936), in all its modalities, is emphasized as an actual practice, and not as "rules" or erudition. This approach to schooling includes the various arts as well as an extended learning of mathematics as a transdisciplinary tool. Disciplinary competencies are integrated with social domains of daily life, in order to develop life competencies in health, social participation, communication, environmental conservation, technological skills, and recreation. Sciences are to be learned by *doing* and *thinking* in the conditions and situations in which their practice take place (obviously not in the classroom). The same goes for life competencies, which can also be integrated with language enrichment and artistic activities.

Implications and Future Directions

The perspective described in this chapter has several implications for the science of behavior, particularly as increased attention is given to topics related to human language and cognition. As described in the chapter, the language used throughout various areas of science has implications for the conduct of subsequent work. That is, how we talk about what we do may impact subsequent research, and ultimately how we approach various applied topics. While this chapter is more theoretical in nature when compared to other chapters in this volume, it is clear that several lessons pertinent to both research and practice can be gleaned. More generally, as the perspective described in this chapter is relatively less well known among many applied behavior analysts, the potential implications of this body of work remain to be seen.

Conclusion

Language is used in various ways throughout science. The present chapter considered some of the ways in which language impacts science—in particular psychology and behavior science—and provided some guidance for the proper use of language in science. While largely a theoretical chapter, it also considered applied issues and concluded with a consideration of the topic of education and schooling. Behavior scientists of all sorts are encouraged to analyze the language of science and practice and consider the extent to which it impacts their work and various areas of research and practice more generally.

Study Questions

1. How are technical and ordinary language different?

2. Explain why language is a *conventional* practice.

3. How does the author distinguish between "alive" and "dead" language?

4. Comment on the relationship between the products of language and language itself.

5. What does the author mean when he suggests that linguistic response systems become detached from the conditions in which they were originally learned?

6. Why does the author have concerns about the term "understanding"?

7. How did the borrowing of language from biology result in a reductionistic conception of behavior?

8. What is the author's concern about Kantor's logical model?

9. The author suggests that ABA did not amount to a true technology of behavior change in applied situations. Explain.

10. What are some of the author's concerns about operant principles in applied circumstances?

11. Summarize some of the author's concerns about the traditional approach to education and schooling.

CHAPTER 8

Observational Learning

Mitch Fryling

California State University, Los Angeles

Rocío Rosales

University of Massachusetts Lowell

Natalia Baires

Southern Illinois University, Carbondale

Link and Preview

It probably goes without saying that we all learn a great deal from observing things in our environment. While this is obvious to both laypersons and scientists from various disciplines, the topic of observational learning—the focus of this chapter—is often not given extensive treatment in behavior analysis. The present chapter focuses on observational learning, reviews conceptual foundations and recent literature, and provides implications for practice. We believe it is an important part of the story for understanding a comprehensive account of language and cognition in behavior analytic perspective.

Observational learning (OL), generally defined, involves behavior change as a function of observing happenings in one's environment. OL is a conceptually challenging topic, one with significant theoretical and applied implications. Indeed, most learning environments require learners to have an OL repertoire. For example, teachers often model a particular task to a classroom of students with the hope that students will engage in the modeled behavior themselves at a later time. Social development also seems to involve OL, as when a child learns how to play and interact with their peers by observing others. Clearly, the absence of an OL repertoire would be detrimental to one's development; learning would have to occur directly, with a trained therapist or teacher providing specific instructions, prompting, and differential reinforcement. This is not only costly but also a slow, cumbersome process that interferes with other learning opportunities. For these reasons, developing the prerequisite skills needed to learn from observation is an essential consideration for behavior analytic practitioners.

Moreover, learning from observation seems to be involved in day-to-day living more generally. For example, humans live in social environments, and their relationships with other people are greatly enhanced if they observe the behavior of others in different situations, and if their behavior is subsequently changed as a function of those observations. For instance, if we observe a coworker to be overwhelmed at work, we may offer them help or wait before asking them to take on an additional task. Alternatively, noticing that our significant other is sad or disappointed about something that happened may require the careful observation of their behavior with respect to the matter in prior interactions. As these examples highlight, *observing relations among various factors in one's environment* fosters subsequent derived relational responding. In this sense, OL may be considered a foundation of language and cognition more broadly.

Our commitment to developing a comprehensive and coherent natural science of behavior requires us to address OL more systematically in behavior analysis. Moreover, as mentioned, OL is also a topic with considerable clinical implications. Indeed, to the extent that individuals can learn to learn from observation, they may develop skills more quickly, including subtle repertoires that can be difficult to instruct directly (e.g., social skills), and adapt more efficiently to ever-changing environments. This chapter provides an overview of behavior analytic research and scholarship in the area of OL. We will begin by discussing conceptual work in the area, followed by a review of various areas of research in OL. Special emphasis is given to the emergence of derived stimulus relations as a function of OL, as this is a particularly promising area for additional research. The chapter concludes with implications for future research and practice.

Conceptual Analysis of Observational Learning

Our section on the conceptual foundations of OL begins with an overview of the work by Bandura and colleagues, which was central to the social cognitive perspective, followed by a review of behavior analytic conceptual analyses of OL.

Bandura's Theory

Generally, Bandura's research program demonstrated something simple yet very important—that behavior can develop as a function of observing a model. Bandura's work also demonstrated that it is not just modeling that is important, but that the consequences of the model's behavior also play a critical role. In particular, participants who observe a model being punished are found to demonstrate less behavior change relative to those who observe a model being reinforced or receiving no programmed consequences at all (e.g., Bandura, 1965). Another issue fundamental to Bandura's work is the *delayed* performance of the observer after observing a model; a great deal of OL seems to be demonstrated long after the model has engaged in the behavior. In this sense, behavior seems to occur in the absence of a current environmental stimulus (we'll address this more in the next section). Following from this, Bandura's research began to investigate cognitive[3] factors to account for this delayed performance. For example, in one experiment (Bandura, Grusec, & Menlove, 1966), one group of observers was told to describe what they were observing, another was told to count while they were observing, and a third group was not given any instructions. The results showed that those who described what they were observing engaged in more OL than those who didn't, suggesting the importance of "cognitive" factors in OL.

While the consequences of the model's behavior have been found to influence the extent to which observers *engage* in the observed behavior themselves, observers can *describe* what they observe irrespective of this (e.g., Bandura, 1965). To Bandura, this suggested that *learning* from observation occurs regardless of observed consequences, whereas *performance,* demonstrated by the engagement in the modeled behavior, is dependent on the consequences of the model's behavior. All of this led to the development of a theory of OL (e.g., Bandura & Jeffrey, 1973). According to the theory, the initial learning of behavior is accounted for by attention and retention processes, whereas the performance of observed behavior is determined by factors involved in motor reproduction and motivational factors. Following an input-output cognitive-type model, the general theory is that observed events are taken in by the individual and stored within the individual, and that these stored experiences (e.g., *images* or *symbols* in cognitive theory) later emerge to guide behavior.

Behavior Analytic Conceptualizations of Observational Learning

Deguchi (1984) provided an alternative explanation of the outcomes described in the OL literature based upon Skinner's radical behaviorism (Skinner, 1974a). Generally, Deguchi highlights that much of the literature on OL has given little attention to the dynamic reinforcement history of the observer. The majority of experiments conducted by Bandura involved typically developing children, who are likely to have a rather extensive history of reinforcement for imitating observed behavior. Moreover, that history of reinforcement is likely to have involved an intermittent schedule of reinforcement, rendering it particularly resistant to extinction and likely to persist during brief postobservation probes during OL experiments. This sort of reinforcement history may explain the popular notion of **one-trial learning** found in the OL literature (i.e., behavior change that results from a single observation).

---

3   From a behavior analytic perspective, these factors are not *cognitive* in the sense that they are something other than behavior; rather, these factors are conceptualized as additional behavior to be accounted for in learning from observation.

Deguchi (1984) also accounts for the delayed performance found in the OL litera-ture by turning to reinforcement histories. Imitative behaviors may not always be rein-forced if they occur immediately after the modeling (as when it is very obvious that one is simply imitating). In accounting for the alleged cognitive events in Bandura's theory, Deguchi describes the influence of instructions on behavior. Bandura's research showed that individuals who were instructed to do various things during observations were more or less likely to learn from observation, depending on the particular instructions. To Deguchi (1984), this is simply seen as the impact of instructions on behavior (more on this below). Finally, reinforcement histories are again used to explain the role of observed consequences. Specifically, the consequences of the model's behavior likely have dis-criminative stimulus functions, with observers having a probable history of reinforce-ment for engaging in observed behavior only when the model is reinforced and especially not when the model is punished. For example, observing someone receive social rein-forcement for engaging in a particular behavior may set the occasion for an observer to engage in that behavior themselves at a later time. Deguchi's work is especially noteworthy for emphasizing the reinforcement history of the observer in accounting for OL.

Palmer (2012) discussed OL in the context of describing **atomic repertoires**. Palmer suggests that much of our complex behavior can be explained by appealing to smaller, fine-grained units of behavior, which may occur both overtly (behavior others can see easily) and covertly (behavior others cannot see easily). Atomic behavior may include imitative, echoic, and tacting repertoires. Pertinent to OL, Palmer explains the one-trial learning phenomenon by suggesting that atomic repertoires occur at the moment of observation. Then, at a later time when part of the original observational context is present, the atomic behavior occurs again and may set the occasion for other behavior. For example, if someone is learning new job duties and observes a model engaging in a particular behavior in a particular situation, when that situation, or even part of that situation, arises again in the observer's experience, they may be more likely to engage in the observed behavior themselves. To Palmer, the theoretical implication of this is that behavior occurring as a function of a single observation is not occurring for the first time with no history of reinforcement. Rather, the behavior has occurred before, at least in some form, and was reinforced at that time, and this history accounts for subsequent behavior change.

While the observer's reinforcement history is central to the behavior analytic account of OL, behavior analysts have also elaborated on the stimulational aspects of OL. Masia and Chase (1997) provide an overview of how conditional discrimination processes, generalization, and functional classes (e.g., stimulus equivalence) may partici-pate in OL. In considering **conditional discrimination**, the authors provide an example of how instructions can function as conditional stimuli that alter the extent to which someone learns from observation. For example, instructions such as "You will be tested on this later," "Don't do it this way," or "Especially focus on X" can alter the extent to which observers engage in observed behavior. Masia and Chase also make the connec-tion to rule-governed behavior, and note that this literature may also inform our interpretation of OL. Considering language and rules more specifically, Fryling, Johnston, and Hayes (2011) note that observers likely have a long history of reinforcement for describing relations in their environment (rule generation) and engaging in subsequent rule following with respect to those descriptions. At the same time, Fryling et al. discourage the assignment of causal or mediational status to this sort of behavior. In other words, the authors do not suggest that this behavior *causes* OL. Rather, this sort of rule generation is to be considered a product of specific attention to what is observed, and such attention is surely required to learn from observation.[4]

Generalization processes may also contribute to OL (Masia & Chase, 1997). Masia and Chase provide an example of an individual with a history of getting burned on the stove who later observes someone get burned from a campfire. In this case, the observer may avoid getting too close to the campfire as a result of the observation *and* the similarity of the campfire to their own experiences with the hot stove. Similarly, the functions of observed consequences may also be impacted by generalization processes, as when we observe someone become very afraid after some event, and as a function of our own experiences of being similarly afraid in entirely different circumstances, we learn to avoid what was observed (i.e., because the consequences are morphologically similar). Generalization processes highlight that it is not just observation, but observation *and* the similarities between what is observed and our own experiences, that impacts OL.

Finally, Masia and Chase (1997) describe how the concept of **functional classes** may contribute to OL. The stimulus equivalence literature has shown how stimuli may develop the stimulus functions of other stimuli, even when those stimuli share no physical similarities. Importantly, such stimulus functions do not simply emerge, they are a product of an individual history of responding with respect to relations among stimuli and responses. For example, given a particular history, a number of very different stimuli may develop the stimulus functions of being "bad" (e.g., smoking, failing school, lying). At a later time, an individual with such a history may observe someone engaging in a different behavior (e.g., swearing) while also being told that the behavior is "bad." As a consequence of this observation and the derived stimulus functions of the word "bad," the individual may avoid the observed behavior and the context in which it occurred. As this simple example highlights, derived stimulus relations are likely to participate in OL.

Elaborating on the stimulational aspects of OL, Fryling et al. (2011) provided an analysis of OL derived from **interbehaviorism** (Kantor, 1953) and **interbehavioral psychology** (Kantor, 1958). Fryling et al. (2011) specifically emphasize the unique field orientation of the interbehavioral position (Kantor, 1958), and especially highlight the dynamics involved in the development of stimulus functions and the role of observing and describing stimulus relations. As noted, the OL literature requires behavior analysts

---

4   Importantly, Fryling et al. (2011) also consider nonhuman animal demonstrations of OL and note that nonhuman animals are unlikely to engage in this sort of rule stating. In other words, the fact that nonhuman animals learn from observation further suggests that we should be careful in our consideration of verbal behavior in accounting for OL. The finding that those who describe their environment may learn more from it should only suggest that careful attention to what is observed greatly enhances OL.

to describe how past observations influence behavior at a later time, often in the absence of an obvious stimulus. In the interbehavioral perspective, this phenomenon can be explained with Kantor's concept of stimulus substitution. Generally, **stimulus substitution** occurs when one stimulus develops the functions of a stimulus that is no longer present as a result of an individual's history of responding with respect to relations among those two stimuli (such relations occur in space and/or time, and may occur among stimuli, settings, responses, and variations thereof). For example, one may think about an old friend when visiting a place that they frequented with that friend (i.e., respond to the friend even when the friend is not physically present). In this case we would say that aspects of the setting developed substitute stimulus functions for the friend. Similarly, previously observed behavior that occurred in a particular setting or situation may be occasioned by stimuli that substitute for past observations. That is, previously observed behavior may be present by virtue of stimulus substitution (see Fryling et al., 2011, for a more detailed overview of stimulus substitution).

Conceptual work in behavior analysis has provided an alternative to Bandura's theory of OL. While the behavior analytic literature differs in some ways regarding the conceptualization of OL, there is a similar focus on environmental factors and how these influence OL. This focus on understanding functional relationships in the natural environment is conceptually coherent with our aims as a natural science and offers specific practical advantages over cognitive perspectives. Most obviously, the behavioral perspective points to environmental factors that may be altered and studied in efforts to promote learning from observation in various situations.

Observational Learning Research in Behavior Analysis

While behavior analysts have begun to provide a comprehensive theoretical account of OL, a number of behavior analysts have also conducted research in the area of OL. The following sections provide an overview of behavior analytic research on OL, including both general OL research and that which specifically focuses on derived stimulus relations. Implications for research and practice are provided throughout.

Assessment of Observational Learning

The majority of the behavior analytic research in the area of OL may be considered assessments of OL, wherein researchers collect preobservation baseline data, implement an observational intervention, and then conduct postobservation assessments of behavior change. A number of topics have been researched this way in the literature, with recent examples including children's preferences (Leaf et al., 2012; Leaf et al., 2016), the acquisition of verbal operants (Storlie, Rehfeldt, & Aguirre, 2015), and parents learning skills to work with their children (Eid et al., 2017). Researchers have also examined factors that may impact OL. For example, Castro and Rehfeldt (2016) assessed the extent to which learning from observation is influenced by the observer's relationship to the model (also see Singer-Dudek & Oblak, 2013, described below).

Observational Learning and Prerequisite Skills

Given the importance to day-to-day functioning of developing an OL repertoire, it is important to consider prerequisite skills. As outlined by Taylor and DeQuinzio (2012), examples of these prerequisite skills include attending, delayed imitation, and identifying and discriminating among contingencies. Related to **attention**, OL involves attending to multiple stimuli (e.g., observing both a modeled response and the subsequent consequence), dividing attention among various stimuli, and engaging in sustained attention.

Imitation, specifically **delayed imitation**, is also pertinent to OL. Two essential components are required in order for imitation to occur within the context of OL: history of reinforcement and a generalized imitative repertoire (Taylor & DeQuinzio, 2012). Imitation skills that are reinforced will be maintained, while a generalized imitative response class will ensure that novel responses occur without the need for direct instruction or a continuous schedule of reinforcement. Delayed imitation is critical as responses often need to be emitted long after the observation of a model. For example, a child may observe a teacher solving a problem during instruction one day, and on a later day be asked to solve a problem in a similar manner in the absence of the model.

Finally, observers' behavior must demonstrate **discrimination** between observed contingencies of reinforcement and punishment. Such discrimination facilitates the development of complex stimulus control such that observers engage in modeled behavior that is reinforced, and not that which is observed to be punished. For example, a child may learn to engage in an appropriate social behavior (e.g., calmly asking for something) after observing that behavior be reinforced, and not engage in a socially inappropriate behavior (e.g., yelling) after observing such behavior fail to be reinforced.

Developing Observational Learning Repertoires

Several researchers have pointed to the need for more research in the area of developing OL with individuals who lack OL repertoires (e.g., Greer, Singer-Dudek, & Gautreaux, 2006; Townley-Cochran, Leaf, Taubman, Leaf, & McEachin, 2015). In one study that focused on developing OL repertoires, Pereira Delgado and Greer (2009) investigated the effects of teaching children without OL repertoires to monitor peers in order to learn from observation. In Experiment 1, two children were taught to monitor peers while those peers were being taught textual behavior (i.e., "reading" in traditional terms). After the participants who were monitoring the peers learned to select a green cube when the peer responded correctly and a red cube when the peer responded incorrectly, both participants demonstrated improvements in OL. Interestingly, while the participants only monitored a peer learning textual responses, postmonitoring probes demonstrated that OL improved while observing the same peer learning to tact fruits and while observing a different peer learn textual behavior.

Experiment 2 of Pereira Delgado and Greer's (2009) research replicated the first experiment but with oral spelling as the target behavior. After learning to monitor a peer's behavior as in Experiment 1, all three children improved oral spelling as a function of observing a peer being taught by a teacher. Interestingly, two of the three observing participants in Experiment 2 learned at the same speed as or faster than their peer who was being taught directly.

Taylor, DeQuinzio, and Stine (2012) also investigated the effects of teaching children to monitor their peers' behavior while those peers were instructed to engage in previously mastered textual behavior (i.e., reading sight words). Monitoring conditions involved imitating peers' responses after being asked, "What did he say?" and engaging in a matching response (i.e., placing a chip under the correct word on a matching board). Specifically, during training a teacher presented a sight word to the peer and said, "Read" while the participant observed. Correct responses were reinforced with a token and praise from the teacher. The teacher would then remove the word card and ask the participant, "What did he say?" requiring an imitative response. The teacher corrected the participant's incorrect imitation responses by re-presenting the word to the peer to read again and again asking the participant, "What did he say?" If the participant still provided an incorrect response, the teacher did not require a matching response and began a new trial. For incorrect responses during the matching task, a least-to-most prompting hierarchy was utilized, where tokens were not delivered and a new trial followed. An exposure condition was also included with separate sight words, with procedures identical to the monitoring condition with the exception that monitoring responses were no longer required. Results indicated that training improved all participants' monitoring responses. Tests for OL also demonstrated that all participants learned from observation when they were required to monitor their peers' behavior. Moreover, two of the three participants demonstrated learning during the exposure condition, suggesting that the effects of the training influenced behavior where monitoring was no longer required.

More recently, MacDonald and Ahearn (2015) evaluated a broad assessment and training package for OL. First a preassessment was conducted, which involved assessing OL across five different tasks, each with three variations. In tasks where OL was found to be deficient, participants were taught specific prerequisite skills that have been suggested in the literature (Taylor & DeQuinzio, 2012), including attending, imitation, delayed imitation, and consequence discrimination. After participants mastered a specific variation within a particular type of task, the experimenters conducted an assessment to test for generalization across the other variations of the task. If generalization across task variations did not occur, the participant then went through the training with that particular variation and, upon mastery, generalization across untrained variations was again assessed. This pattern of testing and training continued until participants demonstrated mastery across all task variations. Once this had occurred, the researchers assessed generalization across task types. Finally, if generalization across a particular task type did not occur, the researchers initiated training for that task area, as described above. This continued until the participants demonstrated mastery across all task types and variations. (Yes, this study involved a lot of steps!)

Results demonstrated that the amount of training required for mastery of each prerequisite skill varied across skills and participants. In addition, five of the six participants demonstrated generalization across task types and across variations of the task within each type. One participant did not demonstrate generalization across task types, but did demonstrate generalization across variations of tasks within each type. In general, the protocol by MacDonald and Ahearn (2015) is noteworthy as it details how OL might be assessed across skills, and also how generalization probes can be systematically incorporated into an OL training program. Again, given the importance of developing an OL repertoire, the evaluation of procedures to develop OL after it has been found to be deficient is an important area for further research in behavior analysis.[5]

Emergence of Conditioned Reinforcers Through Observation

An additional type of OL involves the conditioning of reinforcers through observation (Greer et al., 2006). Greer and Singer-Dudek (2008) assessed whether neutral stimuli (discs and strings) would function as conditioned reinforcers after children observed a peer be reinforced with those items. First, the researchers demonstrated that the neutral stimuli did not have an effect on the participants' performance (skills already in the participants' repertoires) or learning (acquisition of new skills). Then, the researchers implemented an observational intervention that involved the participants' working side by side with a peer on the same task, with trials being presented simultaneously. An opaque partition was between them, however, such that the participants could see only their peers' head and shoulders and the cup where reinforcers were delivered, not their peers' responses. The researchers placed discs or strings in the peers' cup contingent on correct responding, and did not correct errors. Participants' cups remained empty after both correct and incorrect responses (i.e., their access to the previously neutral stimuli was restricted). Findings demonstrated that the observational intervention resulted in the conditioning of the discs and strings as reinforcers.

Singer-Dudek and Oblak (2013) expanded upon the findings of Greer and Singer-Dudek (2008) by specifically evaluating the role of peer presence on the acquisition of conditioned reinforcer functions from observation. The researchers compared two variations of the methodology used by Greer and Singer-Dudek: a no-peer condition where participants worked side by side with an empty chair, and a peer-present condition where participants worked side by side with a peer. In both conditions the neutral stimuli were

---

5   There are a number of topics that may be related to developing observing responses more broadly. For example, Keohane, Pereira Delgado, and Greer (2009) described a number of protocols that facilitate the development of observing responses.

placed in the translucent cup, in front of either the peer or the empty chair, while the participants had no access to the stimuli (strings or toothpicks). Results showed that conditioned reinforcement functions emerged for both maintenance and acquisition tasks only after the peer-present observational intervention, indicating peer presence is important. In addition, similar results were obtained across participants who observed familiar (two participants) and unfamiliar (one participant) peers, suggesting that peer familiarity was not critical. While OL is generally regarded as learning new behavior as a function of observing a model engage in that behavior, this line of research demonstrates that reinforcers may also be conditioned through observation. Importantly, **derived stimulus relations** have also been shown to develop as a function of observation, and the final section reviews this literature specifically.

Observational Learning Research in Derived Stimulus Relations

A growing body of research in OL has examined the extent to which untrained or derived stimulus relations emerge as a product of observation. Sidman (1971) was the first to demonstrate the development of derived stimulus relations when he taught an individual with severe intellectual disability to relate dictated names to their corresponding pictures and also to their corresponding printed texts. Following this direct teaching, the individual labeled the pictures used in the training, read the corresponding text when these stimuli were presented in isolation, and matched the pictures to the text and vice versa. These additional relations were performed without direct teaching. The emergence of these skills demonstrated that a stimulus class consisting of dictated names, pictures, and printed words was formed, and that the stimuli were functionally equivalent (Sidman, 1971; Sidman & Tailby, 1982). This teaching paradigm has demonstrated efficacy for teaching a wide variety of language and cognitive skills to typically developing populations and those with disabilities (Rehfeldt, 2011). The paradigm has wide implications because it can lead to efficient use of instructional time (see chapter 10 for a specific overview of stimulus equivalence). This efficiency can be further enhanced when a participant observes another learner performing conditional discriminations, and these observations lead to subsequent formation of stimulus classes. To date, only a handful of studies have directly evaluated the impact of OL on stimulus equivalence relations (MacDonald, Dixon, & LeBlanc, 1986; Ramirez & Rehfeldt, 2009; Rehfeldt, Latimore, & Stromer, 2003).

Stimulus Equivalence and Observational Learning

Training approaches to teach derived stimulus relations to learners with developmental disabilities will often include a variety of **match-to-sample** (MTS) tasks. During

MTS tasks, a learner is presented with an array of stimuli (termed **comparison stimuli**) and instructed to select the one that corresponds to a stimulus that has been previously or simultaneously presented (termed a **sample stimulus**). Responses are reinforced when the learner makes a correct selection. Teaching may consist of two or more directly trained relations (e.g., A-B and B-C) followed by tests for many more untrained relations (e.g., A-A, B-B, C-C, B-A, C-B, A-C, and C-A).

MacDonald, Dixon, and LeBlanc (1986) were the first to examine the role of OL in stimulus class formation. They recruited four adults with moderate and severe intellectual disability and taught them to match arbitrary visual stimuli. Each participant was taught one set of sample-comparison stimulus relations (e.g., B1-A1, B2-A2) until they demonstrated a mastery criterion. The participant then observed another participant perform a second set of sample-comparison stimulus relations (e.g., C1-A1, C2-A2) such that each observed relation had one stimulus in common with a relation that had been directly taught to participants. During tests for derived relations, all participants demonstrated at least one such relation between the modeled stimuli.

Rehfeldt et al. (2003) replicated and extended this work with individuals with autism and other developmental disabilities. Participants were taught to conditionally relate a set of stimuli and were also required to observe a peer learning conditional discriminations with a different set of related stimuli. The experimenter verbally prompted the participants to observe the model by saying, "Watch [name]," and provided verbal praise when the participant observed the peers. This prompt was effective in establishing attending for all participants in the study (Rehfeldt et al., 2003). The experimenter praised the model while the observer watched the model perform conditional discriminations. All participants demonstrated stimulus class formation for the stimuli that were directly trained and improved posttest scores relative to pretest scores for the stimuli that they observed a peer learning. A second experiment replicated these results using stimulus sets from similar overarching categories and words that could not be discriminated easily by form or shape. Results showed that participants demonstrated emergent performance for all stimulus sets they were trained on, and also displayed some of the relations that they had observed a peer learning.

Finally, Ramirez and Rehfeldt (2009) explored the impact of OL to teach Spanish vocabulary words to typically developing children. In their experiment, one child was taught conditional discriminations between dictated names and their corresponding pictures across three stimulus sets while a second child observed. Results showed the emergence of symmetrical relations in the form of labeling the pictures used in training by both children. Collectively, the results of these studies show support for the use of arranging observation of peers as an attractive approach to teaching conditional discriminations that may result in derived stimulus relations. All three studies used an MTS procedure, and each reported mixed success in establishment of derived stimulus relations. These results suggest that the MTS training procedure may not be effective for all learners and that alternative procedures should be evaluated.

Stimulus-Pairing Procedure

One alternative to MTS training that has received empirical support in recent years is a **stimulus-pairing observation** (SPO) procedure (also termed **stimulus-pairing training** or **respondent-type training**; Rosales, Rehfeldt, & Huffman, 2012; Smeets, Leader, & Barnes, 1997; Smyth, Barnes-Holmes, & Forsyth, 2006). This procedure involves the observation of a stimulus briefly presented in isolation, followed by an **inter-stimulus interval** (ISI) and then presentation of a second stimulus. Thus, the procedure involves pairing of stimuli with no overt response requirement from the participant other than attending to the stimuli presented by the experimenter. Presentations of stimuli may occur on a computer screen or in vivo. These stimulus pairings are followed by tests for derived stimulus relations (Leader & Barnes-Holmes, 2001a, 2001b). Since there is no mastery criterion requirement in the SPO procedure, presentation of stimulus pairs typically occurs for a predetermined number of trials before tests for derived stimulus relations are presented.

The SPO procedure may be more efficient than MTS in terms of time required for learning stimulus relations. It is possible that in MTS tasks, responses are under various types of stimulus control, including irrelevant features of comparison stimuli or varied position of stimuli (Fields, Garruto, & Watanabe, 2010). If participants learn stimulus relations through an SPO procedure, instructors can potentially decrease some of these errors. However, studies that have directly compared the efficacy of MTS and SPO have reported mixed results, with neither procedure showing facilitation of derived stimulus relations for all participants (Clayton & Hayes, 2004; Fields, Reeve, Valeras, Rosen, & Belanich, 1997; Kinloch, McEwan, & Foster, 2013).

Leader and Barnes-Holmes (2001b) demonstrated the efficacy of SPO to teach typically developing five-year-old children academically relevant stimulus relations. The visual stimuli paired were fractions (A stimuli), the corresponding pictorial representations for each numerical property (B stimuli), and the corresponding decimals (C stimuli). The fraction-pictorial representation pairing (A1-B1, A2-B2) was conducted first, followed by the decimal-pictorial representation pairing (C1-B1, C2-B2). Tests for derived stimulus relations subsequently demonstrated that all participants were successful in matching the fractions to their corresponding decimals (A1-C1, A2-C2) and the decimals to fractions (C1-A1, C2-A2). Two follow-up experiments demonstrated that participants also established relations between pictures that were not specifically targeted in training.

Rosales et al. (2012) also recruited typically developing children learning English as a second language and examined the effectiveness of the SPO procedure to teach a small vocabulary set. Participants were required to attend to the experimenter presenting an auditory stimulus paired with a visual (object) stimulus in isolation for a predetermined number of trials. Tests for emergence of stimulus relations demonstrated that the participants acquired most of the listener relations targeted (i.e., selecting a stimulus when named in an MTS format from an array of three items) and some speaker relations (i.e., naming the stimulus when presented in isolation). The experimenters then conducted

multiple exemplar instruction (MEI; involving direct teaching of tact relations with novel stimulus sets, followed by probes with the original training set) in an attempt to demonstrate the emergence of the untrained relations and reported moderate success.

The findings of the SPO literature reviewed thus far are exciting and demonstrate support for the SPO procedure to establish derived stimulus relations in typically developing learners. The utility of the SPO procedure may be most evident for learners with autism and other developmental disabilities due to the potential savings in training time. However, only a handful of studies have examined the possibility of the SPO as an instructional procedure for this population. For example, Takahashi, Yamamoto, and Noro (2011) used SPO to teach relations among names (printed words), faces, and Kanji symbols to two boys with autism. The experimenters paired two visual stimuli (faces and printed words) in succession on a computer screen for one participant, and an auditory and visual stimulus (Kanji symbol plus corresponding auditory stimulus) for a second participant. Following SPO, the experimenters administered subsequent MTS tests to assess emergent relations among these stimuli for each participant. Results indicated the SPO procedure was effective in producing increases in correct responses across all participants, but the study did not directly compare the efficacy of SPO with MTS procedures.

Vallinger-Brown and Rosales (2014) extended the applied research on the SPO procedure for learners with autism by directly comparing the effectiveness of MTS and SPO to facilitate the emergence of untrained responses in children with autism. All participants were exposed to both training conditions, with different sets of stimuli. During the MTS procedure, participants were presented with a sample auditory stimulus and were required to select the correct corresponding visual stimulus from an array of six images presented on an iPad. During the SPO procedure, participants were presented simultaneously with an auditory and visual stimulus and required to observe the screen throughout the training. Results of this study showed mixed results, with one participant demonstrating untrained stimulus relations following training in both procedures and two participants demonstrating minimal increase in performance relative to baseline following the MTS procedure. Finally, a transfer of stimulus control procedure was used to directly teach the target relations to all participants. These authors noted that a possible prerequisite skill for success with the SPO procedure may be overt or covert echoic responding, but this was not directly evaluated in the study.

A similar study by Byrne, Rehfeldt, and Aguirre (2014) further confirmed the effectiveness of an SPO procedure to teach speaker and listener responses (i.e., selection-based responding) to learners with autism. This study also demonstrated the value of MEI to help establish some of these trained and untrained relations. However, these results counter the notion that echoic responding may play a role in levels of accuracy following training with the SPO procedure because the participant who emitted the fewest number of echoic responses during training performed at optimal levels during tests for untrained relations. The authors acknowledge the possibility that this participant may have been engaging in covert echoic responding, but further investigation is needed on this topic.

Future research on the effectiveness of the SPO procedure should systematically examine the prerequisite skills needed for this procedure to be effective. Some research has demonstrated prerequisite skills for learners to benefit from OL more generally (MacDonald & Ahearn, 2015), and it would be interesting to determine if these skills are similar to those that may be required for the formation of derived stimulus relations from observation. Another alternative for learners with more advanced language repertoires may involve indirect measures such as posttraining interviews with participants to inquire directly about procedures used to learn the relations. Given the relative ease with which the SPO procedure can be implemented and the parallels it has to naturalistic instruction, further research in this area seems warranted. If derived stimulus relations may develop through sequential or simultaneous presentation and observation of related stimuli, there are broad implications for its use in practice.

Extended Implications of Observational Learning

Aside from derived stimulus relations, research in OL and specifically on the use of the SPO procedure has demonstrated that transfer of stimulus functions can also occur (Smyth et al., 2006). Smyth and colleagues demonstrated this phenomenon using the SPO procedure in an experiment with participants who self-identified as spider-fearful. The participants were exposed to four stimulus pairings and subsequently tested for a transfer of function for reports of self-arousal in the presence of stimuli that were never directly paired. A second experiment demonstrated differential responding on self-reported levels of arousal when videos of spiders where shown to spider-fearful and non-spider-fearful participants. These results demonstrate the utility of the SPO procedure and offer support for a derived-relations model of the acquisition of anxiety responses (Smyth et al., 2006). Related studies also show support for the notion that conditioned fear or excessive avoidance behavior, which is a defining feature of anxiety disorders, may emerge through observation (Cameron, Roche, Schlund, & Dymond, 2016; Cameron, Schlund, & Dymond, 2015). Clearly, OL has implications for understanding a wide range of psychological phenomena.

Summary of OL Research in Derived Stimulus Relations

While more research is needed, the existing research demonstrates that learners can acquire more skills via OL and derived stimulus relations interventions than by directly observing a model performing those skills (MacDonald et al., 1986; Ramirez & Rehfeldt, 2009; Rehfeldt et al., 2003). That is, OL can also lead to the formation of derived stimulus relations and transfers of stimulus functions (Smyth et al., 2006). In addition, the basic and applied research on the SPO procedure provides some initial support for its use to teach conditional discriminations and establish untrained relations among stimuli for typically developing populations (Leader & Barnes-Holmes, 2001b; Rosales et al., 2012) as well as learners with developmental disabilities such as autism (Byrne et al., 2014; Takahashi et al., 2011; Vallinger-Brown & Rosales, 2014). Moreover, there is growing support for the participation of OL across a wide range of psychological happenings.

Implications and Future Directions

Behavior analytic work in the area of OL has a number of exciting implications for both research and practice. An extensive amount of learning occurs from observation; thus, the development of an OL repertoire is of great importance. Moreover, developing the skills to learn from observation permits individuals to learn *faster*, and therefore to learn *more*, and to adapt to changing circumstances more quickly. Given this, we encourage practitioners to become familiar with the suggested prerequisite skills described in the research literature, assess for their presence, and program for their development when deficits are identified. We also recommend that generalization be assessed regularly, both across variations of particular skills and across skill domains, with the ultimate goal being the development of a highly generalized OL repertoire (e.g., MacDonald & Ahearn, 2015). Behavior analytic researchers may contribute to this important area by evaluating prerequisites more systematically in research studies and by studying various interventions to promote OL with specific learner profiles. Given the importance of developing an OL repertoire, this area demands considerable attention from behavior analysts.

Practitioners should also consider the use of observational interventions in the development of derived stimulus relations. A growing body of research has shown how OL can lead to the development of derived stimulus relations, with multiple skills being learned in a highly efficient manner. As with OL more generally, more specific attention to prerequisite skills is needed in this area, so that both practitioners and researchers develop a better understanding of *when* to use such programs, and further, how to better prepare clients for participation in such programs. This, in addition to the results of studies on the development of conditioned reinforcers through observation, highlights that OL may involve much more than observers' engaging in modeled behavior at a later time.

It seems likely that some type of OL participates in a great range of common psychological events. As mentioned in this chapter, observational processes have been shown to play a role in the development of fears, for example. It is possible that observational processes contribute to the benefits of mindfulness-based interventions as well, as such interventions often involve the deliberate focus on particular features of one's environment. To the extent that some psychological problems are a product of a lack of attention to and observation of stimulus relations in one's environment, interventions may be aimed at promoting such observation. Importantly, however, Greer et al. (2006) noted that several terms within the OL literature seem to be used in various ways, and additional conceptual clarity may be needed as the research in this area continues to evolve.

Conclusion

Observational learning is a conceptually interesting topic with a number of clinically important implications. Our aim in writing this chapter was to provide readers with an overview of the behavior analytic work in OL, including theoretical foundations, an overview of research in the area of OL, a consideration of OL's role in derived stimulus relations, and implications for future research and practice. We hope that this chapter impacts clinical work and stimulates further research in the area of OL.

Study Questions

1. Why is observational learning a socially important topic for behavior analysts to be familiar with?

2. How does Bandura distinguish between *learning* and *performance*?

3. How does reinforcement history explain some of the findings in the observational learning literature?

4. How might "atomic behavior" explain learning from observation?

5. Describe two of the processes outlined by Masia and Chase (1997) to explain observational learning.

6. What are two important prerequisite skills for observational learning?

7. Describe one of the peer-monitoring interventions reviewed in the chapter.

8. How is the literature on conditioning reinforcers through observation different from other research in the area of observational learning?

9. Describe the stimulus-pairing observation procedure. What makes it different from match-to-sample training procedures?

10. Comment on the "extended implications" of observational learning.

11. What is one theme for practitioners to take away from the chapter? Comment on why this is an important topic in clinical practice.

CHAPTER 9

Generative Responding Through Contingency Adduction[6]

Kent Johnson

Morningside Academy

Elizabeth M. Street

Central Washington University

Link and Preview

The present chapter focuses on a topic that is central to the behavior analysis of language and cognition: generative responding. The chapter presents an overview of conceptual foundations, provides references to seminal work in the area, and addresses numerous implications for the design of instructional programs. While much of the content focuses on the topic of education specifically, the processes involved relate to the consideration of language and cognition in behavior analysis more generally.

Generativity is the study of the conditions that produce novel, untaught responding in new circumstances, without directly programing them. Not only is the study of generativity important for a scientific understanding of complex human behavior, it is also important from a practical perspective. Educators cannot possibly teach everything a student needs to learn in order to be an effective independent adult. Even full mastery of the K–12 curriculum will not do the trick. Successful adults engage in untaught blends and recombinations of behavior they previously were taught in order to meet the requirements of contexts not previously presented in instruction. In order to engage in untaught blends and recombinations that meet current contingency demands, people must have component repertoires relevant to those new situations that can be blended and

6   The authors would like to thank Marta Leon, Director of Editorial and Instructional Design for Learning A–Z for her data analysis and helpful suggestions related to Headsprout Reading.

recombined. The new situations must function as an effective teacher. As Ferster (1965)[7] noted,

> It may seem a paradox that the listener (student) needs essentially the same repertoire as the speaker (teacher) if communication is to be effective. What, then, was communicated? Actually an instruction was communicated, a rearrangement of existing verbal behavior so that new combinations can occur.

This analysis is also consistent with Skinner's concept of composition, discussed in *Verbal Behavior* (Skinner, 1957, p. 123, pp. 344–352).

This conceptualization has driven our **generative instruction** model of teaching and learning. The thrust of generative instruction is to arrange instruction of key component skills, facts, concepts, and principles in such a way that students will engage more frequently in more complex academic behavior without direct teaching. We have discovered that complex behavioral repertoires emerge without explicit instruction when well-selected component repertoires are appropriately sequenced, carefully instructed, and well rehearsed.

Our model was developed at Morningside Academy in Seattle, a laboratory school for typical and near-typical elementary and middle school students who struggle to acquire foundational reading, writing, math, thinking, reasoning, and problem-solving repertoires. Our students have not previously reached their potential; many have been diagnosed with learning disabilities such as dyslexia, dysgraphia, dyscalculia, or ADHD. All have average to above average intelligence test scores. Morningside is not a school for children with significant emotional problems, behavioral problems, developmental delays, or autism spectrum disorders. One hundred thirty public partner schools and agencies in the United States, Canada, and Europe have adopted our generative instruction model to date (Johnson & Street, 2004, 2012, 2013, Street & Johnson, 2014).

We will report our discoveries and investigations of **generative responding**, or **untaught responding**, in academic skill development as well as thinking, reasoning, and problem-solving development. The data that we will share have come from many classrooms across the United States, as well as an associated instructional design company. Both of us authors are educational practitioners, so neither of us has conducted detailed or exhaustive controlled studies.[8] Yet our descriptive data show such consistent patterns that we want to share them with the wider behavioral community

---

7   Paper read at the 50th anniversary Conference of the Graduate School of Education, the University of Pennsylvania, 1965. Reprinted in Ferster, Culbertson, and Boren (1975, p. 565). Extracted pages available from the first author of this chapter, a student of Ferster's in the 1970s.

8   Morningside Academy is a third level, scientifically driven service organization (Johnston, 1996) consisting of a laboratory school and current outreach to 130 schools and agencies throughout the US and Canada through Morningside Teachers' Academy. It is not a level 2 organization, such as a university, that conducts controlled research in applied settings. "The priority of applied practice is to deliver effective service, not to answer experimental questions" (Johnston, 1996). A comprehensive science is strongest when it integrates basic research and applied research and modifies applied research procedures to develop successful protocols of service delivery.

in the hopes that other practitioners will join us in our inductive explorations and that researchers will join us by conducting controlled studies of the phenomena that we have confirmed in our multiple settings.

Generativity and Contingency Adduction

The work of three groups of behavior analysis investigators has influenced our work in generative instructional design: Epstein, Skinner, and their colleagues' studies of generativity; Andronis, Goldiamond, and their colleagues' research on contingency adduction; and Haughton, Barrett, Binder, and other precision teachers' work in behavioral fluency. Here, we will briefly describe the first two groups' influences, and later in the chapter we will describe the third group's influence.

Dr. Robert Epstein, a student of B. F. Skinner's, described a series of animal laboratory experiments that were intended to provide a behavioral interpretation of "insight," akin to Kohler's gestalt psychology of the mental life of other animals (e.g., Epstein, 1985; Epstein, Kirshnit, Lanza, & Rubin, 1984). Epstein and his coworkers found that pigeons that were individually taught to push a small box around an experimental chamber, to step on the box, and to peck at an object—all in separate training sessions—would solve the problem of pecking at the object when it was out of reach. When presented with the problem, the birds would demonstrate a series of "insightful" maneuvers, much like Kohler's apes, revealing that behavior analysis can account for such behavior in other animals. In remarkably similar behavior patterns, birds would observe the experimental chamber, move the box under a banana, step on the box, and peck the banana. Only birds that received instruction in all three of the component skills successfully solved the problem. Epstein (1985) described the phenomenon as a "spontaneous" (unprompted, not arranged) interconnection of existing repertoires to solve a problem. The existing repertoires were learned separately, under the same contingencies that prevailed in the problem situation. He later expanded this work to show the emergence of novel behaviors in humans under similar circumstances and used the term "generativity" to name the phenomena. Epstein (1993, 1999) also developed a computer-based algorithm for simulating the shifting probabilities of competing behaviors as the interconnection process unfolds. If Epstein's pigeons were humans, most people would say that they "figured out" how to solve their problem, that they showed "insight," and that they were "very creative" or "clever." From this colloquial perspective, generative instruction is meant to produce students who are clever, creative, insightful problem solvers.

In contrast to Epstein's studies, which showed how component teaching can be added to an existing repertoire to solve a specific problem, Andronis, Layng, and Goldiamond (1997) used the term **contingency adduction** to describe a related but different phenomenon: Behaviors learned under one set of contingencies can be selected or *recruited* by new, very different contingencies that present a new and different problem. The performance is reinforced in the new situation by a different effect on its environment than the effects achieved when the originally established behaviors were emitted. That is, the recruited behaviors form new combinations or blends that serve a new or different function in a new context, solve a new problem, and meet the requirements for success in a new situation, different from the requirements for success under which those recruited behaviors were previously learned. According to Andronis et al. (1997), the moment of reinforcement of a behavior established with one set of conditions by an entirely different set of conditions marks the "Aha!" moment of contingency adduction. No direct instruction or programing of the adduced behavior or behavioral repertoire occurs. Adduction can occur only once, after which the performance becomes part of a student's behavioral history, available as needed to meet reinforcement requirements, and available for further recombining and blending with other components during contingency adduction in future problem solving and discovery learning.

Novel behavior produced by recruitment is different from novel behavior produced by shaping of successive approximations. The new, adduced behavior "comes pre-shaped, and is selected or recruited by different contingencies than those responsible for the initial shaping of the behavior" (Layng, Twyman, & Stikeleather, 2004a, p. 99). Andronis et al. (1997) used the term "contingency adduction" rather than "adduction" to emphasize that a student does not adduce the performance, the new contingency does. The new contingency shares common features with the original contingencies that produced the performance. The term "adduction" is applied in its definitional sense: adduct means "to bring together similar parts," and adduction means "the act of adducing or bringing forward" (Webster's New Collegiate Dictionary, s.v. "adduct" and "adduction," respectively). In the context of academic skill development, contingency adduction allows a teacher to skip one or more subsequent instructional steps on a curriculum ladder because the student can already engage in the performance required by an instructional objective.

Examples of Contingency Adduction: Five Variations We Have Programmed

Johnson and Layng (1992) first provided empirical evidence for contingency adduction in fractions problem solving, eliminating the need for instruction. Four students enrolled in a Morningside summer school program for neighborhood children at Malcolm X College in Chicago were assessed in solving word problems with fractions. The number of correct responses ranged from three to seven out of fourteen assessment problems. Other assessments showed similar deficits in lower-level, whole number word problems and fractions computation skills. The students were placed in instructional sequences in which they were taught the skills required to solve whole number word problems and to add, subtract, multiply, and divide fractions and mixed numbers (i.e., combinations of whole numbers and fractions). Both the whole number problem solving and fractions computation skills were then shaped to accuracy and fluency criteria with separate instructional sequences. After the students had practiced the lower-level skills until they had reached high frequencies of correct responding, they were given a **contingency**

adduction probe: Could they now solve a similar set of fraction word problems correctly when simply given the instruction, "Can you do these problems now?" with no instruction in fractions problem solving? Three of the four students correctly solved all fourteen word problems and one solved thirteen of the fourteen problems correctly. The same test environment in which their previous performance had failed now resulted in a highly successful adduction of a new repertoire, "for free" as we say colloquially. Adduction was not a product of gradual shaping but appeared fully established as a function of establishing its component parts and providing a new instruction. With no fraction problem solving instruction necessary, fluency building was prescribed to assure retention of this adduced repertoire.

Let us examine this example closely to see how it meets the requirements of contingency adduction. Applying Tiemann and Markle's (1990) method of concept analysis to contingency adduction reveals three critical features, listed in table 9.1. Two relevant behaviors were in the students' behavioral histories—whole number word problem solving and fractions computation—thus meeting the first requirement for contingency adduction. A new, different contingency was presented—fractions word problems—with the instruction, "Can you do these problems now?" illustrating the second criterion. Finally, the previously established behaviors, whole number word problem solving and fractions computation, formed a new behavioral sequence that served a new and different mathematical function, solving word problems involving fractions. Solving fractions word problems meets the new reinforcement requirement. Neither of the originally established behaviors was sufficient to meet the new contingency requirement. Solving fractions word problems under these conditions is adduced behavior.

Table 9.1. Three Critical Features of Contingency Adduction

Contingency Adduction Criteria	Notes
1. One or more behaviors are reinforced under one set of contingencies (conditions, circumstances).	It/they become(s) part of the behavioral history of the learner.
2. A *different* set of current contingencies (conditions, circumstances) *recruits* one or more behaviors in a person's history (#1).	**Recruitment** is the occurrence and reinforcement or selection of that behavior in the new circumstance.
3. A *novel stimulus control relation* is formed from the behaviors in the person's history, one that serves a *new and different function or purpose* than the function served when the behaviors were first learned and reinforced.	The moment of recruitment and reinforcement (#2) is the moment of contingency adduction.[9]

---

9   Once a behavior has been recruited and reinforced, it becomes part of the behaver's history; thus, there is only one moment of contingency adduction related to a particular S-R relation, and there is only one moment of contingency adduction related to a particular behavior.

A complete concept analysis (Tiemann & Markle, 1990) includes both critical features and variable features. Each example of a concept contains features that vary from instance to instance while maintaining membership in the concept class. We have so far discovered five variations of contingency adduction that meet the requirements for membership in the concept class. Table 9.2 describes these five variations, and table 9.3 shows three methods for designing instruction to produce contingency adduction that we have engineered so far. Space allows us to give only one or two examples of academic skill development for each variation, but we encourage readers to generate many more examples.

Table 9.2. Some Variations of Contingency Adduction

Variation	New Antecedent Condition	What Occurs	Text Example
1. Adduction of a new sequence of previously learned behavior	A combination of stimuli, each of which controls different behaviors	A new **sequence** of already established component behaviors occurs.	Fractions word problem solving without instruction, as a function of new antecedent requirements, and previous instruction in whole number word problem solving and fractions computation
2. Adduction of a new blend of previously learned behavior	A combination of stimuli, each of which controls different behaviors	A new **blend** (a new topography) of already established behaviors occurs.	Saying consonant blends without instruction, as a function of new antecedent requirements and previous instruction in consonant sounds
3. Adduction of a component of previously learned behavior from context	A component of a previously encountered ("familiar") stimulus	A **component** of already established behavior occurs.	Saying consonant sounds without instruction, as a function of new antecedent requirements and previous instruction in consonant blends

4. Adduction of new vocabulary from context, adduction by process of elimination	A new stimulus, presented together with previously encountered stimuli that serve as nonexamples based upon a prior history of instruction	(a) A new response occurs from the set of new and previously encountered stimuli. (b) The sequence of training restricts response alternatives to the one remaining stimulus, correlating the new stimulus to the requirements for responding contained in the instruction.	Saying new vocabulary words, pictures, and definitions, as a function of new antecedent stimuli and prior instruction in other vocabulary words, pictures, and definitions
5. Adduction of new **equivalence** relations	A new arrangement of previously encountered stimulus-response relations	(a) Already established behavior not previously occasioned by the new antecedent stimulus occurs. (b) The sequence of training events restricts response alternatives, linking a stimulus from one previously established stimulus-response relation to a behavior established in a different stimulus-response relation.	(1) Saying untaught fractions, decimals, and percent equivalence relations, as a function of prior instruction in some fraction, decimal, and percent equivalence relations. (2) Selecting untaught picture-definition equivalents and word-picture equivalents, as a function of prior instruction in word-definition equivalents. (3) All relational operants?

Table 9.3. Three Procedures for Designing Instruction to Produce Contingency Adduction[10]

Procedure	Text Examples
Combined stimulus procedure	(1) Sequence adduction of fractions problem solving (2) Blended topographies adduction of consonant blends
Exclusion procedure (oddity-from-sample procedure)	(1) Component adduction of consonant sounds (2) Adduction of vocabulary words, pictures, and definitions
Equivalence procedure	(1) Saying fraction, decimal, or percent equivalent of another fraction, decimal, or percent (2) Selecting definition-picture equivalents and word-picture equivalents

VARIATION 1

Returning to our example of fractions word problem solving, we see in Variation 1 (see table 9.2) that a *new sequence* of previously established behaviors was adduced by the contingencies of presenting word problems with fractions. Consulting table 9.3, we see that the adduction of the fraction word problem-solving sequence was produced by a combined stimulus procedure. The combined stimulus process occurs naturally when students read text and encounter new words that are recombinations of sounds they have mastered. Students regularly decode thousands of new words after learning the forty-six sounds of letters and key letter combinations (Alessi, 1987). These new math and reading performance sequences allow the instructor to skip instruction for solving fractions word problems and sight word reading and move on to the next more advanced instructional objectives in the math and reading curriculum ladders, saving lots of time and effort.

VARIATION 2

Layng and colleagues (2004a) reported a second variation of novel behavior that meets the three requirements for membership in the concept class contingency adduction. It occurs in our interactive, animated Internet reading program, *Headsprout Early Reading* (http://www.headsprout.com). The program explicitly teaches consonant sounds, such as /c/, /r/, /f,/ /l/, /s/, /p/, /t/, and /n/. Later, the program says, "I bet you can figure out

---

10   We are eager to hear from others who can tell us how they have engineered other procedures.

new sounds all by yourself!" Students are then presented combinations of the directly taught sounds, such as /sn/, /cr/, /sl/, /fl/, /pl/, /sp/, /tr/, and /st/ and asked to listen to and select the correct sound combinations.

Data collected on over 11,000 students showed that between 80% and 95% of students correctly identified the new sound combinations in the absence of instruction (i.e., "for free").[11] Let us again examine table 9.1 closely to see how this example meets the requirements of contingency adduction. Isolated consonant sounds were in the students' behavioral histories, thus meeting the first requirement. A new, different contingency was presented—consonant blends with the instruction, "I bet you can figure out new sounds all by yourself!"—illustrating the second criterion. Finally, the students formed new consonant blends from the previously established isolated consonant sounds, serving a new or different reading function. To meet the new reinforcement requirement, students had to select the correct consonant blends when spoken by the program. None of the originally established consonant sounds were sufficient to meet the new contingency requirement. Correctly selecting consonant blends when heard under these conditions is adduced behavior. In this example we see that *a new blend* of previously established behaviors was adduced by the contingencies of presenting consonant sounds together, the second variation listed in table 9.2. Consulting table 9.3, we see that adduction of consonant blends from consonant sounds was produced by a combined stimulus procedure.

One student in the fractions problem-solving example made an error in the contingency adduction probe, and 5% to 20% of the 11,000 students in the consonant blends example did not successfully adduce the correct behavior in the first adduction probe. One or more component repertoires may emerge during an adduction probe. We call each response to an adduction probe a **candidate response**. Sometimes a candidate response is reinforced and becomes adduced behavior. When a candidate response is not reinforced, it is not adduced and does not become part of the selecting environment for further new repertoires.

VARIATION 3

We have engineered a third variation of novel behavior that meets the three requirements for membership in the concept class, contingency adduction. It occurs when *a component* of a previously learned behavior, but not the composite behavior itself, meets the requirement for reinforcement. Another sequence from instruction in *Headsprout Early Reading* illustrates this process (Layng et al., 2004a). Some individual consonant sounds are adduced by segmenting previously taught consonant blends. For example, the sound /n/ is adduced from the previously taught sight word "an." As the program narrator says, "Some sounds have other sounds inside them!" "An" moves to the left side of the screen and "n" is presented on the right side. The narrator then says, "Click on the sound

---

11   After two failed contingency adduction probes, *Headsprout Early Reading* provides direct instruction in consonant blends.

that does *not* say "an." The student responds "away" from the previously learned sight word "an," and clicks on "n." The narrator then says, "Yes, n." Then "n" is presented alongside of "an" and "a." The program says, "Click on 'n.'" When the student clicks on "n," the program says, "Yes, n." This is the moment of contingency adduction. Six consonant sounds are taught this way: /n/, /c/, /l/, /f/, /r/, and /p/. Four dyads, /an/, /cl/, /fr/, and /ip/, were taught earlier, from which these six consonant sounds were segmented. Data collected on almost 33,000 students showed that they correctly segmented between 86% and 97% of the new isolated consonant sounds from the sound combinations "for free" (without instruction). Eighty-nine percent to 98% of the sounds were isolated on the first attempt, depending upon the sound.

Four sound combinations were in the students' behavioral histories, thus meeting the first requirement for contingency adduction in table 9.1. A new, different contingency was presented, isolated consonant sounds, with the instructions "Some sounds have other sounds inside them!" and "Click on the sound that does not say [the letter combination]," illustrating the second criterion. Finally, the previously established behaviors, four sound combinations, were segmented into six isolated consonant sounds, serving a new or different reading function. Selecting the correct isolated consonant sounds from the sound combinations and other, incorrect isolated sounds met the new reinforcement requirement. None of the originally established sound combinations were sufficient to meet the new contingency requirement. Correctly selecting isolated consonant sounds when heard under these conditions is adduced behavior.

Adduction of a component of previously established behavior is the third variation listed in table 9.2. Consulting table 9.3, adduction of these six consonant sounds from previously established consonant blends was produced by an **exclusion procedure**, specifically an oddity-from-sample procedure (Layng et al., 2004a). The student "responds away" from a previously learned stimulus, allowing a new stimulus, the only remaining stimulus available, to recruit the novel behavior that meets the requirement for reinforcement.

VARIATION 4

A fourth variation of contingency adduction is illustrated in the second Internet program in the Headsprout system, *Headsprout Reading Comprehension* (http://www. headsprout.com). One feature of the program teaches students new vocabulary words in groups of four. The program teaches thirty-one groups of four words, or 124 words, in total. Each word has a correlated definitional word or phrase already in the student's repertoire, plus a picture illustrating the word. The fourth word in each group is learned through an exclusion training procedure in the following manner. After learning the first three vocabulary words with a different procedure, described below, the fourth vocabulary word, definition, and picture are introduced. The new vocabulary word appears in a row along with two of the previously learned words, and the new definition appears below them. The student must "respond away" from the two previously learned words and select the remaining new word that correctly corresponds to the new definition presented below the words. In subsequent instructional frames, the new definition appears in a row along with two of the previously learned definitions, and the new word or the new picture appears below them. The student must "respond away" from the two previously learned definitions and select the remaining new definition that correctly corresponds to the new word or picture presented below the definitions. Likewise, other frames present the new picture in a row along with two of the previously learned pictures, and the new word or definition appears below them. The student must "respond away" from the two previously learned pictures and select the remaining new picture that correctly corresponds to the new word or definition presented below the pictures. Whenever the student clicks on the unfamiliar word, definition, or picture, the program narrator says, "Right! That's the word/definition/picture that goes with that word/definition/picture!"; this is the moment of contingency adduction. Data from twenty students show that just over 96% adduced correct answers on the first trial through exclusion training (Joe Layng, personal communication, August 14, 2017).

This example embodies the three critical features required for membership in the concept class contingency adduction described in table 9.1. Table 9.2 lists this fourth variation, and table 9.3 identifies it as adduction produced by an exclusion procedure. A large number of studies have systematically replicated the exclusion effect with typically developing children, children with disabilities, and undergraduate students learning word-object relations. Most recently, exclusion procedures were used with two-year-old children learning adjectives (Ribeiro, Gallano, Souza, & de Souza, 2017). Our work also helps to extend the generality of using an exclusion procedure.

VARIATION 5

A fifth variation of contingency adduction is familiar to behavior analysts: **stimulus equivalence**. Much research exists to support equivalence-based instruction, reviewed in chapter 10 in this book (e.g., Fields et al., 2009; O'Neill, Rehfeldt, Ninness, Munoz, & Mellor, 2015). From a contingency adduction perspective, in stimulus equivalence procedures, one component of a previously encountered stimulus-response relation occurs with new instructions to relate it to a component of another stimulus-response relation that has also already been learned. For example, at Morningside we ask students to memorize the equivalences among certain fractions, decimals, and percentages as a **tool skill** for learning algebra. Students memorize the following equivalents among tenths, fifths, quarters, thirds, and halves: $1/10 = .1 = 10\%$, $1/5 = .2 = 20\%$, $1/4 = .25 = 25\%$, $1/3 = .33 = 33\%$, $2/5 = .4 = 40\%$, $1/2 = .5 = 50\%$, $3/5 = .6 = 60\%$, $2/3 = .67 = 67\%$, $3/4 = .75 = 75\%$, and $4/5 = .8 = 80\%$. Each of these ten sets of equivalence relations contains three equivalents to master (i.e., fraction to decimal, fraction to percent, decimal to percent), totaling thirty relations, which are much more efficiently mastered in a stimulus equivalence paradigm. When we teach students to memorize ten fraction-decimal equivalents and ten decimal-percent equivalents, then present the ten fractions with appropriate instructions (e.g., "Write the percent equivalents of these fractions"), the adduced performance yields these ten relations "for free."

This example of adduction by equivalence meets the requirements of contingency adduction described in table 9.1. Adduction by equivalence is the fifth variation listed in table 9.2. As Ferster said in 1965 (see the quote at the beginning of this chapter, excerpted from Ferster, Culbertson, & Boren, 1975), the instruction rearranged the student's existing repertoire. This time the instruction, "Write the percent equivalents of these fractions," rearranged a component of students' math repertoires, linking a stimulus from one previously established stimulus-response relation to a behavior established in a different stimulus-response relation. In other words, the sequence of instructional events—memorizing fraction-decimal equivalents, then memorizing decimal-percent equivalents—restricted response alternatives when students were presented with fractions plus the instructions to provide the percent equivalents. Knowing the decimal equivalents of fractions restricted their responses to the instruction to the percent equivalents of the decimals.

Stimulus equivalence is also incorporated in the procedures for teaching vocabulary in *Headsprout Reading Comprehension* (http://www.headsprout.com). To review, vocabulary words are taught in groups of four. Each word has a correlated definitional synonym or phrase already in the student's repertoire, and a picture illustrating the word. Earlier we described how the fourth word in the group is learned through an exclusion procedure. The other three words in each group are learned through exposure plus stimulus-equivalence practice, in the following manner.

Each word is visually presented with its definition in a sentence, along with its picture. The narrator reads the sentence, then the student reads it. After this exposure, stimulus equivalence is leveraged in a practice format that adduces more formal word-definition equivalents, definition-picture equivalents, and word-picture equivalents. Students are presented with a new vocabulary word and, below it, the familiar definition equivalent in an array of several other definitions. When they select the correct definition, the narrator says, "Right! [New word] means the same thing as [familiar definition]." Students also practice the reverse relation. When presented with a familiar definition, students must select the correct new word from an array of words. Likewise, students practice the other legs of the word-definition-picture equivalents: definition-picture equivalents and their reverse, and word-picture equivalents and their reverse. Thus, the stimulus-equivalence procedure in these segments is exposure-initiated rather than contingency shaped.

Data from twenty-four students from one of the thirty-one vocabulary segments shows that they correctly selected the appropriate word when given the definition, picture when given the definition, word when given its picture, and the reverse of these relations 95% of the time on the first trial. Their average number of errors was 1.29. Data from nineteen students from a second vocabulary segment shows that they correctly selected the appropriate answer 97% of the time on the first trial. Their average number of errors was 0.79

Table 9.3 lists adduction of new equivalence relations from previously established equivalences as the third procedure that we have engineered so far to produce contingency adduction. We are curious about the degree to which contingency adduction analysis extends to other relational operant investigations, which is why we have added "all relational operants" with a question mark to table 9.2 as a third text example of the fifth variation of contingency adduction.

Some Complex Classroom Examples of Contingency Adduction

The adduction examples we have presented so far clearly indicate specific antecedent procedures responsible for their occurrence. Many classroom examples are not so clear-cut, representing combinations of more than one of the variations of adduction that we have discussed. For example, after reading comprehension instruction in drawing a conclusion based on information in a text, students may encounter an adduction activity that asks them to make a skillful prediction at a certain point in a text, a new comprehension skill that has not been taught. To be successful, students must draw a conclusion from previously read text in a story—for example, that a character is shy and timid because they fail to speak up when others make false accusations about their past behavior. Then students must go beyond their conclusion and use a new event in a story—another accusation by a different character—to predict that when the character hears the false accusation they will fail to object to it by providing an accurate account of their own behavior. The combined stimuli of a new story event, a new accusation, and the instruction to make a prediction adduce a prediction about a future outcome in the story.

In writing instruction, after learning how to modify nouns with adjectives and how to write dependent clauses, students may encounter an adduction activity that asks them to write sentences with appositives, without any additional instruction beyond a model sentence or two. For example, after learning how to construct sentences such as "The surly, arrogant candidate lost the election to a grassroots candidate," the student may adduce appositive sentence writing and write, "The candidate for state representative, a surly and arrogant man, lost the election to a grassroots candidate." Excellent research-based methods for teaching grammar through sentence combining such as those described by Linden and Whimbey (1990), Whimbey, Johnson, Williams, and Linden (1993/2017), O'Hare (1973), and Archer, Gleason, and Isaacson (2008) greatly enhances the power of adducing sentence writing.

To illustrate the information described thus far in the chapter, below we present an example of a teacher's use of adduction in the classroom.

A Case Study in Adduction

Morningside teacher Marianne Delgado designed a generative process to teach students how to adduce definitions of unfamiliar vocabulary words by using four reading comprehension procedures: (a) using context clues to infer the meaning of a word, (b) describing the connotation and mood that a word evokes, (c) writing multiple forms of the word corresponding to various parts of speech, and (d) writing the word in a complete sentence that indicates its meaning (Delgado & Johnson, 2010). Using context clues to determine the meaning of "writhing," students copied the sentence in which the unknown word occurred from the text, read the sentences that immediately preceded and followed the sentence containing the unknown word, and wrote their best guess of the word's meaning. For example, when students read, "LeGleo peered through the spyglass and viewed the writhing mass, shuddering as he spied rats moving on every piece of the decrepit ship," one student copied the sentence, read the sentences before and after it, and recorded this best guess: "I think writhing must mean wiggling as if the rats are moving constantly. He shuddered so I know he didn't like it."

To describe the connotation and mood that "bedraggled" evokes, Delgado instructed the students to decide whether the word had a positive or negative connotation and give an instance in which they would use the word in daily conversation. One student wrote, "I think bedraggled has a negative connotation, because it was how (story character) Rikki Tikki Tavi appeared after he had been in a flood. I would use *bedraggled* if I was describing how I got caught in a rainstorm while waiting for a bus." When writing multiple grammatical forms of a word, one student wrote, "cache–noun, used with in. He stored the dynamite in a cache. Cache–verb, cached, caching, caches. He cached the code in secret files deep in the computer." When writing sentences that show they know the meaning of a word, students were instructed to surround the word with words that might be contained in a definition and with words that would describe a picture of the word in action. For example, one student wrote, "On my trip to the farm I saw two oxen wearing a *yoke* that was attached to the plow behind the animals," and "On my trip I saw two *fledglings* in a nest that hung over a masonry wall built with stones from the riverbank."

Delgado conducted multiple informal assessments of her procedures with different subsets of the vocabulary words she taught throughout the school year. For some new vocabulary words, students followed the adduction process outlined above; for other words, students practiced flashcards with new words on one side of the cards and teacher-given definitions of the words on the other sides. When given a multiple-choice test of words and definitions, students who adduced word definitions performed as well as students given words and teacher definitions, averaging 4.3 correct of five test items, compared with 4.1 correct of five items for the words they learned by practicing flashcards. Later, when asked to use an accumulation of twelve previously adduced words to write a story, and twelve words learned from flashcards to write another story, students correctly used an average of 10.4 of the twelve adduced words, compared to only 8.9 correct of the twelve words learned from flashcards.

The differences in the flashcard and adduction procedures became even more obvious on two retention tests, using a different set of new vocabulary words from those reported above. On one retention test of words memorized from flashcards, students used 8.5 words correctly out of twelve words in November, but six months later their performance declined to an average of 7.1 out of twelve correctly used words. However, on a retention test of adduced vocabulary words, students wrote an average of 9.8 words correctly in November, and maintained correct usage six months later, averaging 9.3 correct words. When asked to write two separate paragraphs employing six different adduced words and six different flashcard words they had learned six months earlier, students used an average of 5.2 of the six adduced words correctly, but only 4.5 of the six flashcard words correctly.

Delgado and another Morningside teacher, Nicole Erickson (Delgado, Erickson, & Johnson, 2015) replicated these results. Delgado and Johnson (2010) had implemented the adduction procedure with students who performed above grade level in reading and writing. Those students had adduced vocabulary words in the course of preparing a presentation in a project-based learning class. In the study that is reported in Delgado et al. (2015), Erickson successfully used the adduction procedure with corrective readers who performed below grade level in reading and writing. Her students simply required more explicit instruction and correction procedures to master the four reading comprehension procedures.

In addition to designing instruction to promote contingency adduction, we can teach **generative repertoires** such as thinking, reasoning, and problem solving that themselves will facilitate contingency adduction within a sequence of components and composites.

Generative Repertoires

Colloquially speaking, generative repertoires are at work when we "figure out" how to do things we've never done before, draw new conclusions, infer new knowledge, "have insights," and so on. From a behavior analytical perspective, current contingencies occasion generative repertoires: supplementary verbal behavior from the problem solver that may lead to repertoires not previously taught. The student's generative repertoires rearrange current circumstances to prompt generative responding that is based upon new combinations and blends of behavior in our current relevant repertoires. At Morningside, teaching generative repertoires is a high priority.

One important influence is the work of Arthur Whimbey and his colleagues. Their book *Blueprint for Educational Change: Improving Reasoning, Literacies, and Science Achievement with Cooperative Learning* (Whimbey et al., 1993/2017) makes the case that much of novel responding comes from the ability to reason or to engage in analytical thinking. Whimbey et al. reason that many nonanalytic thinkers don't engage in the careful process of analyzing what they read or hear or think, a process that, they assert, analytical thinkers use routinely. Specifically, Whimbey et al. provide examples of how nonanalytical thinkers don't read carefully or draw clues from what they read. They say that nonanalytical thinkers don't question their first assertions or draw pictures to represent complex problems as their more analytical classmates do; rather, they guess at answers that seem, on the surface, to be correct. Whimbey and his colleagues show how these habits lead to incorrect assumptions and ultimately incorrect answers. Our observations confirm these findings. In addition we find that some students don't engage in self-questioning and that some have very disorganized and nonsequential thinking.

Whimbey et al. (1993/2017) then build the case for making overt the reasoning processes of good analytical thinkers that most often occur out of view of an observer. They suggest that one of the reasons that some students don't acquire good reasoning skills is that they don't get to see or hear what the good analytical thinker is doing privately, in order to be able to learn from or imitate it. It is this thesis that set the stage for Whimbey and his colleagues to develop their seminal **think aloud pair problem solving** (TAPPS) method of reasoning from a given problem. TAPPS builds on the notion that effective analytical thinkers engage in a dialogue with themselves. Deciding what to buy at a grocery store, solving a math word problem, and making predictions while reading a mystery all may involve self-dialoguing. This notion aligns perfectly with a radical behaviorist way of thinking. We can apply what we know about observable behavior to events like thinking that we cannot see—that's the radical component of radical behavior analysis.

A significant amount of thinking is private verbal behavior: conversing with oneself as a speaker and listener in the same skin, as Skinner (1953) put it. Skinner called thinking **precurrent behavior**, a sequence of behaviors that prime and prompt final solution behavior. The self as speaker prompts and probes their own behavior and generates stimuli to supplement other behavior already in their repertoire. The self as listener confirms, rejects, or prompts new speaker behavior. The specific consequences of thinking may advance problem solving closer to the solution, having a meaningful effect on the thinker; the thinking behavior will thus be automatically reinforced.

Whimbey et al. (1993/2017) use a problem taken from the Whimbey Analytical Skill Inventory, a test that Whimbey and colleagues constructed and tested for its ability to separate analytical from nonanalytical thinkers. They also provide a "script" of the think-aloud dialogue used by a particularly analytical problem solver—a male lawyer, in this case—to solve the problem, shown in the text box below. The lawyer's dialogue illustrates several of the characteristics of a good problem solver, including his concern for accuracy and how he achieves it: writing a segment of the alphabet to help him find the correct answer, pointing to letters as he counts them in the partial alphabet he has written on the paper before him, making marginal notes on what he has concluded at each point in his analytical thinking rather than trusting his conclusions to memory, and, finally, because the problem asks him to "Circle the consonant that is farthest to the right in the word," saying, "Which is my right hand? This is my right hand. So this direction is right," as he points to his right to be sure he is going in the right direction as he counts off letters in the word. Similar examples are used to teach students the value of drawing pictures and other similar routine skills of good problem solvers.

An Expanded Version of a "Think Aloud" from Whimbey et al. (1993/2017)

OK. The problem says, "If the word sentence contains fewer than nine letters and more than three vowels, circle the first vowel. Otherwise, circle the consonant that is farthest to the right in the word."

I'm going to start from the beginning.

If the word sentence contains fewer than nine letters...

Well, the first thing I need to do is to count the letters in the word "sentence." OK. 1, 2, 3, 4, 5, 6, 7, 8. I think eight is right, but just to be sure, I'm going to count again, and this time, to make sure that I don't miss any letters, I'm going to touch the letters in order with my pen as I say each number. 1, 2, 3, 4, 5, 6, 7, 8. OK, so the word 'sentence' has eight letters in it, which is fewer than nine. So, I'm going to write the word "yes" above that part of the question so I won't forget.

But that's not all. The problem says, "If the word sentence contains fewer than nine letters and **more than three vowels**, circle the first vowel." I already know that the word sentence contains fewer than nine letters, having determined that it actually contains eight letters. That was the first test. So what is the second test? Oh, here it is. It says "**and** more than three vowels." Because the instructions say **and**, it means that for me to circle the first vowel, the word sentence must pass both tests: it must have fewer than nine letters **and** more than three vowels. So the next thing I need to do is to count the number of vowels in the word sentence.

But first, which letters are vowels? Oh yes. They are a, e, i, o, and u.

Are there any of those letters—any vowels—in the word "sentence?" Oh, I see three of them, here and here and here. OK. I need to count them. I'll use my pen. There are 1, 2, 3. OK. There are three. Now, I want to read the part of the problem that deals with this again. It says, "more than three vowels." Well, "sentence" does have three vowels, but it doesn't have more than three. So I'll write a "no" above that part of the problem. And since I have answered only one of the questions "yes," I now know that my answer will be wrong if I circle the first vowel.

So, now what do I do? Let me read the rest of it. "Otherwise, circle the consonant that is farthest to the right in the word." Okay, now I know what to do. But wait, which direction is right? Oh yes, I know that this is my right hand so this direction will be to the right. So the letter that is farthest to the right is an "e." But an "e" is a vowel, so I need to keep moving back from the end until I come to a consonant. Oh, here is one. It's the "c" right before the final "e." Now what was I to do with it? Oh yes, I was to circle it. So that's what I'll do.

In addition to creating the inventory that successfully separates analytical reasoners from nonanalytical ones, Whimbey has either authored or coauthored at least four analytical reasoning workbooks: *Analytical Reading and Reasoning* (2nd ed.; Whimbey, 1990), *Mastering Reading Through Reasoning* (Whimbey, 1995), and *Analyze. Organize. Write.*

(rev. ed.; Whimbey & Jenkins, 1987), as well as *Problem Solving and Comprehension* (6th ed.; Whimbey & Lochhead, 1999), the classic book, first published in 1970, that outlines the TAPPS procedures and provides hundreds of practice problems. Numerous programs have used Whimbey and Lochhead (1999) along with Whimbey's TAPPS program to improve their students' analytical reasoning. For example, Xavier University, a historically black college in New Orleans, teaches a five-week summer program called SOAR (Stress on Analytical Reasoning). Over its first dozen years, students enrolled in SOAR made pre- to posttest gains averaging twelve points on the Preliminary Scholastic Achievement Test (equivalent to gains of 120 points on the Scholastic Achievement Test) and three grade levels on the Nelson-Denny Reading Test. Students enrolled in SOAR during those first years were more than twice as likely to pass science and math in the college sequence than unenrolled students, and more African American students were accepted in medical and dental schools from Xavier than from any other US college (Whimbey et al., 1993/2017). Another example of the success of TAPPS comes from the chemical engineering department at McMaster University—a very selective engineering university in Canada—which has a specific program devoted to teaching problem-solving processes using TAPPS as a primary teaching method (http://www.chemeng.mcmaster.ca/mcmaster-problem-solving-mps-program). Both of these programs, which began before the turn of the century, continue today. Other research shows that TAPPS improves reading comprehension, vocabulary acquisition, writing and editing skills, math performance, direction following, understanding assignments, standardized achievement test scores, aptitude, and even intelligence quotients (Whimbey et al., 1993/2017). Reading between the lines, it also holds promise for setting the stage for students to adduce new repertoires.

Morningside Academy's principal, Joanne Robbins, modified Whimbey's TAPPS program to make it appropriate for younger students at Morningside learning to *think aloud* in their *problem solving* (Robbins, 2011). Robbins's (2014) teacher-training program, which she has designed, field-tested, and revised, is called *Learn to Reason with TAPS: A Problem Solving Approach*. As Johnson (2015) reported in *The Journal of Organizational Behavior Management*, to reduce students' anxiety about the procedure, Robbins introduces **talk aloud problem solving** (TAPS) in a cooperative learning setting and engages students initially in content-free and typically enjoyable exercises such as solving logic problems, puzzles, or brainteasers. The program teaches students how to function in only one of the problem-solving roles—the problem solver or the active listener—at a time. The ultimate goal of the program is for each student to adopt the practices of both a good problem solver and an active listener.

The five qualities of a problem solver include

1.   shows a positive attitude,

2.   works carefully,

3.   breaks the problem into parts,

4. actively works the problem, and

5. never just guesses.

The five qualities of an active listener include

1. follows along,

2. gives encouragement,

3. catches mistakes,

4. leads and hints instead of giving an answer, and

5. reviews for accuracy.

After roles are assigned, each partner in the team receives a card displaying their role. Students learn specific dialoguing practices for each quality. One student—the Problem Solver—performs aloud as the other partner—the Active Listener—provides reinforcement, corrections, and shaping. As students master both the speaker and listener roles, they receive a variety of problems to solve independently, although, even then, they are required to comment out loud on their own speaking, as a listener would. At this stage, the student is practicing combining their speaker and listener repertoires in the same skin into a controlled intraverbal chain. During this phase of the teaching process, Morningside teachers provide reinforcement, corrections, and shaping in a manner similar to what they did when students played only one of the roles for a particular problem. According to Johnson (2015), "Finally, each student practices covertizing the speaker and listener routines while maintaining problem solving fluency. Of course, by encouraging students to covertize the speaker and listener routines, teachers can only see the outcomes of the private dialogue in a correctly solved problem" (p. 143). As Morningside Academy has routinized its own TAPS procedures, students have been providing evidence that they understand its importance in working through many challenging problems, puzzles, logic questions, and even everyday problems that arise. For example, we've witnessed students—deciding where to go for a special lunch or what to do on their break—say, "Let's TAPS that!"

Morningside instructional designers are in the process of developing several generative procedures, including routines for questioning teachers and peers (e.g., Robbins, Layng, & Jackson, 1995), a constructivist approach called "questioning the author" (Beck, McKeown, Hamilton, & Kucan, 1997), and pragmatic natural philosopher and educator John Dewey's (1933) method for reflective thinking, descriptions of which are beyond the confines of this chapter. Besides strengthening our students' problem-solving repertoires, designing generative repertoire procedures reduces the need to design instructional procedures that directly promote contingency adduction and provides more opportunities for using commercially available instructional materials that are not generative in nature.

Frequency Building of Component Skills and Application to Learning Complex Skills

The third group of behavior analysis investigators who influenced our generative instruction model was Eric Haughton's behavioral fluency group, which included Beatrice Barrett, Carl Binder, Annie Desjardins, Michael Maloney, and Clay Starlin, among others. Haughton in particular was interested in the rather explicit nature of the relation between practice to fluency and generative responding. The present authors eventually became part of this group. Before the discoveries of contingency adduction, the behavioral fluency group discovered a wealth of Standard Celeration Chart evidence showing that accuracy of a response class is insufficient for smooth progress through a curriculum sequence. Building component elementary or "tool" skills such as letter sounds and math facts to certain frequencies made it easier to develop useful frequencies of complex skills that require the synthesis of these component skills, such as word and passage reading and computational arithmetic. Eric Haughton (1972) described many Standard Celeration Charts that illustrated these relations, discovered while he was coaching teachers using precision teaching in elementary schools in Canada. Importantly, he calculated the relation between the frequency of saying sounds correctly and oral reading frequency across the Standard Celeration Charts of many teachers representing many students. The correlations ranged from .6 to 1.0. Notably, the correlation between number writing frequency and computation averaged 0.9! Low tool skill frequencies clearly predicted low frequencies and higher errors in more complex reading, math, and writing performance.

Over time, Haughton and his teachers discovered three outcomes of effective classroom practice: (1) when tool skill frequencies reach between 100 and 200 per minute, more complex skills will accelerate faster and require less error correction, and students will progress through curriculum steps at a faster rate; (2) errors are much easier to correct when overall performance on a given skill is higher than fifty to sixty per minute; and (3) students can successfully engage in independent practice without risk of practicing errors when they can perform at approximately half the proficiency level for a given skill (Haughton, 1980). A large number of precision teaching investigations since 1980 have also supported the conclusion that increased performance frequencies improve application (e.g., Evans & Evans, 1985; Johnson & Layng, 1992, 1994; Maloney, Desjardins, & Broad, 1990; Mercer, Mercer, & Evans, 1982). By application, precision teaching means "integration of component response classes into composite response classes" (Binder, 1996, p. 178).[12] One controlled study has examined the relation between the frequency of prerequisite tool skills and complex skills that incorporate them. Van Houten (1980) measured the frequency of long multiplication (e.g., 42 x 26) and long division (e.g., 342 ÷ 12) problems completed in ten minutes. During some conditions students also practiced multiplication and division facts during another part of the school

---

12   In precision teaching, the original meaning of "application," the "A" in the acronyms for fluency such as RAPS, REAPS, and RESSA, was clearly about component skills facilitating composite behavior. The "A" has nothing to do with performing a skill in a new context.

day, and during other conditions they did not. Results showed that students' frequencies of completing long multiplication and long division problems increased only in the conditions in which they also practiced multiplication and division math facts. When math facts practice did not occur, frequencies of long multiplication and division remained the same. Math fact frequencies rose from thirty to forty per minute at the beginning of the experiment to sixty to seventy per minute at the end of the experiment, highly correlated with increases in long multiplication and division frequencies.[13]

Since precision teaching investigations and data are focused on the relation between growth in tool skill frequencies and growth in more complex skill frequencies, it is not possible to draw conclusions about whether **tool skill frequency building** produced *adduction* of more complex skills *in the absence of instruction*. We can say that tool skill frequency building made it appear much easier to learn subsequent more complex skills that required the synthesis of these skills. By *easier*, precision teachers are talking pragmatics: more complex skills will accelerate faster and require less error correction, and students will progress through curriculum steps at a faster rate. Tool skill frequency building enables composite behavior instruction by ensuring that the frequencies of the components are sufficient for them to be easily applied in larger composites, *after at least some instruction in the composite*. Instruction is presumably still necessary but is briefer and requires less error correction. From these data we can conceptualize *degrees of generativity in responding* and a *continuum of instruction* ranging from many demonstrations and opportunities for guided practice and feedback to a few tips and quips, or no help at all. It appears that the amount or dose of instruction required for students to build high frequencies of complex skills with fewer errors was much lower when students had higher frequencies of their component skills.

Collateral Emotional Effects of the Moment of Contingency Adduction

The moment of contingency adduction often produces collateral positive emotional effects. The student's adduced performance may be accompanied by "Aha," smiling, and other overt responses if the student *tacts* the correspondence between their novel behavior and the criteria for reinforcement in the new situation. Aha tacts usually follow

---

13   We should note that many investigations have demonstrated that building component frequencies accelerates composite skill instruction and performance with children and adults with disabilities. The first author did significant work in designing instruction to teach activities of daily living skills such as handwashing and teeth brushing to adults with developmental disabilities in an institution. Teaching focused on practicing tool skill components of these activities, such as reaching, touching, grasping, placing, releasing, pushing, pulling, shaking, squeezing, and tapping; and informally demonstrating their combination to students. Neither task analysis nor chaining procedures were necessary. Even sales and customer service staff have learned to engage in lengthy problem-solving conversations with customers by focusing on product knowledge facts (Binder & Bloom, 1989; Binder & Sweeney, 2002). Many of these investigations have been published; however, we cannot describe them here. Instead, we will stick to our goal of describing generative responding in academic skill development.

sudden and dramatic shifts in stimulus control where the student's performance changes from unsuccessful candidate responses to adduced responses that match the teacher's score sheet. If engineered well, inductive, discovery learning can be enormously more fun for students and teachers than didactic, expository learning.

One reason constructivist-style education dominates current educational practices is likely the aesthetically pleasing outcomes discovery learning in principal can produce. However, constructivist lessons are often not successful for all students. Student outcomes often do not meet high standards, continuing a sorting machine philosophy of education where the best students rise to the top while others are left behind. Often these problems are masked by cooperative learning arrangements in which a few students in a small group do the majority of the learning while the others are left puzzled. Discovery learning lessons also often proceed at a slow pace of learning, bogged down with errors and collateral negative emotional effects. Behavior analysis in education may gain a competitive foothold in current thinking about education by investigating and proposing methods based on a thorough analysis of the conditions under which generative responding through the process of contingency adduction can be arranged.

Contingency Adduction and Behavioral Evolution

The behavioral process of contingency adduction (or comparable accounts of generative responding) is essential to a plausible account of the origins of the vast number of behaviors emitted by organisms, especially humans, during the course of their lives. Behavioral accounts that incorporate only the basic behavior principles of reinforcement, shaping, and stimulus control are insufficient, as evidenced by the large majority of skeptics who find behavioral accounts too elementary and too naive (e.g., Chomsky, 1959). Figure 9.1 depicts a more plausible account. In the course of an organism's behavioral evolution, various contingencies operate simultaneously and continuously on the many behaviors in an organism's history. Novel behavior relations are the outcome of these dynamics. In each new situation or circumstance, contingencies recruit current relevant component repertoires from an organism's history. Novel adduced repertoires are selected from the combinations and recombinations of component behaviors in an organism's history to meet the requirements of those current reinforcement contingencies. These adduced repertoires become part of the selecting environment for further new repertoires required in subsequent new circumstances, and so on, thus producing increasingly complex behavior. When current contingencies are not at sufficient strength, contingency adduction is often facilitated when the student engages in generative repertoires, such as TAPS, best guess study skills, and other analytical routines. Good instructional design assures that students practice generative repertoires to heighten their occurrence in the presence of novel contingencies.

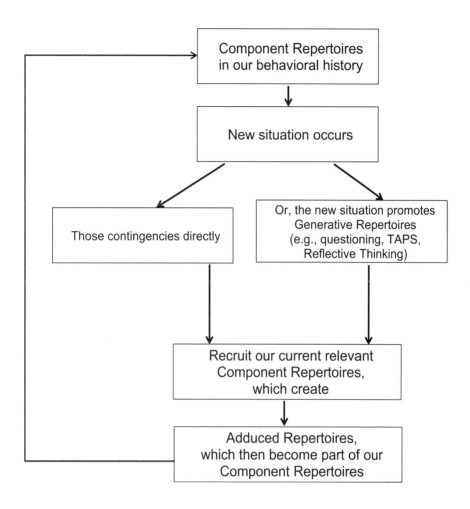

Figure 9.1 Behavioral evolution.

The quote below, by Charles Ferster (1965)[14], conveys the essence of contingency adduction as it applies to instruction.

> The essential point is that the speaker (teacher) does not build the repertoire in the student. He can only prompt, modify, or rearrange verbal behavior that the listener (student) already has. Thus, the interaction between speaker and listener (teacher and student) is most effective when their repertoires are close but not identical. *The listener (student) is well prepared for the speaker's (teacher's) influence when he would have said the same thing given another ten minutes* (italics added).

---

14   Paper read at the 50th anniversary Conference of the Graduate School of Education, the University of Pennsylvania, 1965. Reprinted in Ferster et al. (1975, p. 567). Extracted pages available from the first author.

Implications and Future Directions

Our work with contingency adduction has substantially informed our generative instruction model of academic instruction and our other clinical work with children and youth (Johnson & Layng, 1992, 1994; Johnson & Street, 2004, 2012, 2013; Layng, Twyman, & Stikeleather, 2004a, 2004b; Street & Johnson, 2014). Generative instruction makes teaching and learning more efficient. Eliminating the need for explicitly teaching composite performances reduces time to mastery of a typical curriculum by one-third or more. Generative instruction also provides explicit practice in problem solving without instruction as required in the real world. Direct and explicit teaching alone avoids teaching students how to think and creates dependency upon teachers and instruction for learning. And if we teach ourselves as well as constructivists how to engineer discovery learning effectively, we can heighten the aesthetically reinforcing effectiveness of discovery learning by making reinforcement denser and more probable. Then maybe we'll command a bigger role in American general education—a role that constructivists now claim and that we once claimed in the 1960s and 1970s.

In light of these advantages, we recommend that behavioral instructors revise their typical behavioral instruction protocols such as discrete trial training, direct instruction, and precision teaching in the following manner:

1. Focus instruction on component behaviors to facilitate untaught mastery of complex behavior.

   • Deconstruct the current holistic activities and real-world composite behaviors identified in today's academic curriculum frameworks and standards. Use component/composite analysis to break down the composite behaviors (Binder, 1996; Haughton, 1980; Johnson & Layng, 1992). We have identified over forty foundational component behaviors in reading, writing, and mathematics (Johnson & Street, 2013).

   • Design and present explicit instruction for each component behavior, using the demonstrate-guide-test model described by Gilbert's (1962a, 1962b) Mathetics and Engelmann and Carnine's direct instruction (Engelmann & Carnine, 1982; Marchand-Martella, Slocum, & Martella, 2004) to build highly accurate performance.

   • Design and present frequency-building activities for each component, using Lindsley's precision teaching (Binder, 1996; Johnson & Street, 2012, 2013; Kubina & Yurich, 2012) to build high frequencies of performance.

2. Build complex repertoires from the component behaviors thus established by engineering discovery learning.

   • Sequence instruction so that composite activities follow component instruction.

- After teaching the sequence of component behaviors, design and present a **contingency adduction moment**: one or more composite behavior activities that incorporate the component behaviors that you have explicitly taught. When presenting the composite activity, provide a blend of brief context-setting instruction and connections to natural, real-world problem solving to assure that the activity functions as a motivative operation.

- Use a delayed prompting procedure to guarantee that the composite activity will recruit the components and adduce the complex untaught composite, instead of directly teaching it.

3. Delayed prompting is essentially an upside-down version of explicit instruction; begin with a test phase ("Can you do this now?) and proceed to prompting and guiding, then full-blown demonstrations, as needed.

- Reinforce the new performance to produce adduced behavior.

- Teach generative repertoires such as TAPS, questioning, and reflective thinking to facilitate contingency adduction and discovery learning.

4. Use these procedures for corrective, remedial instruction as well as instruction for new learning. Trouble in algebra does not mean we should intensify instruction and practice in algebra. Component/composite analysis and student performance assessment will reveal the components of algebra that are absent, error-prone, or at frequencies too low to be useful in solving algebra problems. Such nonlinear analyses reveal that the problem that a student presents—in this case, trouble in algebra—is not the main problem to solve.

Conclusion

Generative behavior is behavior that occurs in novel forms under novel circumstances without direct instruction. That behavior analysts can program for generative responding is important, because educators cannot possibly teach every academic skill that a student needs to learn. The purpose of generative instruction is to arrange for the teaching of a number of component skills so that students will demonstrate new forms of complex academic skills that combine several component skills. Research on generativity, contingency adduction, and behavioral fluency have all contributed to the development of the generative instructional model. Five variations of contingency adduction have been programmed in classroom settings and are incorporated into the Headsprout Internet reading program. Results for the Headsprout Early Reading program have shown that a large proportion of students identified new sound combinations in the absence of instruction and formed new consonant blends. Likewise, many students showed the emergence of new vocabulary skills following their completion of the Headsprout Reading Comprehension program. Whimbey and colleagues have provided a framework for analyzing novel behavior in terms of analytic thinking and problem solving. Importantly, for all forms of generative repertoires, the speaker or teacher does not build the repertoire but prompts, modifies, or rearranges verbal behavior that the listener or student already has in the repertoire.

Study Questions

1. What is generativity? Explain in your own words.

2. What are the practical benefits of generative responding? Why is it socially important?

3. Describe two areas of research that have influenced the authors' generative instruction model.

4. Explain "contingency adduction."

5. What are the three critical features of the concept class contingency adduction?

6. How does exclusion learning facilitate contingency adduction? Give an example.

7. Describe two of the examples of contingency adduction reviewed in the chapter.

8. What is the main idea behind the development of TAPPS/TAPS methods?

9. What are the five qualities of problem solvers and active listeners as described in the chapter?

10. What is one of the main conclusions from the precision teaching research described in this chapter?

11. Describe the implications for teaching provided by the authors at the end of the chapter.

12. What is a "contingency adduction moment"? Give an example.

13. The authors say that trouble in algebra doesn't necessarily mean that more practice in algebra is needed. What point are the authors making with this example?

CHAPTER 10

Equivalence-Based Instruction: Designing Instruction Using Stimulus Equivalence

Daniel M. Fienup[15]

Teachers College, Columbia University

Julia Brodsky

The Graduate Center of the City University of New York

Link and Preview

The discovery of a behavior process known as stimulus equivalence was important for behavior analysts because it set the stage for an analysis of conditions under which novel patterns of responses may emerge in the absence of explicit instruction. The present chapter introduces the concepts of stimulus equivalence classes and elaborates upon how the formation of equivalence classes relates to the concepts of stimulus and response generalization. The chapter also describes instructional procedures that have been used in both the laboratory and educational settings for producing equivalence relations.

The challenge of education is to engineer antecedents and consequences to produce accurate performance under appropriate stimulus control conditions. An educator must begin the design of instruction by determining the stimuli that should evoke the desired academic response(s). At the simplest level, an educator may wish to establish responding in the presence of a **discriminative stimulus** such that the response occurs in the presence of certain stimuli—such as saying "five" in the presence of the numeral five (5) but not in the presence of other stimuli, such as other numerals—thereby demonstrating **stimulus control** (Herrnstein, 1990). At a higher level, an educator may want to develop responding to an open-ended category of stimuli, such as treating the numeral five displayed in different sizes and fonts, as functionally interchangeable (see top portion of figure 10.1). The formation of open-ended categories requires **stimulus generalization,**

---

15   Author Note: A portion of Daniel Fienup's effort was conducted while affiliated with Queens College, CUNY.

or the spread of effect across topographical stimulus dimensions (Herrnstein, 1990; Stokes & Baer, 1977). A more complex type of stimulus control is involved in **concept formation**, which entails responding to a range of nonidentical stimuli that may vary across perceptual modalities—such as the numeral five (5), the letters f-i-v-e, the spoken word "five," and five objects—and treating them as functionally interchangeable (see bottom portion of figure 10.1). Concept formation is quite a different phenomenon from stimulus generalization because of the range of stimuli involved. At the level of concept formation, educators may look to the long history of basic and applied studies dealing with the formation of classes of physically disparate stimuli for guidance in teaching such repertoires. This area of research is known as **stimulus equivalence** (Sidman, 1994).

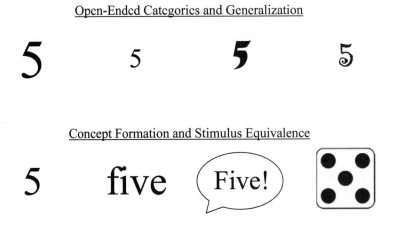

Figure 10.1 A depiction of stimulus generalization and stimulus equivalence.

Equivalence-based instruction (EBI) is a generative instructional design tool that incorporates the principles of stimulus equivalence, which bears resemblance to logical deduction (Fienup, Covey, & Critchfield, 2010). Typically conducted via **match-to-sample** (MTS) procedures, EBI teaches classes (sets) of stimuli containing three or more stimuli each (e.g., A, B, and C). To reduce the amount of direct teaching while maintaining high levels of academic output, educators consider how to link a small subset of stimulus-stimulus relations to expand to a new, larger set of stimulus-stimulus relations. EBI is concerned with the design of instruction to teach functional interchangeability between topographically dissimilar, but thematically similar, stimuli.

The trajectory of stimulus equivalence research is atypical. Many behavioral technologies are inspired by the findings of basic research. Initial stimulus equivalence research was conducted in the applied field, where the phenomenon was discovered and studied by Murray Sidman and his colleagues (Sidman, 1971; Sidman & Cresson, 1973), who taught reading comprehension to learners with an intellectual disability (ID) and Down syndrome. Questions generated in applied settings led researchers to further study this phenomenon in laboratory settings, where the majority of research in this area has been conducted. In the last few decades, while basic researchers have continued conducting research in highly controlled settings, parallel applied and translational research has studied the application of this technology to the design of educationally relevant academic instruction (Rehfeldt, 2011). Areas of instruction have included spelling (De Rose, de Souza, & Hanna, 1996), matching names and faces (Cowley, Green, & Braunling-McMorrow, 1992), geography (e.g., Hall, DeBernardis, & Reiss, 2006), and mathematics (Lynch & Cuvo, 1995). These skills have been taught to participants with a variety of diagnoses, such as Down syndrome (Sidman & Cresson, 1973), fragile X syndrome (Hall et al., 2006), ID (Sidman, 1971), autism spectrum disorders (Stanley, Belisle, & Dixon, 2018), brain injury (Cowley et al., 1992), and visual impairments (Toussaint & Tiger, 2010).

Lynch and Cuvo (1995) conducted a study that typifies EBI. These researchers taught fraction-decimal mathematics classes to general education fifth and sixth graders. The stimuli in the classes included numerical representations of fractions (A stimuli); pictorial analogues, which were grids composed of 100 squares with a particular number of squares filled in black (B stimuli); and numerical representations of decimals (C stimuli). There were twelve separate fraction-decimal classes included in training. For example, class one contained the stimuli 1/5 (A), a pictorial analogue with 20 of 100 squares filled in (B), and 0.20 (C). Figure 10.2 displays examples of taught and derived stimulus-stimulus relations in this study. The researchers used MTS procedures to teach AB and BC relations and test for the emergence of derived relations.

During AB training, the researchers presented a sample stimulus and the participant selected the sample (**observing response**) to produce four comparison stimuli. In AB training, fractions (A) served as samples and pictorial analogues (B) served as comparisons. Of the four comparison stimuli presented during a trial, one was from the same class of stimuli, and selecting this stimulus resulted in an audible "yes" generated by the computer program. Three comparison stimuli were from classes other than the sample, and selecting those comparison stimuli resulted in no effect—that is, the stimuli remained until the participant clicked the correct comparison stimulus. Following mastery of all twelve AB relations, the researchers applied the same training procedure to BC relations where pictorial analogues (B) served as sample stimuli and decimals (C) served as comparison stimuli. Prior to and after the instruction, the researchers tested stimulus-stimulus relations that were expected to emerge from the instruction. Two of these relations were **symmetry** (BA, CB) and tested for whether sample-comparison conditional discriminations resulted in bidirectional transfer whereby the participant made accurate responses when samples became comparisons and comparisons became samples. One derived relation was **transitivity** (AC) and represented an association between two stimuli not directly taught, but related through a mutual stimulus (in this study, the B stimuli). A final derived relation was **equivalence** (CA), or combined symmetry and transitivity, which involved both bidirectional transfer and a novel association.

Prior to instruction, participants showed low levels of class-consistent (accurate) responding. After learning the AB and BC conditional discriminations, participants showed the emergence of equivalence classes by responding with high accuracy to symmetry, transitivity, and equivalence probe trials, thus demonstrating the ability to accurately relate fractions and decimals (see figure 10.2). This is an important educational outcome because participants treated three topographically different stimuli as interchangeable, and this socially significant repertoire resulted from teaching just two overlapping relations. Thus, the teaching strategy appeared to be time efficient, in that several skills emerged after only a few were taught.

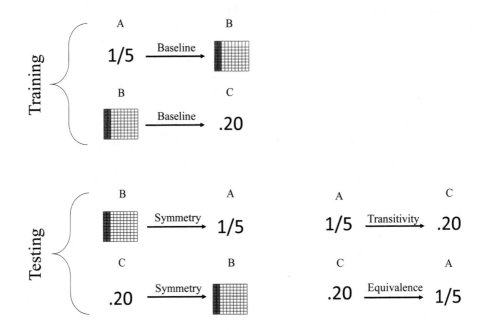

Figure 10.2 Trained relations (top row) and tested derived relations (bottom row) based on Lynch and Cuvo (1995).

Equivalence Procedures as Instructional Design Choices

In this section we will review different components of EBI and the supporting research base. Many instructional design features of the study conducted by Lynch and Cuvo (1995) are worth noting. The first is that by teaching two relations (AB, BC), the researchers observed the emergence of four derived relations (BA, CB, AC, CA). The number of untaught emergent relations shows the power of stimulus equivalence and why educators and clinicians may be interested in adopting this technology. For example,

Lynch and Cuvo (1995) observed the emergence of relations between fractions and decimals that were never directly taught. The effect of programming for and observing the emergence of derived relations has been replicated across a large number of different content areas and populations, including college students learning about single-subject research designs (Lovett, Rehfeldt, Garcia, & Dunning, 2011) and neuroanatomy (Fienup, Mylan, Brodsky, & Pytte, 2016), and learners with disabilities mastering reading and spelling (de Rose et al., 1996) and coin equivalences (Keintz, Miguel, Kao, & Finn, 2011). Broad reviews of equivalence applications (Rehfeldt, 2011), and those specifically with college students (Fienup, Hamelin, Reyes-Giordano, & Falcomata, 2011; Brodsky & Fienup, 2018) and individuals with autism (McLay, Sutherland, Church, & Tyler-Merrick, 2013), summarize the variety of concepts researchers have taught using EBI.

The derived relations reported in EBI studies represent properties of equivalence classes, and the presence of these properties establish that a class of stimuli function interchangeably. The properties established in the Lynch and Cuvo (1995) study were symmetry, transitivity, and equivalence. One additional property is **reflexivity**, whereby a stimulus bears a relation to itself, akin to identity matching (see Sidman, 1994). Lynch and Cuvo (1995) did not test for the property of reflexivity, nor do most studies involving typically developing participants, but this property is important to establish and test in applications with individuals with IDs (e.g., Sidman & Cresson, 1973).

Match-to-Sample Procedures

Lynch and Cuvo (1995) made an instructional design choice by implementing simultaneous MTS procedures (see top portion of figure 10.3) to conduct AB and BC conditional discrimination training. In **simultaneous MTS procedures**, the sample and comparison stimuli are present at the same time. Lynch and Cuvo required an observing response to the sample stimulus to ensure a participant was attending to the sample, and then the comparison stimuli appeared while the sample remained on the screen. A variation of this procedure is **delayed MTS** (see bottom portion of figure 10.3), in which the sample disappears once clicked, and the comparison stimuli appear immediately (zero-second delay) or after some time (Arntzen, 2006). Indeed, most of the EBI applications we are aware of utilize a simultaneous MTS procedure. This is interesting because basic research has shown that delayed MTS results in higher levels of equivalence class formation. Arntzen (2006) conducted a series of experiments with adult learners comparing simultaneous MTS and delayed MTS arrays with delays between zero and nine seconds. Results showed that longer delays between the offset of the sample stimulus and the onset of comparison stimuli resulted in higher numbers of participants demonstrating equivalence classes. To the best of our knowledge, this phenomenon has not explicitly been studied in the context of EBI and teaching academically relevant equivalence classes, although there are examples of delayed MTS procedures used in EBI research (e.g., Lane & Critchfield, 1998; Stromer & Mackay, 1992).

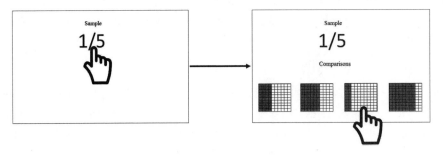

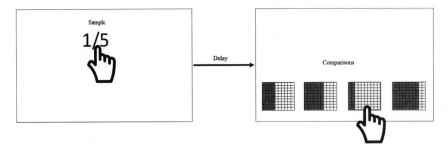

Figure 10.3 Simultaneous MTS (top row) and delayed MTS (bottom row).

Training Structure

Lynch and Cuvo (1995) made an instructional design choice to arrange the training structure of the fraction-decimal classes as a **linear series** (LS), whereby A sample stimuli were conditionally related to B comparison stimuli, and B sample stimuli were conditionally related to C comparison stimuli (see left portion of figure 10.4). The B stimulus was the node, or stimulus that connected the other two, which served as both a comparison stimulus and sample stimulus in different training phases. Basic researchers have rigorously tested other training structures. The other training structures are colloquially described as **one-to-many** (OTM; middle portion of figure 10.4) and **many-to-one** (MTO; right portion of figure 10.4), or technically named **sample-as-node** and **comparison-as-node**, respectively.

In an OTM training structure, given stimuli ABC, an instructor teaches AB and AC relations and tests for the emergence of (1) BA and CA symmetry relations and (2) BC and CB equivalence relations. In this case, A stimuli serve as samples on all training trials and A stimuli are the node, hence the technical name sample-as-node. In an MTO training structure, an instructor teaches BA and CA relations and tests for the emergence of (1) AB and AC symmetry relations and (2) BC and CB equivalence relations. The naming of a particular relation depends upon the training structure used.

You may notice that the BC relations mentioned here represent a trained relation in the LS example and an equivalence relation in OTM and MTO examples. The way to distinguish between these relations is to first note the trained relations (see black lines in figure 10.4) and then consider whether a derived relation (red lines) entails (1) bidirectionality (symmetry), (2) associations between novel stimuli without bidirectionality (transitivity), or (3) associations between novel stimuli with bidirectionality (equivalence). Researchers have directly compared training structures and their effect on the probability of forming equivalence classes. With typically developing adults, the OTM training structure produces the highest levels of derived relations, followed by the MTO training structure (Arntzen, Grondahl, & Eilifsen, 2010; Arntzen & Holth, 1997, 2000). With children and individuals with IDs, the MTO training structure is the most successful arrangement, followed by OTM (Saunders, Drake, & Spradlin, 1999; Saunders, Wachter, & Spradlin, 1988). In basic research studies that directly compared training structures, the LS structure has reliably produced the lowest level of class-consistent responding; however, several applied EBI studies have used the LS training structure with success (e.g., Lynch & Cuvo, 1995; Fields et al., 2009).

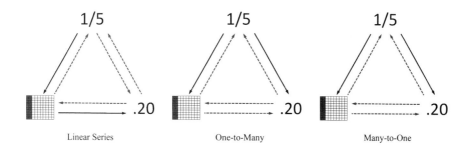

Figure 10.4 The linear series, one-to-many, and many-to-one training structures.

Training Protocol

Another instructional design choice by Lynch and Cuvo (1995) was how to order training and testing phases, referred to as training protocol (see figure 10.5). Lynch and Cuvo programmed all training phases (AB and BC) consecutively and prior to conducting tests of derived relations. During testing, probes for symmetry and transitivity were conducted first, followed by equivalence probes. The training protocol used in Lynch and Cuvo mimics a **simultaneous (SIM) protocol** (see top portion of figure 10.5). In this protocol, all training phases are grouped and all testing phases are grouped, with no overlap between (Fields, Reeve, Adams, Brown, & Verhave, 1997). Another training protocol is the **simple-to-complex (STC) protocol** (see middle portion of figure 10.5), which intersperses training phases and derived relations probes. Across the whole program, derived relations are tested individually, and tests are arranged from the simplest type of derived relations (i.e., symmetry) to the most difficult (i.e., equivalence; Adams, Fields, & Verhave, 1993). Lynch and Cuvo's (1995) protocol would have looked a bit different if conducted as an STC protocol. The authors taught AB, then BC, and then tested for BA, CB, AC, and BC, respectively. In an STC protocol, the test for symmetry of AB would have directly followed AB training. With three-member classes, performance differences produced by the SIM and STC protocols is minimal, but the difference becomes more obvious as class sizes increase (see Fienup, Wright, & Fields, 2015).

The SIM and STC protocols are the most commonly used in basic and applied studies, although other protocols have been discussed. The **complex-to-simple (CTS) protocol** completes training phases consecutively and then tests for the emergence of derived relations individually, starting with the most complex relations (for a description see Adams et al., 1993; for an applied example see LeBlanc, Miguel, Cummings, Goldsmith, & Carr, 2003). The **hybrid protocol** (Imam & Warner, 2014) includes training in consecutive phases, and tests are ordered from simple to complex (see bottom portion of figure 10.5). In other words, the hybrid protocol includes SIM training and STC testing. The first work on training protocols was conducted by Adams et al. (1993) and showed that when instructors taught relations between arbitrary stimuli (e.g., nonsense syllables), the STC protocol produced a very high number of participants who demonstrated equivalence classes. This outcome was considerably better than previous studies utilizing SIM and CTS protocols. Fienup et al. (2015) directly compared the SIM and STC protocols while teaching college students neuroanatomy classes. The researchers found that when teaching three-member (ABC) and four-member (ABCD) classes, participants who completed the STC protocol always formed classes during the first administration of the final test of equivalence. However, fewer participants who completed the SIM protocol formed three-member classes (75%), and this number dropped further with four-member classes (42%). Additional research has demonstrated that the breakdown of testing is potentially more important than whether training and testing are interspersed. Imam and Warner (2014) compared the SIM protocol to the hybrid protocol and found that ordering test phases from simple to complex dramatically influenced whether an individual formed equivalence classes. This procedure mimics the testing order used by Lynch and Cuvo (1995) and may explain why Lynch and Cuvo found high performance during tests of equivalence class formation.

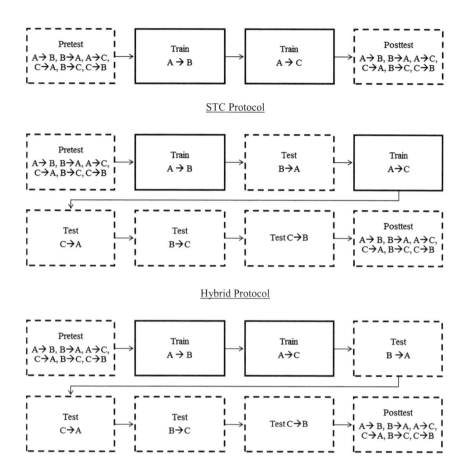

Figure 10.5 The SIM, STC, and hybrid training protocols. Dashed boxes represent testing probes; solid boxes represent training phases.

Generalization of Class-Consistent Responding

Lynch and Cuvo (1995) conducted generalization trials and paper-based generalization tests using novel fraction-decimal classes. Frequently, EBI researchers test for generalization across stimuli, responses, and time. For example, Trucil, Vladescu, Reeve, DeBar, and Schnell (2015) taught portion size estimation using EBI, and tested for generalization by asking participants to estimate portions of novel foods, demonstrating stimulus generalization. Such tests underscore the educationally relevant outcomes produced by EBI. Reyes-Giordano and Fienup (2015) conducted MTS EBI and tested derived relations in computerized MTS, multiple-choice, and fill in the blank formats. The outcomes suggested response generalization. Albright, Reeve, Reeve, and Kisamore (2015) taught participants statistics concepts and demonstrated maintenance one week after equivalence training. Fienup et al. (2016) demonstrated that learning neuroanatomy classes via computerized EBI resulted in higher course exam performance a few weeks later as compared to no equivalence training, demonstrating a combination of stimulus and response generalization and maintenance.

Successful performance on generalization measures demonstrates that instructors may choose to use EBI teaching procedures even when the target response topography may differ from the training topography. This is educationally important because many curricular goals include writing and talking about stimuli. However, teaching in this modality may be difficult, and the results of the EBI literature suggest the MTS training often results in improved writing and discussion of educational stimuli (e.g., Walker, Rehfeldt, & Ninness, 2010). Additionally, the research has shown that when maintenance tests are administered, participants continue to respond in a class-consistent manner in both the experimental settings (Albright, Schnell, Reeve, & Sidener, 2016; Trucil et al., 2015) and the naturalistic educational settings (e.g., Fienup et al., 2016); however, some booster training may be required to maintain responding (Walker & Rehfeldt, 2012). Such generalization outcomes may be beneficial in clinical work, where a therapist can train concepts such as classes of animals using EBI in a client's home, but the learner may generalize to writing about classes of animals at school or speaking about classes of animals with peers on the playground.

EBI Applications

Researchers have demonstrated the utility of EBI in teaching a wide variety of socially significant behaviors across a number of individuals of varying skill levels. Sidman (1971) first demonstrated equivalence relations in a learner with ID. The learner had a preexisting repertoire of matching spoken words to pictures. After Sidman taught the learner to match spoken and printed words, the learner was then able to match words to their corresponding pictures, thereby demonstrating reading comprehension. In a follow-up study, Sidman and Cresson (1973) taught two young adults with Down syndrome reading comprehension, but unlike in the 1971 study, the participants did not have a preexisting spoken word-picture repertoire. The researchers taught the participants to choose pictures and written words when presented with dictated words and observed the emergence of reading comprehension—matching pictures and written words. This study replicated and extended the original 1971 study and experimentally demonstrated the emergence of transitive relations and equivalence classes contingent upon teaching specific, linked conditional discriminations.

Much of the applied literature represents a replication and extension of the Sidman and Cresson (1973) procedures to teach different repertoires. For example, Keintz et al. (2011) taught coin equivalences to children with autism, which is an important step in teaching functional use of money. Coin names served as A stimuli, physical coins served as B stimuli, printed prices served as C stimuli, and dictated prices served as D stimuli. Following training, participants were able to engage in a number of derived skills, such as matching coin names with prices. Such a procedure could also be used to teach equivalences with paper-based currency in addition to coin-based currency in clinical practice.

A number of studies have involved utilizing EBI with children and adults with disabilities. LeBlanc et al. (2003) taught classes that involved US state names (A), pictures of states (B), and state capital names (C) to children with autism. Hall et al. (2006) replicated and extended the work of LeBlanc et al. (2003) and Lynch and Cuvo (1995) by teaching geography and mathematics skills to children with fragile X syndrome. Stanley et al. (2018) taught adolescents with autism a number of academic content areas, including chemical compounds (technical names, compound symbols, common names), units of measurement (yards, feet, inches), and historical figures (names, pictures, facts, country of origin). EBI procedures have also been used to help adults with brain injury match names and faces (Cowley et al., 1992) and recognize emotions (Guercio, Podolska-Schroeder, & Rehfeldt, 2004), as well as teach Braille to children with degenerative visual impairments (Toussaint & Tiger, 2010). Using EBI to address these socially significant repertoires benefits both clients and clinicians by saving valuable instructional time, allowing the clinician to progress to teaching other skills with the saved time.

Several studies have focused on language and language arts skills, including the initial studies conducted by Sidman (1971) and Sidman and Cresson (1973) of reading competencies. Additionally, researchers have taught competencies such as foreign languages, spelling, and prereading skills. Equivalence researchers have trained other language arts skills in similar ways. For example, Connell and Witt (2004) trained kindergarteners to match uppercase and lowercase letters to the spoken name of the letter and its sound, de Rose et al. (1996) taught reading and spelling skills to first grade children, and Lane and Critchfield (1998) taught letter sounds to individuals with intellectual disabilities.

Much of the basic research related to stimulus equivalence has focused on demonstrating properties of classes or manipulating a parameter of training to observe how it affects the formation of classes. One important feature of equivalence classes is the **transfer of stimulus functions** across stimuli related in an equivalence class (for a review, see Dymond & Rehfeldt, 2000). Researchers have found that once a set of stimuli function interchangeably (as an equivalence class), functions associated with one class member transfer to other class members. For example, Hayes, Kohlenberg, and Hayes (1991) conditioned stimuli to serve reinforcing and punishing consequences by pairing them with verbal feedback. Then, they included the stimuli in a training procedure to form equivalence classes and taught a conditioned reinforcer in one class and a conditioned punisher in another. After equivalence classes were formed, the researchers found that stimuli in a class with a conditioned reinforcer took on reinforcing functions and stimuli in a class with a conditioned punisher took on punishing functions. Unfortunately, there have not been enough applications that explore the use of transfer of function to solve socially important skill acquisition deficits. An application of these findings in clinical work might involve establishing classes of "safe" (e.g., toys, books) and "dangerous" (e.g., knives, matches, guns) stimuli and corresponding approach and avoidance responses to a stimulus from each class, which should then transfer to other members of the safe and dangerous classes.

Two important applications of transfer of function are reported in the literature. One exemplar was conducted by Taylor and O'Reilly (2000). In this study, the researchers taught individuals with disabilities to engage in a behavior chain at a grocery store (e.g., get basket, collect food items, and check out). After this, the participants engaged in an MTS task that matched various grocery store stimuli—the written and spoken word "SUPERMARKET," pictures from the inside of a familiar supermarket, and pictures from the inside of a novel supermarket. In effect, the researchers developed a grocery store class using an MTS procedure after establishing a discriminative function (i.e., how to shop) to some members of the class (e.g., images of the inside of the trained/familiar supermarket). When the participants were then taken to a novel grocery store, they were able to engage in the behavior chain with high levels of accuracy similar to individuals taught using multiple exemplar training (i.e., taught the behavior chain in multiple grocery stores) and with higher levels of accuracy than participants who completed single-exemplar training (i.e., taught the behavior chain in one grocery store). Training in one supermarket and teaching supplementary classes may have saved instructional time and resources. Such a procedure could be expanded to teach other activities of daily living to clients, such as borrowing books from the library, calling others on a phone, ordering at a restaurant, and using public restrooms. In another example of transfer of function, Rosales and Rehfeldt (2007; also see Rehfeldt & Root, 2005) began by teaching participants to mand for preferred items using pictures of the desired item. The researchers taught participants to mand by engaging the participant in a behavior chain that led to a reinforcing outcome and withholding a step in that chain to create an opportunity to mand. For example, one behavior chain included listening to music. The participant had to mand for headphones by handing a picture of headphones to the researcher in order for the chain to continue and result in the opportunity to listen to music. After manding was established in the participant's repertoire, the researchers used EBI to teach the participant three-member equivalence classes that included pictures, spoken names, and written words of those same desired items. Next, during the behavior chain, the researchers omitted the pictures but made the written words available to participants. The researchers observed that participants were readily able to mand using both vocal and written words. In other words, once Rosales and Rehfeldt (2007) established pictures as discriminative stimuli for manding, the function transferred to other members of the class (the corresponding text).

Much of the recent applied EBI research has focused on college-level content. This phenomenon has been studied in a number of settings, such as the laboratory (e.g., Albright et al., 2015), as part of a course requirement (Critchfield, 2014), as a method of lecture (Pytte & Fienup, 2012), and as an online supplement to in-class instruction (Walker & Rehfeldt, 2012). Several studies have shown that EBI is more effective at concept formation than no instruction. For example, Fields et al. (2009) taught college students four four-member statistics classes using an LS training structure and an STC training protocol. Each class contained a graph displaying an interaction (A), a textual example of an interaction (B), a name of a statistical interaction (C; e.g., crossover interaction), and a definition of that interaction (D). The researchers compared the effects of EBI to a no-instruction control group that completed pre and post assessments with a break in between. Fields et al. (2009) found that participants had comparable levels of performance at pretest, but the EBI group scored significantly higher on the posttest and demonstrated the formation of statistical interaction equivalence classes.

EBI has been shown to be more effective than instructional procedures typically used in the classroom, such as reading a textbook (O'Neill, Rehfeldt, Ninness, Munoz, & Mellor, 2015) and video-taped lecture (Lovett et al., 2011). It is also more efficient than directly teaching all stimulus-stimulus relations in a class (Fienup & Critchfield, 2011). Researchers have had success implementing EBI through various delivery methods. While many researchers deliver this instruction via automated computer tutorials (e.g., Albright et al., 2015), some have had success using paper-and-pencil formats (Walker et al., 2010) or distance education formats, such as Blackboard (Walker & Rehfeldt, 2012) and Adobe Connect (Sella, Ribeiro, & White, 2014), which demonstrates the potential of EBI technology, irrespective of instructional setting or format. Participants have demonstrated equivalence class formation in a variety of response topographies, including computer-based MTS (e.g., Fienup & Critchfield, 2011), paper-based MTS (Fields et al., 2009), clicker-based responding (Varelas & Fields, 2017), selection-based intraverbals (e.g., O'Neill et al., 2015), vocal intraverbals (e.g., Walker et al., 2010), and estimating portions of food (Hausman, Borrero, Fisher, & Kahng, 2014). EBI researchers have taught college students a wide range of socially significant topics, such as neuroanatomy (e.g., Reyes-Giordano & Fienup, 2015), research design and analysis (Fields et al., 2009; Fienup & Critchfield, 2011; Sandoz & Hebert, 2016; Sella et al., 2014), functions of behavior (Albright et al., 2016), portion size estimation (e.g., Trucil et al., 2015), disability categorization (Walker et al., 2010), and advanced algebra and trigonometry (Ninness et al., 2006, 2009).

Implications and Future Directions

There is robust experimental evidence for the effectiveness of EBI (Brodsky & Fienup, 2018; Fienup et al., 2011; Rehfeldt, 2011). However, this claim comes with a caveat that should shape future research and application: the vast majority of experimental evidence comes from teaching individuals a small set of discrete skills in highly controlled settings. Instruction ranges from teaching children with disabilities three three-member geography classes (LeBlanc et al., 2003), to teaching typically developing children twelve three-member fraction-decimal classes (Lynch & Cuvo, 1995), to teaching college students sixteen three-member neuroanatomy classes (Fienup et al., 2016). These skill sets were taught in settings analogous to controlled laboratory settings, such as a quiet area of a classroom (participant 1; LeBlanc et al., 2003), separate classrooms (participant 2; LeBlanc et al. 2003; Lynch & Cuvo, 1995), and traditional university laboratory space (Fienup et al., 2016). Collectively, the research suggests that EBI is promising for educational applications, but research is needed that is conducted in traditional educational settings and scales this type of instructional design to address the many educational needs of individuals with and without disabilities.

Many educational content areas have yet to be addressed by EBI researchers. Most individuals are in school from ages five to eighteen and increasingly contact higher educational schooling for at least an additional four years. The sum of the EBI research base touches upon a few academic content areas students may come across during this long time of formal education. Two recent studies demonstrate progress toward the goal of scaling EBI. Greville, Dymond, and Newton (2016) trained four five-member (name, image, function, pathology, anatomy) and eight four-member (name, image, function, pathology) neuroanatomy classes to students in their first and second year of medical school. Fienup et al. (2016) taught sixteen four-member neuroanatomy classes that covered one-third of the neuroanatomy content covered in an undergraduate behavioral neuroscience course. These studies represent movement toward broader curricular applications of EBI. We hope to see researchers designing EBI applications that span content across entire courses.

Another glimmer of hope in scaling EBI comes from the publication of Dixon's (2015) PEAK relational training system: Equivalence module (PEAK-E; see chapter 11). The PEAK-E module was designed for children with disabilities and contains 184 different educational goals, spanning repertoires such as demonstrating reflexivity with objects, pictures, and stimuli from different sensory modalities (e.g., gustatory); demonstrating symmetry with pictures and objects or written words and objects; the formation of planetary equivalence classes (with pictures, spoken names, and written names of planets); reading and mathematics classes; and even perspective taking. For a particular skill, the curriculum specifies the training procedures and specific derived relations to be evaluated. This curriculum emphasizes tests of reflexivity, symmetry, transitivity, and equivalence toward the development of higher-order concept learning—something that is omitted from common curricula for children with disabilities.

There is a sizable evidence base demonstrating the efficacy of equivalence work with typically developing college students (thirty-one experiments across twenty-eight papers; Brodsky & Fienup, 2018) and a number of studies evaluating EBI in individuals with developmental disabilities (McLay et al., 2013). Very few studies address EBI as an instructional tool for typically developing children. This problem is related to the scaling issue mentioned above in that many general education topics have not been examined by EBI researchers because the participants included in studies determine the educational content of the studies. Thus, many of the goals listed in national school curricula such as the Common Core (National Governors Association Center for Best Practices & Council of Chief State School Officers, 2010), which is used by forty-two states in the US, have not been evaluated for whether or not they are amenable to EBI. The work conducted by Albright et al. (2015), Lynch and Cuvo (1995), and Ninness et al. (2006, 2009) dealing with mathematics EBI applications strongly suggests this technology could be applied to a wide array of Common Core mathematics competencies. For example, a first grade goal is "tell and write time in hours and half-hours using analog and digital clocks" (see 1.MD[16][15]). In an EBI application, classes could include spoken times (A), written times (B), time displayed on an analog clock (C), and time displayed on a digital clock (D). This set of stimuli is amenable to an OTM training structure where spoken times serve as sample stimuli. One may find that certain relations, like matching spoken and written times, are already in the participant's repertoire and, thus, training could focus on teaching AC and AD relations and testing for the emergence of the remaining relations. Lynch and Cuvo's (1995) procedures could be used to address the third grade goal to "understand two fractions as equivalent (equal) if they are the same size, or the same point on a number line" (see 3.NF). This training could serve as a prerequisite for addressing the fifth grade goal to "use equivalent fractions as a strategy to add and subtract fractions" (5.NF). As a last example, Common Core specifies a goal to "classify two-dimensional figures into categories based on their properties" and provides the following subgoal: "Understand that attributes belonging to a category of two-dimensional figures also belong to all subcategories of that category. *For example, all rectangles have four right angles and squares are rectangles, so all squares have four right angles*" (5.G). Indeed, the educational goals proposed by the Common Core curriculum could benefit from EBI.

Additional research is needed to identify training and testing parameters that promote equivalence class formation toward building robust EBI applications. Currently, a number of instructional design components have empirical support. With adult learners, data exists suggesting that participants should respond with mouse clicks (Kato, de Rose, & Faleiros, 2008) and undergo OTM training structures (Arntzen & Holth, 1997) within the context of the STC training protocol (Fienup et al., 2015), using delayed MTS training procedures (Arntzen, 2006) and a high mastery criterion (Fienup & Brodsky, 2017). With young learners and individuals with disabilities, the only research comparing different EBI components suggests the MTO training structure is best (Saunders et al., 1988, 1999). Clearly, many components of EBI have not been tested, especially with young learners and individuals with disabilities (McLay et al., 2013), which are frequently reported populations in behavior analytic research. Additionally, an astute reader will note that applied researchers have used some components of EBI with success, despite negative findings for that component in the basic research. For example, the LS training structure is reliably found to be simultaneously ineffective in basic research (e.g., Arntzen & Holth, 1997) and effective in applied work (e.g., Fields et al., 2009). What is not communicated in the research is the number of pilot studies conducted by researchers,

---

16   [15] These standard numbers refer to American Common Core educational standards, which can be found at http://www.corestandards.org.

including those conducted in our own lab, to optimize a specific EBI tutorial. This process may hamper adoption by educators, and thus, we encourage researchers to investigate optimal instructional design components of EBI. Specific guidelines for designing EBI applications with different populations would promote mainstream use of EBI.

Beyond the design of EBI components lies a challenge in disseminating actual programs. Many EBI applications are computer based and require the developer to have skills in software design. This may prevent educators from adopting EBI. One solution lies in the development of commercially available EBI applications. A platform where instructors could specify instructional content and disseminate the program to students and clinicians for use on smartphones and tablets would allow for considerable flexibility for learners. Another avenue researchers can pursue is evaluating low-tech procedures or procedures within already-existing educational systems. In terms of low-tech applications, Walker et al. (2010) used a paper-and-pencil-based procedure that entailed completing multiple-choice worksheets for training. Many EBI applications with individuals with disabilities entail MTS discrete trials similar to educational strategies already in place for the individual. In this context EBI adds the programming for and testing of derived relations. Regarding already existing educational systems, Walker and Rehfeldt (2012) demonstrated that the popular course-management system Blackboard could be used to administer quizzes for EBI of single-subject research design. Accompanying task analyses that specify how to create individual quizzes and quiz contingencies for systems like Blackboard and Quizlet (see https://www.quizlet.com) could help speed the dissemination of EBI technology.

Conclusion

This chapter provided an overview of processes involved in stimulus equivalence and a review of instructional research that utilizes stimulus equivalence (EBI). In addition, a number of areas in need of additional research were highlighted. Collectively, EBI research findings show that it is an effective technology for teaching a number of socially significant skill sets to learners on a spectrum of age, skill level, and disability status (Brodsky & Fienup, 2018; Fienup et al., 2011; Rehfeldt, 2011). As research on effective EBI design choices grows, instructors will be able to optimize their equivalence-based teaching procedures. This knowledge base, combined with evidence of scaling and greater accessibility of the technology, has the potential to bring behavior analytic instructional design one step closer to mainstream adoption.

Study Questions

1. How is stimulus equivalence different from generalization?

2. Suppose you are teaching a child letter-name-sound classes. Letters serve as the A stimuli, names of letters serve as the B stimuli, and letter sounds serve as the C stimuli. You teach AB and AC relations (one-to-many training structure). In this scenario, which relations represent symmetry and which relations represent equivalence?

3. If you were teaching a child math quantities (A: spoken name of number, B: numeral, C: quantities of dots), how could you mimic the training procedures of Lynch and Cuvo (1995) to teach math quantity classes? What relations would you directly teach and what specific relations would you expect to emerge as a function of that training? (See figure 10.2 for assistance.)

4. What is training structure? How would you differentiate instruction based on this variable and the clientele you work with?

5. What is a training protocol? What evidence suggests one should use one training protocol over another?

6. How can you incorporate tests for generalization within an equivalence-based instruction protocol?

7. What is transfer of function? Describe one application that has incorporated transfer of function.

8. How have educators applied equivalence-based instruction to teach college-level content?

9. How could the content of this chapter be applied to teaching classes of stimuli that are not related by sameness (e.g., frames of opposition or comparative frames)?

Relational Frame Theory: Basic Relational Operants

Mark R. Dixon
Southern Illinois University

Caleb R. Stanley
Southern Illinois University

Link and Preview

Chapter 10 provided an overview of the phenomenon known as stimulus equivalence. Chapter 11 builds upon that chapter by delineating arbitrary relations other than stimulus equivalence, all of which play an important role in language and cognition. The concepts of relational framing and derived relational responding are introduced in this chapter, as well as the relevance of both concepts for the understanding of human language. The chapter surveys the types of additional relational frame families, including research in support of each type and educational implications of building repertoires of each.

On the Origin of Relational Frames

An **emergent,** or **derived, relation** is any relation between two stimuli that develops without a direct history of reinforcement. **Derived relational responding** has appeared in the behavior analytic literature for over forty years, with the first demonstration of an emergent relation being traced back to the work of Murray Sidman. In an attempt to teach reading skills to a boy with intellectual disabilities, Sidman (1971) found that when he taught a specific set of relations, new relations would emerge in the absence of direct training. For example, he taught the boy that spoken words (A) were the same as pictures (B) (A-B), and the pictures (B) were the same as the printed words (C) (B-C). Following this training, the boy not only was able to respond to the directly trained relations (i.e., A-B and B-C), but also responded correctly to relations that had not been specifically taught. For instance, he responded correctly by saying the spoken word (A) in the presence of printed words (C) (C-A) and vice versa (see chapter 10). While it is not surprising that the participant made this response, as most individuals would with sufficient training, the most surprising finding was that he made this response in the absence of reinforcement for responding in accordance with that specific relation. Novel responding in the absence of reinforcement poses an interesting question for behavioral science. Sidman theorized the boy responded correctly to these untrained relations because the stimuli had become equivalent, and he coined this phenomenon **stimulus equivalence**. As a result, many behavioral scientists began researching this phenomenon in an attempt to explain it. Over the years, numerous conceptual and theoretical debates ensued, each offering an account that attempts to explain the phenomenon. **Relational frame theory** (RFT; Hayes, Barnes-Holmes, & Roche, 2001) is one such attempt.

Since stimulus equivalence was first popularized, the connection between derived relational responding and language has been obvious. One of the first studies to evaluate this connection was conducted by Devany, Hayes, and Nelson (1986), who compared the performance of three groups of children on tests of stimulus equivalence. Groups consisted of typically developing children with full language, children with an intellectual disability who demonstrated expressive language, and children with an intellectual disability who had more severe language deficits. The researchers exposed the children to a series of trainings in the form of conditional discriminations, then tested them on their ability to form equivalence relations. The findings showed that all children who formed equivalence classes also demonstrated language, whereas those who did not form equivalence classes were without language. Additionally, since all children were exposed to the same trainings and reached the same mastery criteria prior to the equivalence tests, failure to form equivalence was not due to the inability to learn the conditional discriminations. Instead, the evidence pointed to a relationship between language and stimulus equivalence.

Most early literature on derived relational responding consisted of establishing relations among stimuli based on their physical features, referred to as **nonarbitrary relational responding**. Lowenkron (1989) provided one of the first demonstrations that this type of relational responding could be brought under contextual control. In this study, Lowenkron required participants to select between sets of stimuli dependent on background color. For example, selecting the comparison stimulus that was the same as the sample in the presence of a blue background would result in reinforcement, and selecting a comparison stimulus that was larger or longer than the sample in the presence of a green background would also result in reinforcement. The background color eventually came to exert contextual control over the participants' responses, even when the participants were presented with novel stimuli.

Steele and Hayes (1991) expanded on the findings of Lowenkron's (1989) study by examining if relational responding to arbitrary stimuli could be brought under contextual control. In their study, the authors exposed participants to a series of trainings in which participants were taught relations between arbitrary stimuli using contextual cues of same, opposite, and different. The results showed that the relational responses were brought to bear on the stimuli due to the contextual cues. This suggested that humans not only demonstrate relational responding to stimuli based on their physical properties, but also demonstrate relational responding to arbitrary stimuli based on the presence of a contextual cue. This had implications for language development since this pattern of responding may explain the process by which words acquire their meaning—through their relation with other stimuli in the presence of a contextual cue. For example, imagine that a young child with limited verbal capabilities is taught to select a picture of a fox from an array when asked "Show me the same as fox." In this example, the word "same" serves as a contextual cue that specifies the relational response that would be reinforced in the presence of the word "fox"—selecting the picture of the fox. When this relational response is made, the functions of the stimuli are altered depending on the contextual cue. In this example, the word "fox" acquires the same stimulus functions as the picture of the fox, and the child is likely to respond to the word "fox" as though it is the same as the picture, even when this visual stimulus is absent. In this way, the word "fox" essentially acquires the meaning of the picture and vice versa, which provides an explanation for the process in which words can acquire meaning.

Further support for the relationship between language and relational stimulus equivalence was found when experimenters followed a sixteen-month-old infant over the course of an eight-month period. In this study, Lipkens, Hayes, and Hayes (1993) documented the development of language as well as the infant's performance on tests of stimulus equivalence and exclusion when presented a series of relational tests. The data showed that the child was able to respond correctly to both tests of equivalence and exclusion following the various trainings of the study, despite the limited verbal repertoire of the child at the time. These findings yielded two significant implications. First, because the child had little to no verbal repertoire, it suggested that derived relational responding was not dependent on language mediation, and therefore, language was not necessary for derived relational responding to occur. Instead, although derived relational responding is not dependent on language, language may be dependent, at least in part, on derived relational responding. The second major implication was that the child responded correctly to the tests of exclusion even though no training had been conducted to that specific test. This could not be readily accounted for by the stimulus equivalence model and suggested other explanations may be necessary to account for this pattern of responding.

The prevailing notion at the time the studies described above were conducted was that language gave rise to derived relational responding, and derived relational responding was dependent on language. Relational frame theorists believed that language was dependent on and resulted from a form of relational responding called **arbitrarily applicable relational responding** (AARR). Steele and Hayes (1991) provided this evidence in their study when they demonstrated that AARR could be brought under contextual control. These studies served to provide the first empirical support for the core assumptions behind RFT, and, while the origins can be traced back to stimulus equivalence, not everything is equal.

Fundamental Concepts in Relational Frame Theory

RFT holds that emergent relations result from the behavior of **relating**. Relating means responding to one event in terms of another event (Hayes, Barnes-Holmes & Roche, 2001). For instance, if an individual was taught to select a black square in the presence of an identical black square and a triangle when presented with the statement "Which is the same?" they are relating, or making a relational response. In this example, the individual was responding to a stimulus in terms of its physical or formal similarities (i.e., the shape of the stimulus) to another stimulus. This type of relational responding is referred to as nonarbitrary relating. In nonarbitrary relational responding, stimuli are related in terms of their physical properties, such as color, shape, size, weight, texture, smell, and so on. An example of nonarbitrary relational responding involving size would be if a clinician is teaching a child the concept of bigger and smaller, whereby the child is taught to select the largest block from an array of three blocks of varying size when presented with the statement "Which is the biggest?" In this example, the child is responding to each of the blocks in terms of their size to one another. An interesting feature of nonarbitrary relational responding is that is it not limited to humans, as many other species have been trained to respond relationally to the physical properties of stimuli. For instance, nonarbitrary relational responding has been observed in birds (Towe, 1954), fish (Perkins, 1931), and mammals (Harmon, Strong, & Pasnak, 1982).

RFT posits that relational responding is much more than responding to the physical or formal characteristics of a stimulus. Rather, relational responding can come under the control of cues that can be modified based on social convention, known as **arbitrarily applicable relational responding** (AARR). In contrast to nonarbitrary relational responding, AARR is not dependent on the physical or formal properties of a stimulus to make a relational response, but instead relies on a contextual cue that specifies the relation between the stimuli. For example, imagine a child is being taught differences in coin values. During training, the child is verbally told that a dime (A) is more than a nickel (B) (A-B), and a nickel (B) is more than a penny (C) (B-C). Without having ever been directly taught the relation between the dime (A) and penny (C), the child will derive that the penny is less than the dime (C-A) and the dime is more than the penny (A-C). Without ever having seen the stimuli, the child can make this response because the contextual cue (i.e., more than) is controlling this pattern of responding. In fact, the nonarbitrary stimulus properties seem to compete with this pattern of responding, as the physical size of the dime is less than that of the penny. In this example, the individual is responding to the stimuli based solely on the contextual cue.

The above example highlights the notion that in the presence of a contextual cue, individuals can respond relationally to any stimuli, regardless of the actual physical properties of those specific stimuli. Additionally, unlike nonarbitrary relational responding,

AARR is a pattern of responding belonging only to humans, with no other animal species having exhibited this type of relational responding. Several studies have attempted to establish equivalence classes in nonhuman animals (e.g., Murayama & Tobayama 1997; Yamamoto & Asano, 1995), but with little success. It has been documented that with extensive training, certain species of animals have occasionally responded with high accuracy in accordance with reflexive and symmetrical relations (Oden, Thompson, & Premack, 1988; Pack, Herman, & Roitblat, 1991), few have demonstrated responding in accordance with transitivity (D'Amato & Colombo, 1985; Tomonaga, Matzusawa, Fujita, & Yamamoto, 1991), and none have demonstrated high levels of correct responding in accordance with stimulus equivalence. Because AARR is a pattern of responding unique to humans, RFT rests on the assumption that AARR is the core of complex human language and cognition, with our advanced verbal repertoires arising from arbitrarily applicable relational responses. As such, an understanding of the principles and concepts underlying RFT can aid in the identification of the specific environmental variables responsible for these repertoires, which has applied utility in that interventions can be developed to establish and strengthen these behaviors.

PROPERTIES OF A RELATIONAL FRAME

Most literature on derived relational responding refers to a pattern of responding relationally as a "relational frame." This term is often used as a noun, but it refers to the action of framing events relationally, or responding to one event in terms of another (Hayes & Hayes, 1989). Specific patterns of relational responding constitute different types of relational frames. For example, responding to one stimulus in terms of its similarities to another stimulus is one pattern of relational responding, while responding to one stimulus in terms of its differences from another stimulus is another pattern of relational responding, both of which represent distinct types of relational frames. A relational frame consists of three defining properties: (1) mutual entailment, (2) combinatorial entailment, and (3) transformation of stimulus function. **Mutual entailment** occurs when an individual responds to one stimulus in terms of another stimulus. For example, imagine a child is presented with a block and a ball and is taught to select the ball (B) when asked, "Which one is the ball?" (A), and is provided reinforcement for making the correct response (A-B). As depicted in figure 11.1, mutual entailment occurs when the individual responds by saying "ball" (A) when shown the actual physical ball (B), without ever having received reinforcement for producing the vocal utterance in the presence of that stimulus (B-A).

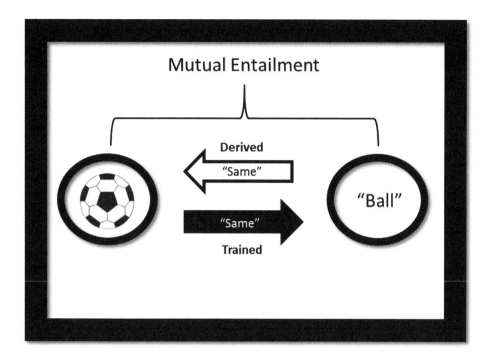

Figure 11.1 Mutual entailment.

Combinatorial entailment adds another level of complexity and refers to a derived stimulus relation in which two or more stimulus relations mutually combine (Hayes & Chase, 1991). Stated another way, combinatorial entailment occurs when an individual responds to a stimulus in terms of another stimulus based on mutually entailed relations with other stimuli. Using the previous example, imagine that the mutually entailed relation between the physical ball (A) and the vocal utterance "ball" (B) has already been established. An additional mutually entailed relation can develop if the individual is directly taught to respond with the vocal utterance "round toy" (C) when presented with the question "What is a ball?" (B) (B-C). In the absence of direct training, they will demonstrate mutual entailment by saying "ball" (B) when asked, "What toy is round?" (C) (C-B). If the child has a sufficient repertoire of relational responding, they will additionally demonstrate a combinatorially entailed response. In this example, the child would respond with the vocal utterance of "round toy" (C) when presented a ball (A) and asked, "What shape is this?" (A-C), and by selecting the ball (C) when presented an array containing a ball and a block and asked, "Which one is the round toy?" (A) (C-A; see figure 11.2).

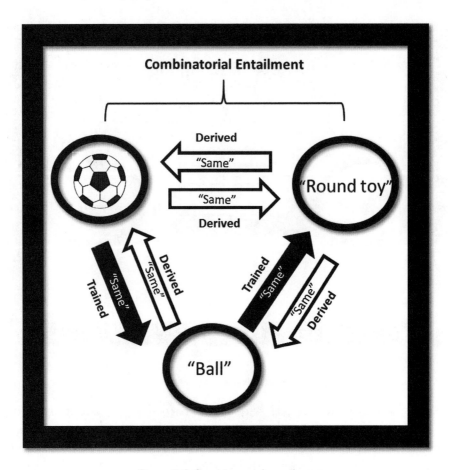

Figure 11.2 Combinatorial entailment.

The final property of a relational frame is the transformation of stimulus function. The **transformation of stimulus function** (see also chapter 10) is an ongoing process that occurs contingent on the development of mutually entailed and/or combinatorially entailed relations. The transformation of stimulus function occurs when a certain stimulus in a relational network has certain functions and serves to modify the functions of other stimuli in that relational network in accordance with the derived relation (Hayes, Barnes-Holmes, & Roche, 2001). More simply stated, the transformation of stimulus function is demonstrated when the function of a stimulus is changed due to a mutually and combinatorially entailed relationship with other stimuli. As a result, this stimulus will not only evoke new behavior, but also evoke the behavior in novel contexts because of its relational history with other events. Building on the previous example, imagine that the mutually entailed and combinatorially entailed relations between a ball and the vocal words "ball" and "round" are established (A-B, B-C, A-C, and C-A). The child may be able to request "ball" or a "round toy" when asked, "What do you want to play with?" or ask for a ball in the absence of prompts. This pattern of responding represents a transformation of stimulus function because neither the question nor wanting to play with the toy would have evoked the request for the ball prior to the establishment of a relational history.

Now, imagine the child from the previous example is presented with an entirely novel item that they have never interacted with before. They are taught that this new item is called a JES. If the child was asked, "Would you like to play with the JES?" it is likely that the child will not respond to this question. If the child was taught a JES is similar to, but also better than, a ball, the child may now be more likely to engage with the item because it has been related to an already preferred stimulus, and the new stimulus is better than the already preferred item. Although this example contains an arbitrary word with no actual meaning, it is no more arbitrary than any other novel words that we are exposed to each day. Every word ever encountered throughout the duration of an individual's life was at one time an arbitrary stimulus, void of any function or true meaning. It was not until that arbitrary stimulus participated in relational networks with other stimuli that the functions transformed. The functions of those once arbitrary stimuli acquired meaning based on their relationships with known stimuli, without a direct training history. The transformation of stimulus function gives rise to a true understanding of the stimuli encountered in our daily lives. In the above example, the resulting transformation of stimulus function allowed for the reinforcing experience of interacting with a potentially preferred tangible stimulus. The transformation of stimulus function may also allow for an individual to solve problems or respond in terms of abstract relational events. Once relational responding has been firmly established in an individual's repertoire, stimuli can be related to almost any other stimuli, resulting in a near limitless amount of transformations of stimulus function, depending on whatever complex combination of contextual cues happen to be present at any given moment.

RELATIONAL FRAMING AS A GENERALIZED OPERANT

Demonstrating derived relational responses to stimuli in the absence of a history of reinforcement is a hallmark characteristic of mutual and combinatorial entailment. Emitting derived responses, however, first relies entirely on a history of differential reinforcement for relating events to other events in this way. Responding in accordance with mutual entailment, along with combinatorial entailment and the transformation of stimulus function, comes about due to a history of differential consequences and multiple exemplars. In this way, relational framing is probably best conceptualized as generalized operant behavior. When an individual is provided a sufficient number of exemplars and receives reinforcement for making mutually and combinatorially entailed relations, they will then begin to make these responses seemingly naturally, and in contexts in which they were not initially trained. Furthermore, as the individual is taught new stimulus relations, more untrained stimulus relations will begin to emerge in the absence of direct training. This pattern of responding allows for faster learning and facilitates the development of more complex relational repertoires.

Initial research on derived relational responding as a generalized operant was scant, with most articles consisting of conceptual and theoretical discussions on the topic (e.g.,

Barnes-Holmes & Barnes-Holmes, 2000) or demonstrating the emergence of combinatorial relations in individuals with existing relational repertoires (e.g., Healy, Barnes, & Smeets, 1998; Healy, Barnes-Holmes, & Smeets, 2000). Recently, however, numerous empirical articles have emerged supporting derived relational responding as operant behavior. Some researchers have even established derived relational responding repertoires when they were previously nonexistent (Barnes Holmes, Barnes Holmes, Smeets, Strand, & Friman, 2004; Berens & Hayes, 2007).

A more recent study conducted by Belisle, Dixon, Stanley, Munoz, and Daar (2016), for example, sought to teach perspective-taking skills (i.e., deictic relational responding) to three children with autism and evaluate if this pattern of responding would generalize to novel stimuli. The researchers used a two-sided picture card, which depicted a different picture on each side, to test the children's ability to make different types of perspective-taking responses. To evaluate perspective-taking abilities, the child was first shown both sides of the picture card and the card was positioned so that the participant and the assessor could see opposite sides of the picture card; then the assessor would ask a question that required the participant to perform perspective taking. Baseline performance indicated that the participants failed to respond correctly when presented with certain perspective-taking tasks. The researchers then conducted training for one set of picture cards until the participants could respond accurately to the required tasks. Following training, the participants were exposed to a set of picture cards containing novel stimuli (i.e., stimuli that differed from those taught in training) to evaluate whether they demonstrated this pattern of responding with this new set of cards. Two of the three participants demonstrated high levels of responding to the novel set of picture cards, while the third participant required additional training to reach the same criterion. Because the stimuli in the second set of picture cards were not formally similar to those used in the first set, correct responding to the second set cannot be interpreted as stimulus generalization, but rather suggests this pattern of relational responding as a generalized type of operant behavior. These findings contribute to the growing body of literature supporting derived relational responding as generalized operant behavior, which develops from and is shaped by a history of differential consequences.

An RFT Account of Language and the Response from the Behavior Analytic Community

The first behavior analytic account of language was provided by B. F. Skinner (1957) in his book *Verbal Behavior*. In this analysis, Skinner proposed that language arises in the same way as any other operant behavior—it is reinforced. Skinner defined verbal behavior as behavior that is reinforced through the mediation of a listener who has been trained to provide reinforcement to the speaker. Therefore, a speaker's verbal responses are dependent on the consequences the speaker contacts from the listener. While this account of verbal behavior served the behavior analytic community for over fifty years, some believe there are challenges with this definition. First, Skinner's definition of verbal behavior may not be entirely functional. A functional definition requires that the definition be stated in terms of the history of the individual organism and the current environment. Skinner's definition of verbal behavior incorporated the history of conditioning of a listener; therefore, the definition no longer depends solely on the history of the speaker. Furthermore, this definition focuses only on the role of the speaker and considers the listener's behavior nonverbal. In addition, Skinner's definition of verbal behavior may be too broad. With Skinner's definition it is not hard to classify almost any behavior as verbal behavior. For example, imagine a rat that has been trained to press a lever and, contingent on a lever press, is provided food by a researcher. Using Skinner's definition, the rat's behavior would meet the criterion for verbal behavior. The speaker's (i.e., rat's) behavior (i.e., lever press) is reinforced through the mediation of the listener (i.e., researcher). Given this example, most basic operant experiments where an animal's behavior is reinforced by an experimenter would also meet this criterion. In other words, Skinner's definition of verbal behavior provides no meaningful way to discriminate between all basic operant research ever done with rats and pigeons and the complexity, generativity, and variability of human language.

An alternative account of language came in the form of a collection of works on derived relational responding titled *Relational Frame Theory: A Post-Skinnerian Account of Human Language and Cognition* (Hayes, Barnes-Holmes, & Roche, 2001). In this book, the authors present the foundational concepts of RFT along with the accumulation of publications supporting it over years of research. In addition to the fundamental concepts of RFT, the book offered an alternative account to human language and cognition. According to RFT, language arises due to framing events relationally, and this pattern of responding is the core of human language and cognition. Our complex verbal repertoires are the result of relational responding in the presence of a contextual cue that comes to control this pattern of responding to stimuli, regardless of the physical or formal properties of the stimuli. In short, RFT holds that AARR gives rise to language. This definition of language addresses some of the concerns surrounding Skinner's definition described above. For example, RFT provides a functional definition of language in that it is no longer dependent on an understanding of a second person's history of reinforcement in order to determine whether a first person's behavior is verbal. In RFT the behavior of both the speaker and listener is considered verbal. The speaker produces verbal stimuli that are a product of framing events relationally, and the listener responds in accordance with these relationally framed events.

The Hope Relational Frame Theory Provides

A core foundational assumption of RFT is that relational training can give rise to complex networks of untrained stimulus relations. For example, imagine that a three-member stimulus equivalence class has been established between a set of stimuli (e.g., A→B→C). From training only two relations (A-B and B-C), another four relations (B-A, C-B, A-C, & C-A) emerge without the need of explicit training. Now, imagine that stimulus A is then established as being different from stimulus D (A-D). By establishing this single relation between stimulus A and stimulus D, all other stimuli within the same equivalence class as A are then also related to stimulus D, which results in a total of nine untrained stimulus relations. Now, if stimulus D was then related to a completely different set of stimuli, an even greater number of relations would be made between the new stimuli and all other previously related stimuli. This example demonstrates that with only a few directly trained relations, the number of relations that emerge is exponential. With every stimulus we have ever encountered being related to every other stimulus we have and will encounter, it becomes clear just how generative relational responding can be.

Because relational responding is so generative, it has particular utility in terms of skill acquisition. Rather than directly training every single response to an individual, trainers can set up programming so that untrained relational responses can be derived. For example, imagine that you are trying to teach a child to tact a novel stimulus, and you want to train vocal and printed words to this stimulus. Rather than teaching every single relation among the stimuli, which would be undoubtedly time consuming, you could set up the stimulus relations so that only two relations would need to be trained for the other relations to emerge. The generative nature of relational responding could be particularly useful in situations where limited resources are afforded or time constraints exist. For instance, a study conducted by Stanley, Belisle, and Dixon (2018) sought to use procedures based on RFT to teach academically relevant material to individuals with autism. One of the skills taught involved unit conversion between yards, feet, and inches. Rather than teaching every single relation between yards, feet, and inches, the researchers arranged the stimuli so that training consisted of teaching conversion of inches to yards and feet to yards. Once these were taught to criteria, the researchers tested for the emergence of the unit conversion of inches to feet and feet to inches. The participants responded with high accuracy to these specific relations, despite the fact that they had not been directly trained. This study demonstrates the generative nature of derived relational responding. Rather than teaching every single relation among the stimuli (i.e., a total of six relations), the researchers arranged the stimuli so that only two relations were directly trained and the remaining relations were derived. Although this represents only a single demonstration of this phenomenon, a clinician could replace the stimuli with stimuli individualized to their client, while retaining the same arrangement, in order to facilitate the emergence of derived relations.

Types of Relational Frame Families

There are a number of different ways in which stimuli can be related to one another. Take, for example, an apple and a cat. Initially, it may appear as though these two stimuli are not related to one another at all. But upon further inspection, these two seemingly unrelated stimuli can be related to one another in countless ways. For example, it might be easy to think of ways in which these two stimuli are different from each other. Perhaps the color of the two stimuli is different (e.g., the cat is black and the apple is red), or maybe the cat has hair, whereas the apple does not. The cat may be bigger and weigh more than the apple. Both the cat and the apple are the same because they are living organisms; however, the apple is classified as a fruit, whereas the cat is classified as an animal. Relations such as same, different, more or less than, opposite, temporal relations, and many more resulted from only a single example. Within the RFT literature, stimulus relations have typically been categorized into nine distinct families of relations: (1) coordination, (2) opposition, (3) distinction, (4) comparison, (5) hierarchical, (6) temporal, (7) spatial, (8) conditionality/causality, and (9) deictic. In this chapter, relational frames are categorized into six families, with the frame families of temporal, spatial, and conditionality/causality grouped into the frame family of comparison, since these topographies are compared relative to each other across a wide variety of dimensions (i.e., time, space, size).

COORDINATION

The first type of relational frame family is the frame of **coordination** (see figure 11.3). This relational frame has been considered to be the simplest relation and the first to emerge in an individual's repertoire. The frame of coordination appears to serve as the foundation on which other frames are built (Hayes, Barnes-Holmes, & Roche, 2001). The frame of coordination deals exclusively with sameness and similarity. The examples from equivalence research described in the beginning of the chapter are examples of frames of coordination. An example of similarity (but not equivalence) would be if an individual was taught that a pen is similar to a paint brush. In this instance, the pen and paint brush are not exactly the same physically but are the same in terms of their function—they both are utensils used to produce markings on a page.

The relational frame of coordination is the most researched type of stimulus relation, encompassing approximately 73% of the literature on derived stimulus relations (Rehfeldt, 2011). Research for this type of frame dates back over forty years, beginning with Sidman (1971). Since then, abundant basic and applied studies have been published, a list far too exhaustive to outline in this chapter. However, basic research on this relational frame includes demonstrations of contextual control over transformations of stimulus functions in frames of coordination (Dougher, Perkins, Greenway, Koons, & Chiasson, 2002), relating equivalence classes to other equivalence classes (Barnes, Hegarty, & Smeets, 1997), the transformation of respondently conditioned stimulus functions in accordance with arbitrarily applicable relations (Roche & Barnes, 1997), and many others (e.g., Barnes-Holmes, Barnes-Holmes, Roche, & Smeets, 2001a; Healy et al., 2000; Valverde, Luciano, & Barnes-Holmes, 2009). Researchers have used instructional procedures grounded on the frame of coordination in a variety of areas, including teaching fraction-decimal relations (Lynch & Cuvo, 1995), second languages (Haegele, McComas, Dixon, & Burns, 2011; Joyce, Joyce, & Wellington, 1993), and accurate portion size estimates (Hausman, Borrero, Fisher, & Kahng, 2017) to children and adolescents, as well as to college students (e.g., Critchfield & Fienup, 2010; Fienup, Covey, & Critchfield, 2010;

Sella, Ribeiro, & White, 2014; Walker, Rehfeldt, & Ninness, 2010). In addition, coordination has demonstrated particular utility for skill acquisition in individuals with disabilities and has been used to teach name-face matching to adults with brain injuries (Cowley, Green, & Braunling-McMorrow, 1992), as well as to teach US geography (LeBlanc, Miguel, Cummings, Goldsmith, & Carr, 2003), music skills (Arntzen, Halstadtro, Bjerke, & Halstadtro, 2010), monetary values (Keintz, Miguel, Kao, & Finn, 2011), academic skills (Stanley et al., 2018), and emotions (NoRo, 2005) to individuals with autism. (See chapter 10 of this volume for more on frames of coordination as it pertains to equivalence-based instruction.)

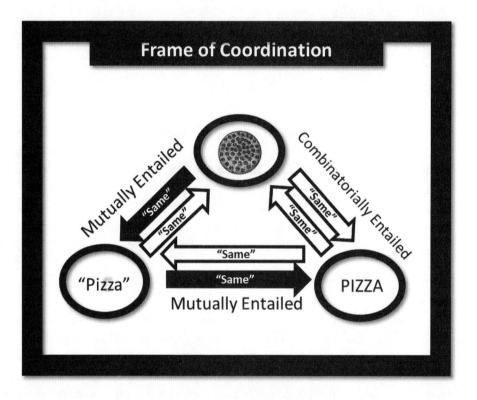

Figure 11.3 Frame of coordination.

DISTINCTION

The relational frame family of **distinction** refers to relating one stimulus in terms of its differences to another stimulus. For example, if an individual is taught that the text C-U-P is the same as the vocal utterance "cup" and then taught that this vocal utterance is different from the vocal utterance "bowl," the individual will then respond not only as though the vocal utterance "bowl" is different from the vocal utterance "cup," but also that it is different from the text C-U-P and vice-versa (see figure 11.4). Again, notice in this example that the relation of sameness must first be established or exist in the individual's repertoire before the relation of difference develops. An additional component of the frame of distinction worth noting is that the relevant dimension by which the stimuli are being differentiated is usually not specified. We do not know exactly which specific features of the stimuli differ, only that they differ in some way. Using the previous example, it is not clear how exactly a bowl and a cup are different, since they are different along several properties (e.g., shape, color, size, texture). Successful AARR does not require this specification; it only requires responding accurately to the contextual cue "different." As a more clinically oriented example, a clinician might target this pattern of responding if attempting to teach a child olfactory discrimination (i.e., discrimination of different scents). The clinician could present a sample scent (e.g., vanilla), followed by a sequentially presented identical scent and a nonidentical scent (e.g., cinnamon) and the discriminative stimulus "Which is different?" If the child received reinforcement following a correct relational response, it would strengthen this pattern of nonarbitrary relational responding. Although this may appear as a trivial skill not worth targeting, it has potential applied utility for individuals with limited verbal repertoires who have difficulty responding accurately to problems involving the contextual cue of different.

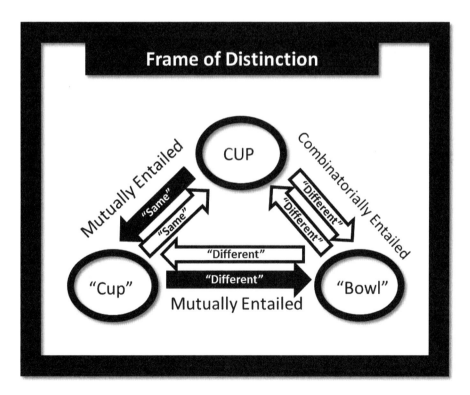

Figure 11.4 Frame of distinction.

Research on the frame of distinction dates back to the first demonstration of AARR, in which participants' responses to arbitrary stimuli were brought under contextual control (Steele & Hayes, 1991). Several basic studies on the frame of distinction have been conducted since then (e.g., Roche & Barnes, 1997), most of which have been demonstrations of basic behavioral phenomena that support underlying theory of RFT, lending further empirical support for the theory. For instance, a study conducted by Dixon and Zlomke (2005) sought to evaluate relational frames of coordination, opposition, and distinction using computerized training procedures consisting of a series of conditional discriminations. During the first part of their study, participants were shown two stimuli on the screen and asked to choose between two arbitrary colored response options that served to describe the stimuli as same, opposite, or different. This procedure established relations of same, opposite, and different between these stimuli. Participants were then exposed to a series of tests to determine if they were able to correctly respond to the derived, symmetrical relations they were initially trained on. All participants demonstrated high levels of correct responding to the tests, as well as when presented with novel stimuli. This study demonstrated that procedures other than match-to-sample can be utilized as a means of establishing relational responding. Although there are several basic and translational studies on the frame of distinction, most demonstrations were conducted with typically developing participants who likely could already respond in accordance with the frame of distinction. Currently, there have been no studies that have successfully established a frame of distinction in individuals previously lacking this pattern of responding. Therefore, substantial applied research is necessary to provide empirically based methodology for teaching these behaviors. A particular population that would greatly benefit from applied procedures for establishing relational framing of distinction is individuals with autism, given that these individuals often have deficits in their relational repertoires.

OPPOSITION

The relational frame family of **opposition** deals with relating one stimulus in terms of another stimulus based on the contextual cue of opposite. For example, if a child was taught an elephant is big and then taught big is the opposite of small, the child will subsequently respond to the elephant as the opposite of small (see figure 11.5). The relational frame families of opposition and distinction are similar to one another, yet differ based on the relevant dimensions of the stimulus (Rehfeldt & Barnes-Holmes, 2009). With the frame of opposition, the stimuli are being differentiated based on some reference point along a continuum of a relevant dimension, with each event at opposing ends of the continuum. In a frame of distinction, the stimuli are also differentiated based on a relevant dimension, but the dimension remains unspecified and is not often implied. For example, an elephant is the opposite of a mouse because each are at differing ends on the continuum of the specified dimension of size. In contrast, the statement "the elephant is different from the mouse" does not indicate which dimension they are being differentiated upon (e.g., size, shape, color).

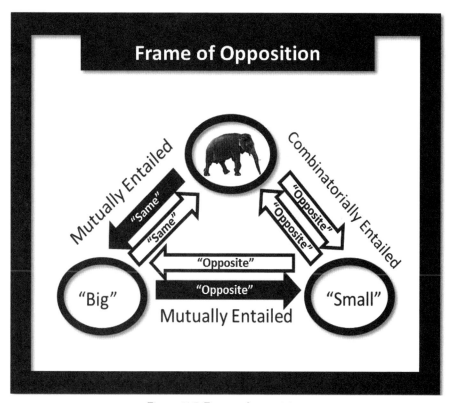

Figure 11.5 Frame of opposition.

Numerous studies have been published on the frame of opposition, both basic and applied. For example, Dymond, Roche, Forsyth, Whelan, and Rhoden (2007) conducted a study demonstrating the transformation of avoidance response functions in accordance with the relational frames of same and opposite. In this experiment, participants were first exposed to a relational training procedure to establish same and opposite relations among arbitrary stimuli. Once relational networks were established, one stimulus from the network was established as discriminative for an avoidance response that canceled a scheduled presentation of an aversive image/sound. Results showed that for participants exposed to the relational training procedure, other stimuli in the network acquired discriminative functions in accordance with the relations of sameness and opposition. In other words, stimuli that were related in a frame of sameness or coordination were discriminative for the previously taught avoidance responses, whereas those that were related in a frame of opposition were not.

Other basic research on the frame of opposition has demonstrated the transformation of consequential function in accordance with the frame of opposition (Whelan & Barnes-Holmes, 2004), as well as generalized responding to the contextual cue of opposite (Healy et al., 2000). Furthermore, Barnes-Holmes, Barnes-Holmes, and Smeets

(2004) conducted a study in which children who were lacking the frame of opposition were exposed to a set of relational trainings that resulted in the emergence of generalized responding in accordance with the frame of opposition. The authors of this study accomplished this by first exposing the participants to a series of training and testing phases, which involved establishing opposite relations among several paper coins and presenting a problem-solving task to the participant. The problem-solving task required the participant to select the coin that could be used to buy as many or as few sweets as possible, which the participant could only accomplish if they could respond in accordance with relational frames of opposition. After a series of trainings, the experimenters were successful in establishing relational responding in accordance with opposition, and this responding generalized to presentations involving novel stimuli and to novel experimenters. These findings support the assumption that relational responding is a generalized operant behavior. Similar studies have been conducted with children with disabilities, and the results suggest that relational training procedures are effective in establishing relational responding of opposition with this population as well (e.g., Dunne, Foody, Barnes-Holmes, Barnes-Holmes, & Murphy, 2014).

COMPARISON

The relational frame of **comparison** deals with relating one stimulus in terms of another based a specific quantitative or qualitative dimension. Common examples of responding in accordance with this relation include more/less, better/worse, bigger/smaller, and faster/slower. Countless other comparative relations among stimuli can exist. It is important to note that the relevant controlling variable for any particular response is relative to the comparison being made; it is not inherent in any property of a particular stimulus. For example, if you showed an individual a large book and a medium-sized book and asked, "Which is bigger?" they would select the large book rather than the medium book. Now, if you presented the medium-sized book alongside a small book, the person would select the medium-sized book. In this example, the medium book is only smaller when it is being compared to a larger stimulus, thus illustrating how a direct relational comparison must be made between the stimuli (see figure 11.6). A more clinically relevant example might involve teaching monetary values of coins to a child, such as the relations among the values of a quarter, a penny, and a dime. To accomplish this, a clinician could present the dime as a sample stimulus along with an array containing a penny and a quarter, while reinforcing the learner's selection of the quarter when asked, "Which is worth more?" The clinician could then repeat the stimulus arrangement except reinforce the learner's selection of the penny when asked, "Which is worth less?" This arrangement would effectively establish the quarter as more than the dime and the penny as less than the dime, while simultaneously allowing for the derivation of the relationship between the quarter and the penny.

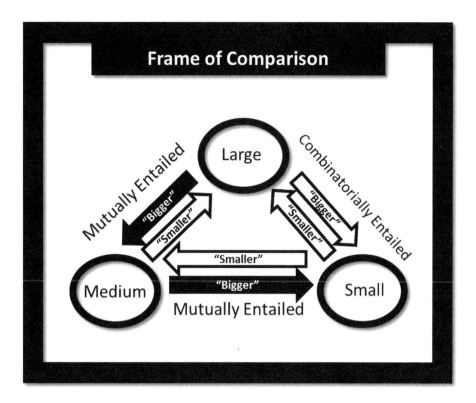

Figure 11.6 Frame of comparison.

Like the relational frame of coordination, the relational frame of comparison has a well-established empirical base. Several basic studies have been conducted demonstrating the emergence of AARR in terms of this frame and the resulting transformation of stimulus functions (e.g., O'Hora, Roche, Barnes-Holmes, & Smeets, 2002; Vitale, Barnes-Holmes, Barnes-Holmes, & Campbell, 2008; Whelan, Barnes-Holmes, & Dymond, 2006). In a study conducted by Dougher, Hamilton, Fink, and Harrington (2007), for instance, the experimenters exposed college students to a series of trainings that established a frame of comparison using arbitrary stimuli. They then taught the participants that stimulus "A" was smaller than stimulus "B," and stimulus "C" was the largest stimulus. The experimenters then paired stimulus "B" with mild shock using respondent conditioning. Next, the experimenters presented the participants with each of the three stimuli and measured changes in their skin conductance. The results showed changes in skin conductance were greater for stimulus "C" than for stimulus "B," and were smaller for stimulus "A" than for stimulus "B" for six out of eight participants. This exemplifies the transformation of stimulus function for the "A" and "C" stimuli, since only "B" was paired with shock. Recent applied studies on this frame have demonstrated that the frame of comparison can be established in typically developed children's repertoires when it is lacking (Berens & Hayes, 2007), and this pattern of responding can generalize to novel stimuli and trainers (Barnes-Holmes, Barnes-Holmes, Smeets, et al., 2004). Data from these studies support AARR as an operant behavior and demonstrate the utility of multiple exemplar training in establishing relational frames. Other studies on the frame of comparison have demonstrated utility in populations of those with disabilities, such as autism (e.g., Dunne et al., 2014).

HIERARCHICAL

Hierarchical relations consist of responding to a stimulus in terms of its *membership to* or as being *part of* another stimulus (see chapter 13 in this volume). In other words, hierarchical relations denote belongingness between a group of stimuli and a common categorical relation, and they are often stated in the form of "stimulus A is an attribute of stimulus B" or "stimulus A is contained by stimulus B." For example, if an individual was taught that cats and dogs belong to mammals, and snakes and lizards belong to reptiles, they would respond to mammals as containing cats and dogs, and reptiles as containing snakes and lizards (see figure 11.7). Similarly, if the individual was taught that mammals and reptiles belong to animals, the individual would respond as though animals contained dogs, cats (both of the mammals), snakes, and lizards (both of the reptiles). Notice, however, that although all dogs are animals, not all animals are dogs. The functions of belongingness flow top down, not bottom up, which is a defining characteristic of hierarchical frames. This type of responding may be the closest to providing an understanding of complex topics such as abstraction and concept formation.

Research on the relational frame of **hierarchy** is less established than the other relational frames, with few empirical demonstrations reported in the literature (see chapter 13). One of the first demonstrations of a hierarchical relation was conducted by Griffee and Dougher (2002), who taught college students a series of relations to arbitrary stimuli and conducted subsequent tests to determine the extent to which the participants formed hierarchical relations. The findings suggested that relational responding could be brought under contextual control consistent with that of hierarchical relations. Furthermore, results showed all stimuli at the bottom of the hierarchy shared functions with stimuli at the top of the hierarchy, but the stimuli at the top of the hierarchy did not share the functions of those at the bottom.

Additional studies have emerged demonstrating the utility of multiple exemplar training to teach hierarchical relations (e.g., Gil, Luciano, Ruiz, & Valdivia-Salas, 2012, 2014). A recent study conducted by Mulhern, Stewart, and Elwee (2017) found a correlation between age, intellectual performance, and hierarchical responding. These data suggest hierarchical responding seems highly correlated with intellectual performance, and hierarchical relational frames tend to develop over the course of several years as individuals age. Although the previously mentioned studies add empirical support for hierarchical relations, further research is necessary on this frame. With the exception of the study by Mulhern et al. (2017), all the previously mentioned studies were conducted with typically developed adults, which limits the generalizability of the data to other populations. Future research can evaluate different procedures for establishing hierarchical relations in children, since children likely have simpler verbal repertoires than adults. Further research is needed on this relational frame in terms of applied demonstrations in populations with disabilities. Research has yet to be conducted that evaluates the effectiveness of procedures in establishing hierarchical frames in individuals lacking this repertoire (see chapter 12 for more on hierarchical frames).

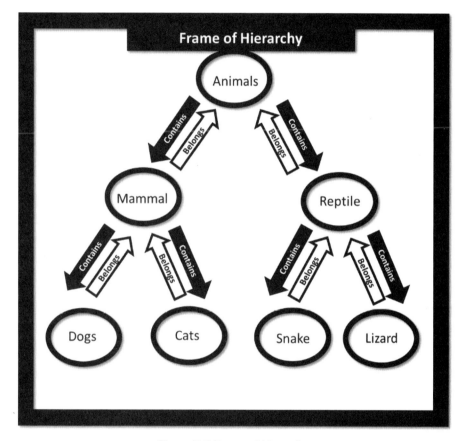

Figure 11.7 Frame of hierarchy.

DEICTIC

Deictic relational frames involve responding to a stimulus in terms of its perspective to the speaker themself. Deictic responding appears to be central to perspective taking and is often under the contextual control of pronouns, such as I/you, me/she, us/them, and so on. Perspective taking can also include spatial relations of here/there and temporal relations of now/then, since one is always speaking here and now and others are always listening there and then. Given that deictic relational responding requires some form of perspective taking by the speaker, this pattern of relational framing is essential for the development of an understanding that different people see different things. Although this seems like a relatively simple skill, it is often deficient in individuals with disabilities such as autism, Down syndrome, and other developmental and intellectual disabilities. Therefore, clinicians can teach deictic relational responding to these individuals in an effort to facilitate the development of many perspective-taking skills.

Studies have reported a relationship between an individual's perspective-taking abilities and intellectual functioning (Gore, Barnes-Holmes, & Murphy, 2010). Individuals who respond with low accuracy to perspective-taking tasks typically have lower intellectual functioning and verbal ability. Other studies have found that those with schizophrenia (Villatte, Monestès, McHugh, Freixa i Baqué, & Loas, 2010) and social anhedonia (Vilardaga, Estévez, Levin, & Hayes, 2012; Villatte, Monestès, McHugh, Freixa i Baqué, & Loas, 2008) demonstrate difficulty responding in accordance with deictic relations, suggesting a potential connection between the two. Several studies have reported successful results in terms of establishing this type of responding in typically developed individuals (e.g., Barnes-Holmes, Barnes-Holmes, & McHugh, 2004; Heagle & Rehfeldt, 2006; Weil, Hayes, & Capurro, 2011) as well as those with neurodevelopmental disabilities (e.g., Belisle et al., 2016; Jackson, Mendoza, & Adams, 2014; Rehfeldt, Dillen, Ziomek, & Kowalchuk, 2007) and schizophrenia (O'Neill & Weil, 2014). Taken together, results from these studies suggest that deictic relating is amenable to training via multiple exemplar training. Research on deictic relations could benefit from additional studies establishing single and double reversals in nontypically developed individuals, especially in terms of here/there and then/now relations. (See chapter 17 for more on perspective taking.)

Implications and Future Directions

Within only a few decades, RFT has generated a significant amount of research, and the number of studies published on derived relational responding and RFT continues to increase (Dymond, May, Munnelly, & Hoon, 2010). There are areas, however, in which additional research would be beneficial, one being cross-sensory stimulus relations (i.e., stimulus relations encompassing more than one sensory modality). Much of the literature on derived relational responding focuses primarily on establishing stimulus relations between visual and vocal stimuli, with little attention given to the olfactory, gustatory, and tactile sense modes. While studies demonstrating cross-modal relational frames exist (e.g., Belanich & Fields, 1999; Dixon, Belisle, Stanley, Munoz, & Speelman, 2017; Toussaint & Tiger, 2010), the limited research does little in providing a well-documented framework for program development by clinicians. Despite the limited demonstrations, movement toward broadening RFT's applications—such as the incorporation of cross-sensory stimulus relations—can be seen with the development of a curricular application based on the theory and concepts underlying RFT, known as the Promoting the Emergence of Advanced Knowledge (PEAK) Relational Training System. PEAK consists of four modules, each designed to target a specific type of learning. The final two modules, the PEAK-Equivalence (Dixon, 2015) and PEAK-Transformation (Dixon, 2016) modules, are directly based on the concepts and principles underlying stimulus equivalence and RFT. These modules incorporate these principles and concepts into (1) an assessment designed to identify an individual's potential relational framing deficits and (2) a curriculum designed to teach the skills identified as deficits by the assessment. There are 184 different programs within the curricula for each of the modules that clinicians can use to teach relational framing skills to their clients. With the programs encompassing a broad range of relational skills, including cross-sensory relational responding, the overarching goal of the PEAK is to establish relational framing as a generalized operant behavior. Clinicians can utilize this technology to facilitate relational framing repertoires, and researchers can use the programs as a framework to answer empirical questions.

A second avenue for future RFT research would be to conduct longitudinal studies. Longitudinal studies would be beneficial for, and add to the existing empirical support for, RFT in a number of ways. First, having longitudinal studies that document the development of relational frames and language would allow for a better analysis of the contribution of relational framing to language development. RFT holds that relational framing emerges first and gives rise to language, or more precisely, that language *consists of* relational framing. Although Lipkens et al. (1993) conducted such an analysis and obtained results supporting this perspective, their data is limited to only a single child. Longitudinal studies would yield meaningful data in terms of whether language or relational framing emerges first. Second, longitudinal research could be afforded to populations that are often lacking complex verbal repertoires. Having longitudinal studies conducted in this area would allow researchers to evaluate the effect relational training may have in producing more complex verbal responses in these individuals.

Researchers may also conduct randomized controlled trials (RCTs) of various RFT-based procedures. While most studies in behavior analysis feature the use of single-subject designs, RCTs would add an additional level of scientific credibility outside of the behavior analytic community. RCTs would also allow researchers to compare the relative effectiveness of RFT and other approaches for producing changes in larger and longer-term repertoires. For example, researchers may compare RFT-based procedures with traditional verbal behavior therapy and control groups to evaluate which form of training is most effective and efficient in producing sophisticated verbal repertoires. RCTs may also be utilized to compare groups of people who receive varying amounts of relational training to evaluate if a dosage effect is present.

Finally, future research can be conducted evaluating the relationship between neurological data, derived relational responding, and language. Numerous studies have evaluated the relationship between derived relational responding and language using functional MRIs (fMRIs; Hinton, Dymond, Von Hecker, & Evans, 2010; Ogawa, Yamazaki, Ueno, Cheng, & Iriki, 2010; Schlund, Cataldo, & Hoehn-Saric, 2008; Schlund, Hoehn-Saric, & Cataldo, 2007) and electroencephalograms (EEGs; e.g.,

Barnes-Holmes et al., 2005; Roche, Linehan, Ward, Dymond, & Rehfeldt, 2004; Yorio, Tabullo, Wainselboim, Barttfeld, & Segura, 2008). Most of these studies involve exposing participants to a series of relational tests while documenting which areas of the brain are activated during exposure to these tests. Rather than documenting which areas of the brain are activated when exposed to relational procedures, future research could attempt to link neurological data with observed behavioral performances.

Conclusion

Sixty years ago, Skinner proposed the first behavior analytic account of human language. This analysis has served as the primary account of language for the behavior analytic community since that time; however, the definition of verbal behavior and the analysis itself was not without limitations. RFT offers an extension that addresses some of the potential limitations of Skinner's analysis. An RFT account of language holds that AARR is the core of language. It becomes increasingly hard to dismiss RFT as the evidence supporting it continues to grow. If the evidence supports the utility of an RFT approach for producing analyses and outcomes that are not possible using Skinner's verbal operants alone, then the utility of continued work using only Skinner's verbal operants may require reexamination.

Since the emergence of RFT in the 1980s, a substantial body of evidence has been established that supports the underlying theoretical and conceptual foundations of RFT. Additionally, RFT has demonstrated ubiquitous utility in terms of teaching skills to individuals and promoting responding that is generative of numerous other behaviors. Although RFT has generated a significant amount of empirical support, many areas could benefit from further empirical exploration. As we move forward in our pursuit of understanding language and cognition, it is imperative that behavior analysis continue to research and scientifically evaluate the underpinnings of language and cognition, while making data-driven decisions rather than appealing to dogma.

Study Questions

1. What characterizes an emergent or derived relation?

2. Distinguish between nonarbitrary relational responding and arbitrarily applicable relational responding.

3. From an RFT perspective, what gives rise to complex human language and cognition?

4. What is a relational frame?

5. What are the three defining properties of a relational frame and how do they differ from one another?

6. According to RFT advocates, what are some potential limitations of a purely Skinnerian approach to language?

7. What are the different types of relational frame families discussed in this chapter?

8. In terms of applied utility, what is the primary advantage offered by programming for the emergence of derived relations?

CHAPTER 12

Assessing and Teaching Complex Relational Operants: Analogy and Hierarchy

Ian Stewart

National University of Ireland, Galway

Shane McLoughlin

University of Chichester, UK

Teresa Mulhern

National University of Ireland, Galway

Siri Ming

Private Practice

E. B. Kirsten

National University of Ireland, Galway

Link and Preview

The preceding chapter surveyed the different types of relational operants. To supplement that discussion, the current chapter focuses exclusively on two in particular, analogy and hierarchy. As was the case with the operants described in chapter 11, the discussion in this chapter is inspired by relational frame theory (Hayes, Barnes-Holmes, & Roche, 2001). Regardless of theoretical focus, the implications for behavior analytic instructional procedures focused upon analogical and hierarchical reasoning are clear.

As has been discussed previously, **relational frame theory** (RFT) has introduced the idea that derived arbitrarily applicable relational responding, or relational framing, is an operant repertoire that underlies human language and cognition. Substantial research findings now support this thesis, including studies on diverse patterns of derived relational responding that show a consistent correlation with complex human performance (e.g., Dymond & Roche, 2013; Zettle, Hayes, Barnes-Holmes, & Biglan, 2016). Much of the work has been focused on relatively simple relational operants (primarily equivalence but also others such as opposition and comparison). However, RFT research has also modeled and investigated more complex derived relations, including analogy and hierarchy, in both children and adults as well as in populations of both typically developing individuals and those with developmental delay. The aim of this chapter is to consider the research on these two particular relatively complex operants.

Analogy

A critical feature of analogy ("A is to B as C is to D") is the transfer of existing knowledge from one context to another through an assessment of the relationship or overlap between them. It is a core component of higher-order language and cognition, including scientific and mathematical skills (e.g., Polya, 1954) as well as problem solving more generally (e.g., Brown, 1989) and is commonly used as a metric of intellectual potential (e.g., Sternberg, 1977). In more basic, functional analytic terms, analogy may underpin much of our untaught behavior in novel contexts because it allows us to use existing knowledge of familiar contexts to guide behavior in new or unfamiliar ones. Examples of this abound in educational and scientific domains. Consider for instance "electron (A) is to nucleus (B) as earth (C) is to sun (D)." This shows the basic process involved in analogy whereby an individual's familiarity with a known domain (e.g., the solar system) can be used to teach them about important aspects of a second unknown domain (e.g., atomic structure). Furthermore, analogy is not just confined to education and science but is evident in diverse situations in everything from the understanding of figurative speech (e.g., "arguing with him is fighting a losing battle") to dealing with new procedures or technologies (e.g., "using that new application is like reading a map").

Based on its perceived importance, the study of analogy has long been a key area within mainstream cognitive research (e.g., Bod, 2009; Gentner, 1983; Vosniadou & Ortony, 1989). In this field, the general consensus is that analogy involves a transfer of relational information from a domain that already exists in memory (usually termed the "source," the "base," or the "vehicle") to a domain to be explained (termed the "target," or the "topic"; see, for example, Vosniadou & Ortony, 1989). Furthermore, over the years a variety of theories have been produced in accordance with this conceptualization (e.g., Christie & Gentner, 2014; Corral & Jones, 2014; Gentner, 1983; Gentner, Holyoak, & Kokinov, 2001; Holyoak & Thagard, 1989; Keane, 1997; Lu, Chen, & Holyoak, 2012; Sullivan & Barner, 2014).

Until the 1990s, behavioral psychologists showed little or no interest in analogical reasoning. The advent of RFT has changed this. RFT posits derived relational responding as the core operant pattern underlying human language and cognition, including all of the complex performances of which we are capable, such as analogy. Equivalence (or coordination) relations are seen as the simplest relational pattern that can be derived and most likely the first to be acquired (e.g., Lipkens, Hayes, & Hayes 1993). In this case, if a learner is told that A is the same as B, then they will readily determine that B is the same as A, even though this has not been directly taught. In this case, the word "same" cues a coordination relation between A and B and enables the learner to derive the mutually entailed B-A coordination relation, assuming an appropriate training history. Furthermore, if this learner is then taught to match B and C, then a more complex mutually entailed A-C equivalence relation can also be derived. Multiple other derived relations have also been empirically shown, including for example, comparison (e.g., "if A is more than B, then B is less than A"), opposition (e.g., "if A is opposite of B, then B is opposite of A"), temporality (e.g., "if A is before B, then B is after A"), and so on. Of key importance from an RFT perspective is the fact that derived relations are arbitrary, and thus the relations need not be based on formal properties of the stimuli. For example, the C and A terms in derived equivalence don't go together because they look like each other in some way (just as the word "cat" does not resemble an actual cat) but based on a learned generalized relational pattern.

A key feature of analogies is that they involve the derivation of an equivalence relation between derived relations themselves. Hence in the analogy "A : B :: C : D," the task is to derive a relation between A and B and between C and D, and also to derive an equivalence relation between these two relations themselves based on the fact that they are the same type of relation. Consider the analogy presented in figure 12.1, denoted as "chair : stool :: glove : sock."

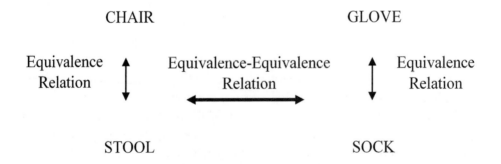

Figure 12.1 A representation of the analogy denoted as "chair : stool :: glove : sock" showing the relations between the elements.

From an RFT perspective, "chair" and "stool" participate in a relation of equivalence (because both are furniture), while "glove" and "sock" also participate in a relation of equivalence (because both are items of clothing). A correct analogical response involves the derivation of these two equivalence relations and the derivation of a further equivalence relation between the relations (i.e., "chair" is equivalent to "stool" in the same way as "glove" is equivalent to "sock" because each are members of the same respective class).

In accordance with this conception, Barnes, Hegarty, and Smeets (1997) reported the first RFT model of analogical reasoning as the derivation of equivalence relations between equivalence relations, or **equivalence-equivalence responding**. In this study, the experimenters first gave participants **match-to-sample** (MTS) training and testing for the induction of several equivalence relations between arbitrary (nonsense syllable) stimuli. In a subsequent, critical stage, they exposed the participants to equivalence-equivalence (analogical) testing, which was similar to the equivalence testing but comprised two different types of trials, referred to as similar–similar and different–different trials, respectively. During the former (similar-similar) trial, the sample stimulus was always a compound of a combinatorially entailed relation of sameness (e.g., B1C1), and the two comparisons included both a compound stimulus formed by a combinatorially entailed relation of sameness (e.g., B3C3) and one formed by a combinatorially entailed relation of distinction (e.g., B3C4). Different–different trials entailed the same comparisons, but this time the sample stimulus was a combinatorially entailed relation of *distinction*, not *sameness*. In the language of RFT, this equivalence-equivalence test was designed to see if participants would relate two derived coordination or distinction relations to each other in accordance with a derived frame of coordination (i.e., relationally frame one relation as being coordinated with another relation). Findings were that a range of participants, including adults as well as nine- and twelve-year-old typically developing children, readily passed this analogical-type test.

A considerable quantity of studies has now extended this work. One aspect on which several follow-up studies have focused is the importance of formal, or nonarbitrary, properties in analogy. Consider again the analogy from figure 12.1: "chair: stool :: glove : sock." In this example, the arbitrary equivalence relation between the words "chair" and "stool" is based, to some extent, on the coordination of physical properties shared by the actual stimuli with which the words are coordinated (i.e., both actual items have legs and a flat platform for sitting on). Similarly, the arbitrary equivalence relation between the words "glove" and "sock" is based on the shared physical properties between the clothing items (i.e., both are made of soft material and fit on parts of the body). Thus, although the two equivalence relations and the equivalence-equivalence relation are entirely arbitrary (there are no formal similarities shared by the words or shared between the words and the actual objects), they can readily be traced back to shared nonarbitrary features. In simple terms, the nonarbitrary features are brought to bear automatically in the derivation of the coordination relations.

A study by Stewart, Barnes-Holmes, Roche, and Smeets (2001) was the first to capture this dimension of analogy, by showing equivalence-equivalence relations based on stimuli that differed along various physical dimensions including, for example, color. Stewart, Barnes-Holmes, Roche, and Smeets (2002) subsequently demonstrated that relating derived relations could allow the discrimination of a common physical similarity between the relations and that this in turn could produce transformation of functions in a separate task. For example, the researchers exposed participants who had previously sorted a series of wooden blocks according to color instead of shape to an analogical protocol in which all trials involved the discrimination of common shapes across the equivalence-equivalence network. After that, participants changed the way they sorted the blocks so that they sorted according to shape. This arguably modeled the experience of "insight" via analogy, whereby analogical responding facilitates a new more effective response to the environment. One more recent study by Ruiz and Luciano (2015) showed that participants would choose equivalence relations involving common physical properties as more closely related and thus more suited to form an equivalence-equivalence relation than equivalence relations involving different physical properties.

RFT research has extended the equivalence-equivalence model in a number of other ways also. For example, a number of researchers have used a method known as the **relational evaluation procedure** (REP) to demonstrate a much more generative model of analogy than in the original (i.e., Barnes et al., 1997) study (Stewart, Barnes-Holmes, & Roche, 2004). Other researchers have measured relating derived relations, as a model of analogy, using reaction times and **event-related potentials** (ERPs). This work showed that, based on presumed lower levels of complexity, derived similar-similar relations were emitted with greater speed than derived different-different relations and were underpinned by different patterns of neural activity (Barnes-Holmes et al., 2005). This outcome is similar to findings seen elsewhere in the neurocognitive literature (Luo et al., 2003) and suggests that the derivation of relations between relations recruits similar neural resources to solving analogies in conventional format. Subsequently, Lipkens and Hayes (2009) demonstrated the derived relating of opposition and comparative relations and showed that directly teaching an analogy between two relations allowed participants to derive a number of untaught analogies between novel stimuli. Finally, Ruiz and Luciano (2011) extended the RFT model of analogy by teaching and testing **cross-domain analogies**, defined as the derived relating of relations across separate relational networks. Whereas the research reviewed thus far focused exclusively on within-domain analogies (e.g., "overcoming a difficult personal problem is like overcoming a difficult work problem"), cross-domain analogies involve the transfer of knowledge from one domain to a completely unrelated domain (e.g., "overcoming a difficult personal problem is like reaching the top of a mountain"). Ruiz and Luciano (2011) found that such analogies could be established via a history of **multiple exemplar training** (MET) and that performance on the model strongly correlated with that on a standard analogy test.

For the present purposes, perhaps the most relevant extension of Barnes et al. (1997) is research assessing derived relations between relations in young children. If RFT researchers are correct that equivalence-equivalence responding represents a basic empirically controlled form of analogy, then it might be expected that performances based on equivalence-equivalence responding would coincide with those recorded on more traditional analogy tests used by mainstream researchers.

For cognitive developmental psychologists, one key issue has always been at what age children become able to engage in analogical reasoning. Because of the view that the relations contained within analogies are complex (often referred to as "higher-order"), it was traditionally believed that children under twelve could not solve analogies (e.g., Piaget, Montangero, & Billeter, 1977). According to Piaget, higher-order relations were present only in formal operational thinking, which is not fully developed until adolescence. Apart from providing empirical evidence supporting this claim, Piaget also tried to identify the incorrect strategies that younger children in his studies may have used to try to solve the analogies. One type of incorrect answer was indicative of simple associations rather than higher-order relations. For example, consider the task "Bicycle is to handlebars as ship is to _____?" In this case the relationship between A and B refers to "steering mechanism," so the correct answer is "rudder." However, children would often select "bird" based on the logic that "both birds and ships are found on lakes." In doing so, they were focused only on the "lower-order" relation in the incomplete pair (C and D); they ignored the first pair (A and B) and thus also missed the higher-order relation between relations.

Goswami and Brown (1990) have also closely examined the types of simple associations to which children incorrectly default in the context of analogies. Their research deployed pictorial stimuli, presenting three of the stimuli from an A : B :: C : D analogical pattern as an incomplete pattern and an additional four stimuli as response options. Consider, for example, the following sequence: "Bird is to nest as dog is to _____" with the options "doghouse," "cat," "another dog," and "a bone." The correct (analogical) choice involves selecting the doghouse, based on the common relation of habitat. The remaining, incorrect options in this case include the bone as a simple associative choice (as dogs and bones frequently go together), the other dog as a match on the basis of "surface similarity" derived primarily from perceptual features, and the cat as a "category match." Findings showed that children between ages four and nine performed at levels significantly above chance, with accuracy positively correlated with age. On this basis, Goswami and Brown (1990) concluded that children as young as four or five can show analogical reasoning, and that increasing age allows them to respond less on the basis of simple associations and more in accordance with higher-order relations.

One possible confound that may have influenced outcomes in both the Piaget et al. (1977) and Goswami and Brown (1990) studies, however, concerns the level of the children's familiarity with the target pairs and the relations between them. In Piaget's research, the children's analogical reasoning skills may have been underestimated because they did not have adequate experience or knowledge of concepts such as steering mechanisms, for example. Regarding the findings of Goswami and Brown, it is possible that age differences may have reflected differences in levels of experience with birds, nests, and so on, rather than in relational competence.

As it happens, data from Goswami and Brown (1989) shed light in this regard. This study involved a series of item analogies based on causal relations (e.g., cutting, wetting, and melting), with which most three- or four-year-olds are familiar. Consider the task

"Playdoh is to cut playdoh as apple is to _____." The experimenters presented tasks such as this to children in conjunction with other tasks that probed their familiarity with the target causal relations. For example, they showed the children three pictures of items that had been causally transformed (e.g., cut playdoh, cut bread, cut apple) and asked them to select the causal agent responsible for the transformation (e.g., a knife, water, the sun). Results showed a strong correlation between scores on the analogies and on the control tasks, thus suggesting the importance of familiarity with target relations for analogical reasoning. This implies, first, that relational knowledge and analogical competence codevelop, and second, that where relational knowledge is high, children even as young as four may derive the target relations and respond in accordance with analogy. Conversely, where relational knowledge is inadequate, associative, and likely incorrect, strategies will dominate.

Carpentier, Smeets, and Barnes-Holmes (2002) used the equivalence-equivalence paradigm to provide a functional analytic test of the emergence of analogical responding in young children. They assessed a range of age groups including adults, nine-year-olds, and five-year-olds. Across several experiments, adults and nine-year-olds successfully demonstrated equivalence-equivalence relations, but the five-year-olds did not. Only when the latter were exposed to equivalence-equivalence type tests in which the composite equivalence relations were directly taught as opposed to being derived did they subsequently demonstrate the target performance. Further empirical support for these findings was reported in follow-up research by Carpentier, Smeets, and Barnes-Holmes (2003).

The fact that five-year-olds in Carpentier et al. (2002) did demonstrate derived analogical relations seems consistent with Goswami and Brown's (1990) research; however, in contrast to the outcomes of the latter, extensive relational pretraining was required. As such, the issue of whether five-year-olds can genuinely show analogical reasoning based on the core processes described here (i.e., the derivation of relations between derived relations) seems as yet open. From the RFT perspective, derived relational abilities should be relatively well honed by age five, and five-year-olds should also have a robust general relational knowledge base. As such, it might be predicted that they could solve at least some analogy tasks, though it would need to be ascertained that such performances are based on derived equivalence-equivalence rather than on some simpler associative basis. In any event, RFT would predict that explicit exemplar training in equivalence-equivalence responding should greatly boost performance on traditional analogy tasks.

As an example of the potential application of the RFT approach to analogy in an applied arena, one relatively recent study used MET to teach children with autism to solve novel metaphors (Persicke, Tarbox, Ranick, & St. Clair, 2012). Metaphor is a subtype of analogy in which a primary function of the relational process is to highlight particular nonarbitrary properties of the analogical target that are shared with the vehicle. For example, the aim of a metaphor such as "He's as busy as a bee" is to highlight how busy the target is by comparing it (he, in this case) to an insect known for being fast moving and productive. Persicke et al. (2012) taught children with autism to solve novel metaphors (e.g., "This apple is candy") through induction of the following steps: (1) stating properties of the target (i.e., apple—it's fruit, grows on trees, tastes sweet), (2) stating properties of the vehicle (i.e., candy—it's food, tastes sweet, rots your teeth), and (3) identifying the property shared between the two, thus identifying the metaphor's meaning (in this case, that the apple tastes sweet). RFT would suggest that a number of relational performances were involved. Teaching the children to relate each stimulus in the metaphor to its respective properties might be seen as instances of equivalence or possibly hierarchical relating, while comparing the inferred properties of the two stimuli in the metaphor arguably consisted of both distinction relating (for nonidentical properties) and coordinate relating (when the shared property was identified). All participants learned to solve novel metaphors, and their responding generalized to novel, untaught metaphors.

In conclusion of the discussion of analogy, in spite of the core importance of analogical reasoning within higher cognition, there remain limited instructional protocols to help establish the necessary skills. From an RFT point of view, the core repertoire of analogy is the capacity to derive relations between relations. As such, a protocol such as that implemented by Carpentier et al. (2002) that targets equivalence-equivalence responding and related composite skills may be useful in establishing the basis of analogical abilities.

Hierarchy

The second complex repertoire under discussion in this chapter is hierarchical relational responding, which RFT sees as underlying responding in accordance with conceptual hierarchies (see figure 12.2). One key example of conceptual hierarchies is **hierarchical classification**, in which classes of stimuli are treated as members of larger classes (e.g., "poodle" is classified as a member of the category "dog," while "dog" is classified as a member of the category "animal," and so on; see e.g., Griffee & Dougher, 2002; Slattery, Stewart, & O'Hora, 2011). Another example is **hierarchical part-whole analysis**, in which elements are treated as parts of larger, more inclusive "wholes" (e.g., "nail" is categorized as part of "finger," while "finger" is categorized as part of "hand," and so on; e.g., Slattery & Stewart, 2014; Stewart, Slattery, Chambers, & Dymond, 2018).

Responding in accordance with conceptual hierarchies is a fundamentally important repertoire with regard to understanding and navigating the world (Bornstein & Mash, 2010; Furrer & Younger, 2008; Gelman, 1988; Kalish & Gelman, 1992; Lin & Murphy, 2001; Markman, 1989; Proffitt, Coley, & Medin, 2000). For example, a young child sufficiently skilled in this repertoire who learns the category of a new person in her environment can derive likely properties of that person, and compare and contrast with other already known people and make predictions about what to expect (e.g., "Jenny is a doctor like my father; that means she treats people who are ill and probably works in a hospital, like he does; she probably knows a lot about medicine and how to treat sick people"). This type of responding can thus facilitate rapid learning and understanding. Furthermore, it is critical for promulgation and promotion of key skills needed in the educational arena, including, for example, logical and scientific thinking. For instance, the understanding of taxonomies (e.g., within biology or chemistry) is heavily dependent on hierarchical organization. As such, hierarchical conceptual responding is a very valuable repertoire in educational terms.

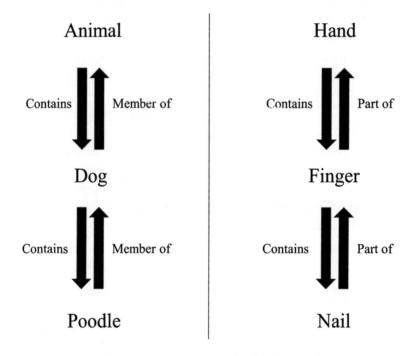

Figure 12.2 Examples of conceptual hierarchies: left, classification hierarchy; right, analytic hierarchy.

A substantial quantity of research on conceptual hierarchies has previously been provided by mainstream cognitive-developmental researchers (e.g., Blewitt, 1994; Deneault & Ricard, 2006; Greene, 1994; Inhelder & Piaget, 1964). The main focus of such work has been hierarchical classification, in which stimuli are organized into a hierarchy of classes within classes. Theorists from this tradition see this phenomenon as involving three core features, namely transitive class containment, asymmetrical class containment, and unilateral property induction.

Transitive class containment refers to classifying a stimulus (A) as a member of a higher-order class (C) on the basis that it is a member of a subclass (B) that is a member of that higher-order class. For example, if a child is taught that "poodle" (A) is a type of "dog" (B), then they may also classify "poodle" as an "animal" (C) on the basis that "dog" (B) is a type of animal. **Asymmetrical class containment** refers to the fact that a higher-order class (e.g., "animal") contains a lower-order class (e.g., "dog") but not vice versa (i.e., "dog" does not contain "animal"). **Unilateral property induction** refers to the concept that properties or features of a higher-order class (e.g., "animal") will also be found in a lower-order class (e.g., "dog") but not vice versa. For example, all animals breathe and thus dogs breathe; however, while dogs have four legs, not all animals do (e.g., Halford, Andrews, & Jensen, 2002). Learning to respond in accordance with these properties is seen as critical for being able to think and derive effectively, especially in the educational arena. At the same time, while important, hierarchical classification may be just one variety of conceptual hierarchical responding. Markman and colleagues (e.g., Markman & Seibert, 1976), for example, compared classification (class/member) type hierarchy with analysis (part/whole) type hierarchy (involving the analysis of a stimulus [e.g., a face] into its parts [e.g., eyes, nose, mouth]). They found that younger children responded with higher accuracy to questions based on analysis hierarchy than to those based on classification hierarchy; accordingly, the authors argued that analysis hierarchy develops earlier than classification hierarchy.

Until recently there has been relatively little research on hierarchical responding by behavior analysts. The first such study was one on hierarchical classification by Griffee and Dougher (2002), who modeled features of responding in accordance with a natural language hierarchy (e.g., robin–bird–animal). This work was an important first step in providing a bottom-up model of hierarchical classification. However, Griffee and Dougher did not explicitly test for the three features that cognitive developmental theorists had suggested were important in hierarchical classification. A more recent study by Slattery et al. (2011) tested the Griffee and Dougher (2002) model for the presence of one of these features, namely, transitive class containment, and found that only two out of eight participants showed this pattern. Though Slattery et al. subsequently adapted the protocol such that participants did begin to show behavior consistent with transitive class containment, they recommended an alternative approach to modeling hierarchical responding including classification using RFT.

Within RFT, hierarchical conceptual responding can be conceptualized and modeled as a pattern of hierarchical relational framing. As with other frames, the latter might be hypothesized to originate in the teaching of nonarbitrary relations. For example, one such nonarbitrary relational pattern that might be important is containment: A child might learn, in one context, to describe things as being physically inside other things (e.g., "my hand is in my glove") and in another, to describe things as containing other things (e.g., "the house contains the doll"). This repertoire might then come under contextual control (i.e., of cues such as the words "in" and "contains") and generalize, developing into more abstract patterns such as classification (i.e., responding to "members" as being contained in "classes") or analysis (i.e., responding to "parts" as being contained within "wholes"). Accordingly, hierarchical responding can be investigated by establishing arbitrary stimuli as cues using nonarbitrary training and then using those cues to establish hierarchical relations (e.g., "member/class") between arbitrary stimuli and gauging additional derived relations and/or properties.

To date, a number of studies have modeled hierarchical responding as hierarchical relational framing. The first of these was conducted by Gil, Luciano, Ruiz, and Valdivia-Salas (2012). In this study, nonarbitrary relational training was used to establish contextual cues for both hierarchical ("includes," "belongs to") as well as "same" and "difference" relations. In the case of the hierarchical cues, for example, participants were exposed to two-dimensional picture stimuli inside two-dimensional outline stimuli and were taught to choose the former in the presence of the "belongs to" cue and to select the latter in the presence of the "includes" cue. In later stages, these cues were used to test expected transformation of functions of arbitrary stimuli via hierarchical relations. As an example, the researchers taught participants that stimulus X.1 had the property of being cold and that it contained a number of other arbitrary stimuli including A1 and B1. They then tested them for whether a stimulus C1, previously derived as being in the same class as A1 and B1, was also cold, and the participants showed this predicted transformation of functions. This study demonstrated a number of empirical and methodological innovations, including (1) the establishment of contextual cues for containment relations and (2) the demonstration of a format in which instructors require learners to select contextual cues for particular frames in order to probe the learners' responding in accordance with multiple stimulus relations (same, different, belongs to, includes). More recently, Gil, Luciano, Ruiz, and Valdivia-Salas (2014) extended this initial study by showing additional patterns of derived hierarchical relations and by providing an improved set of controls over participants' performance.

Both Gil et al. (2012) and Gil et al. (2014) modeled hierarchical responding as broadly conceptualized. As indicated above, however, mainstream research has suggested a number of varieties of hierarchical responding, including hierarchical classification and hierarchical analysis, and these varieties may have functionally important differences. Accordingly, a number of more recent studies have focused on using an RFT approach to investigate particular varieties of conceptual hierarchy.

Slattery and Stewart (2014) used relational framing to model hierarchical classification specifically and to probe for the three core features said to characterize it, namely, transitive class containment, asymmetrical class containment, and unilateral property induction. In Phase 1 of their study, they established arbitrary shapes as contextual cues for hierarchical relational responding, similar to Gil et al. (2012, 2014). In contrast to the Gil et al. studies, however, the core of this training involved a very simple set of colored shape stimuli that might be grouped together only along particular physical dimensions. This aimed to facilitate tight control over the nonarbitrary relational pattern supporting the establishing of the contextual cues, so as to facilitate hierarchical classification in particular, and more specifically, by inducing relating of abstracted common physical properties ("classes") with examples of shapes that included those particular properties ("members"). In Phase 2, the cues thus established were used to teach and test a hierarchical relational network of nonsense syllables. Nine out of ten participants who completed the protocol exhibited predicted patterns of derived relational responding and transformation of functions in accordance with all three of the properties of hierarchical classification by showing asymmetrical mutual entailment, transitive combinatorial entailment, and unidirectional transformation of functions.

Another more recent study has extended Slattery and Stewart's (2014) approach by using a similar two-phase protocol to demonstrate and investigate hierarchical analysis rather than hierarchical classification and to examine whether the properties of this pattern of relational framing would differ from those implicated in hierarchical classification (Stewart et al., 2018). The key difference between this study and the previous one was in Phase 1, which established contextual cues. In Slattery and Stewart's (2014) study, the relations that were relevant in teaching the contextual cues were between concepts based on the abstraction of common physical properties ("classes") and examples of shapes that included those particular properties ("members")—for instance, between the concept "green" and particular shapes that were green. In the Stewart et al. (2018) study, in contrast, the relations that were relevant in teaching the contextual cues were between shapes made up of a number of different parts ("wholes") and examples of the parts themselves ("parts")—for example, between a shape made up of a red triangle, a yellow star, and a green circle (the "whole") and a yellow star (a "part"). As in the previous study, Phase 1 established the functions of contextual cues, and then in Phase 2, these cues were used to teach and test for derived relational responding and transformation of functions. Findings showed a similar pattern of mutual and combinatorial entailment but, in contrast with Slattery and Stewart's (2014) results, the absence of any consistent pattern of transformation of functions. The authors argued that although in part this was predictable—because, in contrast with classification hierarchy, analytic hierarchy is not associated with any particularly clear-cut pattern of transformation of functions—further research would be useful for testing ways in which particular patterns of function transformation might be induced.

These examples of RFT work on hierarchical relational responding show that verbally competent individuals engage in hierarchical relational framing and that this form of behavior underlies patterns of responding in accordance with conceptual hierarchies, including both hierarchical classification and analysis. Recent research has extended this work in directions that are of direct relevance to the current focus on the early development and establishment of these repertoires.

One example is a study by Mulhern, Stewart, and McElwee (2017), who measured patterns of relational framing linked with categorization in a large sample of young (three- to eight-year-old) typically developing children. The protocol correlated framing performance, including nonarbitrary and arbitrary containment and arbitrary hierarchy, with linguistic and cognitive potential as measured by standardized instruments. To assess nonarbitrary containment, the researchers presented children with differently colored boxes in which smaller boxes were physically contained inside larger boxes, and asked the children whether one particular box was inside another or contained the other. To assess arbitrary containment, they presented children with a number of differently colored circles that were physically the same size as each other. The researchers then told the children about one or more "containment" relations between the circles and probed for the derivation of further relations in the absence of any physical containment relations being demonstrated (hence, these tasks probed for arbitrary relations). For example, for mutual entailment tasks, they told the children that one particular colored circle (e.g., the green one) contained another particular colored circle (e.g., the red one) and then tested for predicted derived responding (in this case, that the red one was inside the green one). Finally, to assess arbitrary hierarchy, the researchers presented children with real and nonsense words on a computer screen, told them about one or more "hierarchical class" type relations between the stimuli, and probed to see whether they could correctly derive further relations. For example, for mutual entailment tasks, they told the children that one particular nonsense word (e.g., "tol") was a type of animal and then tested to see whether they could endorse the correct entailment relation (in this case, that the class "animal" contained "tols" as members). As for the previous task, this was an arbitrary relational task because the stimuli representing classes and members did not show any physical relationship of relevance to the task. Results showed expected variation in level of relational categorization skill based on age, as well as strong correlations between relational performance and scoring on standardized measures.

Another recent study, following on from the latter, used an adapted version of the protocol used in Mulhern et al. (2017) to assess and teach relational framing of categorization in young typically developing children and to assess the impact of training on relevant measures of language and categorization (Mulhern, Stewart & McElwee, 2018). In two experiments, the researchers assessed and instructed children in mutual and combinatorial entailment and transformation of functions of hierarchical relations. In Experiment 1, they assessed and instructed five-year-olds in arbitrary containment, while in Experiment 2, they assessed and instructed six-year-olds in arbitrary hierarchy. Both experiments employed a multiple baseline design across responses and participants and compared children receiving instruction with controls. In both experiments, correct responding increased to criterion levels on introduction of teaching, and both generalization and maintenance were observed. Additionally, in both cases the instructional group showed better performance than the controls on measures of language and categorization. Such results suggest that hierarchical framing can be systematically taught and has potential intellectual benefits, though additional research using larger samples and conventional analysis is needed to confirm the latter.

Apart from this work, researchers have also recently applied RFT to the assessment and teaching of **class inclusion responding**, a sub-repertoire that falls under the umbrella of hierarchical classification skill. In a typical example of such a task, the researcher first shows a child an array of stimuli in a particular class that includes two different subclasses, with a greater quantity of one subclass than the other. They then typically ask the child whether there are more members of the more populous subclass or more members of the class. For example, they might show the child an array of red and blue flowers with more red flowers than blue flowers and ask, "Are there more red flowers or are there more flowers?" The aim of the task is to ascertain if children can respond to a stimulus as simultaneously belonging both to a class as well as to a subclass contained in it.

Ming, Mulhern, Stewart, Moran, and Bynum (2018) used an RFT paradigm to assess and train this ability in three typically developing preschoolers (Experiment 1) and three individuals with autism spectrum disorders (Experiment 2). In each of the two experiments, the researchers first assessed the three participants, who failed to demonstrate class inclusion. They then gave them nonarbitrary relational instruction using a nonconcurrent multiple baseline design. More specifically, they showed the participants how the two sets of stimuli used on a particular trial (e.g., pictures of cats and pictures of dogs) might be arranged into separate transparent boxes representing each of the two classes, and then how both of the boxes might themselves be put into a larger transparent box representing the overarching class (i.e., animals). The rationale was that this demonstration of the physical containment relations involved could support establishment of the appropriate relational repertoire. In both experiments, relational teaching successfully established the target repertoire, and subsequent testing demonstrated both maintenance and generalization to untrained stimulus sets.

In conclusion, with regard to conceptual hierarchy, as is the case with analogical reasoning, there remain relatively limited instructional protocols to help establish the necessary skills. We have described a number of approaches based on recent empirical studies that might be employed in this context. However, much further exploration and refinement of these protocols is needed in order to further this work.

Implications and Future Directions

There are a number of topics that require further research related to the current chapter. With regard to the area of analogy, discussed earlier in this chapter, further work is warranted to explore the utility of a protocol that targets equivalence-equivalence responding and related composite skills with young children and individuals with developmental delays. Research exploring generalization and extension beyond core abilities is also needed. For example, once a core repertoire is in place, then MET using more traditional picture-based tasks such as those used by cognitive developmental psychologists might be deployed. Research improving the functional utility of such tasks is also warranted (see, for example, Carpentier, Smeets, Barnes-Holmes, & Stewart, 2004). In addition, in the case of both analogies and metaphors, instructors might query underlying formal or nonarbitrary properties during assessment and highlight these properties during instruction, with a particular emphasis on these in the teaching of metaphor.

Turning to conceptual hierarchy, the Mulhern et al. (2017, 2018) protocols, which evaluated and established containment and hierarchical relational responding, focused on hierarchical classification only while not exploring hierarchical analysis. Furthermore, even in the exploration of hierarchical classification, much further investigation is needed. For example, the protocols used focused on contextual cues for hierarchical relational framing per se (e.g., type of, contains) exclusively. This is reasonable in the case of simpler frames such as coordination or comparison. However, hierarchical relational framing is more complex than these frames in that derivation in accordance with the full scope of hierarchy should implicate other simpler frames also. For example, in addition to framing appropriately in response to the cues of "type of" and "contains," other important aspects of this pattern might also be tested. When two stimuli are framed as being part of the same class, then they should also both be framed as being different from other stimuli framed within a different class and equivalent to each other, in at least some contexts, independent of their physical properties. Such a pattern of responding might be expected from someone with a sufficiently advanced repertoire of hierarchical classification. The Mulhern et al. protocols did not test for such relations; adjusting it so as to do so might be expected to improve its reliability and validity as a test of classification. This would be one useful direction for future work. Despite the fact that further work is needed, however, the protocols described in some of the studies discussed, including especially those focused on assessment and teaching of hierarchical relational frames in children and individuals with developmental delay, do indicate the potential of RFT as an approach to this important repertoire.

Conclusion

The repertoires on which this chapter has focused, namely analogical reasoning and conceptual hierarchical responding, are simultaneously complex but also of central importance in terms of the development of sophisticated thinking and reasoning skills. This chapter indicates that there is potential in adopting an RFT approach to the assessment and instruction of these skills. Key aspects of RFT exemplified in these studies include nonarbitrary relational support, MET of relational patterns, and consistency of contextual control. This work is starting to allow sophisticated behavior analytic investigation of these protocols, which can capture key aspects of the features of these phenomena. Although relational framing paradigms have been discussed and outlined in traditional cognitive developmental literature, developing a functional analytic conception of these repertoires can readily facilitate practically oriented behavior change.

Study Questions

1. What are the core features of analogy as conceptualized by relational frame theory?

2. What part do nonarbitrary features play in analogy? Give an example of an analogy and describe the nonarbitrary features involved.

3. List and briefly describe three ways in which researchers have extended the findings of Barnes, Hegarty, and Smeets (1997).

4. What is the significance of the findings of Carpentier, Smeets, and Barnes-Holmes (2002) with regard to the debate concerning the age at which children become capable of analogical reasoning?

5. What are the three defining properties of hierarchical classification as explored by cognitive developmental researchers?

6. How did Stewart, Slattery, Chambers, and Dymond (2018) extend Slattery and Stewart's (2014) protocol?

7. How did Mulhern, Stewart, and McElwee (2017) assess hierarchical relational framing of categorization?

8. What is class inclusion? Briefly describe how Ming, Mulhern, Stewart, Moran, and Bynum (2018) have approached class inclusion using an RFT paradigm.

CHAPTER 13

Rule-Governed Behavior and Verbal Regulation

Jonathan Tarbox
University of Southern California and FirstSteps for Kids

Vincent Campbell
University of Southern California and FirstSteps for Kids

Savannah Pio
University of Southern California and FirstSteps for Kids

Link and Preview

The present chapter focuses on an important topic in the behavior analysis of language and cognition, rule-governed behavior. While it may seem obvious that much of the behavior of humans is influenced by rules (or "instructions"), there are a number of interesting issues and implications related to this topic. This chapter provides an overview of conceptual foundations, reviews basic and applied research, and suggests several areas for future research and practice in the area of RGB.

The demonstration of the power of direct-acting contingencies of reinforcement to influence behavior is among the greatest contributions of the science of behavior analysis. Indeed, the basic principles of behavior analysis can largely be described as a collection of the ways in which immediate environmental contingencies directly impact the behavior of organisms. However, for humans with complex verbal behavior, the picture is somewhat more complicated. B. F. Skinner (1969) made the observation that talking about the future can affect one's behavior in the present. In particular, rules that describe contingencies can control behavior *as if* the behavior had contacted the contingencies described, *even though it never has in the past.* For example, this book might provide you with a web address that links you to study materials on the Internet, along with a statement that, if you study those materials (behavior), you are likely to get a better grade on the exam (consequence). You might then follow that rule by going to that web address and studying those materials, although you have never engaged in that behavior at that website in the past and so you never could have received reinforcement for it. Put simply, verbally competent humans, starting around the age of three to five (Bentall, Lowe, & Beasty, 1985), can work toward a verbally constructed future that they have never had—and may never have—direct contact with. This is the essence of **rule-governed behavior** (RGB).

Skinner (1974a) pointed out that RGB is critical to human civilization. Aside from cases of observational learning (see chapter 8), without RGB, every individual human would have to contact virtually every direct consequence in order to learn. In some cases, this would be merely inefficient, as in learning to cook without recipes. In other cases, this would be downright deadly, as in learning to avoid poisonous animals and foods, and so on. The earliest developments in agriculture likely involved RGB behavior of some sort because it necessarily involved behaving with respect to a verbally constructed future (e.g., planting today to prepare for harvest time several months away) that was too delayed and infrequent to control behavior directly. Even the development of a behavior as rudimentary as building a hut today because it might rain next week likely involved some participation of RGB, and engaging in behaviors such as these undoubtedly contributed to the survival of the cultures that induced their members to do so. But aside from immediately practical matters of survival and convenience, RGB is critical to creating and maintaining all of the higher-order pillars of civilization. Virtually all laws, for example, are rules that describe behaviors to be avoided and the aversive consequences of failing to do so (Skinner, 1989). The laws of science, as Skinner pointed out, are essentially "rules for effective action" with respect to the natural world (1974a, p. 259). Skinner (1969) explained that rules are largely how knowledge is passed down from one generation to another, so that each generation can learn from its elders, rather than only through trial and error. Without RGB, humanity would quite literally have to reinvent the wheel every generation.

Despite the critical role that RGB plays in civilization, rules can also come to influence behavior in maladaptive ways. Control by rules often overrides control by prevailing contingencies of reinforcement (Baron & Galizio, 1983). For example, a participant in a laboratory experiment may follow the rule "I need to press fast," even though they continue to fail to earn reinforcers on a **differential reinforcement of low rate** (DRL) schedule, or a gambler may continue to follow the rule "I'm going to win; I just need to play one more spin," while losing all their money in a slot machine. Because of the power of rules to influence behavior and because of the ubiquity of rules in daily life, a thorough understanding of what rules are and how they control behavior is likely critical to a comprehensive applied science of behavior. We now turn to a discussion of what, exactly, RGB is.

Defining Rule-Governed Behavior

Rule governed behavior is behavior that occurs due to contact with an antecedent rule and *not* due to prior contact with the contingencies the rule describes (Skinner, 1969). RGB can be contrasted to **contingency-shaped behavior,** which is behavior that occurs due to prior contact with contingencies, *not* contact with rules. For example, if you are told, "Pressing the lever slowly will earn you points," and you then press the lever slowly, that slow rate of lever pressing is likely rule governed, assuming you have not participated in a similar experiment in the past. If you had been given no instructions and you tried pressing the lever quickly and received no points and then tried pressing the lever slowly and then received points, subsequent slow pressing might be primarily contingency shaped. Note that exactly the same topography of behavior (i.e., slow pressing) may be rule governed or contingency shaped purely on the basis of the history and function of the behavior.

Outside of the laboratory, behavior is rarely 100% contingency shaped or 100% rule governed. People talk to themselves frequently about what they are doing and are in constant contact with contingencies, so most behavior is likely partially controlled by both rules and contingencies. A laboratory example might be if the experimenter told you, "Try pressing fast or slow and see what works," and you then follow the rule and come in contact with the contingencies and then continue to press slowly. In this case your slow pressing might be partially controlled by the word "slow" in the experimenter's instructions, partially controlled by the points you received for slow pressing, and perhaps partially controlled by a rule you constructed yourself during that experience with the contingencies (e.g., "Aha, it works better when I press slowly; the experimenter was telling the truth").

What Is a Rule?

If RGB is defined as behavior that occurs due to contact with a rule, then a scientific account requires a technical definition of a rule. Skinner at various times described a rule as a discriminative stimulus (1969, p. 148), as a "contingency specifying stimulus" (1969, p. 169), and as an antecedent that altered the function of other stimuli (1957, p. 359). A rule cannot be a discriminative stimulus because a discriminative stimulus is defined as a stimulus that was present in the past when a behavior was reinforced, and RGB, by definition, has not occurred or been reinforced in the presence of that rule in the past. So it is likely more appropriate to state that rules affect behavior *as though* they were discriminative stimuli. Stating that a rule is a contingency-specifying stimulus gets more to the heart of what rules seem to do—they tell the listener what contingencies are likely to bear on their behavior. But this definition was problematic for decades because we did not yet have a technical definition, in terms of behavioral principles, of what is meant by specification (Hayes, 1991).

Contemporary Accounts of Rules and Rule-Governed Behavior

The crux of the challenge with rules is that they have the function of discriminative stimuli, even though they have never been directly established as such. For the first several decades of research in behavior analysis, little or no research was done that showed that a stimulus can come to have a function other than that which was directly taught. In cases of stimulus generalization, a stimulus comes to function *as though* it were a discriminative stimulus even though the behavior was never reinforced in its presence (e.g., someone tacts all examples of apples as "apple" after learning to tact just a few apples as "apple"), but this is due to the physical similarity between the teaching stimuli and the generalization stimuli (e.g., all apples are round). Rules do not need to be physically similar to other rules that have had the same function in the past. To demonstrate this easily, we could present to you any random combination of action words (e.g., clap, jump, smile), any random combination of temporal words (e.g., before, after, first, last), and any random sequence of the words "do" and "don't," and if you were attending carefully, you could follow the rule, even though you certainly have never done that same sequence of actions in response to a physically similar instruction in the past. In lay terms, you understand the *meaning* of the novel rule, apart from responding to how it is physically similar to rules you have followed in the past.

A functional analysis of meaning, in terms of behavioral principles, was lacking for decades in behavioral research (Parrott, 1984b). Skinner (1957) was clear that the meaning of a word was to be found in the contingencies of reinforcement for the behavior of the speaker (or listener), but what are those contingencies? Starting in the 1970s, Dr. Murray Sidman began research on reading comprehension that later came to be called **stimulus equivalence** (see chapter 10 for in-depth explanation of equivalence). When words participate in equivalence relations with objects, an analysis of these relations may comprise a functional analysis of the "meaning" of those words (Catania, 1997) or of speaking with meaning and listening with understanding (Parrott, 1984b). For example, an English-speaking child learns to tact cars as "car," and then derives the response of pointing to a car when hearing the word "car" (i.e., listener response).

Equivalence research provided a partial explanation for how rules can control behavior *as though* the person had contacted the contingencies described in the rule, because the research showed how words come to have the functions of other stimuli, *as though* the words were those stimuli themselves. For example, the word "clap" can have some of the same functions as seeing someone clapping (e.g., you yourself can clap when you hear the word "clap"). However, rules do not simply provide words that are equivalent to action. Rules also provide words that specify **contingent relations** between antecedents and behaviors (e.g., "If it's raining, take an umbrella"), between behaviors and consequences (e.g., "Clean your room and then you can go out and play"), and between antecedents, behaviors, and consequences (e.g., "If mom is already mad [antecedent], and you ask her for something [behavior], then she is going to say no and you won't get to have it [consequence]"). **Relational frame theory** (RFT; see chapter 11) provides an account of how humans learn to respond to the relations between stimuli in multiple ways, including *conditional* or *causal* relations. According to RFT, the ability to respond to one stimulus as conditional, or contingent upon another, is itself generalized operant behavior learned through multiple exemplar instruction. For example, over perhaps hundreds or thousands of exemplars of a child's parents saying conditional statements that involve two stimuli (e.g., "First eat your veggies, then you get dessert"), the child then responds to new such statements *as though* she has contacted those statements in the past, even though she has not. The antecedent stimuli that are present that cue the contingent relation (e.g., "First/then," "If/then," "If and only if") become functionally substitutable for a stimulus that is discriminative for the actual contingent relation so that the child can respond to those cues as though he has contacted the relation they describe in the past, even though they have not (Tarbox, Tarbox, & O'Hora, 2009).

Figure 13.1 depicts relations involved in a rule that describes an antecedent, a behavior, and a consequence. Such a rule likely involves, at a minimum, (1) an equivalence (or coordinative, in RFT terminology) relation between the word for the antecedent and the actual antecedent, (2) an equivalence relation between the word for the behavior and the actual behavior, and (3) an equivalence relation between the word for the consequence and the actual consequence, plus (4) a conditional relation between all of the above, cued by the words "if" and "then" (Barnes-Holmes, O'Hara, et al., 2001). The complexity of the contingency described by the rule can be increased by cueing additional relations. For example, rules might describe what *not* to do (i.e., frames of distinction), *when* to do something (i.e., temporal frames), that consequences will be bigger or smaller than in the past (i.e., comparative frames), and so on.

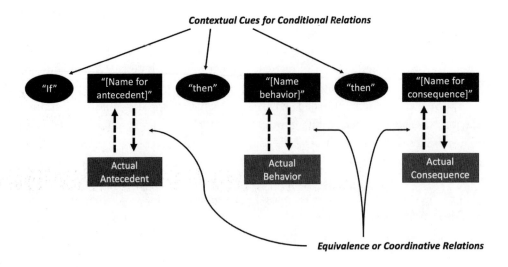

Figure 13.1 Schematic of the minimum relations constituting a complete rule that describes an antecedent, behavior, and consequence.

Dimensions and Characteristics of Rules

The defining feature of a rule would seem to be that it *functionally* describes a contingency to the listener's contacting it, but a virtually endless range of complexity is possible, presumably limited only by the complexity of the verbal and relational repertoire of the listener contacting the rule. Peláez (2013) proposed a framework for analyzing some of the key dimensions of rules that are likely to impact whether a listener will follow the rule: (1) explicitness, (2) accuracy, (3) complexity, (4) source, and (5) time (immediate, delayed, or remote).

The **explicitness of a rule** refers to how clearly and completely the rule describes the contingency. For example, "Clean your room by five o'clock or you lose your cell phone" clearly describes the behavior, when it needs to occur (the antecedent), and the consequence to be avoided. A less explicit version of a similar rule might be "Get some cleaning done, OR ELSE." More explicit rules are more likely to be followed than less explicit rules.

The **accuracy of a rule** is the degree to which the rule describes the actual contingency the listener will experience if they follow the rule. All other things being equal, more accurate rules are probably more likely to be followed, particularly if the listener has a history of contacting and following other accurate rules from similar sources in the past.

The **complexity of a rule** refers to how many variables and relations between variables the rule entails. In the example above, a more complex rule might be "Clean your room *more* than you cleaned it last time, by five o'clock, or you lose your cell phone." That rule is more complex because it also entails the comparative relation *more* between the behavior to be executed now and a behavior executed in the past. All other things being equal, a less complex rule is probably more likely to be followed than a more complex rule.

The **source of the rule** refers to who the speaker is. All other things being equal, rules are more likely to be followed when they are delivered by speakers who have a larger history of mediating reinforcement for following rules they have delivered in the past. Listeners can also derive and speak their own rules, in which case they act as both the speaker who delivers the rule and the listener who listens to it and then follows it (or fails to). Individuals who have a larger history of reinforcement for deriving and following their own rules are probably more likely to follow their own rules, relative to those have less of such a history.

The element of **time** refers to temporal components of the rule. For example, a rule can describe a contingency with a long-delayed or an immediate consequence for behavior (e.g., "If you smoke cigarettes today, you will get cancer in twenty years" versus "If you drink poison, you will die right now"). All else being equal, rules that describe more immediate consequences are probably more likely to be followed than rules that describe more delayed consequences. Another temporal component that could affect the likelihood that a listener will follow the rule is the duration of time that passes from the time the listener contacts the rule to the time the listener has the opportunity to follow the rule. For example, rules that describe what to today or tomorrow are probably more likely to be followed than rules that describe what to do next week, month, or year. Peláez (2013) notes that little research has systematically analyzed these components of rules and that much future research is needed. We return to a brief discussion of these parameters in the "Practice Recommendations" section later in the chapter.

Functional Units of Rule Following

Zettle and Hayes (1986) and Hayes, Zettle, and Rosenfarb (1989) proposed three functionally distinct types of rule following, based on the history that established each repertoire as well as how it functions in the present moment: (1) pliance, (2) tracking, and (3) augmenting.

Pliance is a repertoire of rule following that was acquired due to a history of socially mediated arbitrary reinforcement for following rules. This repertoire is likely established when parents reinforce a child's behavior of doing what they are told by meting out positive and negative reinforcement that is not related in any meaningful way to the natural consequences of the child's behavior. For example, "First take a bath and then I will read you a book," or "Finish your chores or I'll take away video games." The reason for the term pliance," which comes from the word "compliance," is that this repertoire is acquired through arbitrary reinforcement of compliance, per se.

Tracking is a repertoire of rule following that is acquired due to a history of following rules and then coming into contact with the contingencies that the rules describe. Examples include "Take a bath so you are not smelly and your friends don't make fun of you," "Clean your room so that the next time you want to find your toy, you will be able to find it easily," or "Put your shoes on before you go outside and play, so your feet don't get hurt by stepping on sharp rocks." The relation between the behavior and the reinforcer is the primary distinction between pliance and tracking. In pliance, the relation is arbitrary—the consequence is simply whatever the authority figure chooses to use to modify the listener's behavior. In tracking, the consequence is a natural consequence of the behavior. In lay terms, pliance is more like obedience, whereas tracking is more like following accurate advice. Research has shown that individuals may be more likely to form and follow rules that describe actual contingencies, as opposed to just doing what authority figures tell them to do, when authority figures exert less of a presence through monitoring compliance (Donadeli and Strapasson, 2015). To the extent that behavior analysts want to help clients form and follow rules that accurately help them achieve valued goals, this research implies that it may be beneficial to sometimes help clients "figure things out themselves," rather than always directly telling them what to do.

Augmenting is a repertoire of rule-following in which the rule transforms the function of stimuli for the listener. In particular, contact with rules can transform previously neutral stimuli to have novel reinforcing and/or discriminative properties. For example, when being trained by a behavior analyst, a parent of a child with autism might contact the rule "Doing extinction for your child's tantrums is moving him closer to making friends and succeeding in school." Contact with this rule may help mitigate the aversive functions of hearing their child's crying. In addition, the sound of their child crying during a tantrum may have a transformed discriminative-like function of evoking increased effort on the part of the parent, as opposed to avoidance. Augmenting seems to be particularly relevant to behavior that involves what is often referred to as "values" in lay terms (Hayes, Barnes-Holmes, & Roche, 2001). For example, the function of losing money, which is clearly aversive, may be transformed into a source of positive reinforcement via contact with a rule such as "If you donate money to this charity, you will help treat children who have cancer." Rules that control augmenting behavior are referred to as "augmentals." It is worth noting that augmentals have much the same effect as motivating operations (Laraway, Snycerski, Michael, & Poling, 2003), so it may be reasonable to think of augmentals as verbally motivating operations made possible by derived relational responding.

It is important to note that, although repertoires of pliance, tracking, and augmenting likely develop in that respective order in typical child development, the distinction is not intended as implying that one is better or more adaptive than another. In any given person, if one of the repertoires of rule following is excessively strong or rigid, it could have negative consequences. For example, if one's pliance repertoire is excessively strong or rigid, they might only do what they are told, which could severely limit their creativity, career advancement, social relationships, and so on. If one's tracking repertoire is overly strong or rigid, they might never comply with authority figures, even when to do so is critically important (e.g., police, supervisor at work). Finally, if one follows augmentals too rigidly, it can lead to negative life outcomes. For example, the augmental "No pain, no gain" can be useful when followed to a reasonable degree (e.g., moderate exercise) but can be damaging when applied too rigidly (excessive exercise that produces injury) or under contextual circumstances that lead to harm (e.g., in a physically abusive intimate relationship).

Basic Research on Rule-Governed Behavior

In this section, we describe some of the classic basic studies on RGB and some of the major findings, thereby laying the groundwork for our later discussion of applied research and practice recommendations.

Sensitivity

Among the earliest findings in basic research on RGB was that RGB tends to be less sensitive to changes in contingencies, compared with contingency-shaped behavior.

Kaufman, Baron, and Kopp (1966) provided participants with instructions that occasioned behavior that was appropriate to reinforcement schedules but found the behavior was insensitive to changes in those contingencies. Shimoff, Catania, and Matthews (1981) studied schedule sensitivity in two groups of college students by giving one group clear instructions on how to respond by pressing a lever on a DRL schedule. The other group was given no specific instructions; instead their lever-pressing behavior was gradually shaped to occur at a low rate on the DRL schedule. The researchers then changed the reinforcement schedule to reinforce high-rate responding, without giving any new instructions. The lever pressing of the group that was not given explicit rules (e.g., whose behavior was shaped by contingencies) increased in rate when the DRL contingency was removed, whereas the group whose behavior was directly instructed by explicit rules describing DRL did not. The results suggested behavior that is primarily rule governed tends to be less sensitive to changes in contingencies than behavior that is primarily contingency shaped, all other things being equal.

Instructed Versus Derived Rules

A small amount of research has found that the origin of a person's rules may affect how sensitive those rules are to changes in environmental contingencies. For example, participants who were directly instructed on what rules to follow were less sensitive to unsignaled changes in reinforcement schedules than participants who developed their own rules to follow based on past direct contact with contingencies (Catania, Shimoff, & Mathews, 1989). Hayes, Brownstein, Haas, and Greenway (1986) compared sensitivity to contingencies in groups of participants who had been given accurate rules, minimal rules, or partially accurate rules. When confronted with changes in contingencies, participants who had been given accurate rules were less sensitive to these changes than those who were given minimal or only partially accurate rules. Put simply, when participants were given accurate rules describing reinforcement contingencies and they apparently behaved with respect to those contingencies, they actually were not behaving sensitively to the contingencies because their behavior did not change when the contingencies changed. Participants whose behavior was either mostly contingency shaped or controlled by self-derived rules were far more sensitive to changes in contingencies.

Rules Describing Behavior Versus Contingencies

Matthews, Catania, and Shimoff (1985) conducted an experiment with undergraduate college students responding on multiple **random ratio** (RR) and **random interval** (RI) schedules of reinforcement. The researchers taught participants to derive rules that described either behavior (e.g., "press fast" or "press slow") or contingencies (e.g., "The button works after a random number of presses"). They then reversed the actual contingencies, and participants who had been taught to create rules that described behavior continued to follow their old rules, even when the rule was inaccurate. However, participants who had been taught to derive rules that described contingencies were more likely to adjust to the new contingencies. The results suggest that rules that encourage attending to the environment, rather than merely executing specific behaviors, may produce behavior that is more sensitive to changes in the environment.

Applied Research on Rule-Governed Behavior

Despite the tremendous importance of RGB to human civilization, there has been surprisingly little research conducted on applying what we know about RGB to solving problems of social significance. However, what little research currently exists has addressed a rather broad range of topics, and we describe some of this research below.

Gambling

Problem gambling is an interesting behavioral phenomenon because most games, particularly slot machines, by mathematical necessity, do not allow players to win in the long term. While reinforcement is occasionally delivered, if a gambler plays for long enough, it is absolutely certain that they will lose money overall. It is also apparent that, although reinforcement occurs occasionally, the much more frequent direct consequence of gambling is money loss, which would presumably function as extinction or punishment. The fact that most people are not problem gamblers may support this analysis. However, researchers estimate that between 1% and 2% of the US population meets diagnostic criteria for pathological gambling disorder, while up to approximately 14% of the population engages in problem gambling behaviors (Cunningham-Williams et al., 2005). Furthermore, the effects of problem gambling can be severe, so it would seem that, for these individuals, some variables other than direct consequences are likely contributing to gambling.

Dixon (2000) conducted one of the first studies to apply an analysis of RGB to gambling behavior. The study involved manipulating the delivery of rules in a simulated roulette game in which participants were sometimes allowed to place their own bets and the experimenter sometimes dictated where bets would be placed. The dependent variable of interest was the amount of chips wagered. Participants consistently wagered more chips when they had control over chip placement versus when the experimenter did, despite there being no difference in the probability of winning. When the experimenter provided the participants with accurate rules (e.g., "I cannot pick numbers that make you lose"), the difference in wagering between participant-controlled versus experimenter-controlled trials decreased substantially. The implications of this study are that gambling behavior may be largely influenced by inaccurate rules that gamblers follow, rather than solely by the reinforcement schedule entailed in the game. In addition, the results imply that interventions that target these rules have the potential to affect gambling behavior.

Public Health

Public health is an area in which RGB is implicated, almost by definition. It is very rarely the case that members of the public receive adaptive, immediate, direct-acting consequences for their health- and safety-related behaviors. Indeed, the immediate consequences of many health- and safety-related behaviors are *maladaptive*. For example, the immediate consequences of smoking, taking off a helmet, having intercourse without condoms, drinking alcohol, consuming illegal drugs, consuming high-calorie processed foods, and so on, can be highly reinforcing. And since the vast majority of typically developing adults do not have professional staff following them during all hours, it is not possible to deliver professionally mediated direct consequences for most behaviors related to public health. RGB would seem particularly relevant to the area of public health, then, and a few researchers have studied rules and/or analyzed how rules might be involved in strengthening and weakening safe and healthy behaviors.

Jonah and Grant (1985) evaluated the effects of a Selective Traffic Enforcement Program (STEP) in Ottowa, Canada, that involved intensive public education about the benefits of seat belt use and the law requiring it, as well as stepped-up enforcement of seat belt laws via traffic citations. The program was theorized to work via two mechanisms: (1) increased probability of punishment for driving without a seat belt, and (2) increased awareness of this contingency, as well as of the greater safety that seat belts afford. The results of the evaluation showed that seat belt use increased from 64% to 84%, that driver casualties declined by 14%, and that these results were maintained two years after the intervention. For individual drivers who received a speeding citation and then drove more slowly, one might attribute the effects of this intervention to direct-acting punishment, not RGB. However, for anyone whose behavior changed before receiving a citation, the changed behavior was likely largely rule governed. Rules such as "I have to wear a seat belt so I don't get a ticket" and/or "I have to wear a seat belt so I don't get killed in a crash" plausibly helped mediate the effects of the public safety campaign.

Mathews and Dix (1992) hypothesized that RGB may be relevant to influencing how cartoonists depicted characters wearing seat belts in nationally syndicated newspaper cartoons. In a personal letter to eight cartoonists, the experimenters described the importance of drawing cartoon characters wearing seat belts, for the purpose of modeling safe behaviors to the public. The percentage of cartoon characters depicted wearing seat belts increased from 15% to 41%, but the effects were inconsistent across cartoonists. However, the cost of the intervention was essentially zero, and the effect was to alter stimuli contacted by hundreds of thousands of people; therefore, the cost/benefit ratio may have been high. The effects of writing letters to cartoonists must be largely due to RGB. Several of the cartoonists confirmed something of this sort when they wrote back to the researchers, stating that they felt good about "doing the right thing."

Higher Education

A few studies have examined how rules may participate in policies designed to have large-scale effects on student outcomes. Robertson and Peláez (2016) studied the effects of a graduation success initiative (GSI) on rate of retention and on-time graduation in undergraduate college students. The GSI was a university-wide policy that required that students declare a major upon entering school. It was hypothesized that doing so would set the occasion for students to develop rules regarding which classes they needed to take to graduate on time and behave accordingly. Overall, the GSI produced a sixteen-point increase in on-time graduation.

Rules as Supplements to Behavior Intervention Plans

It seems probable that adding rules to effective behavior intervention plans could make those intervention plans work more rapidly, because less direct contact with contingencies may then be needed. However, very little research has systematically evaluated the added benefit of including rules in behavior intervention plans. Watts, Wilder, Gregory, Leon, and Ditzian (2013) compared differential reinforcement of other behavior (DRO) with rules to DRO without rules for decreasing excessive engagement with high-preferred toys in four children with autism. During DRO without rules, the therapist delivered a reinforcer if the child did not engage with a preferred toy for twenty seconds. In the DRO with rules condition, the therapist informed the child that they would receive a reinforcer if they did not touch the preferred toy for twenty seconds. The DRO with rules condition was highly effective for all participants and decreased the behavior more rapidly than the DRO without rules for three of the four participants. For the fourth participant, the DRO without rules condition was not effective at all. It is likely that many other applied behavior analysis studies have also included descriptions of contingencies but did not include that information in the methods section of the manuscripts and/or did not systematically evaluate whether the inclusion of instructions was an effective component of the intervention. Much more research is needed on the effects of rules on larger behavior intervention plans.

Although adding rules to interventions may enhance effectiveness, it is possible that it could have unwanted effects as well. Because rules can decrease the sensitivity of behavior to contingencies, some researchers have suggested that the use of rules as part of interventions should be considered carefully (Hayes, Brownstein, Haas, & Greenway, 1986). Particularly when the goal of an intervention is to strengthen a repertoire that should then be sensitive to natural contingencies, it may not be optimal to use rules to establish particular behaviors early on. For example, when teaching social skills, one could use rules to establish particular topographies quickly (e.g., "Introduce yourself," "Introduce a topic of conversation"), but those behaviors may not then be sufficiently sensitive to actual social contingencies. As a person matures and navigates different social contexts and groups, what works and what doesn't work will change from time to time and context to context. If there are methods for establishing social skills that primarily rely on contingencies, these might be preferred over reliance on rules.

Establishing Repertoires of Rule Following

Most or all of the basic and applied research described above has evaluated RGB in people who already demonstrate a repertoire of rule following. Very little research has established repertoires of RGB in people who did not already demonstrate it. Tarbox, Zuckerman, Bishop, Olive, and O'Hora (2011) used an RFT analysis to design an intervention for establishing the simplest repertoire that might reasonably be conceptualized as rule following: accurately following novel rules that describe antecedents and behaviors. The experimenters used multiple exemplar instruction to teach children with autism, ages three to seven, to follow simple rules that described mastered antecedent stimuli and mastered motor responses. For example, therapists would hold up picture cards and present instructions such as "Clap if this is a carrot" or "If this is a fire truck, then touch your head." During half of the trials, the described antecedent was present, and during the other half it was not (randomly determined). Although the picture cards were known (i.e., participants could respond accurately to them as listeners, in other words, receptively) and the motor responses were known (i.e., the participants could respond accurately to the motor response instructions), the participants could not respond accurately to the if/then conditional statements contained in the instructions. During baseline, participants almost exclusively displayed the motor response described in the rule, regardless of whether the antecedent described in the rule was present. Nontechnically speaking, the participants did not "understand if/then conditionality" or they lacked "cause and effect reasoning." The experimenters taught participants multiple exemplars of rules describing antecedents and behaviors until generalization was observed across untaught rules. Results were variable, but all six participants acquired the skill of responding to untaught rules describing antecedents and behaviors by the end of the study. Although the study was not designed to address pliance directly, the repertoire established in the study might reasonably be analyzed as pliance because the reinforcers included were never related directly to the behaviors described in the rules, nor were the reinforcers described in the rules at all. Instead, the same generalized reinforcers (e.g., food, praise, tokens) were used across all rules that were presented.

In a follow-up study, Wymer, Tarbox, Beavers, and Tullis (2016) extended multiple exemplar instruction to rules that described behaviors and consequences. In the multiple exemplar teaching, a therapist presented rules such as "If you do [behavior], then you get [consequence]." On half of the trials, the described consequence was preferred (e.g., "If you clap hands, you get a ball"), and on the other half, the described consequence was nonpreferred (e.g., "If you stomp your feet, you get broccoli"). Preference was determined at the outset of each session by a mini preference assessment. All three participants rapidly acquired the generalized repertoire of following untaught rules that described preferred and nonpreferred consequences. Although this study was not designed to address tracking directly, the rule following that the study established might be considered tracking because the rules described behaviors and the consequences those behaviors would produce if executed. Put simply, the children with autism were not given reinforcers merely for doing what the experimenter told them to do, but rather, were given whatever reinforcers they chose, based on whether they executed the described behaviors or not. Taken together, the two studies described above provide evidence that a basic repertoire comprising the ability to follow antecedent-behavior and behavior-consequence rules is teachable to children with autism via instruction with multiple exemplars.

When Rule-Governed Behavior Is Maladaptive

Despite the many advantages of RGB, there are potential hazards associated with it as well. Researchers have pointed out that the rigidity that rules can engender can be maladaptive (Hayes, Brownstein, Zettle, Rosenfarb, & Korn, 1986). In other words, even when a rule occasions an adaptive behavior (e.g., "I have to study to do well in school"), if it is followed too rigidly, it may prevent the person from contacting the actual contingencies, for example, overstudying may not actually produce a higher grade and may decrease contact with important social or family relationships. A small number of studies have attempted to directly address the relation between overly rigid RGB and maladaptive behavioral outcomes.

Wulfert, Greenway, Farkas, Hayes, and Dougher (1994) interviewed undergraduate college students using the Scale for Personality Rigidity and divided participants into high-rigidity and low-rigidity groups based on their scores on the scale. They then gave participants a lever-pressing task consisting of a multiple DRL and fixed ratio (FR) schedule. After the participants demonstrated stable responding, the examiners switched the reinforcement schedule to extinction. Half of the participants in each group received accurate instructions about extinction, whereas the other half continued to receive instructions telling them to respond on an FR schedule. Participants in the high-rigidity group continued to respond as though they were on an FR schedule (they continued to follow the FR instructions), whereas participants in the low-rigidity group demonstrated decreased rates of lever pressing (their behavior was sensitive to extinction, as opposed to continuing to follow an inaccurate rule). The implication of these results is that individuals who are reported to "have higher rigidity" are likely to engage in behavior that is more sensitive to control by rules and less sensitive to the contingencies for their behavior. In other words, these individuals may be more likely to follow old rules, even when those rules do not accurately describe real contingencies and even when following those rules may not be in their best interest.

McAuliffe, Hughes, and Barnes-Holmes (2014) compared rigidity of rule following in participants with and without reported depressive symptoms. In the first experiment, the researchers initially gave participants accurate rules that described how to respond on high- or low-rate reinforcement schedules, and participants in both groups responded appropriately. However, when the researchers provided inaccurate rules later, participants who reported higher depressive symptoms rigidly followed old inaccurate rules, despite a lack of reinforcement. The behavior of participants who reported lower depressive symptoms changed when the provided rules were not effective, thereby showing greater sensitivity to contingencies.

In the second experiment, McAuliffe et al. (2014) compared rules that modeled pliance versus tracking. In the pliance condition, experimenters asked participants to read the experimental instructions out loud, and then the experimenters told the participants that they would be watching them carefully and that they would check to see how many points they earned after the experiment. In the tracking condition, experimenters asked the participants to read the instructions silently, and the experimenters could not see the instructions. In addition, experimenters did not indicate that they would watch the participants; they merely told participants to earn as many points as they could. In the pliance condition, participants with higher depressive symptoms were significantly less sensitive to reinforcement contingencies than were participants with less depressive symptoms. However, in the tracking condition, participants with higher depressive symptoms were indistinguishable from participants with lower depressive symptoms. The results suggest that, even when a person has a history of maladaptive, rigid rule adherence, their RGB may be amenable to disruption through strengthening tracking behavior. The larger applied implication of this study is that strengthening repertoires of tracking, as opposed to pliance, may help establish more flexible, sensitive repertoires of behavior. These repertoires could be beneficial to people facing new challenges for which old rules have not prepared them, such as a parent with a newly diagnosed child with autism, or a child with autism encountering new social contingencies in high school or college.

Research on Say-Do Correspondence

Several decades of research have focused on making positive reinforcement contingent on correspondence between what people say and what they do. Space does not permit a comprehensive review of the literature, but readers are encouraged to read Bevill-Davis, Clees, and Gast (2004) for an in-depth review. In an early study, Risley and Hart (1968) implemented a "do-say" teaching procedure in which they first gave preschool children an opportunity to engage in a specific low-frequency play behavior (e.g., playing with blocks and paint), referred to as the "do" component, followed by an opportunity to verbally report which play behaviors they engaged in (the "say" component). The researchers delivered reinforcement contingent upon correspondence between doing and saying, resulting in an increase in those low-frequency play behaviors. Furthermore, these results were maintained, and correspondence was maintained even after it was no longer required for reinforcement, suggesting the strengthening of a generalized operant of accurately describing what one did (e.g., say-do correspondence).

Similar results have been replicated across more socially significant behaviors (Rogers-Warren & Baer, 1976), subsequent studies have replicated the finding of generalization (Ward & Stare, 1990), and a small amount of research has been done on investigating say-do correspondence as generalized repertoires of RGB (Luciano, Heruzo, & Barnes-Holmes, 2001). Overall, the literature on say-do correspondence suggests that relatively young children (i.e., preschool age) can be taught to talk to themselves and others about what they are going to do and that, when reinforcement is provided for accurately predicting their behavior (or describing it after the fact), increases in targeted nonverbal behavior can be produced. Furthermore, the generalization observed in multiple studies seems to suggest that such procedures may establish a generalized repertoire of say-do correspondence. It seems plausible that such behavior may be closely related to, perhaps even a subtype of, RGB, and future research should more explicitly investigate this connection.

Practice Recommendations

The literature on RGB is still in its infancy, particularly in the applied realm. We look forward to a more productive future of research in this area and offer the following preliminary recommendations for practitioners.

Establishing Repertoires of Rule-Governed Behavior

The studies by Tarbox and colleagues (2011) and Wymer and colleagues (2016) provide a relatively straightforward framework for how the repertoire consisting of the ability to follow novel rules can be taught to someone who does not already display it: treat that ability like a generalized operant and teach it through multiple exemplar instruction until generalization to untaught exemplars is demonstrated. The following are practical tips for establishing initial repertoires of rule following:

1. **Assess prerequisite skills.** Learners should already accurately follow a large variety of one-step instructions, should demonstrate a large variety of auditory-visual conditional discriminations (i.e., "receptive labels" or listener behavior), and should likely already display generalized derived symmetry (in RFT jargon, "generalized derived mutually entailed relations of coordination").

2. **Start small.** First teach rules that describe only antecedent-rule relations or only behavior-consequence relations. After learners demonstrate generalization to novel rules, teach the other repertoire. After they demonstrate generalization to novel rules in the second repertoire, consider teaching rules that describe relations between antecedents, behaviors, and consequences.

3. **Expand complexity.** After learners can reliably follow novel rules that describe antecedents, behaviors, and consequences, consider adding in other relational operants. Consider gradually fading in less probable consequences (i.e., not always fixed ratio one). Consider gradually fading in delays between the presentation of the rule and the antecedent described in the rule (i.e., opportunity to follow the rule), and consider gradually fading in delays between the behavior described in the rule and the consequence described in the rule.

4. **Be flexible.** Adjust how instructions are presented, what type of reinforcers are used, how many exemplars are taught at once, and any other relevant procedural details, in order to maximize the learner's response to teaching.

Consider Dimensional Characteristics of Rules

When intervening on a client's RGB and/or when using rules as a component of larger intervention packages, consider the dimensional characteristics of the rules you are providing. As discussed earlier, Peláez (2013) suggests that the following characteristics are likely to impact how effective rules are: (1) explicitness, (2) accuracy, (3) complexity, (4) source (who the speaker is), and (5) time (immediate, delayed, remote). For example, when delivering rules that describe the contingencies of a classroom-wide behavior management program in a school setting, to maximize effectiveness, it might be wise to consider delivering those rules clearly, honestly, simply, from a trusted source (e.g., teacher or principal who has a history of delivering honest rules), frequently (not just at the beginning of the semester), and—for rules that describe consequences—with a relatively short delay (e.g., as opposed to consequences that occur only at the end of a month or semester).

However, as learners are successful with rules that optimize the dimensions described above, consider gradually fading them out. The real-life settings in which clients live will rarely continue to deliver optimal rules, and clients would be well served to learn to become sensitive to rules with less optimal dimensions. As Peláez (2013) notes, little research has systematically evaluated these characteristics of rules, but these dimensions are likely a useful resource for designing and problem solving interventions that contain rules.

Teaching Rules for Flexible Rule-Governed Behavior

Little or no research has been done on how to establish rules that optimize a client's RGB repertoire, but some general practice recommendations are worth discussing and should serve as directions for future research. It seems likely that, all other things being equal, flexible rule following and deriving is probably more adaptive than rigid rule following and deriving. For example, in most challenging situations, a rule like "I need to try different approaches and see what works" is probably going to be more adaptive than

"I have to get it right" or "I have to just do what I am supposed to do." Therefore, it might be worthwhile both to model these types of rules during regular everyday interactions with clients and also to explicitly teach them. It is possible that even varying the topography of rules from one moment to the next might help foster rule flexibility. For example, rather than always saying, "Try to finish your work quickly," one might present a variety of similar rules, such as "Work fast," "Go like a racecar," "Work like lightening," and so on. In addition, there is some evidence to suggest that rules that are more general may engender behavior that is more flexible and sensitive to contingencies, relative to rules that are more specific and prescriptive (Hayes, Brownstein, Haas, & Greenway, 1986). For example, when teaching conversational skills, a rule like "Try noticing what your friends are into" might engender more flexible responding than "Ask your friend what they want to talk about."

Implications and Future Directions

Rule-governed behavior is an area of behavior analysis that is widely acknowledged as important and yet, at the same time, largely ignored in research and practice. This circumstance could be partially due to the previous lack of a behavioral conceptual analysis of rules and RGB that suggested a clear road ahead for studying RGB. Such a practical analysis is now available in RFT, and research has started to very slowly progress. A separate, highly productive line of research is that of **acceptance and commitment therapy** (ACT). ACT is a behavior analytic treatment approach designed to loosen the rigidity with which rules control behavior, particularly rules that evoke responding toward shorter-term, smaller negative reinforcement (e.g., avoidance of social anxiety in the moment) at the cost of longer-term, larger positive reinforcement (e.g., meaningful social relationships). To a very large extent, ACT works by disrupting control of overt behaviors by maladaptive and rigidly held rules and increases control both by less-verbal, direct-acting, short-term contingencies as well as by verbally constructed, long-term positive reinforcement contingencies referred to as "values." Space does not permit a full treatment of ACT here (see chapter 15 for more on ACT), but it is worth noting that the ACT literature has largely developed separately from the applied behavior analysis literature and so the potential of ACT work, which is designed to make repertoires of RGB more flexible and adaptive, has hardly been tapped in terms of its contributions to the mainstream ABA literature. Future researchers should bridge this gap by dismantling package interventions such as ACT and identifying the specific ways in which they affect RGB, weakening maladaptive RGB and strengthening flexible and adaptive repertoires of RGB.

Little or no previous research has investigated the role of RGB in rigidity in autism, but a connection seems plausible. Rigidity might be conceptualized as behavior that is relatively insensitive to environmental contingencies, which is also a well-documented feature of RGB. Future research might investigate how RGB correlates with rigidity in autism and, in particular, whether the rigidity of RGB, itself, is related to overall rigidity in people with autism. More important than mere correlations would be research that attempts to loosen the rigidity of behavioral repertoires displayed by people with autism. One fruitful direction for such research might be to attempt to increase the sensitivity of behavior to contingencies, perhaps by providing strong differential reinforcement for behaviors that contact environmental contingencies versus those that follow rules. For example, perhaps a player who follows the rules of a game might earn a small preferred consequence (e.g., brief praise), whereas a player who invents new rules to the game might earn a much larger reinforcer (e.g., more praise and extended play time). A second and perhaps complimentary direction for research in decreasing the rigidity of RGB in individuals with autism might be to use rules to enhance the flexibility of the individual's RGB itself. For example, one might present rules such as "It's fun to do things differently," "Let's try a new way," and "Let's see what happens if…" while providing strong positive reinforcement for stating, following, and ultimately deriving novel rules of this sort. Much more research in this area is needed.

Conclusion

We hope that the conceptual analyses and practice recommendations presented in this chapter will spur continued research into RGB, as well as program development by practitioners, thereby contributing to a fuller scientific understanding of human behavior. Such an understanding is likely to be relevant to most repertoires of socially significant, verbally influenced behavior, and would be especially relevant to the treatment of autism spectrum disorders. Overly rigid rule following seems to be at the core of many difficulties displayed by more verbal individuals with autism and perhaps at the core of many of the challenges that parents of individuals with autism face as well (Gould, Tarbox, & Coyne, 2017).

Study Questions

1. Rules that describe contingencies can influence behavior even when the individual has never contacted the contingency. Explain this with an example.

2. Comment on the benefits of RGB and explain how humanity would have to "reinvent the wheel" every generation in the absence of RGB.

3. How can RGB also contribute to maladaptive behavior?

4. Provide an example that highlights the difference between rule-governed and contingency-shaped behavior.

5. Why is it difficult to conceptualize a rule as a discriminative stimulus?

6. How does equivalence research contribute to our understanding of rules?

7. Provide an example that includes each of the five components proposed by Peláez (2013).

8. How are the concepts of pliance, tracking, and augmenting useful in the analysis of RGB?

9. Explain and comment on the results of the study by Shimoff, Catania, and Matthews (1981). What is the primary implication of these results?

10. Describe two of the studies in the section titled "Applied Research on Rule-Governed Behavior."

11. What are some areas for future research in the area of RGB, behavioral rigidity, and autism?

12. What are the four recommendations for practice related to establishing RGB?

13. What do the authors recommend in the section titled "Teaching Rules for Flexible Rule-Governed Behavior"?

CHAPTER 14

Problem Solving

Thomas G. Szabo
Florida Institute of Technology

Link and Preview

The present chapter builds upon the previous chapter on rule-governed behavior by focusing on a repertoire that is fundamental to the daily lives of humans—solving problems. The chapter also expands upon prior chapters on relational frame theory and contrasts a behavior analytic approach with cognitive work in the area. The author provides an overview of recent research on problem solving and describes implications for practice.

Skinner's operant analysis of problem solving provides a rich scaffold from which to help learners develop skills for generating novel solutions in situations where they lack an effective response. Despite Skinner's conceptual advances, many efforts to teach problem solving within a behavior analytic framework do not veer far from nonbehavioral approaches. Nevertheless, in recent years, some authors have begun investigating ways to utilize the more intricate aspects of Skinner's analysis in applied studies with children. Relational frame theory offers additional tools that can be used to teach problem-solving skills.

Problem solving is likely critical to everyday human functioning, given that everyday situations rarely provide the perfect environment to support behavioral repertoires exactly as they are first learned. For example, children may need to derive new ways of solving simple problems during play, adolescents may need to come up with novel solutions to complex social conflicts, and adults must find creative solutions to family and work challenges on a regular basis. Many of these situations seem to require a person to execute a new behavior, which they were never directly taught to do, often involving a novel combination of two or more previously learned behaviors in composites that were never directly learned. Despite the importance of problem solving, like many constructs, it is not clearly understood and has not been addressed adequately in behavior analytic conceptual or empirical work. Empirical evaluations of this process are rare in the behavioral literature. Nevertheless, the rudiments of a conceptual analysis were proposed by B.

F. Skinner many decades ago, and a small amount of behavioral research has been done on the topic.

This chapter reviews behavioral and nonbehavioral research on teaching problem solving and related skills, including research using common-sense approaches, and discusses the usefulness of extending Skinner's examination of problem solving with pragmatic verbal analysis, an approach derived from the experimental analysis of human behavior. Additionally, the chapter discusses pragmatic approaches informed by **relational frame theory** (RFT; Hayes, Barnes-Holmes, & Roche, 2001) and concludes with recommendations for practitioners.

Conceptual Approaches to Problem Solving

This section of the chapter reviews conceptual foundations for the study of problem solving, including Skinner's analysis and common cognitive and constructivist approaches.

Skinner's Analysis of Problem Solving

Skinner (1953) proposed that a problem is a situation in which an organism in a state of deprivation or aversive stimulation has no immediately available response that will reduce the deprivation or terminate the aversive condition. The solution to the problem, according to Skinner, is the response that reduces or terminates this nonoptimal condition. In turn, solving the problem involves manipulating the variables of which behavior is a function such that the solution can be emitted. Skinner's interpretation of problem solving involves two parsimonious steps: (1) an establishing operation is in effect, and (2) variables are manipulated until a response that terminates the establishing condition is produced. However, Skinner suggests that in many cases, a third step will be needed in which supplementary stimuli in the form of probes and prompts will be required to occasion the problem-solving response. For example, one might talk to oneself about various potential solutions, draw a diagram, write a list, and so on, all of which produce supplementary stimuli, to which one might then respond with a successful solution.

Cognitive and Constructivist Approaches to Problem Solving

In contrast to Skinner's focus upon manipulatable environmental variables, constructivist accounts focus on the architecture of the mind (Piaget, 1970), and cognitive accounts focus on information-processing models of problem inputs that lead through various mental processes to a solution output (Siegler, 1983). Reese (1994) reviewed fifty-seven applied psychology or education papers dealing with problem solving from these nonbehavioral traditions and identified seven shared steps described in common sense terms by researchers. The sequence of steps Reese documented throughout the constructivist and cognitive problem-solving literature is as follows: Difficulty is Felt, Define the Problem, Gather Information, Identify Possible Solutions, Select a Plan, Carry Out the Plan, Test the Outcome, and Change the Plan.

Skinner's two-step approach underscores the parsimony of easily controlled antecedent and consequent variables as opposed to hypothesized developmental levels at which the steps outlined above can be used or cognitive maps inferred with which to make use of these steps. Yet despite the elegance of Skinner's interpretation, many applied behavior analytic treatments of problem solving examined herein make use of a sequence of steps that are conspicuously similar to those emerging from the cognitive and constructivist perspectives (e.g., Agran, Blanchard, Wehmeyer, & Hughes, 2002; Bernard-Opitz, Sriram, & Nakhoda-Sapuan, 2001; Briscoe, Hoffman, & Bailey, 1975; Cote et al., 2014; Hughes, 1992). Perhaps this is unsurprising: there may be pragmatic utility to breaking down Skinner's composites into common-sense component repertoires. However, the applied science of behavior analysis aims to be conceptually systematic (Baer, Wolf, & Risley, 1968) for the purpose of identifying redundancies and inconsequential variables. Thus, restating these steps in technical terms would be a useful procedure for analysts interested in paring the steps down to those that are necessary and sufficient. For example, the steps discussed above could be recast as follows: Establishing Operation in Effect, Tact the Problem, Arrange and Sample Multiple Discriminative Stimuli-Reinforcement Probabilities, Environment Selects the Most Probabilistically Effective Solution, Emit Behavior, Contact Reinforcers, and Environment Refines the Selection of an Optimal Solution.

In some cases, tacting the problem may be unnecessary. In others, arranging multiple three-term contingency matrices may be redundant because only the putative establishing operation, discriminative stimulus, and reinforcer are needed to evoke effective action. To date, no investigators have conducted component analyses to determine the conditions under which any of these steps are necessary or sufficient in and of themselves.

Behavioral Studies with Common-Sense Approaches

This section reviews behavioral research that follows a more traditional approach to studying problem solving. The studies are grouped into four subsections: a) teaching problem solving in unstructured community settings, b) the self-determined learning model of instruction, c) using video models to teach social problem solving, and d) teaching problem solving strategies for complex categorization tasks.

Teaching Problem Solving in Unstructured Community Settings

In an early community psychology study involving lower-income policy board members, Briscoe et al. (1975) taught participants a three-step procedure that included stating the problem, finding solutions to the problem, and implementing the action to the solution. The experimenters employed supplementary prompts in the form of cue cards and faded in the instructional sequence. In accordance with Skinner's suggestion that successful problem solvers generate verbal stimuli to supplement other behavior in their repertoire, they taught participants to vocalize several possible options and the response to be made that would solve the problem at hand in upcoming board meetings.

Problem and solution tacts as well as action behaviors increased during teaching and during follow-ups. However, some limitations were noted. First, participants did not maintain these skills at high levels. Second, follow-up sessions were conducted with the experimenters present; thus, it is not clear whether the problem-solving behaviors would have been maintained in the absence of an outside observer. Third, the authors reported that although the participants learned the skills they were taught, no data were collected as to whether the skills used by participants led the board to successful accomplishment of its objectives. Fourth, it is important to note that the problem-solving repertoire Briscoe and colleagues taught was really a rule-following repertoire. That is, participants followed the rule to generate options, but there were no contingencies that brought these options under stimulus control, and no attempt was made to assess the degree to which problem solving that followed this pattern was maintained or increased in frequency over time. Finally, although the procedure involved an establishing operation and manipulating variables that facilitate the successful emission of a solution response, the manipulated variables were preselected by the investigators. Since it is unknown whether the solutions helped the board accomplish its aims, it is not entirely certain whether the procedure led to behavior under the control of relevant features of the environment. Taken as a whole, this was an important example of community behavioral psychology with specific, measurable behavioral outcomes, in contrast to frequently reported mental health approaches with affective gains (e.g., Perkins & Zimmerman, 1995). Nevertheless, the study offered only preliminary evidence of the utility of a behavior analytic approach to problem solving, as is likely the norm in a study that is perhaps the first in a particular area of research.

The Self-Determined Learning Model of Instruction

A number of investigators have employed multiple variants of the **self-determined learning model of instruction** (SDLMI; Agran et al., 2002; Cote et al., 2014; Hughes, 1992; Wehmeyer, Palmer, Agran, Mithaug, & Martin, 2000). Common throughout these and other studies from this group of researchers is the use of scripted problem-solving instruction delivered by a teacher that follows a sequence predetermined by the investigator. Hughes (1992) taught individuals with severe intellectual disabilities to verbalize five statements: the problem, a generic class of solution response, a specific solution behavior, the outcome, and a self-reinforcing statement. Wehmeyer et al. (2000) and Agran et al. (2002) taught students with mild disabilities to vocalize answers to the questions "What is my goal?" and "What can I do to make this happen?" and, after emitting a response, to vocalize answers to additional questions, "Did I meet my goal?" and "Do I need to adjust my goal or plan?" Cote et al. (2014) taught elementary students with autism a variation that included identifying problems, determining possible solutions, choosing best solutions, emitting a response, and self-evaluating.

Each of these studies provided evidence that vocal rehearsal of a problem-solving strategy in the presence of an establishing operation could lead to successful utilization of the tactics involved in the strategy. In each of these approaches, too, manipulation of variables with the supplemental support of formal prompts and verbal probe stimuli proved useful. However, as was the case in Briscoe et al. (1975), solving the problem did not result from participants' manipulating variables until the environment selected an effective response. Rather, the experimenters taught a predetermined package of steps, and only after the preplanned response was emitted did participants evaluate the outcomes. Perhaps rather than problem solving in the Skinnerian sense, the participants learned to follow rules describing particular scripted sequences of behaviors. In these studies, problems were solved by the investigators, who constructed external stimuli used to assist others. Skinner described such approaches as "public products of problem solving" (Skinner, 1969, p. 139) that are useful in the accumulation and transmission of social wisdom. As in the constructivist and cognitive models, these top-down efforts solve the problem for others but do little to assess whether learners have developed a problem-solving repertoire that they employ independently in novel situations.

An additional limitation of this body of research is that the majority of studies included problems that were perhaps not really problems in the Skinnerian sense. In particular, most of the problems consisted of the participants' engaging in behaviors that were less problematic for the learners themselves than for others (e.g., engaging in stereotypy in the classroom). Skinner's analysis of a problem requires that the solution to the problem be reinforcing to the person solving the problem. The participants' solving the problem in the studies described above probably amounted more to reinforcement for caregivers than for the participants themselves.

Using Video Models to Teach Social Problem Solving

A slightly closer approximation to teaching what Skinner conceptualized as problem solving is found in Bernard-Opitz et al. (2001). In this study, investigators showed children with autism animated social problems, each with a choice of possible solutions and an additional option to produce novel, unprompted solutions. The experimenter showed and discussed pictures presenting both appropriate and inappropriate responses, prompted innovative solutions by a light and the question, "Do you have any good ideas?" and reinforced novel answers. Probes in which prompts and reinforcers were withheld showed gains, but the study did not assess generalization to novel contexts outside of the laboratory. Additionally, although the rate of appropriate solution selections increased, the authors did not supply data on the rate of alternative solutions generated by learners during probes. Thus, as in the previous studies, children were successfully taught to select previously modeled appropriate answers to social conflict questions, but they were not taught to manipulate variables that would make it possible for them to emit an optimal response of their own.

Teaching Problem-Solving Strategies for Complex Categorization Tasks

Skinner (1957) defined the **intraverbal** as a verbal operant that bears no formal similarity to or point-to-point correspondence with the antecedent verbal stimulus that evokes the response and is maintained by nonspecific social reinforcement. Learning to categorize stimuli when asked to do so can be conceptualized as intraverbal responding that can be hastened by using a verbal problem-solving strategy. Sautter, LeBlanc, Jay, Goldsmith, and Carr (2011) taught typically developing preschoolers a problem-solving strategy for categorization that involved self-prompting with intraverbal chains. The authors found that multiple tact instruction, intraverbal instruction, and mediating-response teaching were necessary but insufficient for producing a problem-solving repertoire. When learners were offered mediating-response prompting (instructional rule-use prompts and pictorial-tact prompts), intraverbal categorization increased and prompt fading was successful. An important finding was that participant use of audible self-prompts, evident initially, declined with use of the problem-solving strategy.

In a follow-up study, Kisamore, Carr, and LeBlanc (2011) examined one of Palmer's (1991) predictions that visual imagining could be taught as a problem-solving strategy to facilitate intraverbal categorization. The authors taught typically developing preschoolers the same prerequisite skills as before (multiple tact instruction, intraverbal instruction) and followed this with visual imagining instruction, visual imagining prompting, and visual imagining prompting plus a rule during probes. In the final phase, experimenters prompted participants with a rule statement prior to beginning the phase. Rules such as "You can *imagine* [italics added] all the places where animals go and tell me what you see" (Kisamore et al., 2011; p. 263) decreased the number of problem-solving prompts needed and appeared to augment visual imagining.

As in Sautter et al. (2011), teaching was necessary but insufficient. Modeling and prompting generated learners' self-prompting and self-probing for supplemental stimuli that occasioned an imaginative response to solve the problem. Skinner's analysis of operant seeing, or "seeing in the absence of any identifiable external support" (Skinner, 1953, p. 271), involves the learner's performing speaker and listener roles simultaneously and the presence of a self-rule-following repertoire. The combination of these skills might have led to automatic reinforcement, curtailing the need to acquire social reinforcement by solving problems vocally aloud. Nevertheless, also as in Sautter et al. (2011), it is unclear whether participants actually used the strategy of visual imagining, since this is a covert and currently unmeasurable behavioral repertoire.

To summarize the work reviewed thus far, applied behavioral literature that explicitly harnesses Skinner's account of verbal problem solving is limited. Many studies appear on the surface to use Skinner's analysis, but upon close examination, they do not meet the inductive criteria that Skinner established. Said differently, many studies provide top-down rules by which instructor-defined solutions are generated in a lock-step manner when learners follow a particular rubric. Although these approaches are grounded in environmental determinants of behavior and are laudable because they do not require an appeal to cognitive structures or innate information-processing formulas, the extent to which they establish generative repertoires of problem solving is unclear. The two studies attempting to teach problem-solving strategies for complex categorization tasks are exceptions in that participants in both experiments used problem-solving strategies to generate their own, novel supplemental stimuli that evoked effective solution responses. It is upon the shoulders of these studies that we now turn to RFT extensions of Skinner's analysis of verbal behavior and applied RFT problem-solving studies.

Pragmatic Verbal Analysis

From an RFT lens, Skinner's definition of problem solving, which "makes the appearance of a solution more probable" (Skinner, 1953, p. 247), limits the term to contexts in which there are obstacles to be avoided or removed. Taken at face value, a rat that pushes a box until it is flush with a cabinet, stands on the box, and pulls a chain to shift a bag of nuts on a counter until it falls to the floor is engaging in problem solving. Although this could be considered one aspect of problem solving, it is a noncomplex form that involves no verbal behavior. Yet in Skinner's conceptualization, it is the intersection of contingency-shaped and rule-governed behaviors that will lead to the most promising lines of applied research (Skinner, 1969), so this same line of reasoning applied to human problem solving would likely be fruitful.

Accounts of problem solving based on RFT analyze problem solving as a verbal repertoire consisting of framing events relationally under the antecedent and consequent control of an absence of effective action (Hayes, Gifford, Townsend, & Barnes-Holmes, 2001). This repertoire involves verbally relating stimuli in ways such that their functions are altered. Verbal problem solving defined as such involves pragmatic verbal analysis. Hayes, Gifford, et al. (2001, p. 90) define **pragmatic verbal analysis** as "framing relationally under the control of abstracted features of the nonarbitrary environment that are themselves framed relationally." In other words, tacting features, functions, and classes of stimulus events leads to tacting features, functions, and classes of the tacts themselves.

This categorization of one's verbal behavior is the procedure by which supplemental stimuli are generated such that discriminated, generalized, and abstracted relations among arbitrary and nonarbitrary stimuli can be brought to bear upon action. Effective verbal problem solving, then, involves such tacting of one's own tacts and conjoint actions, which is perhaps what is meant by the common sense terms "self-reflection" and "self-evaluation." For example, given an establishing operation of being unable to read without glasses and no eyewear at hand, an individual might generate formal probes such as "Where have I been in the last hour that I might find my glasses? I'll check the closet, pantry, and garage." Tacting the locations where the individual has been in the past hour is the first aspect of pragmatic verbal analysis. The second step is to tact features, functions, or classes of these and other tacts that have been successful in the past. To do this, the individual might generate additional supplementary prompts, such as "These are all dark places (feature) where I didn't need glasses, so what are some places I've been recently where I might have stopped to read something (function)?"

When verbal problem solving generalizes to novel contexts, it may be because verbally abstracted physical dimensions of nonarbitrary stimulus events come to serve as relational cues for the frame of coordination between them. In other words, tacting a relation between two stimulus events cues action with respect to that relation. A professor who tells himself, *When I read too many source materials, it's like I'm flooring the gas pedal in my car; I need to find ways to prepare lectures more efficiently* is solving an intellectual problem by comparing it to a physical one. Pragmatic verbal analysis thus produces the context in which acting in accordance with multiple relational frames (i.e., coordination, distinction, opposition, hierarchy) between verbal and physical events become repertoires that promote problem solving.

Strategic Versus Valuative Problem-Solving

From an RFT lens, it can be useful to differentiate strategic from valuative problem solving. In **strategic problem solving**, novel solutions are generated based upon previously successful ones and well-established networks of verbal relations. The result is the formation of linear, step-like problem-solving heuristics, such as those discussed earlier. For example, to solve a problem, a learner might ask themself, *What is the problem, what are two solutions, and what are the pros and cons of each?* **Valuative problem solving** involves the use of relational framing in contexts where no previous verbal history can be brought to bear. Therefore, valuative problem solving results in a number of possible outcomes that can be contacted briefly, either by metaphorical extension or by direct contingency sampling, until the contingencies of reinforcement reveal and select the optimal solution. For example, a writer composing verse about the swells of emotion may insert lines using alliteration and rhyme into a poem and sample each one repeatedly for its effect at bringing the listener's attention to the equivalence between cadences of ocean and emotion.

The important contribution of RFT to these two types of problem solving is the categorization of framing repertoires (i.e., equivalence, distinction, opposition, conditionality, temporality, locality, hierarchy, and deixis). These repertoires have been well documented in at least 288 empirical studies to date (O'Connor, Farrell, Munnelly, & McHugh, 2017) and are discussed at greater length in chapters 11 and 12. They are skill sets that can be taught with multiple exemplars to improve the effectiveness and efficiency of strategic problem-solving repertoires. In other words, relational operants permit for an analysis of the broad and temporally drawn-out behaviors described by Skinner into smaller, more easily analyzed and potentially more easily taught units.

Reducing Delay Discounting

The ability to delay gratification is widely acknowledged to be an important predictor to many socially relevant outcomes (e.g., Dixon, Buono, & Belisle, 2016), and situations that demand self-controlled responses might reasonably be conceptualized as situations that require problem-solving behavior that makes impulsive responding less likely. A prediction from the RFT literature is that the ability to delay responses is, in itself, a problem-solving skill that can be acquired by multiple exposures to tasks involving conditional framing. Given Skinner's analysis, the problem is that the delay to reinforcement is aversive, and the only available response that reduces the aversive condition is an impulsive choice. An ideal solution would be a response that both reduces the aversive stimulation and decreases reliance upon the nonoptimal impulsive choice. Dixon and Holton (2009) evaluated the RFT prediction that such conditions can be met with pragmatic verbal analysis instruction. The authors asked five individuals with gambling disorder to complete a relational responding task involving learning conditional discriminations aimed at transforming the functions of irrelevant stimuli to alter subsequent delay discounting. Arbitrary color stimuli were related to quantitative gambling stimuli in conditional discrimination instruction involving worse than/better than relations. Following teaching and testing, discounting occurred less often; that is, the participants responded to arbitrary color stimuli correlated with larger, later payoffs more than to those correlated with smaller, sooner rewards. This study provides very preliminary support to the possibility that a pragmatic verbal analysis approach to instruction can reduce impulsive responding to the present situation due to the intrusion of stimulus functions transformed via language and due to the increased salience of larger but temporally remote reinforcers after relational instruction. Put more simply, gamblers' impulsive behavior in this study seemed to lessen as they were taught to "reflect back" on poorer and better choices made in the past.

Teaching Metaphorical Reasoning

Metaphorical language is a particularly strange form of verbal behavior because it necessarily involves calling a thing something other than what it literally is. When considered from a behavioral perspective, a speaker might tact a nonverbal stimulus metaphorically by labeling it with a label that is conventionally reserved for tacting a completely different stimulus. For example, a speaker might tact a particularly strong person as a "horse." Depending on the history of the listener with respect to metaphorical verbal behavior, it could be quite challenging to produce a socially successful listener response. An RFT analysis might prove useful for addressing the behavior of the listener. Specifically, effective metaphorical "reasoning" by the listener in such cases may be a skill that will reduce an establishing operation present when an individual is unable to comprehend metaphor used in typical conversation. In order to successfully "think through" a novel metaphor uttered by a speaker, a listener may manipulate verbal variables in accordance with coordination, distinction, and hierarchy frames to solve the problem of how to respond intraverbally to speaker metaphors.

Based on the analysis described above, Persicke, Tarbox, Ranick, and St. Clair (2012) taught children with autism to attend to relevant contextual cues surrounding a metaphor and to engage in reciprocal relational responding to respond correctly to metaphorical questions. The metaphorical questions involved asking the participants to explain the meaning of metaphors that combined two seemingly unrelated stimuli by identifying the shared feature of the two stimuli. To do this, the experimenters prompted the participants to talk to themselves about the features of one stimulus (i.e., hierarchical relating) and then the features of the other stimulus (hierarchical relating), and then identify which feature was the same between the two stimuli (coordinative relating), thereby providing the answer to the "meaning" of the metaphor. For example, participants might respond to the question "If I told you that the snow was a blanket, what would I mean by that?" with something like "Snow is cold, white, and it covers things, and blankets are warm, they cover you, and they belong on your bed—you must mean that the snow was covering things!" The experimenters instructed the participants on multiple exemplars of metaphors until they demonstrated accurate responding on the first trial of new metaphors that had never before been taught. Two children demonstrated generalized accurate responding after multiple exemplar instruction plus visual prompts (which were faded out), and a third reached mastery criteria after multiple exemplar instruction alone. That the findings generalized to untaught metaphors demonstrates that metaphorical reasoning may be taught to children with language deficits and that once learned, it may be a flexible, generally applicable skill that solves the problem inherent in an aversive condition when a speaker is using an unfamiliar turn of phrase. This strategy for teaching metaphorical reasoning is a kind of pragmatic verbal analysis that facilitates a generalized problem-solving repertoire. That is, participants produced supplemental stimuli to categorize arbitrary and nonarbitrary events in accordance with relational frames of hierarchy, coordination, and distinction and thus solved the problem of how to respond to metaphor.

In summary, research informed by an RFT perspective on problem solving as pragmatic verbal analysis is still in its infancy, but the initial results are promising and consistent across studies. The general findings would appear to be that one's own behavior, one's current circumstances, and one's verbal construction of near future circumstances are all environmental variables to which one can be taught to respond verbally. Put another way, the ability to talk to oneself about one's own behavior, one's current circumstances, and which behaviors are likely to produce preferred future circumstances seems to be a complex repertoire of relational verbal behavior that is teachable via multiple exemplar instruction.

Relevance of Rule Deriving

Chapter 13 addressed **rule-governed behavior** (RGB), and rule following in particular, to a thorough degree, and that will not be repeated here. However, rule deriving may be particularly relevant to problem solving and warrants discussion. **Rule deriving** is a repertoire of behavior consisting of creating rules that describe potential future behaviors and future environmental circumstances and then responding with respect to the rules one just derived. It differs from rule following in that rule following generally entails the delivery of rules by someone else (often an authority figure), whereas rule deriving entails articulating novel rules oneself. Rule deriving fits well in Skinner's analysis of problem solving in that it likely comprises some of the behavior that Skinner posited to occur after the appearance of a problem and before the appearance of the solution. That is, some of what one likely does to modify one's own environment such that a solution is available is talk to oneself about how one might modify one's environment and what the outcomes might be. For example, if a child's favorite toy is not working (i.e., problem) and the child then says to themselves, "Maybe I could check the batteries, or maybe I could ask an adult, or maybe it's just broken—I'll check the batteries!" (problem solving behavior), and then checks the batteries and replaces them (solution) and the toy then works (reinforcer), then it would appear that rule deriving may have played an important role in the chain of problem-solving behaviors.

It is also worth noting that rule-deriving behavior of this sort might provide a behavior analytic way to analyze and teach some of the stages of problem solving proposed by cognitive researchers, including "identify possible solutions and select a plan," as socially meaningful overt behaviors, as opposed to hypothetical constructs. In addition, the RFT analysis of pragmatic verbal analysis described earlier also fits well with an analysis in terms of rule deriving because rule deriving is likely an important part of the self-directed verbal relating that characterizes that repertoire. For all of these reasons, it would appear that rule deriving could be a useful area for further research and conceptual analyses into problem solving.

Unfortunately, very little research has been done on rule deriving, so it is not possible to say with any degree of certainty how the repertoire is acquired or how relevant it is to problem solving. In a recent study on rule deriving, Monclus, Uribio, and Szabo (2016) taught three children with autism (five, seven, and fourteen years of age) to derive their own rules for solving social behavior problems after viewing multiple video models of related situations. To occasion rule formation, the models turned away from the problem, pressed a red button, and looked into the camera as they vocalized options and selected a response. They then pressed the button again and emitted the solution in context. The experimenters then exposed the participants to situations that resembled the problems modeled in videos and instructed them to press a red button, turn to face the experimenter, and derive an if/then statement about the contingencies. All three participants responded effectively to 80% or more of the situations they were exposed to, although two needed a supplemental prompt before responding in at least one of the probes. To assess whether nonverbal behavior (such as handing a toy to a sibling) was under the control of covert rules and whether verbal reports were functionally equivalent to the covert rules, the authors conducted three control procedures known as the silent dog method (Arntzen, Halstradtro, & Halstradtro, 2009; Taylor & O'Reilly, 1997). In the first control, duration from instruction to completion was measured in three novel problems. The second control involved measuring response duration when self-talk was interrupted by another speaker. In the third control, participants taught a confederate to solve the problem using the same rules that they had derived when faced with a similar situation. One participant, a seven-year-old girl, successfully solved all problems and, based on results obtained during the silent dog control procedure, appeared to have done so using self-generated rules.

The types of problems solved by participants in this experiment have applied significance. In addition, pragmatic verbal analysis procedures used to teach problem solving resulted, in some cases, in a generalized repertoire of rule deriving. This is one of the few studies that have attempted to analyze the relationship between covert and overt problem solving and the aspects of pragmatic verbal analysis necessary for establishing this repertoire. More work in this area is needed, yet there seems to be great potential for generating a range of procedures for teaching self-directed verbal relating and precise protocols for teaching rule deriving in context.

Implications and Future Directions

The literature reviewed in this chapter is a promising start to the behavior analytic study of problem solving, but it is probably fair to say that the field of applied behavior analysis is far from conclusively answering how problem-solving skills can be taught. Accordingly, there are a number of implications that can be drawn with regard to both research and practice.

Research Directions

The topic of problem solving presents a number of opportunities for future research and practice. Few studies have examined problem solving from the perspective of pragmatic verbal analysis as described in this chapter. Given this, it seems that entire lines of research are needed to explore this area. In addition, more research is needed in the area of rule deriving, including further conceptual analysis. This work not only is conceptually interesting but has large social implications given the importance of problem solving in day-to-day life.

Practice Guidelines

Despite the limited empirical data on the most effective methods to teach problem solving from an applied behavior analytic perspective, clients receiving applied behavior analytic services, across a wide variety of populations and diagnoses, would benefit from enhanced problem-solving skills. Therefore, we believe it is prudent for practitioners to address such deficits when needed (also see Najdowski, 2017, for a practitioner's manual that includes guidance on teaching problem solving). Based on conceptual analyses from Skinner (1953, 1969), Hayes, Gifford, et al. (2001), and the empirical literature reviewed herein, I offer the following recommendations to guide ABA practice in developing problem-solving repertoires:

1. Identify relevant establishing operations and controlling variables of the desired problem-solving behavior.

2. Provide supplemental stimuli (prompts and probes, both formal and thematic) to aid discrimination. Fade these stimuli when learners can respond independently to desired controlling variables.

3. Teach learners to vocally generate their own prompts and probes. When learners vocalize their problem solving, teachers can shape both verbal and nonverbal responses. The aim is to improve the probability that learners will learn to manipulate only those variables most relevant to their immediate context.

4. After problem-solving skills are acquired, teach learners to reduce the magnitude of their self-prompts and probes. This is important for at least two reasons. First, many learning environments do not tolerate vocal self-talk. Second, when problem solving is competitive, inscrutability is advantageous.

5. Scripted problem-solving instructions serve as strategic supplements. These stimuli can be introduced in various forms so that behavior develops contextual sensitivity to the necessary and sufficient script components for each new problem scenario. The aim of varying these supplemental stimuli is to induce behavioral flexibility (response generalization). Therefore, *fade out scripts as quickly as possible* and consider using *variable multiple exemplars of scripts*, as opposed to only a single script format.

6. Specific elements of traditional problem-solving scripts may or may not be relevant in a given context. For example, emitting a self-reinforcing statement (Hughes, 1992) could be beneficial in situations where solutions do not contact

reinforcement immediately, but not in other circumstances. Another aspect of scripts is what has been termed "strategic problem solving" (Hayes, Gifford, et al., 2001). One type of strategic script is systematic evaluation of the outcomes of problem-solving strategies, which seems to be crucial for future refinement of and generation of new problem-solving strategies.

7. Program for and reinforce stimulus generalization. That is, reinforce the use of problem-solving strategies across novel environments to solidify and contextualize the problem-solving repertoire.

8. Teach learners to respond in accordance with coordination, distinction, opposition, hierarchy, temporal, location, and numerical relational frames. Pragmatic verbal analysis may add appetitive functions to otherwise aversive problem situations. Practice of this kind has also been shown to increase the salience of larger, temporally remote reinforcers.

9. To improve existing problem-solving repertoires and improve the control exerted by the environment, teach learners to self-prompt in accordance with coordination, distinction, opposition, hierarchy, temporal, location, and numerical relational frames.

10. Foster the development of a pragmatic verbal analysis repertoire by asking learners to tact verbally abstracted physical dimensions of nonarbitrary stimuli and to tact their tacts in relational classes. For example, teach children to experiment to see whether baking soda or sugar produces a livelier volcano; then ask them to experiment to see whether smiling or frowning produces livelier conversations. Over multiple exemplars, tacts regarding the relationship between abstracted properties of stimuli will serve as relational cues for behavior in accordance with frames applicable to the context. In the example above, a successful intervention might result in a child's telling you later that he is experimenting to see whether looking in peoples' eyes or looking away results in more people offering to play with him.

11. Where possible, create problem-solving contexts in which learners contact proprioceptive feedback. Problem solving can be taught in physicalized contexts and later prompted in more abstract, verbally demanding situations. As in other learning scenarios, establish contingencies for learners to vocalize physical problem-solving procedures during learning activities and diminish the magnitude of their vocalizations during performances. Fostering the dynamic interplay of rule governance and contingency shaping in this manner can lead to flexible, generally applicable problem-solving behavior.

12. Problem solving, as analyzed here, involves self-directed verbal behavior and evaluation. When acquiring these skills, some learners might emit overly critical or negative self-directed verbal behavior. Avoid establishing excessive or overly

harsh evaluation of one's own behavior (e.g., "I am stupid," "I always mess up"). If you hear responses such as these, express empathy. Let the learner know that solving problems is hard and that you make mistakes too. Encourage learners to be "kind" to themselves by saying things such as, "I caught my mistakes and now I have a solution that works!"

13. As with everything we do in applied behavior analysis, use powerful positive reinforcement and make learning fun. In early stages of instruction, use prompts that are effective enough to prevent repeated errors, thereby preventing teaching from becoming aversive.

Conclusion

The present chapter provided an overview of the important topic of problem solving. Traditional behavior analytic approaches were considered relative to those informed by cognitive and constructivist foundations. After reviewing behavioral studies derived from more traditional foundations, an analysis of problem solving based on relational frame theory—pragmatic verbal analysis—was reviewed. A summary of select research related to this conceptualization was provided, as was an analysis of rule deriving in the context of problem solving. The chapter concluded with implications for further research and guidelines for practice.

Study Questions

1. Why is problem solving a socially important behavioral repertoire?

2. How does Skinner define a problem?

3. Provide an example of a problem using Skinner's conceptualization.

4. What are the two steps involved in Skinner's interpretation of problem solving?

5. List the cognitive steps to problem solving as well as their behavior analytic translation.

6. What was the primary shortcoming of the study by Briscoe, Hoffman, and Bailey (1975)?

7. Comment on the research described in the section "Teaching Problem-Solving Strategies for Complex Categorization Tasks"; be sure to include a strength and weakness of this line of research.

8. Distinguish between the RFT emphases on strategic and valuative problem solving.

9. Describe one of the studies in the section on reducing delay discounting or teaching metaphorical reasoning.

10. What is rule deriving and how does it pertain to the understanding of problem solving?

11. Comment on two of the recommendations for practice. Explain why these two recommendations stand out to you as especially interesting and important.

CHAPTER 15

Second- and Third-Wave Behavior Therapy

Emily K. Sandoz

Department of Psychology, University of Louisiana at Lafayette

Gina Q. Boullion

Department of Psychology, University of Mississippi

D. Owen Rachal

Department of Psychology, University of Louisiana at Lafayette

Link and Preview

This chapter extends the analyses of verbal and nonverbal behavior that compose the body of this book into a greater degree of complexity and a wider scope—specifically, those involved in the second- and third-wave behavior therapies. The content of this chapter consists of behavior analytic treatment approaches that are generally applied outside of the scope of practice of mainstream behavior analysts. With a focus on the variety of complexity of the typically developing human behavioral repertoires, this chapter presents the possibility of extending mainstream behavior analysis both scientifically and practically. In particular, the chapter describes acceptance and commitment therapy, a contemporary behavior analytic third-wave therapy, and addresses the implications for the science and practice of applied behavior analysis.

Behavior analysis has long been challenged with two related issues: (1) the role of private events in the analysis of human behavior, and (2) the application of behavior analysis for the adult outpatient population (e.g., Anderson, Hawkins, & Scotti, 1998; Breger & McGaugh, 1965; Golden, 2009; Wolpe, 1978; Wulfert, 2002; Wynne, 2004). These challenges are particularly salient when considering behavior therapy from a behavior analytic perspective, as individuals seek behavior therapy due to concerns about private events and their impact on behavior, concerns that are relevant for many of the clinical populations that behavior analysts serve.

Behavior Analysis and Private Events

Despite the common impression that behaviorists somehow deny the occurrence of behaviors like thinking and feeling (e.g., Shevrin & Dickman, 1980), the issue of private events in behavior analysis has received much direct and consistent attention in the literature. In 1945, Skinner proposed private events as part of the stimulating conditions that might occasion operant behavior. By 1969, he had clarified the role of private events in his behavioral analysis, including them as part of the behavior being analyzed (Skinner, 1969; pp. 221–268). In fact, for Skinner, the inclusion of private events was an important distinction between methodological and radical behaviorism (Skinner, 1953). Over the years, many behavior analysts clarified (e.g., Branch & Malagodi, 1980; Creel, 1980; Moore, 1980) or extended (e.g., Zuriff, 1979) Skinner's work on private events, while others offered distinct alternative positions on private events from interbehavioral (e.g., Parrott, 1983, 1986) and molar (e.g., Rachlin, 1984) perspectives.

Behavior analysts' positions on the role of private events in radical behaviorism still vary widely with respect to (1) the relevance of private events to a behavioral analysis and (2) the causal status of private events. Many accept Skinner's position, discussing private events not as causes but as still relevant as private behavior, private physiological stimuli, or descriptors of a likelihood of engagement in a particular behavior (see Moore, 2009). Some (e.g., Baum, 2011a, 2011b; Rachlin, 2011) discard private events as irrelevant to the scientific analysis of behavior. Some (e.g., Palmer, 2009, 2011) emphasize the role of private events in scientific interpretation, distinct from analysis but necessary for maintaining a comprehensive science. Others (e.g., Fryling & Hayes, 2015) dispute the distinction of some events as "private," instead positing all psychological events as wholly unique and in-kind observable. And still others (e.g., Dougher, 2013) point to the workability of the inclusion of private events in behavior analysis as it is clinically applied in behavior therapy.

Clinical Behavior Analysis and the Rise of Behavior Therapy

Less consistent attention has been given to **clinical behavior analysis**—the application of behavior analysis to serve adults seeking to address psychological difficulties in outpatient treatment (see Kohlenberg, Tsai, & Dougher, 1993; c.f., Kohlenberg, Bolling, Kanter, & Parker, 2002). Behavior analysts have long been interested in the kinds of difficulties that typically bring adults into outpatient treatment (e.g., anxiety, depression, or other struggles categorized as "psychopathology"). This is evident in early conceptual behavioral accounts of psychopathology. For example, Skinner (1953) rejected the disease model of psychopathology, describing disordered behaviors in terms of the reinforcing context. From the Hullian tradition, Dollard and Miller (1950) provided a book-length account of psychoanalytic principles in terms of drives. This interest is also evident in experimental studies supporting early animal models of psychopathology. For example, Estes and Skinner (1941) attempted to model anxiety along with its disruption of behavior under appetitive control in rats, a study that created the foundation for research on conditioned suppression.

From early on, these behavioral accounts of psychopathology came with behavioral accounts of treatment and behavior change in psychotherapy. Both Skinner's (1953) and Dollard and Miller's (1950) texts, for example, included not only descriptions of psychopathology, but also descriptions of psychotherapy processes in behavioral terms. Neither proposed new approaches or formats to psychotherapy. Instead, they attempted to understand the phenomenon of psychotherapy as it existed at that time in terms of behavioral principles. These conceptual accounts also translated into empirical investigations of psychotherapy from a behavioral perspective in two veins—understanding how these traditional psychotherapies worked, and applying behavioral principles in ways that might work better.

Several lines of inquiry sought to empirically account for psychotherapy processes and outcomes in behavioral terms. This work mostly involved exploring the verbal contingencies at play in the therapy room. Krasner and colleagues conceptualized and modeled experimentally psychotherapy processes using a series of verbal conditioning studies (see Krasner, 1963). Kanfer and colleagues conducted a series of clinical interview and analogue studies manipulating interviewer behavior to directly shape interviewee verbal behaviors (e.g., Kanfer, 1959; see Kanfer, 1961; Kanfer & McBrearty, 1962; Kanfer, Phillips, Matarazzo, & Saslow, 1960; Phillips, Matarazzo, Matarazzo, Saslow, & Kanfer, 1961). As behavior analysts explored the clinical relevance of verbal conditioning processes, however, many came to challenge the central tenet of psychotherapy—that changing verbal behavior in the therapy room could result in broad, generalizable behavior change outside of the therapy room (e.g., Zax & Klein, 1960). In fact, a number of behavior analysts responded to this challenge by rejecting not just the theories behind psychotherapy, but the focus on manipulating verbal contingencies to change verbal behavior at all. And behavior therapy was born.

First Wave of Behavior Therapy

In its first wave, **behavior therapy** all but abandoned the focus on manipulating verbal behavior, focusing instead on changing the direct contingencies controlling the behavioral excesses and deficits classified as psychopathology. Offered as a distinct alternative to psychodynamic psychotherapy, the original behavior therapy movement united behaviorists from disparate traditions around a focus on changing direct contingencies in accordance with specific scientific values. In short, behavior therapists held that behavior change interventions should be

1. supported by coherent theories derived from empirically established basic principles, and

2. comprised of well-established, empirically supported procedures (Hayes, 2004).

Thus, the well-established basic behavioral principles of operant and respondent conditioning were applied in techniques such as counterconditioning, aversion therapy, negative practice, reactive inhibition, and systematic desensitization (see Bandura, 1961; Eysenck, 1960, 1964; Metzner, 1963; Wolpe, 1958, 1961). The evidence supported the effectiveness of these interventions in terms of reducing subjective ratings of distress and maladaptive behavior (e.g., see Grossberg, 1964). Further, research efforts sought to clarify the mechanisms of change in behavioral terms (e.g., see Rachman, 1967, for an early review of systematic desensitization), supplementing data from effectiveness studies with data from animal (e.g., Wilson & Davison, 1971) and analog (e.g., Ross & Proctor, 1973) studies.

With these early successes, behavior therapy grew in prominence. It did not, however, take clinical behavior analysis with it. In fact, interest in the behavioral mechanisms of talk therapy faltered, lying dormant for almost two decades (Kohlenberg et al., 2002). This can be attributed to two issues. First, doubt grew regarding the clinical significance of changing verbal behavior in the therapy session (e.g., see Grossberg, 1964), which characterizes much of the behavior the therapist directly observes and manipulates in adult outpatient treatment. Second, clinical behavior analysis did not rise to behavior therapists' original challenge that psychotherapy be based on evidence supporting not only effectiveness but the basic underlying theory. Accounts of verbal conditioning, and the data supporting them, were of limited relevance to (1) most of the problems for which adults sought outpatient treatment, and (2) the fact that discussing these problems in a therapy session could result in improved functioning outside of a therapy session (see Kohlenberg et al., 1993; Kohlenberg et al., 2002). Until these accounts progressed, clinical behavior analysis would have little to offer, leaving behaviorists to either avoid adult outpatient treatment altogether, employ conditioning concepts with imprecision, or incorporate nonbehavioral analyses to support their work.

Second Wave of Behavior Therapy

Meanwhile, behavior therapy continued to evolve independent of clinical behavior analysis. And as the connections between behaviorism and behavior therapy grew strained, behavior therapists became increasingly accepting of accounts of psychopathology and behavior change that incorporated models of cognitive mediation (e.g., Bandura, 1969). Accordingly, the second wave of behavior therapy (e.g., Bandura, 1974; Beck, 1976; Mahoney, 1974; Meichenbaum, 1977) was dominated by approaches that conceptualized specific psychopathologies as attributable to specific cognitive errors. Changing these behaviors, then, involved using language to correct these errors. Technologies from the first wave of behavior therapy were largely retained but were deemed supplementary to new technologies designed to alter dysfunctional beliefs and problematic cognitive processing.

The commitment to the development of empirically supported theories and clinical procedures was also retained in this era of behavior therapy (see Beck, 2005). For example, behavior therapy researchers sought empirical support for the general cognitive theory of depression (e.g., see Haaga, Dyck, & Ernst, 1991), the content specificity hypothesis (e.g., Greenberg & Beck, 1989; Salkovskis et al., 2000), and the efficacy (e.g., Blackburn, Bishop, Glen, Whalley, & Christie, 1981) and effectiveness (e.g., Cohen, Sullivan, Minde, Novak, & Helwig, 1981) of cognitive behavior therapies. And these efforts were largely successful, fostering the dominance of the second wave of behavior therapy over other forms of intervention for some time.

All but absent from this program of research, however, was the development of basic principles of cognitive change (behavioral or otherwise) and their relationship with overt behavior change. As descriptive data grew matching diagnostic categories with cognitive functioning, the burgeoning body of basic data on cognitive processes was rarely consulted (see Beidel & Turner, 1986). As efficacy data piled up, research on cognitive mediation was conspicuously lacking (see Stevens & Pfost, 1983). In short, the basic idea that behavior changed because cognitive errors changed was simply not considered.

In time, behavior therapy research efforts did take a closer look at cognitive mediation. And among the data that emerged was a series of anomalies that seriously challenged this core idea that direct cognitive changes were necessary for behavior change (see Hayes, 2004). Data on changes over the course of treatment suggested that early positive responses to behavior therapy occurred before clients were exposed to key components (e.g., Ilardi & Craighead, 1994). Results from a large component analysis suggested that cognitive components do not incrementally improve the effectiveness of behavior therapy (Gortner, Gollan, Dobson, & Jacobson, 1998; Jacobson et al., 1996). And data that directly examined purported mechanisms of change were inconsistent at best. For example, several data sets suggested that cognitions covary with symptoms, but without evidence of causal links (e.g., Burns & Spangler, 2001). And as these data threatened the cognitive model that supported behavior therapy's second wave, several different bodies of research converged on an alternative.

Third Wave of Behavior Therapy

In applied research on behavior therapy, novel approaches that deemphasized the role of cognitive mediation began to proliferate. For example, attempts to adapt behavior therapy to chronically suicidal patients resulted in the development of **dialectical behavior therapy** (DBT; Linehan, 1987), which integrates the explicit focus on behavior change that characterized first-wave behavior therapies with the shaping of awareness and acceptance of one's immediate experience. Others (e.g., Wells & Matthews, 1994) focused on the increased attention paid to worry, rumination, and other forms of nonproductive cognition. This resulted in the development of the metacognitive therapy (Wells, 2000), which replaces direct strategies to modify cognitive contents with direct strategies to modify counterproductive metacognitive beliefs (e.g., attributing power to unwanted thoughts). In a more traditional wing of behavior therapy, Barlow and colleagues (e.g., Barlow, 1988; Barlow, Craske, Cerny, & Klosko, 1989) incorporated private events into treatment by extending exposure, based on respondent extinction, to interoceptive cues (e.g., physical sensations associated with anxiety).

Meanwhile, in behavior analysis, two streams of basic research provided the foundation for a coherent and productive theory of language and cognition—**relational frame theory** (RFT; Hayes, Barnes-Holmes, & Roche, 2001). First, the data on **rule-governed behavior** (RGB; see Hayes, 1989) suggested that humans will respond to contingencies contacted via instruction (i.e., via a "rule") even when they conflict with directly experienced contingencies (e.g., Galizio, 1979). In light of the rigidity and insensitivity that characterizes psychopathology, RGB was offered as a basic theoretical account that could support continued conceptual and technical development of behavior therapy (e.g., Zettle & Hayes, 1982). Second, the data on stimulus equivalence in verbally able humans (Sidman, 1971) suggested that when the discriminative functions of one stimulus are conditional upon the presence of another stimulus, the two stimuli come to share functions in a bidirectional manner. Further, these bidirectional relationships among stimuli appeared to emerge, untrained, through combinations of directly trained relationships, and are not limited to equivalence. And in this phenomenon that came to be called **derived relational responding** (DRR; see chapter 4 in this volume) was an account of verbal conditioning that both explained rule-governed behavior and extended beyond.

The development of this program of research on DRR as a conceptualization of verbal behavior also opened the doors for a resurgence in clinical behavior analysis (Kohlenberg et al., 2002). Many of the kinds of problems that brought adults to outpatient behavior therapy were analyzable when viewed according to the basic theory of DRR and transformation of stimulus functions. The verbal stimuli that those humans had learned to effectively discriminate in their world came to share functions with the events themselves. With this, new responses could be learned without direct experience. Humans could learn to fear and avoid events without ever having been exposed to them. Likewise, it was clear that the talk that occurred in therapy could evoke responses that were functionally equivalent to the problematic behaviors in clients' lives and shape new, more effective repertoires. And thus, the third wave of behavior therapy was born.

The third wave of behavior therapy has been described by Hayes (2004) as including several elements:

1. an emphasis on empirical support, coherent at multiple levels of analysis;

2. a focus on generalizable principles of behavior change;

3. a sensitivity to context and function of behavior (both public and private) over form;

4. the aim to expand repertoires to produce breadth and flexibility; and

5. a consistency between analysis of client behavior and that of clinician behavior.

In this way, third-wave behavior therapies returned to the scientific strategy and principles that defined the first wave, but with an explicit account of the role of private events. In short, third-wave behavior therapies tend to focus on cognition and emotion indirectly, changing the context to alter the relationships among private events and overt behaviors, such that the functions of those private events are expanded.

The trends that typify the third wave are evident in behavior therapies from varying theoretical orientations. However, two of the third-wave behavior therapies retained explicit philosophical and theoretical foundations within clinical behavior analysis: functional analytic psychotherapy and acceptance and commitment therapy. **Functional analytic psychotherapy** (FAP; Kohlenberg & Tsai, 1991) focuses on using the therapeutic relationship to analyze, evoke, and shape clinically relevant behaviors. **Acceptance and commitment therapy** (ACT; pronounced "act"; Hayes, Strosahl, & Wilson, 1999, 2012) focuses on undermining problematic impacts of DRR and increasing personally meaningful actions in the presence of unwanted private events. The remainder of this chapter will focus exclusively on ACT.

Acceptance and Commitment Therapy

Acceptance and commitment therapy (Hayes, Strosahl, & Wilson, 1999, 2012) applies RFT and the basic findings on DRR to help people engage in their lives in more personally meaningful ways. ACT is based on RFT's idea that most of the behavioral tendencies typically categorized as psychopathologies are acquired and maintained by complex relational networks (Dymond & Roche, 2009). Specifically, repertoires become dominated by behaviors under rule-governed aversive control (Levin, Hayes, & Vilardaga, 2012). Thus, from the ACT perspective, psychopathology is characterized functionally by **psychological inflexibility**—a response class that involves persistent avoidance, excessive rule governance, and subsequent difficulty taking meaningful action (Blackledge & Drake, 2013; Hayes & Wilson, 1994). Psychological well-being, on the other hand, is characterized functionally by **psychological flexibility**—a response class that reflects sensitivity to both immediate contingencies and verbally constructed values (Blackledge & Drake, 2013).

Scientific Strategy and Support

ACT is grounded in a particular extension of behavior analysis called **contextual behavioral science** (CBS; Hayes, Barnes-Holmes, & Wilson, 2012), which is distinguished by its explicit grounding in functional contextualistic philosophy. **Functional contextualism** (FC) emphasizes a pragmatic approach to scientific pursuit, with the aim being to reliably predict the conditions under which behaviors of social significance occur and change those conditions to exert experimental control or influence. FC further holds that ideally, the behavioral analyses that allow for prediction and control do so with precision (a high degree of specificity), scope (broad applicability), and depth (cohering with other levels of analysis). CBS also explicates a reticulated research approach where theoretical, practical, and multifaceted (i.e., basic, analogue, and applied) empirical efforts are mutually influential in fostering CBS's overall progress. The CBS scientific approach has resulted in the rapid proliferation of studies demonstrating support for the efficacy of ACT in fostering behavior change in a number of domains (see Hayes, Luoma, Bond, Masuda, & Lillis, 2006; Powers, Vörding, & Emmelkamp, 2009; Ruiz, 2010) and for psychological flexibility as the mechanism for improvement (Ruiz, 2012).

Processes

ACT is a process-based therapy, defined not by a specific set of techniques but by a focus on increasing the probability of psychologically flexible behaviors. This is quite distinct from the common focus in psychotherapy on reducing psychological distress or changing problematic thoughts. Instead of aiming to reduce or change the aversive private events associated with various diagnostic categories, ACT practitioners elicit these events and broaden their functions by shaping new, personally meaningful behaviors in their presence. This might involve the integration of any number of techniques from first- or second-wave behavior therapies, from other third-wave behavior therapies, or from outside of behavior therapy altogether. Fidelity to the ACT model simply involves assessing and intervening on the repertoire in terms of psychological flexibility.

In order to assist practitioners in the implementation of ACT, psychological flexibility is often conceptualized as involving six interdependent facets (Hayes, Strosahl, Bunting, Twohig, & Wilson, 2004). Each facet describes a functional dimension of behavior that together represent a unified model of behavior change (Hayes, Pistorello, & Levin, 2012). These facets are described as **mid-level terms**. Like psychological flexibility (and inflexibility), they are not proposed as technical terms, but rather serve to orient practitioners to assessing and intervening on functional dimensions of behavior consistent with the underlying technical account described in RFT (Levin et al., 2012). These six mid-level terms are valued living, present moment awareness, cognitive defusion, experiential acceptance, self-as-context, and committed action.

Valued living. Valued living has been described as the primary purpose of ACT (Hayes et al., 1999), such that psychological flexibility and each of the other core processes are evaluated in terms of the extent to which they foster valued living (Hayes, Strosahl, Bunting, et al., 2004). Valued living refers to any behaviors that are acquired and maintained due to their correspondence with a person's verbally established values (Wilson, Sandoz, Kitchens, & Roberts, 2010). Thus, in ACT, clients verbally clarify their chosen purpose, or the abstract qualities they desire their ongoing behavior to have, along with the specific topographies or goals they can track as potential values-consistent behaviors (see Sandoz & Anderson, 2015). These verbal constructions then serve as formative and motivative augmentals, transforming the functions of the inherent stimulus products and natural consequences of values-consistent behaviors so that they serve as intrinsic reinforcers. In this way, values can foster behavior under rule-governed appetitive control in any conditions (Wilson et al., 2010). Values avoid the rigidity and insensitivity typically associated with verbal control by emphasizing abstract qualities of behavior over specific topographies or outcomes (Levin et al., 2012). For example, the value of "being an extraordinary mother" might involve the acute goal of ignoring tantrums. Once established as such, the entire experience of ignoring, including the sound of the child's cries, could be transformed to reinforce the entire class of values-consistent behaviors. Shaping a more flexible repertoire, then, involves shaping verbalization of both purposes across a range of contexts. In practice, intervening on valued living often involves evoking client descriptions of (1) a specific meaningful moment from memory (e.g., a sweet moment; Wilson & Sandoz, 2008) or imagination (e.g., one's own funeral; see Hayes, Strosahl, & Wilson, 1999), (2) some quality of the client's behavior that makes or has made that moment meaningful, and (3) examples of behaviors that would also be characterized by that meaningful quality.

Present moment awareness. ACT practitioners intervene to build present moment awareness, or flexible, focused awareness of public and private events as they occur (Hayes, Strosahl, Bunting, et al., 2004; Hayes, Pistorello, & Levin, 2012; Levin et al., 2012). Psychological flexibility is characterized by sensitivity to a broad range of stimuli in the changing context, whereas psychological inflexibility is sensitive to a narrow range of aversive events. From the ACT perspective, discrimination of events, both public and private, as they occur, will broaden the aspects of context likely to influence behavior. ACT emphasizes both flexibility and focus, as flexibility of awareness without focus is essentially distractibility, and focused awareness without flexibility is essentially hypervigilance. Instead, present moment awareness as trained in ACT allows for focus on particular stimuli that are significant, and for the shifting of attention when necessary for effective values-consistent behavior. In practice, intervening on present moment awareness often involves guiding clients' attention to aspects of the immediate experience. This could be carried out in an eyes-closed meditation (e.g., a breathing meditation) or simply in conversation (e.g., "What do you notice happening in your body as we speak about this?").

Experiential acceptance. Experiential acceptance involves approaching events that have previously functioned as aversive without attempts to manage or control them (Blackledge & Drake, 2013). Psychological inflexibility is characterized by persistent experiential avoidance, when a small number of difficult, unwanted private events exert extensive aversive control over behavior. This emerges through DRR, where individuals learn to tact certain co-occurring private events (i.e., thoughts, bodily sensations, memories) as emotions (e.g., "anxiety") that should be avoided (Hayes, Strosahl, Wilson, et al.,

2004). Building flexibility involves changing the functional relationship between behavior and the difficult, unwanted private events that have previously functioned as aversive (Levin et al., 2012). In ACT, we shape valued living in the context of unwanted private events, as it is often values-relevant contexts that foster vulnerability by eliciting painful private events. In practice, intervening on experiential acceptance often involves use of metaphor to practice approach of unwanted experiences. For example, the therapist might instruct a client to interact with an object that symbolizes their pain as they typically do (e.g., by swatting or pushing it away), then to interact with it as they would a butterfly (e.g., gently letting it land in cupped hands and holding still to observe it; Boone & Cannici, 2013).

Cognitive defusion. Cognitive defusion (originally called "deliteralization"; Hayes et al., 1999) involves awareness of thinking as ongoing behavior, such that the functions of cognitive events broaden and no one verbal function dominates. Psychological inflexibility is characterized by cognitive fusion, where the context supports literal functions (i.e., the content of thoughts) as the dominant source of control over the repertoire (Blackledge, 2007). In this way, cognitive fusion refers to the same phenomenon described in the rule-governed behavior literature and produces the same insensitivity to other sources of stimulation (Blackledge & Drake, 2013). Building flexibility involves disrupting the literal functions such that other functions (e.g., sensory qualities, memories of similar thoughts, other relevant perspectives) can come to influence behavior along with other events in the context. In practice, intervening on cognitive defusion often involves drawing attention to the process of thinking. This could involve reflecting the client's description of thoughts with explicit labeling of them as thoughts (e.g., "So you feel compelled by this thought that you are unlovable") or asking the client to describe thoughts (e.g., "It looked like something shifted for you just then. What's coming up for you as we discuss this?").

Self-as-context. Self-as-context involves awareness of one's own behavior as distinct from other internal or external events, including self-relevant private events (Hayes, Pistorello, & Levin, 2012; Levin et al., 2012). The self emerges through discrimination of one's own behavior as distinct from other events (Skinner, 1974b). Once a client verbally discriminates the self (i.e., as a concept), however, they can easily relate to it, and it can take on functions of other events through DRR. Psychological inflexibility involves private events (e.g., evocative emotions or self-relevant cognitions) coming to dominate functions of the self (Levin et al., 2012). Thus, like a highly generalized rule, these functions can impact behavior in any situation, as the self is an event that is always relevant (i.e., "If me, then…"). Psychological flexibility, however, involves awareness of the self as an event that is present for and relatable to all other events, but is uniquely discriminable and uniquely invariant in terms of its location in time, place, and person (Blackledge & Drake, 2013). As such, building flexibility in ACT involves shaping awareness of self in the presence of private events that vary across time (e.g., memories of the past and concerns for the future), place (e.g., different situations, relationships, roles), and person (e.g., different perspectives on the same event). In practice, intervening on self-as-context might involve having the client list different roles, concepts, labels, or characteristics they associate with themselves (e.g., by completing a list of "I am" sentence stems). Next the therapist might ask the client to notice conflicts among the different descriptions, notice which others would know and which they wouldn't, imagine contexts in which these different descriptions dominate their experience of themselves, and imagine that certain descriptions would not apply in the future.

Committed action. Committed action describes a large response class of values-consistent behaviors for which the stimulus control over different topographics is well discriminated between contexts. The dominance of aversive control that characterizes psychological inflexibility often prevents contact with appetitive events that could serve to discriminate and consequate effective, values-consistent behavior. Building flexibility, then, involves shaping (1) the discrimination aspects of the immediate context related to values and (2) the engagement in values-consistent behaviors as appropriate to that context. In practice, intervening on committed action often involves having a client describe the function of their current behavior, describe immediately available behaviors that would be more values consistent (and likely evoke some discomfort), and set a goal to engage in a chosen behavior more often outside of session (despite the discomfort).

Implications and Future Directions

The material covered in this chapter thus far—and in particular the discussion of ACT—is decidedly relevant to practitioners and to the field of applied behavior analysis as a whole. We explore both of these areas below.

Implications for Practitioners

For behavior analytic practitioners, the implications of the evolution of behavior therapy and ACT can be quite significant. Applied behavior analysis has always been committed to addressing problems of social significance (Baer, Wolf, & Risley, 1968). Behavioral difficulties categorized as psychopathology account for 30 percent of the nonfatal disease burden and 10 percent of the overall disease burden worldwide (World Health Organization, 2016). This is despite the proliferation of psychological treatments and the ever-increasing availability of psychotropic medications. Further, this excludes individuals whose suffering is not categorized by the socioverbal community as pathological. The basic research underlying ACT would suggest that psychological suffering is, in fact, universal, as it is a product of normal learning processes. Despite its universality, however, psychological suffering is of tremendous social significance, and behavior analysis clearly has something to offer. We encourage practitioners, whether trained as behavior therapists or not, to rise to the challenge of the human condition in at least three ways.

First, let us be open to the inclusion of private events as relevant in behavioral analyses. **Mentalism**, or the appeal to private events as causes of overt behavior, is rejected by behavior analysis. However, private events and their relationships with overt behavior can be analyzed and intervened upon from a behavior analytic perspective. Just as with any other behavior outside of the focus of the intervention, considering private events is often unnecessary to gain prediction and influence over the behavior of interest. But when private events are relevant, referring clients to practitioners working from perspectives we reject as mentalist (e.g., cognitive therapists) seems a bizarre course of action. Where our direct analyses of overt behavior alone fall short, let us be open to considering private events in relation to the behaviors of interest, with a focus on shifting the contexts controlling those behavior-behavior relations.

Second, let us consider verbal behavior in terms of DRR and the transformation of stimulus functions. Behavior analysts, like members of any profession, use language to intervene on their clients' behavior as well as that of other stakeholders (e.g., employees, colleagues, students, and parents). The difference, however, is that we have at our disposal, in RFT, an analysis of verbal behavior that accounts for the conditions under which that language might be most effective. We can change behavior by using language to help transform the functions of the contexts in which individuals live and work. Whether training a parent, teaching a class, giving a presentation, or marketing an intervention, let us harness the incredible power of language to increase our effectiveness.

Third, let us consider psychological flexibility as a dimension of the behavioral repertoire, even outside of the behavior therapy setting. Often the rigidity and insensitivity of client behavior is what makes it problematic. For example, a client might talk about trains or dinosaurs regardless of the context or their partner's interest, and at the exclusion of other topics. The psychological flexibility model proposes conditions under which rigidity like this might emerge (i.e., in the context of aversive private events where this pattern allows for temporary escape and avoidance). ACT proposes how we might intervene to improve flexibility without having to avoid contexts that elicit aversive private events. Psychological flexibility, by definition, involves increased sensitivity to direct contingencies and verbally established values to allow for an increase in personally meaningful behavior. This quality of behavior is associated not only with recovery from psychopathology but with thriving in a number of different domains of living. Certainly, this level of engagement in life is relevant to behavior analysts intervening in all sorts of settings with all sorts of clients.

Implications for Our Field

If practitioners are going to easily incorporate these implications into their work, there are developments that behavior analysis as a field must make. First, we need to expand our approaches to assessment. In particular, to the extent that we are dissatisfied with the tools commonly used to assess private events and relationships between private events and overt behavior (e.g., questionnaires), we are challenged to develop new approaches. Second, we need to integrate theory, research, and practical training in complex human behavior into typical behavior analysis curricula in order for the field of behavior analysis to progress and evolve. This text represents an initial effort, yet it is not enough, nor is the work presented in this text complete. Third, we need pioneer behavior analysts to adapt third-wave behavior therapy technologies to the practice of behavior analysis in the various settings in which behavior analysts work. ACT is topographically different when implemented by medical doctors, managers, or coaches, and likewise, most behavior analysts will not seek the training and licensure necessary to incorporate talk therapy into their practice. Behavior analysts, however, do not need to be trained in talk therapy to adapt ACT where it would serve their work. For example, Gould, Tarbox, and Coyne (2017) demonstrated increased overt values-directed behaviors following a brief ACT training intervention implemented by behavior analysts.

Despite challenges, behavior analysis has made substantial progress in how to apply behavior analytic approaches to complex human suffering. It may now be time to integrate these advances into the mainstream of behavior analytic research, training, and practice.

Conclusion

The present chapter considered the historical development of contemporary behavior therapy. Beginning with the consideration of private events in behavior analysis, this chapter provided an overview of the development of clinical behavior analysis, and in particular its role in analyzing the complex problems faced by adults in outpatient psychotherapy. Behavior therapy can be seen as having developed in three phases, or "waves"—each of which was described in this chapter, with particular emphasis given to acceptance and commitment therapy. A number of implications were described, including those focused on practice and the field of behavior analysis as a whole.

Study Questions

1. Define private events. Are they the same as or different from mental events?

2. Can private events be included in the science of behavior analysis? Why or why not?

3. What are some of the defining features of the first-wave behavior therapies?

4. What are some of the defining features of the second-wave behavior therapies? How do these depart from the first wave?

5. What are the some of the defining features of the third-wave behavior therapies? How do these depart from the second wave?

6. Do the third-wave behavior therapies move toward, away from, or make no movement with respect to the foundational philosophy and principles of behavior analysis, compared to the second wave?

7. What is acceptance and commitment therapy?

8. What are some of the defining processes of ACT?

9. Compare and contrast the defining features of ACT with mainstream applied behavior analysis, in terms of being conceptually systematic with behavioral principles, focusing on behavior, focusing on generalization, and insistence on being effective in producing substantial changes in socially significant behavior.

10. What are the implications of ACT for your current practice in applied behavior analysis and for what you see as the future evolution of mainstream applied behavior analysis?

Implicit Cognition and Social Behavior

Dermot Barnes-Holmes

Colin Harte[17]
Ghent University, Belgium

Ciara McEnteggart
Ghent University, Belgium

Link and Preview

Chapter 16 builds upon previous chapters on derived stimulus relations, and relational frame theory in particular. The focus of this chapter—implicit cognition and social behavior—is of great importance as it relates to many of the most pervasive social issues around the world. The authors review research on a number of consequential topics and describe ongoing conceptual development.

The human species is composed of relatively weak and slow-moving primates, and yet we have, in one sense, come to dominate the planet in a very short period of time. Arguably, the propelling force behind our rise in dominance is our ability to learn how to relate stimuli and events in increasingly abstract, or arbitrarily applicable, ways. Irrespective of how this ability evolved so strongly in our species (see Hayes & Sanford, 2014), it appears to lie at the core of human language and cognition (Hayes, Barnes-Holmes, & Roche, 2001). On the one hand, the human ability to engage in abstract relational responding has been the key to our success in developing modern civilization with increasingly sophisticated sciences and technology. On the other hand, abstract relational responding allows humans to categorize other members of their own species into in- and out-groups and to react to members of an out-group in a highly negative manner without having a direct negative experience with any member of that group. Such prejudicial behaviors

---

17   The first two authors contributed equally to the chapter.

appear to be widespread and common among the human species. Indeed, at the time of writing we had just witnessed populist appeal for literally building a wall along the border between the United States of America and Mexico and the withdrawal of the United Kingdom from the European Union to allow for greater control over its borders. And in the last 100 years of human history, we have witnessed two world wars in which millions were slaughtered, and extremist attempts at mass genocide, based, at least in part, on the human ability to categorize out-groups as sufficiently threatening to warrant warfare.

The ability to categorize other members of our species into in- and out-groups may have served us well as small groups of hunter-gatherers, because it supported necessary cooperation within a group against another in competing for potentially limited resources. However, when human groups become increasingly abstract and increase in size (e.g., to nation states) and the level of science and technology allows for the annihilation of millions at the press of a button, the evolutionary value of prejudicial behavior, or social categorization, seems completely lost. Indeed, one could argue that in the modern context of a genuinely globalized world there is only one in-group—the entire human species and even more broadly life itself on this planet.

Clearly, the human ability to engage in social categorization is a potentially lethal behavior that we need to study and to understand if we are to predict and influence it in a manner that will serve to protect life on this planet. The science of psychology, and social psychology in particular, has devoted considerable time and effort in tackling this issue (see Tajfel, 1981, for seminal work). Behavior analysis has been less engaged, empirically, in this area, but its main progenitor, B. F. Skinner, became a household name for publishing books that described how behavioral principles could be used to engineer human cultures in a positive and peaceful direction. Empirical efforts at understanding social categorization within behavior analysis have not been entirely absent, however. As we shall see, relatively early in the study of stimulus equivalence and arbitrarily applicable relational responding, behavior analysts made attempts to create experimental models of human prejudicial behavior. It is fair to say that those conducting this early work had little appreciation of how rapidly social categorization effects can occur in human behavior. Only relatively recently has the "split-second" nature of such responding come to light. As such, the pervasive and uncontrolled nature of human prejudicial behavior is rendered even more threatening because it seems to occur "involuntarily" (because it is so rapid). The area of research that has focused on this phenomenon has been labeled **implicit social cognition**, and the current chapter will provide an overview of this work.

Specifically, this chapter will focus on the research investigating the role of derived relations in the development of social stereotypes, prejudices, and beliefs. We will briefly review the large body of literature that has employed a method derived from **relational frame theory** (RFT; Hayes, Barnes-Holmes, & Roche, 2001), known as the **implicit relational assessment procedure** (IRAP). The social domains upon which we will focus comprise national identity, religion, race, gender, sexuality and sexual preferences, age, body image, and smoking as a stigmatized behavior. We will then discuss the existing conceptual attempts to understand these findings in the context of RFT, including a recently proposed model for analyzing IRAP effects—the **differential arbitrarily applicable relational responding effects** (DAARRE) model.

Implicit Social Cognition

Work on implicit social cognition, from an RFT perspective, actually began in the early 1990s. Specifically, researchers sought to examine social categorization in Northern Ireland, where family names and sectarian symbols are often associated exclusively with either Catholic *or* Protestant communities (Watt, Keenan, Barnes, & Cairns, 1991). The study involved training participants in a series of match-to-sample tasks that were designed to generate derived equivalence relations between Catholic names and Protestant symbols that would be inconsistent with the verbal/social histories of participants who resided in Northern Ireland. The results showed that some Northern Irish residents did indeed demonstrate difficulty in forming these equivalence relations, whereas individuals from outside Northern Ireland did not. Numerous studies since then have reported broadly similar outcomes in which participants with specific preexperimental histories appear to show difficulty forming derived relations that are inconsistent with those histories (e.g., Barnes, Lawlor, Smeets, & Roche, 1996; Dixon, Rehfeldt, Zlomke, & Robinson, 2006; Leslie et al., 1993; Merwin & Wilson, 2005). Interestingly, recent research in this area has also shown that it is possible to undermine these types of effects with appropriate match-to-sample training designed to counter racially biased responding in white children (Mizael, de Almeida, Silveira, & de Rose, 2016).

The general strategy of comparing patterns of responding that are consistent versus inconsistent with participants' preexperimental histories led to more recent efforts to develop behavior analytic procedures that may be used to assess verbal relations. Currently, the most widely used method in this regard is the IRAP (Barnes-Holmes, Murphy, Barnes-Holmes, & Stewart, 2010). In the IRAP procedure, experimenters present pairs of stimuli (e.g., words, pictures, statements) on each trial, require participants to confirm or disconfirm the relation between these pairs within a short response latency window, and provide corrective feedback after each response. In general, the feedback is designed to be consistent with participants' preexperimental verbal histories on half of the blocks of trials, and inconsistent on the other half. For example, an IRAP might require responding "True" to a picture of a flower and the word "pleasant" (history consistent) on one block, and "False" (history inconsistent) on another block. The basic logic of the IRAP is that, all things being equal, participants should show a tendency to respond more quickly on history-consistent, relative to history-inconsistent, blocks. This difference in latencies across the two types of blocks is often referred to as the **IRAP effect** or a positive or negative **response bias**, depending on whether the effect is above or below zero. It is important to understand that the terms "IRAP effect" and "response bias" should not be interpreted as a proxy for a mental construct or implicit attitude in a cognitive or social psychological sense. Instead, these terms simply denote a tendency to respond in one particular direction over another on the IRAP.

There are several response-time measures for assessing implicit cognition, such as the Implicit Association Test (IAT), evaluative priming, and the Extrinsic Affective Simon Task (EAST). However, all of these other measures emerged from the "mainstream" cognitive tradition and therefore cannot be attributed to RFT, or behavior analysis more generally. There is one other task, however, that has emerged within behavior analysis known as the Function Acquisition Speed Test (FAST; O'Reilly, Roche, Ruiz, Tyndall, & Gavin, 2012). The FAST has been used to assess implicit social cognition, but at the time of writing only one published study had used the measure in this domain.

One advantage of the IRAP over many of the other measures is that it allows for a more detailed analysis of the relations being measured. This is made possible through the separation of the measured relations into four individual trial-types. In an IRAP designed to measure racial response biases, for example, the following four trial-types might be presented: White People-Positive-True/False; White People-Negative-True/False; Black People-Positive-True/False; and Black People-Negative-True/False. Therefore, the IRAP permits a functional distinction between, for example, black people as both positive *and* negative, which may be conceptually important in socially sensitive domains.

Social Research

This section will address research within the various social domains listed earlier. We will focus largely on IRAP research because it is clearly contained within the behavior analytic tradition.

National Identity

One of the first published IRAP studies assessed biases toward different nationalities (i.e., Irish, Scottish, American, and African) by native Irish and Irish-American participants (Power, Barnes-Holmes, Barnes-Holmes, & Stewart, 2009). Across two experiments, researchers gave participants an IRAP in which the label stimuli "more likeable" and "less likeable" appeared with a target consisting of two nationalities to be compared in terms of likeability on each trial. In Experiment 1, the pairs were "Irish-Scottish," "Scottish-American," "American-African," "Scottish-Irish," "American-Scottish," and "African-American," and participants were required to choose either "True" or "False" as response options on each trial. As an example, the first trial listed above could be read as "Irish are more likeable than Scottish; true or false?" Results indicated a strong "in-group response bias" for Irish over Scottish, and American over African nationalities. That is, participants tended to respond more quickly when they were required to respond "True" rather than "False" when these two pairs were presented with "More Likeable." In Experiment 2, the target pairs were "American-Irish," "Irish-Scottish," "Scottish-African," "Irish-American," "Scottish-Irish," and "African-Scottish," and the participants were Irish-Americans (i.e., American citizens who claimed Irish heritage). Results indicated an in-group response bias for American over Irish, Irish over Scottish, and Scottish over African. In both experiments, participants' self-report measures rating preferences of these nationalities diverged from the IRAP biases. For example, in the self-report measure, the Irish Americans rated Irish as more likeable than Americans (or any other group), but on the IRAP they responded "True" more quickly than "False" when responding to the "More Likable; American-Irish" trial-type. This study was one of the first to highlight the potential utility of the IRAP in the assessment of potentially sensitive social issues. That is, the IRAP seemed to provide a method for assessing the natural verbal relations at play over and above self-report measures.

Religion

Hughes, Barnes-Holmes, and Smyth (2017) employed the IRAP to assess the biases of Catholics and Protestants in Northern Ireland, a post-conflict context in which sectarian tensions had been the source of violence and discrimination across three decades. Specifically, in a known-groups design, the researchers presented Catholic and Protestant participants in Northern Ireland with one of two label stimuli (i.e., "Catholics" or "Protestants") on each trial with one of six positive (e.g., friendly, safe) or negative (e.g., bad, dishonest) words as target stimuli. The IRAP required responding in a pro-Catholic and anti-Protestant pattern on some blocks of trials (e.g., pressing a key for "True" when "Safe" appeared with the word "Catholic") and a pro-Protestant and anti-Catholic pattern on the remaining blocks of trials (e.g., pressing a key for "False" when "Safe" appeared with the word "Catholic"). The IRAP revealed pro-Catholic and pro-Protestant biases across both groups; however, in-group biases were stronger. For example, the size of the difference in reaction times was larger when Catholic participants were required to confirm rather than deny that Catholics were positive compared to when they were required to confirm rather than deny that Protestants were positive; the opposite was the case for the Protestant participants.

Similar research was also conducted by Drake et al. (2010) on attitudes toward Christians and Muslims in an undergraduate sample in the United States. Results revealed a distinct positive bias for Christians on both the Christian-Positive and Christian-Negative trial-types, and a *negative* bias for Muslims on Muslim-Negative, but no significant effect was observed on Muslim-Positive. Moreover, Scheel, Roscoe, Scaewe, and Yarbrough (2014) found a broadly similar pro-in-group Westerner bias when they assessed attitudes toward Muslims and Westerners in a US-based undergraduate sample.

Race

One of the earliest IRAP studies focused on racial bias and examined the response patterns of white participants toward pictures of black and white individuals (Barnes-Holmes, Murphy, et al., 2010). The researchers presented participants with one of two label stimuli (i.e., "Safe" and "Dangerous") on each trial with a picture of a white or black man holding a gun as a target stimulus. The IRAP revealed pro-white and anti-black biases, although the anti-black effect was restricted to one trial-type (i.e., the *Dangerous-Black* trial-type). Indeed, four other studies have also examined racial bias using the IRAP, and broadly similar positive in-group biases were found for white participants (Drake et al., 2010; Drake et al., 2015; Power, Harte, Barnes-Holmes, & Barnes-Holmes, 2017a). The most recent of these combined the IRAP for examining racial biases with the measurement of electroencephalograms (EEGs; Power, Harte, Barnes-Holmes, & Barnes-Holmes, 2017b). The EEG recordings revealed that the event-related potentials (ERPs; i.e., brain responses) were more positive for the pro-black trials than for the pro-white trials across six of the frontal sites. Indeed, it is interesting that the differential ERP patterns observed in this study were restricted to the frontal sites and that greater positivity was recorded for the IRAP performances that required responding in a manner that was inconsistent with a white in-group racial bias. Specifically, as the authors point out, the findings are broadly consistent with research in the neurocognitive literature indicating that the prefrontal areas of the cortex (i.e., more primitive areas of the brain) may be involved in suppressing emotional reactions that are deemed to be undesirable in some way—in this case a pro-white/anti-black response.

Gender

The IRAP has also been used across a number of studies in the assessment of gender biases. For example, a study by Cartwright, Hussey, Roche, Dunne, and Murphy (2016) evaluated the potential utility of the IRAP for assessing gender binary beliefs. Specifically, participants completed two IRAPs, in which one of two label stimuli were presented (i.e., "Men" and "Women") on each trial. One IRAP presented *positive* masculine (e.g., "competitive") or feminine (e.g., "nurturing") traits as target stimuli; the other IRAP presented *negative* traits (e.g., masculine "aggressive"; feminine "bossy"). Participants also completed a number of self-report measures on sexism and heteronormativity and a hiring task to assess hiring preference. The IRAPs revealed that participants readily paired masculine traits to men (e.g., saying men-competitive-*true*, more easily than false) and feminine traits to women (e.g., saying women-nurturing-*true*, more easily than false), and rejected pairing feminine traits with men (e.g., saying men-nurturing-*false*, more easily than true) and masculine traits with women (e.g., saying women-aggressive-*false*, more easily than true). Interestingly, 83% of participants rated male traits as making someone more hirable. Similar results were found in another study using a FAST (Cartwright, Roche, Gogarty, O'Reilly, & Stewart, 2016).

Indeed, similar gender stereotyping biases have also been found using the IRAP concerning gendered house chores (e.g., chopping wood is for men and cooking is for women; Drake et al., 2010), gendered toys in young boys and girls (e.g., dolls are for girls and toy cars are for boys; Rabelo, Bortoloti, & Souza, 2014), and gendered university disciplines (i.e., men are related to science and arts but women to arts only; Farrell, Cochrane, & McHugh, 2015).

Sexuality and Sexual Preferences

The IRAP has also been used in the assessment of attitudes toward sexuality and sexual preferences. For example, in a study of sexual orientation, Cullen and Barnes-Holmes (2008) assessed biases among a group of heterosexual and homosexual male participants. The IRAP presented one of two label stimuli (i.e., "Straight" and "Gay") along with a positive stereotypical target for straight people (e.g., "normal," "safe") or a negative stereotypical target for gay people (e.g., "abnormal," "dangerous"). The IRAP revealed pro-gay and pro-straight biases for both groups; however, an anti-gay bias was observed on the gay-negative trial-type among heterosexuals only. In three further studies, researchers successfully used the IRAP to predict sexual orientation by asking participants to relate the labels "straight" or "gay" with attractiveness and unattractiveness (Ronspies et al., 2015; Timmins, Barnes-Holmes, & Cullen, 2016).

In a study on sexual stereotyping, Scheel, Fischer, McMahon, and Wolf (2011) reported IRAP findings in which women confirmed more quickly than they denied that traits stereotypical of gay men (e.g., "artistic," "feminine") corresponded with this group; a similar bias was obtained for associating straight men with stereotypical traits (e.g., "assertive," "masculine"). And in a study on BDSM (bondage and discipline, sadism and masochism; or acts of domination and submission) practice, students and clinicians who reported no BDSM tendencies produced greater anti-BDSM/pro-normal IRAP effects than those who reported BDSM tendencies (Stockwell, Hopkins, & Walker, 2017; Stockwell, Walker, & Eshleman, 2010).

Age

One of the earlier IRAP studies examined ageist attitudes among young people and revealed pro-young and anti-old biases in the first experiment (Cullen, Barnes-Holmes, Barnes-Holmes, & Stewart, 2009). A second experiment attempted to assess the *malleability* of the IRAP effects. Researchers randomly assigned participants to either a pro-young or pro-old condition in which they were exposed to pictures of admired old and disliked young people (pro-old condition) or to pictures of admired young and disliked old people (pro-young condition). Participants completed one IRAP immediately after exposure to the pictures and then a second identical IRAP twenty-four hours later. The pro-young condition produced strong pro-young and anti-old effects on both days, whereas the pro-old condition produced relatively weak pro-young effects and relatively strong pro-old effects on both days.

Body Image

A substantial body of IRAP research has also emerged in the domain of body image in recent years. One of the first studies was conducted by Roddy, Stewart, and Barnes-Holmes (2010), and results revealed a pro-slim, but not an anti-fat, bias. This effect was replicated in another study by Roddy, Stewart, and Barnes-Holmes (2011), which also employed facial electromyography (EMG) to gauge emotional responses of participants while they conducted the IRAP, and both measures found a pro-slim bias. Interestingly, in a similar study by Nolan, Murphy, and Barnes-Holmes (2013), this effect was found only among males. Similarly, in a study that employed only female participants and female stimuli, Exposito, Lopez, and Valverde (2015) found no pro-slim or anti-fat bias, potentially suggesting that women demonstrate less weight-related prejudice than men.

Body-image IRAP effects have also been shown to predict body dissatisfaction, body weight, and disordered eating, beyond that of self-report measures (Juarascio, Forman, Timko, & Herbert, 2011). Furthermore, Heider, Spruyt and De Houwer (2015) employed two IRAPs, one assessing actual body image (i.e., I am thin) and one assessing ideal body image (i.e., I want to be thin). Results indicated actual self-thin bias was lower in those with higher levels of body dissatisfaction, whereas ideal self-thin bias was higher in those with higher levels of body dissatisfaction. Similar research on attractiveness, rather than body image, found broadly consistent findings in which pro-attractive biases were observed (Murphy, Hussey, Barnes-Holmes, & Kelly, 2015; Murphy, MacCarthaigh, & Barnes-Holmes, 2014).

Smoker Status

Two published studies have used the IRAP to assess attitudes toward smokers and non-smokers (Cagney, Harte, Barnes-Holmes, Barnes-Holmes, & McEnteggart, 2017; Vahey, Boles, & Barnes-Holmes, 2010). In the first of these, Vahey et al. (2010) presented to adolescents an IRAP in which the labels "smoker" and "non-smoker" appeared with either social acceptance or social rejection words (identified from tobacco marketing campaigns), along with "similar" or "opposite" as response options. Results showed that smokers responded more quickly when confirming that smokers were *similar* to social acceptance words, but no difference emerged between acceptance or rejection words among the non-smokers.

In the second study, Cagney et al. (2017) attempted to conduct a more detailed analysis of attitudes toward smokers using the IRAP in both adult and adolescent smokers and non-smokers, and they also explored the impact of parental smoking status. The results showed a pro-smoker bias for both adults and adolescents smokers, with a neutral bias for non-smokers in both groups. However, adult smokers and non-smokers were more clearly differentiated than the two adolescent groups on the IRAP, whereas the opposite was true in terms of the self-report measures. Post-hoc analyses indicated that non-smokers showed more positive bias scores toward smokers on the IRAP if their parents were smokers (relative to non-smoking parents). Non-smokers also showed more positive bias scores toward non-smokers if their parents did not smoke (relative to smoking parents). Overall, therefore, smoking status and parental smoking status appeared to influence social attitudes toward a socially stigmatized group (i.e., smokers).

Understanding IRAP Effects from a Relational Frame Theory Perspective

As noted at the beginning of this chapter, the behavior analytic basis of the IRAP involves comparing two opposing patterns of relational responding, one of which is deemed to be generally consistent with the preexperimental history of the participant, the opposing pattern, by definition, which is not. The so-called IRAP effect is therefore deemed to reflect this difference in preexperimental relational responding. This is, in essence, the basic assumption underlying the IRAP. Over the years, however, increasingly sophisticated behavior analytic accounts of the IRAP have emerged, and the remaining half of the current chapter will consider these, with a particular focus on social implicit cognition.

The Relational Elaboration and Coherence (REC) Model

The types of effects that have been observed with the IRAP have been referred to as **brief and immediate relational responses** (BIRRs), in that they are emitted within a short response window of time after the onset of each trial. In contrast, **extended and elaborated relational responses** (EERRs) are more complex and emitted more slowly and as such occur over a longer period of time (Barnes-Holmes, Barnes-Holmes, Stewart, & Boles, 2010; Hughes, Barnes-Holmes, & Vahey, 2012). The distinction between BIRRs and EERRs was conceptualized within the context of the **relational elaboration and coherence** (REC) model, an initial RFT approach to implicit cognition (Barnes-Holmes, Barnes-Holmes et al., 2010; Hughes et al., 2012). The basic idea behind the model is that the IRAP (and indeed other implicit measures) produces the types of effects it does because the task forces participants to emit BIRRs rather than EERRs. The latter are generally assumed to be evoked by traditional self-report measures, when participants are not under time pressure to respond to each item in a questionnaire. The strength or probability of the BIRRs emitted toward experimental stimuli is deemed to be *functionally similar* to that of responses toward these stimuli in the participant's preexperimental history, particularly in situations in which individuals have to respond relatively quickly or have little motivation to reflect on how they are responding in that particular moment in time.

Imagine, for example, a white individual who has resided exclusively in white neighborhoods, has no non-white friends or family members, and has been exposed to many media images of black people as violent drug dealers and inner-city gang members. When presented with an IRAP that displayed pictures of black males carrying guns, according to the REC model, BIRRs confirming that black men are "dangerous" and "criminals" are likely to be more probable for this individual than those denying such relations, thus revealing an anti-black racial bias (see Barnes-Holmes, Murphy, et al., 2010). Indeed, this bias might not be observed if the same individual were asked to rate the same pictures of the black men in the absence of time pressure. In the latter context, there is sufficient time to respond in accordance with an extended and elaborated relationally coherent network (i.e., an EERR), which by definition extends beyond the initial BIRR. In this case, the REC model suggests that the individual may fail to report the initial BIRR based on the additional relational responding, such as "It is wrong to discriminate on the basis of race" and "I am not a racist." Hence, the IRAP reveals the BIRR, and a questionnaire reveals the EERR.

It's worth noting some limitations to the REC model. In concluding that the IRAP reveals BIRRs rather than EERRs, the REC model assumes that participants respond to each of the four IRAP trial-types in more or less the same manner. This basic assumption has not been upheld empirically, however, and thus behavior analysts have recently attempted to develop a more sophisticated RFT-based understanding of the behavioral effects observed with the IRAP. In presenting this more recent account, we will focus first on an IRAP that is not relevant to social cognition, but thereafter consider the implications for the social-psychological domain.

Imagine an IRAP that aimed to assess the response probabilities of four well-established verbal relations pertaining to non-socially valenced stimuli, such as shapes and colors. Across trials, the two label stimuli, "Color" and "Shape," could be presented with target words consisting of specific colors ("Red," Green," and "Blue") and shapes ("Square," "Circle," and "Triangle"). As such, the IRAP would involve presenting four different trial-types that could be designated as (1) *Color-Color*, (2) *Color-Shape*, (3) *Shape-Color*, and (4) *Shape-Shape*. During such a *Shapes-and-Colors* IRAP, participants would be required to respond in a manner that was consistent with their preexperimental histories during some blocks of trials: (1) *Color-Color-Yes*, (2) *Color-Shape-No*, (3) *Shape-Color-No*, and (4) *Shape-Shape-Yes*. On other blocks of trials, the participants would have to respond in a manner that was inconsistent with those histories: (2) *Color-Color-No*, (2) *Color-Shape-Yes*, (3) *Shape-Color-Yes*, and (4) *Shape-Shape-No*. Thus, when the four trial-type effects are calculated, by subtracting response latencies for history-consistent from history-inconsistent blocks of trials, one might expect to see four roughly equal trial-type effects. In other words, the difference scores for each of the four trial-types should be broadly similar. Critically, however, the pattern of trial-type difference scores obtained with the IRAP frequently differs across the four trial-types (e.g., Finn, Barnes-Holmes, Hussey, & Graddy, 2016).

The REC model always allowed for the potential impact of the functions of the response options on IRAP performances, in which there may be a bias toward responding "Yes" over "No," for example, and that this interacted with the stimulus relations presented in the IRAP (Barnes-Holmes, Murphy, et al., 2010). As such, one might expect to observe larger differences in response latencies for trial-types that required a "Yes" rather than a "No" response during history-consistent blocks of trials. In the case of the *Shapes-and-Colors* IRAP described above, therefore, larger IRAP effects for the *Color-Color* and *Shape-Shape* trial-types might be observed relative to the remaining two trial-types (i.e., *Color-Shape* and *Shape-Color*). The REC model does *not* predict, however, that the IRAP effects for the *Color-Color* and *Shape-Shape* trial-types will differ (because they both require choosing the same response option within blocks of trials), but in fact our research has shown that they do (e.g., Finn et al., 2016, Experiment 3). Specifically, we have found what we call a **single-trial-type-dominance-effect** for the *Color-Color* trial-type. That is, the size of the difference score for this trial-type is often significantly larger than for the *Shape-Shape* trial-type. This finding has led us to propose an updated model of the relational responding that we typically observe on the IRAP, which we will briefly outline subsequently. A complete description of the model and its implications for research using the IRAP is beyond the scope of the current chapter (but see Finn, Barnes-Holmes, & McEnteggart, 2018). However, it is important to consider the model here simply to highlight how an ongoing focus on relational responding is continuing to contribute toward a behavior analytic approach to human social implicit cognition.

In attempting to explain the single-trial-type-dominance-effect for the *Shapes-and-Colors* IRAP, it is important to note that the color words we used in our research tend to occur with higher frequencies than the shape words in natural language (Keuleers, Diependaele, & Brysbaert, 2010). We therefore assume that the color words evoke relatively strong orienting responses relative to the shape words. Or more informally, participants may experience a type of confirmatory response to the color stimuli that is stronger than for the shape stimuli. Such responses may be interpreted as arising from the Cfunc rather than the Crel properties of the stimuli.[18] Critically, a functionally similar confirmatory response may be likely for the "Yes" relative to the "No" response option (because "Yes" frequently functions as a confirmatory response in natural language). A high level of functional overlap, or what we define as coherence, thus emerges on the *Color-Color*

---

18   According to RFT, many of the functions of stimuli that we encounter in the natural environment may appear to be relatively basic or simple but have acquired those properties due, at least in part, to a history of relational framing. Even a simple tendency to orient more strongly toward one stimulus rather than another in your visual field may be based on relational framing. Identifying the name of your hometown or city from a random list of place names may occur more quickly or strongly because it coordinates with other stimuli that control strong orienting functions (e.g., the many highly familiar stimuli that constitute your hometown). Such functions may be defined as Cfunc properties because they are examples of specific stimulus functions (i.e., orienting) that are acquired based on, but are separate from, the entailed relations among the relevant stimuli; the latter are labeled Crel properties (see Finn et al., 2018).

trial-type among the orienting functions of the label and target stimuli and the "Yes" response option. During history-consistent blocks of trials on the IRAP, this coherence also coordinates with the relational responding that is required between the label and target stimuli (e.g., *Color-Red-Yes*). During history-consistent blocks, therefore, the trial-type could be defined as involving a maximum level of coherence because all of the responses to the stimuli, both orienting and relational, are confirmatory. During inconsistent blocks, however, participants are required to choose the "No" response option, which does not cohere with any of the other orienting or relational responses on that trial-type, and this difference in coherence across blocks of trials yields relatively large difference scores. The model we have developed that aims to explain the single-trial-type-dominance-effect, and a range of other effects we have observed with the IRAP, is named the **differential arbitrarily applicable relational responding effects** (DAARRE) model (pronounced "dare"). In the following sections we will outline the DAARRE model for the *Shapes-and-Colors* IRAP and then consider an example of how the model may apply to the results obtained from an IRAP that targeted social cognition (i.e., race).

The DAARRE Model

A core assumption of the DAARRE model is that differential trial-type effects may be explained by the extent to which the Cfunc and Crel properties of the stimuli contained within an IRAP cohere with specific properties of the response options across blocks of trials. Response options, such as "Yes" and "No," are referred to as **relational coherence indicators** (RCIs) because they are often used to indicate the coherence or incoherence between the label and target stimuli that are presented within an IRAP (see Maloney & Barnes-Holmes, 2016, for a detailed treatment of RCIs).

The basic DAARRE model as it applies to the *Shapes-and-Colors* IRAP is presented in figure 16.1. The model identifies three key sources of behavioral influence: (1) the relationship between the label and target stimuli (labeled as Crels), (2) the orienting functions of the label and target stimuli (labeled as Cfuncs), and (3) the coherence functions of the two RCIs (e.g., "Yes" and "No"). Consistent with the earlier suggestion that color-related stimuli likely possess stronger orienting functions than shape-related stimuli (based on differential frequencies in natural language), the Cfunc property for Colors is labeled as positive and the Cfunc property for Shapes is labeled as negative. The negative labeling for shapes should not be taken to indicate a negative orienting function; rather, it simply indicates an orienting function that is weaker than that of colors. The labeling of the relations between the label and target stimuli indicates the extent to which they cohere or do not cohere based on the participants' relevant history. Thus, a color-color relation is labeled with a plus sign (i.e., coherence), whereas a color-shape relation is labeled with a minus sign (i.e., incoherence). Finally, the two response options are each labeled with a plus or minus sign to indicate their functions as either coherence or incoherence indicators. In the current example, "Yes" (+) would typically be used in natural language to indicate coherence, and "No" (-) to indicate incoherence. Note, however, that these and all of the other functions labeled in figure 16.1 are behaviorally determined, by the past and current contextual history of the participant, and should not be seen as absolute or inherent in the stimuli themselves.

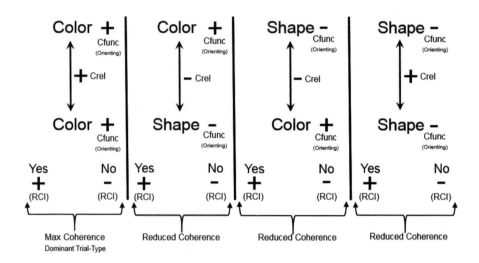

Figure 16.1 The DAARRE model as it applies to the Shapes-and-Colors stimulus set. The positive and negative labels refer to the relative positivity of the Cfuncs for each label and target, the relative positivity of the Crels, and the relative positivity of the RCIs in the context of the other Cfuncs, Crels, and RCIs in that stimulus set.[19]

As can be seen in figure 16.1, each trial-type differs in its pattern of Cfuncs and Crels, in terms of plus and minus properties, that define the trial-type for the *Shapes-and-Colors* IRAP. The single-trial-type-dominance-effect for the *Color-Color* trial-type may be explained, as noted above, by the DAARRE model based on the extent to which the Cfunc and Crel properties cohere with the RCI properties of the response options across blocks of trials. To appreciate this explanation, note that the Cfunc and Crel properties for the *Color-Color* trial-type are all labeled with plus signs; in addition, the RCI that is deemed correct for history-consistent trials is also labeled with a plus sign (the only instance of four plus signs in the diagram). In this case, therefore, according to the model, this trial-type may be considered as maximally coherent during history-consistent trials. In contrast, during history-inconsistent trials there is no coherence between the required RCI (minus sign) and the properties of the Cfuncs and Crel (all plus signs). According to the DAARRE model, this stark contrast in levels of coherence across blocks of trials serves to produce a relatively large IRAP effect.

---

19   Figure 16.1 adapted from D. Barnes-Holmes, Finn, McEnteggart, & Barnes-Holmes [2017]. Adapted by permission of Springer Nature.

Now consider the *Shape-Shape* trial-type, which requires that participants choose the same RCI as the *Color-Color* trial-type during history-consistent trials, but here the property of the RCI (plus signs) does *not* cohere with the Cfunc properties of the label and target stimuli (both minus signs). During history-inconsistent trials, the RCI *does* cohere with the Cfunc properties (minus signs) but not with the Crel property (plus sign). Thus, the difference in coherence between history-consistent and history-inconsistent trials across these two trial-types is not equal (i.e., the difference is greater for the *Color-Color* trial-type) and thus favors the single-trial-type-dominance-effect (for *Color-Color*). Finally, as becomes apparent from inspecting figure 16.1 for the remaining two trial-types (*Color-Shape* and *Shape-Color*), the differences in coherence across history-consistent and history-inconsistent blocks is reduced relative to the *Color-Color* trial-type (two plus signs relative to four), thus again supporting the single-trial-type-dominance-effect.

At this point, it seems important to consider how the DAARRE model might be used to interpret a single-trial-type-dominance-effect that was obtained in an early IRAP study that focused on racial bias. Specifically, Barnes-Holmes, Murphy, et al. (2010) reported four trial-type effects for a study that presented pictures of white and black males carrying guns with words related to safety and danger. The two critical trial-types in this context were *Safe-White* and *Dangerous-Black* because participants were required to press "True" during pro-white and "False" during pro-black blocks of trials. The participants (who were all indigenous white Irish individuals) tended to respond "True" more quickly than "False" on these two trial-types. However, the size of the difference for the *Safe-White* trial-type was approximately twice the size of the difference for the *Dangerous-Black* trial-type. In effect, a single-trial-type-dominance-effect was observed. One could interpret this result as indicating that participants were simply more certain about the safety of white men carrying guns than they were about the danger of black men carrying guns. Our recent work with the DAARRE model, however, suggests that we should be more cautious in drawing such a conclusion. For illustrative purposes, consider the following (speculative) interpretation.

Let us assume that the pictures of the white men and the safety words possessed relatively positive evaluative functions, whereas the pictures of black men and danger words possessed relatively negative evaluative functions. If we translate these assumptions into a figure similar to the one we used above for the *Shapes-and-Colors* IRAP, it quickly becomes apparent that the single-trial-type-dominance-effect may have arisen, in part, from differences in coherence across the two trial-types, rather than purely from racially biased responses (see figure 16.2). Specifically, note that the Cfunc and Crel properties for the *Safe-White* trial-type are all labeled with plus signs; in addition, the RCI that is deemed correct for pro-white trials is also labeled with a plus sign (the only instance of four plus signs in the diagram). In this case, therefore, according to the model, this trial-type may be considered as maximally coherent during pro-white blocks. In contrast, the *Dangerous-Black* trial-type involves a "mixture" of Cfunc and Crel properties; the pictures and words possess negative Cfunc properties but a positive Crel property between them, and participants are required to choose the positive RCI on pro-white blocks.

Similar to the *Shapes-and-Colors* IRAP, therefore, the difference between the size of the IRAP effects may be attributed in part to a relative difference in the coherence among the Cfunc, Crel, and RCI properties of the stimuli presented within the IRAP.

In making this argument it is important to understand that we are not suggesting that IRAP effects are therefore irrelevant procedural artifacts that do not reflect potentially important behavioral histories with regard to racial differences and other social psychological phenomena. Indeed, the relative difference in coherence that we have just suggested using the DAARRE model requires that participants evaluate the pictures of the white men positively and the black men negatively. What the DAARRE model provides, therefore, is the potential for a more precise analysis of the functional relations that are in play when participants are required to complete an IRAP.

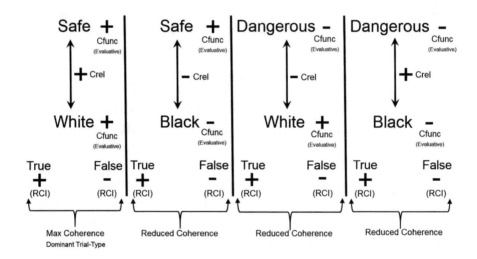

Figure 16.2 The DAARRE model as it applies to the race stimulus set.

Implications and Future Directions

On balance, there has been very little direct study of the variables that may be used to change or manipulate the types of relational responding that appear to be involved in implicit social cognition. One notable exception was the study reported by Cullen et al. (2009) in which exposure to positive and negative exemplars (of old and young individuals) was shown to impact relevant IRAP performances. It seems important, therefore, that future research in this area begin to focus on methods, techniques, and general strategies for changing implicit social cognition that may be deemed problematic in the natural environment. Indeed, it should be noted that some success has been reported in manipulating IRAP effects, or their relationship to other behavioral measures, in the clinical domain (e.g., Bast & Barnes-Holmes, 2015; Bast, Linares, Gomes, Kovac, & Barnes-Holmes, 2016; Hussey & Barnes-Holmes, 2012; Leech, Barnes-Holmes, & McEnteggart, 2017; Ritzert, Forsyth, Berghoff, Barnes-Holmes, & Nicholson, 2015). Future behavior analytic research in implicit social cognition is therefore well placed to explore and develop "interventions" for changing the types of relational responding that seem to be involved in implicit cognition (e.g., Mizael et al., 2016).

Conclusion

The current chapter aimed to provide an overview of the main body of work on what may be described as implicit social cognition, but from a behavior analytic perspective. Much of the empirical research has emerged from RFT and a procedure (the IRAP) arising from the theory. Conceptual analyses, such as those provided by the REC and DAARRE models, have also emerged. The research, both empirical and conceptual, has clearly become increasingly sophisticated since the initial studies reported in the early 1990s, and it appears our understanding of the relational responding involved is gradually becoming clearer. As noted, however, further research aimed at changing implicit social cognition is clearly warranted. Indeed, at a time when there is increasing populist appeal for building walls and withdrawing from a forty-year European Union, there seems to be even greater urgency to tackle the human capacity for categorizing each other in potentially negative and ultimately lethal and toxic ways.

Study Questions

1. Construct a list of the studies on implicit cognition and social behavior that have been published within the behavior analytic literature.

2. Name the methodology that has been used most extensively in the studies you listed in response to question 1.

3. Provide a brief description of one implicit relational assessment procedure (IRAP) that has been used to study implicit cognition and social behavior.

4. Briefly describe the findings from three studies that used the IRAP to examine implicit cognition and social behavior.

5. Briefly describe the relational elaboration and coherence (REC) model.

6. Explain how the REC model proved to be limited in accounting for IRAP findings.

7. Using an appropriate diagram, describe the differential arbitrarily applicable relational responding effects (DAARRE) model.

8. Explain how the DAARRE model accounts for IRAP effects that the REC model does not.

9. Provide an example of a DAARRE model that explains the findings from a study on implicit cognition and social behavior.

10. Provide a brief outline of a study in implicit cognition and social behavior that could be useful in achieving the goals of prediction and influence.

CHAPTER 17

Perspective Taking, Empathy, and Compassion

Carmen Luciano

University of Almería, Spain;
Madrid Institute of Contextual Psychology

Bárbara Gil-Luciano

University of Nebrija, Madrid;
Madrid Institute of Contextual Psychology

Adrián Barbero

Madrid Institute of Contextual Psychology;
University of ICADE Comillas, Spain

Francisco Molina-Cobos

University of Almería, Spain

Link and Preview

This chapter concludes the book and addresses three complex but critically important repertoires of social behavior—perspective taking, empathy, and compassion—from the perspective of traditional psychology, radical behaviorism, and functional contextualism. The authors' analyses suggest a number of directions for practical action and provide fruitful insights for expanding behavior analytic research and practice into an area that has traditionally been dominated by other branches of psychology.

Perspective taking (PT), empathy, and compassion are three ordinary terms that refer to concepts that have existed for centuries, but researchers only began to study them in the last years of the twentieth century. In the last decade, the number of published studies has shown an accelerated curve, and most of them point to the positive impact of the behaviors defining these terms in several domains, including developmental, social, health, clinical, political, and economic arenas. The interplay of one's behavior with others' human behavior involved in PT, empathy, and compassion is at the core of complex inter- and intrapersonal abilities for problem solving, effective living, and evolution. Although the massive trend of papers adds relevant information, it also presents a lack of consensus either in defining these abilities or in identifying the conditions under which they are developed. It is our contention that the behavior of PT is the *core ability in empathy and compassion*. The examples below illustrate this point.

> *Pedro is nine years old. One of his favorite games to play with his friends is to portray their favorite fictional characters or their heroes. He portrays his sister, his teachers, or people from several different professions. When he represents them, he thinks and acts just like they would, while discriminating his own perspective from those of the character he is representing. We might say that Pedro can place himself in the perspective of those characters. On one occasion, Pedro arrives at school and sees that his friend Luis has just wounded his knee. He is bleeding. Pedro goes to him and, even though he does not feel pain in his own knee, he feels like he understands Luis when watching him complain about the pain—Pedro has gone through a similar situation before. He acts as quickly as possible to make his friend's pain go away. He is acting the way others acted when he was injured, and in so doing, he is compassionate toward Luis by assisting him.*

> *Alfonso recently lost his sister in a terrible train accident. Among other things, he feels disconnected and isolated from others, even though everybody worries about him and tries to make him feel better. Suddenly, he hears about his good friend Patricia, with whom he has always had a special relationship. Patricia's father has been hospitalized for several months, struggling between life and death. When they meet, Patricia tells Alfonso what is happening to her. "I don't seem to connect to practically anyone since I have been going through my father's situation." Suddenly, Alfonso connects with Patricia. He feels his own pain, recognizes the similarity to what she is feeling right now, and feels closer to her. He tells her this and discovers that Patricia also feels closer to him.*

> *Maria is an architect who builds houses with a purpose in mind, a purpose derived from enjoying step-by-step creative building so that people will enjoy living in warm houses with adequate lighting, ventilation, and green spaces. She loves making buildings that can offer other people not only beauty but usefulness. It is a compassionate act, an act with personal meaning.*

It is quite possible that, when reading these examples, most of us will realize that they have common elements and that PT (I-You) is fundamental to all of them. In Pedro's case, PT is present for a specific purpose, but it was also present when empathy emerged, in which case, his own emotion was coordinated with the emotional behavior of another person. In another case, PT is present when compassion is also present, like when the motivation of helping others is driven by feeling connected to them. The key question is whether some fundamental behavioral repertoire is critical to all of these examples and, if so, what are the necessary behavior-environment functional relations for these behaviors to take place?

These critical social repertoires described above seem to concern the development of the self and self-knowledge, invoking a functional perspective that Skinner specified long ago. Skinner (1974a, p. 35) wrote, "A person who has been made aware of himself by the questions he has been asked is in a better position to predict and control his own behavior." One relevant derivation would be that, without the development of these complex abilities, our species would have been extinguished. That is, the ability to discriminate one's own emotions and the emotions of others, as well as the chosen action and the responsibility that comes with it, is developed through interactions with others. These interactions promote the building of flexible patterns of interactions with one's own emotions and thoughts so that effective or meaningful actions take place. And perhaps in the absence of these repertoires developing, the development of behavioral patterns defined by suffering or psychological inflexibility may be more probable.

In this chapter, we address PT, empathy, and compassion from the standpoints of traditional psychology, radical behaviorism, and functional contextualism. In doing so, we track the verbal processes involved in all three of these repertoires, along with their implications in applied contexts.

Perspective Taking

Perspective taking refers to the ability to respond to another's perspective without losing one's own perspective. It is known as the ability "to be in the other person's shoes" or as "reading minds." For instance, if Pedro, in the above example, were asked, "How would you feel if you were your sister when she wakes up in the middle of the night with a nightmare?" he would feel somehow similar to his sister and might respond to his feeling by helping his sister in some way.

PT is a key ability that is likely critical for effective daily living interactions. PT has been found to be a core element in many areas that involve relating to others as well as relating to one's own emotions and feelings. PT has been associated with effective social interactions, resolving health problems, effective clinical interactions, improving economic protocols, and spirituality and compassion (Barnes-Holmes, Barnes-Holmes, Roche, & Smeets, 2001b; Biglan, 2015; Hayes, 1984; Luciano, Valdivia, & Ruiz, 2012; Törneke, 2010; Strosahl, Robinson & Gustavsson, 2015; Wilson, Bordieri, & Whiteman, 2012; Villatte, Villatte, & Hayes, 2016; M. Villatte, Vilardaga, & Monestes, 2012). However, in spite of the relevance of PT abilities and the large amount of published research that addresses it, only in the last few decades has PT begun to be approached in a way that focuses on the conditions under which it can be promoted.

The Traditional Approach to Perspective Taking

Early attempts to understand PT were dominated by research coming out of the **theory of mind** (ToM) tradition, which refers to the capacity of inferring the beliefs, intentions, and emotions of others in order to explain and predict their behavior (Premack & Woodruff, 1978). In the classical Sally-Anne ToM task (Baron-Cohen, Leslie, & Frith, 1985), children witness a doll named Sally putting a marble in a box and then leaving the room. Then, another doll named Anne moves the marble to a drawer. Children are then asked where Sally will look for the marble when she returns. Children who have not yet developed ToM abilities cannot distinguish what Sally knows from what they know, and thus respond incorrectly that Sally will look for the marble in the drawer. With some exceptions, most of the research on ToM has been conducted under the cognitive conceptualization of levels, identified as simple and complex visual PT abilities, as the basis of knowledge and true and false beliefs (Howlin, Baron-Cohen, & Hadwin, 1999). ToM has commonly been used to evaluate and train the development of PT abilities, and ToM deficits have been shown in children with autism spectrum disorder (Baron-Cohen et al., 1985) and in persons diagnosed with schizophrenia, schizotypy, and social anhedonia (Corcoran, Mercer, & Frith, 1995; Villatte, Monestès, McHugh, Freixa i Baqué, & Loas, 2008). A large amount of ToM research has been published on PT, but all of it has been dedicated to documenting deficits in PT, as opposed to remediating them. The ToM model has not been fruitful in leading to effective intervention research, arguably because it did not provide the key learning processes involved in ToM that affect PT (see Barnes-Holmes et al., 2001b; McHugh, Stewart, & Hooper, 2012; and Montoya, Molina-Cobos, & McHugh, 2017, for reviews). However, the ToM literature contributed substantially to drawing research attention to the topic of PT, and as well as describing the various overt behaviors involved in PT. This helped lay a foundation for a functional approach to the study of PT.

A Functional Approach to Perspective Taking

Functionally speaking, PT is the ability to notice one's mind (i.e., private behaviors and stimuli) while inferring others' minds, without losing perspective of oneself, the one who is experiencing all the thoughts and emotional content across time and places as a unique experiential *locus* or *self* (Barnes-Holmes et al., 2001b; Hayes, 1984; Kohlenberg & Tsai, 1991; Luciano, Valdivia-Salas, Cabello, & Hernández, 2009; Skinner, 1974a; J. L. Villatte, Villatte, & Hayes, 2012).

Early on in the behavioral tradition, Skinner (1974a) pointed to the relevant role of the self and self-knowledge. He wrote that the self is a locus where a diversity of genetic and environmental conditions converges to organize a unique and characteristic repertory. Earlier, Skinner (1945) provided some of the conditions that give rise to private events as part of the self. And moreover, he emphasized the role of self-awareness as central to the human condition. He wrote that the person who is conscious of himself or herself is in a better position to predict and control his or her own behavior. These ideas crystallize in the proposal of the self of Kohlenberg and Tsai (1991), who specify the problems of the self and the therapy created to overcome such problems, **functional analytic psychotherapy** (FAP). However, there was no specific research on this complex behavior, leaving the interactions to prevent difficulties in the self's behaviors and the client-therapist interactions in an unknown scenario. That is, the verbal processes involved between the therapist's and the client's behavior to build new repertoires were unknown.

The main problem in the difficulty researching self-behaviors probably had to do with the consideration that discriminating one's own behavior was a simple discrimination, rather than one that involved verbal processes. But for that behavior to take place, perspective taking is needed between the one performing the discrimination and the thing being discriminated so that the functions of these events are transformed (Barnes-Holmes, et al., 2001b). Not an easy problem in those times, when there was no effective conceptualization for this complex behavior. The early behavioral view of the self was consistent with the way these behaviors seem to be produced. However, research in this area was almost absent until behavior analysts took a contextually oriented approach to PT and conducted research on the emergence or derived production of functions and behavior. This set the stage for the development of **relational frame theory** (RFT) to give an account of language as relational behavior. And it was then that one of the relational repertoires of behavior, **deictic framing**, was developed and became available to provide a behavior analytic account of PT—one that could be applied to different human behaviors including the problems of the self and the therapeutic relationship.

Perspective Taking as Deictic Framing

The RFT perspective states that language is **framing**, which means responding to one stimulus in terms of the contextual relation established with another stimulus. As described in earlier chapters, framing is a relational operant established through multiple exemplars to abstract a number of relational cues that, when learned, can be arbitrarily applied to any type of stimulus. New relations derive from the effects of this application and indirectly provide or change stimulus functions. Consider, for instance, a child who has learned the relational cues "more than," "less than," and "same as" and is told, "These two toy cars are the same color, red, but the size is different. The big car is as fast as the one you play with at home, but the small one is faster than the big one. Which of them would you choose if you want the fastest?" A child with an intact framing repertoire can respond by picking up the small car the first time without any previous interactions with that car or that particular question. He will also probably be able to learn the rule "These cars are both red, but the small one goes faster than the big one." That is, the small car has acquired a derived appetitive and discriminative function on the basis of the comparative relation applied to the two cars and the sameness relation with directly established functions (the one he plays with at home).

Fully formed human verbal repertoires involve responding to a number of relational cues: coordination (e.g., *same as*), distinction (e.g., *different*), opposition (e.g., *opposite*), comparison (e.g., *more than, less than*), hierarchical (parts of something, or *inclusion*), temporal (*now, then/before, later*), causality (*if…, then*), and deictic (*I-You, Here-There, Now-Then*). Advanced framing ability goes beyond a particular relation to combinations of relations, as is the case when we make or understand analogies or metaphors, or we form problem-solving rules and follow them. The relational behavior that is particularly relevant to PT is what is known as **deictic framing**. Deictic framing specifies a relation in terms of the perspective of the person who is behaving (Barnes-Holmes et al., 2001b), for instance, the perspective *I* versus *Other*; the perspective *I before* and *I later*, or *You before* and *You now*; or the perspective *I here* and *My stomachache, there*. Deictic framing is at the core of most complex human behaviors that involve responding to the relation between oneself and others.

Three deictic frames were identified almost twenty years ago (Barnes-Holmes et al., 2001b): I versus YOU (Other), NOW versus THEN, and HERE versus THERE. However, the most relevant point is that they are not separated, but rather they promote the unique perspective of the I as invariant (even when noticing the Other perspective) and always occurring in the NOW (even when noticing a THEN, in the past or future), and always occurring HERE, NOW (even when noticing I-THERE in other places; Barnes-Holmes et al., 2001b; Luciano et al., 2009). This occurs through the many opportunities that other people in the community provide for the combination of these perspectives. Thus, the perspective of I-Here-Now emerges as invariant through any other perspective that might be involved, for instance, I-Here-Now and You-Here-Now (e.g., *I am here, now, in the kitchen and I notice that you are in the bathroom*), or I-Here-Now and I-Here-Then (e.g., *I am making the pizza now and I will clean the kitchen later*). The establishment of deictic relational cues is a social learning process. In other words, across multiple exemplar training provided by the people around us who ask questions, model responding, and give feedback, we learn to abstract the deictic relational cues I-You, Here-There, and Now-Then in multiple combinations. The questions that Skinner identified to establish self-knowledge are the key verbal interactions that establish deictic framing in young children, for instance, *What I am doing now? What are YOU doing now?* and *What is HE doing now? What am I doing Here?* and *What did I do Yesterday?*

The implications of deictic framing for understanding human behavior are enormous because deictic cues are applied in thousands of ways in daily life. That is, when this repertoire is fluently in place, we can apply the deictic cues when we understand or formulate rules, when we learn to differentiate our own emotions from those of others, when we look back or forward in our life, when we know what the other person knows or sees, when we feel we connect to other people, and so on. We apply deictic cues when we feel what it is being said by another person or we formulate questions and statements such as the following:

"What are you going to do later?"

"You and I cried before, and now I am still crying and you are laughing."

"I was better before than I am now."

"If I were where you are now, I would be able to see what you see, but I cannot from here."

"How do you think your brother is feeling when you pick up his car without asking permission?"

"I cannot feel what you are feeling now. But, you know, if I were in your shoes and had the same history you have had, I would be feeling the same."

Finally, beyond the core role of deictic framing to promote PT and to understand the formation of beliefs about oneself or others is the most relevant role that deictic framing promotes: it is the *formation of the self as a unique and integrative context* for any thought or emotion that develops. That is, deictic framing allows the formation of a hierarchical or inclusion relation between oneself and one's own behavior, which is essential for the human being to be conscious, to be mindful, and to have a sense of spirituality. And this repertoire is what is likely needed to respond to one's own behavior without responding as though I AM it. In other words, the ability to respond to oneself as a context in which behavior occurs is broader and more flexible than responding to oneself by labeling oneself as one's behavior. To respond to a momentary emotion as though there is some space between oneself and that emotion likely allows the opportunity for a flexible response to that emotion. For example, when one experiences rage, one might notice that emotion as something one is experiencing, which could leave room for a variety of responses, rather than defining oneself by the emotion (e.g., "I am just the kind of person who can't control their anger," which may be more likely to evoke a rigid, maladaptive response (e.g., aggression). As a whole, flexible deictic relational framing likely facilitates problem solving and interpersonal relations skills such as empathy and compassion.

Empirical Research on Deictic Framing and Implications

Research on deictic framing has increased in recent years and has been extended to different areas. The developmental domain was the first to be addressed by the analysis of protocols of deictic combinations in order to evaluate and train PT in normal developing children and in children with autism spectrum disorder (ASD). The protocol was designed to target the three deictic relations, I-You, Here-There, and Now-Then, through three levels of complexity (simple, reversed, and double-reversed). A simple trial of I-You would be *If I have a ball and YOU have a cookie, then what do I have and what do YOU have?* Similar simple trials are designed to respond to Here-There (e.g., *I am standing HERE at the door and you are standing THERE at the table*) and to Now-Then as relating I-Now and I-Then (e.g., *Now I am playing with the ball and yesterday I was reading*).

Reversed trials require more complexity. For example, a reversed I-You trial would be *I have a ball and YOU have a cookie, however if YOU were me and if I were YOU, then what would I have?* A reversed Here-There example would be *I am HERE at the door and you are THERE at the window, but if THERE were HERE and HERE were THERE, then where would I be, and where would you be?* The double-reversed trial, in which two deictic relations are reversed, requires still more complexity. Following the above example, the trial would be *I am HERE at the door and you are THERE at the window, but if I am YOU and YOU are me and if HERE is THERE and THERE is HERE, then where would I be and where would YOU be?*

Research has supported a general developmental sequence in the learning of these levels of complexity, with older children and adults showing fewer errors in spatial and temporal reversed and double-reserved relations (McHugh, Barnes-Holmes, & Barnes-Holmes, 2004). Children with ASD have shown difficulties with reversed deictic relations, especially the Now-Then relations, which have been correlated with poor social skills (Rehfeldt, Dillen, Ziomek, & Kowalchuk, 2007). The deictic protocols have also been adapted to evaluate false-belief and deception repertoires, showing a clear developmental trend in both areas (Barnes-Holmes et al., 2001b; Heagle & Rehfeldt, 2006; McHugh et al., 2004; Weil, Hayes, & Capurro, 2011). As a whole, the available research presents a fruitful panorama in remediating deficits in PT. However, at the same time, more natural protocols are needed to increase generalization to the natural setting beyond the specific deictic tasks designed for the protocols (see reviews by McHugh et al., 2012; Montoya et al., 2017; Mori & Cigala, 2016). In this line, researchers use a precise analysis of the deictic relations to detect flexibility in PT using different tasks, such as, for instance, the **implicit relational assessment procedure** (IRAP; Barbero-Rubio, López-Lopez, Luciano, & Eisenbeck, 2016).

Finally, M. Villatte et al. (2012) used the deictic protocol designed by McHugh et al. (2004) to evaluate PT in persons diagnosed with schizophrenia in comparison to persons without such a diagnosis. The performance of the former group was poorer on all reversed and double-reversed deictic relations, and they had more difficulties in taking the perspective of another and correctly attributing the intention of others (M. Villatte et al., 2012). To summarize the above, deictic protocols seem to be sensitive to measuring and treating PT abilities and appear to provide a behavioral foundation underlying classical ToM tasks and other attribution tasks, where no specific processes had previously been identified.

Beyond the relevant impact of the deictic protocol for evaluating and teaching PT or ToM, deictic framing has been identified as being at the core of the process responsible for the formation of thoughts and emotions and, more importantly, of the self as an integrated set of behavioral repertoires. More specifically, deictic framing has been found to be the key ability for the formation of self-rules (thoughts and emotions about oneself and the world and others around one). Developing content about one's own behavior and life require the deictic-I in order to experience and notice that it is a behavior about oneself.

To feel in one's own skin and say sentences to oneself such as *I am very good at this and they are not, I am not good enough, Nobody loves me, I will never have a successful life, I am a person who loves to help others* is not the same as repeating sentences we all know. It means that emotions or feelings become present according to one's history and one can feel who is feeling them, in contrast to other agents, moments, and places. The formation of thoughts about oneself is only possible through multiple interactions with others where the I-You, Here-There, and Now-Then are interchanged. Consequently, the content about oneself and its function depends on one's personal history.

The final point is that deictic interplay is the key to establishing the content and functions of self-rules, and it is the key to establishing a hierarchical perspective between the self-rules and the very person who is noticing the self-rule (the deictic-I). The advantages of self-knowledge and the self have already been mentioned, although the processes were not established. The main point is that having a fluent hierarchical deictic-I repertoire establishes a context where one can be less attached to or trapped by emerging self-rules. That is, such a repertoire allows us to overcome these momentary events and to connect with more relevant and meaningful functions. In other words, with this ability intact, we would react by noticing and integrating the self-evaluations that emerge and we would respond under the influence of those other functions.

Based on this analysis, researchers have designed deictic framing protocols to promote the deictic/hierarchical framing of one's own behavior. In the first of these studies, Luciano et al. (2011) proposed a relational-based account of defusion interactions, typically used in **acceptance and commitment therapy** (ACT; Hayes, Strosahl, & Wilson, 1999). This study compared a deictic-I protocol with a deictic-I protocol plus hierarchical cues in adolescents with problematic behaviors as participants (Luciano et al., 2011). Results showed that the latter protocol had a greater effect than the former on reducing the frequency of problematic behaviors and promoting psychological flexibility at a four-month follow-up. These results have been replicated, improved, and extended using specific experimental tasks (such as analogues of daily situations). For instance, Gil-Luciano, Ruiz, Valdivia-Salas, and Suarez-Falcon (2016) analyzed the effect of these deictic protocols on a behavioral pain tolerance task; López and Luciano (2017) analyzed their effect on attention tasks; and Floody, Barnes-Holmes, Barnes-Holmes, and Luciano (2013) tested the effect on the functions of negative self-evaluative rules. So far, these authors' findings suggest the significant role of hierarchical and deictic-I framing in changing functions to self-content in establishing the ability of noticing and behaving according to what matters. Deictic framing seems to be key in many other psychological phenomena such as empathy, compassion, psychological flexibility, spirituality, transcendence, and mindfulness (Hayes, 1984; Törneke, Luciano, Barnes-Holmes, & Bond, 2016; J. L. Villatte et al., 2012; Wilson et al., 2012).

For instance, psychological flexibility has been defined as behaving on the basis of hierarchical framing with the deictic-I (Törneke et al., 2016). This can be explained as the ability of noticing my own ongoing emotion and thoughts from the deictic

I-Here-Now and my behavior, I-There, at the same time that noticing the integration or inclusion of such behavior as part of ME as the context for the higher-order appetitive functions (valued or meaningful functions) be present and to act accordingly. At this point, it is worth pointing out that several experimental-clinical studies have already been designed according to this view with very positive results (e.g., Ruiz, Riaóo, Suárez, & Luciano, 2016). Moreover, the relevant role of deictic and hierarchical framing has recently been used in a very specific way to approach the therapeutic relationship and clinical problems (Barnes-Holmes et al., 2018) that are central in client-therapist interactions promoted in FAP. In a similar but less specific manner, this role is also present in the relational approach to clinical interactions of J. L. Villatte et al. (2016) and of Törneke et al. (2016).

Putting all this together, deictic framing is involved in the formation of rules, whatever their content, and general beliefs about oneself as a hierarchical experience of ME with the functions coming from one's personal history. And, at the same time, deictic framing is needed to establish the experience of ME noticing whatever self-content is present at the moment (e.g., Barnes-Holmes et al., 2001b; Luciano et al., 2009; Wilson et al., 2012). As mentioned, becoming fluent in framing one's thoughts or emotions in the deictic I-Here-Now and one's thoughts and feelings There-Now establishes a hierarchical perspective (in other places called self-as-context) that enhances flexible repertories. This flexible repertoire serves an important function within a verbal community because we cannot escape from interacting with our own feelings, thoughts, and functions emerging in the context of other people's behaviors and events in the world according to our own personal history. Put simply, it is very easy to become attached to such functions of one's own behavior and, consequently, to act blindly concerning what matters. However, learning to frame in the hierarchical/deictic-I is central to generating psychological flexibility because of its relevance to so many other verbal relational repertoires, as described above.

To sum up, most of the studies on promoting PT have been carried out under the umbrella of deictic framing, pointing not only to the classical ToM tasks but also to the design of more naturalistic deictic protocols. In addition, deictic framing has been identified as being at the core of the emergence and extension of networks of thoughts and emotions, for better and for worse—that is, for the emergence of both positive and negative self-content and for the emergence of a secure or insecure sense of self. Moreover, a good number of experimental and clinical protocols have shown that the combination of deictic and hierarchical framing of one's behavior generates the functional hierarchical context where one connects with one's own emotions and thoughts and experiences the awareness of behaving according to what matters to oneself.

To conclude, PT as deictic framing seems to be at the core of prosocial behavior for good, and this is for better but it might be for worse (the former, as Skinner pointed out years ago, because it places the person in a better position to behave according to what matters; the latter, because PT might also be used for purposes other than prosocial ones). We will now turn our attention toward the deictic processes that might be involved in empathy and compassion.

Empathy

Empathy is a term that was introduced into the German language around 1858, originating from the Greek term "empatheia," meaning "feeling-in," as in merging with an object or being connected to some kind of feeling or emotion. The meaning of "empathy" evolved to underlining the interpersonal connection, and then emphasizing its emotional component; this latter aspect was formulated by Titchener, who pointed to PT as the relevant ability (Batson, 2009; Lanzoni, 2015; Vilardaga, 2009). The interest in studying empathy during the twentieth century reflects its definition in *Reader's Digest* in 1955 as the "ability to appreciate the other person's feelings without yourself becoming so emotionally involved that your judgment is affected" (Lanzoni, 2015).

Today, the large number of studies that have been published on empathy show a vast panorama that crystallize in the lack of consensus about its definition and, more importantly, about the conditions under which empathic behavior develops and could be changed. As Batson (2009) states explicitly, after decades of studying empathy, the difficulty lies in establishing what is being considered as empathy by different researchers. For example, sometimes empathy means labeling or imagining another's thoughts and feelings, whereas other times it means adopting another's position and feeling like the other person feels.

Empathy appears significant in many areas of human functioning. A brief overview shows the link between empathy and emotional intelligence and with functioning well in daily living (e.g., Eisenberg, 2000; Goleman, 1998). It has also been correlated with prosocial behaviors and conflict resolution (Batson, 2009; Garaigordobil & Maganto, 2011), and with improving sports and artistic performances (Sevdalis & Raab, 2014). Conversely, deficits in empathy have been found in children diagnosed with autism (Baron-Cohen et al., 1985) and in people diagnosed with psychosis (Vilardaga, Estévez, Levin, & Hayes, 2012; M. Villatte et al., Monestès, 2012). However, the lack of consensus in defining empathy makes analyzing and studying it a very difficult task.

Traditional Approach and Empirical Context

The numerous different definitions, conceptualizations, measures, and methodologies used to study empathy prevent a precise analysis and interpretation of the results obtained across studies. These same problems hinder the interpretation of studies combining neuroscience and empathy. For example, the review by Zaki and Ochsner (2012) shows that most of the studies have used measures focused on what is happening in the brain when an individual watches videos of people talking about highly personal emotional events. The question here is whether the reaction to such videos is a precise example of empathy. In other words, what is the conceptualization, focus, or goal by which empathy is being defined in these studies? The same problems might be found in those areas oriented to improving empathic skills in practitioners in medical and clinical contexts, where empathy is defined, for instance, by active listening, initiating statements, and discussing and writing about empathy (e.g., Brunero, Lamont, & Coates, 2010; Gerdes, Segal, & Lietz, 2010).

However, even with different definitions of the term "empathy," deficits in empathy have been addressed in children using the ToM protocol (Baron-Cohen et al., 1985) with no evidence of the positive effects of remediating empathic responding beyond the specific task that was directly trained. That is, there was no generalization to novel empathy situations or false-belief tasks, or any signs of promoting social interactions (e.g., Golan & Baron-Cohen, 2006; Silver & Oakes, 2001). Behaviorally oriented program protocols have shown similar results (e.g., Leblanc, Coates, et al., 2003). This means that targeting emotional labels while training in PT does not help the learner to be more effective in responding to their emotional interactions. As Vilardaga et al. (2012) pointed out, the problems with these empathy protocols is that there is no experimental approach to the psychological phenomenon of empathy that allows the production of rules and formulas with increasing levels of precision, scope, and depth. In other words, empathy has often been addressed as either a hypothetical internal construct or an oversimplified overt behavior.

A Relational Framing Account of Empathy

Even the most general meaning of empathy as understanding how others feel, sharing feelings, and responding to those feelings without losing one's own perspective (Valdivia-Salas, Luciano, Gutiérrez, & Visdómine, 2009) reveals dark zones. For example, it is one thing to feel like the other person is feeling, which might be conceptualized as a coordination between one's own feelings and the other's feelings. But the function that such coordination promotes in the very person who is behaving this way is a different thing. That is, feeling like the other person may feel does not have the same function for everyone, and for the person themself, because it depends on the person's history in the present context. For example, let's imagine that Maria feels loneliness framed in coordination with Peter's signals of loneliness to Maria, but, for Maria, this feeling has the function of remaining in the situation and doing something for Peter. However, for Carlos, the same feeling has avoidance functions, and he withdraws from contact with Peter to reduce the effect of the feeling in coordination between them. And, for Esther, these same feelings entail actions to manipulate Peter's behavior.

Perhaps the lack of consensus about what empathy is goes hand in hand with the need for differentiating two elements. Specifically, we should differentiate *feeling* an emotion—in the sense of the function that occurs in response to the other's emotional behavior—from the *function* of this emotion and the particular action under its control. Differentiating the two processes should be a fruitful alternative when evaluating empathic behavior and designing intervention protocols. Following this line, Valdivia-Salas et al. (2009) proposed a promising protocol to establish empathic behavior by translating the core features of empathy into behavioral-relational language with deictic framing as the core ability. In this proposal, deictic framing occurs throughout the process of experiencing the coordination of emotion and responding to it without losing one's own perspective. Three consecutive strategies are indicated to achieve empathy.

A first step is the establishment and understanding of *one's own emotions*. This process is promoted by agents in the verbal community *so that we learn* to verbally discriminate our own private events from others' behavior. That is, the community reinforces the coordination of internal states (e.g., pain when I fall) with a label (e.g., I feel pain) with those of the other (e.g., my brother did not fall and feels no pain). Through multiple exemplars of these types of discriminations, we not only learn to label a name, but we also learn to respond in accordance with deictic framing, such as I-Here-Now and my Pain-There (in the knee), and at other times, I-Here and my Pain-There (in my head), and with other events, I-Here and my Hungry-There, and so on. And very importantly, through these multiple exemplars of discriminating one's own behavior, we learn to discriminate our own experience from the unique perspective of I-Here-Now, so that the self is developed as a hierarchical perspective of many events occurring to me across time and places. This process occurs along with the discrimination of the "YOU" and the respective discriminations.

A second step is the establishment and understanding of *the emotions of others* as another element for empathic responding. This requires a shift in one's perspective to that of another's perspective but without losing the former—that is, *shifting* from I-Here-Now to "as if I were you now" (e.g., responding as if now I were my brother), or "if I were you then and then should be now" (e.g., responding as if I were my brother when he was a baby), and, importantly, without losing the perspective of I-Here-Now. Beyond this shift of moving around the deictic reversal I-You, one must learn to discriminate cues that suggest that some private events are occurring in others. For example, if Luis's mother cries, Luis might feel that she is hurt on the basis of coordination between a particular experience of being hurt with the label "being hurt" and a subsequent action of crying when he was hurt. Luis might also have learned the conditional rule "If something hurts, then I cry."

A third step is to learn *to respond empathically* by virtue of differentiating my own experienced feelings, connected to those of the other person, while at the same time realizing that the experience I am feeling is occurring due to my history with similar experiences, by definition not occurring now, but nonetheless this feeling is occurring, or the functions stemming from it are present. Expressed in relational terms, the following deictic framings are in place: "I-Now-Then (before) and I-Now-Here" and "I-Now-Here and You-Now-Here," and I can react to my emotions in a useful way. That is, when deictic framing develops, the functions of one's behavior (the feeling I am experiencing) change and alter the feeling I am having Now as if being There-Then. This increases the likelihood of valued functions connected to the deictic I-Here-Now emerging and, then, of behaving accordingly. For instance, in our example, the transfer of the emotional functions I-You might make Luis reexperience his pain as being similar to his mother's pain and, at the same time, know that he has not hurt himself like his mother has and that he is the one noticing such a pain as I-Here and my pain as There. As a result, he will be in a good position to help his mother by asking for help instead of crying, as might be the case if he had been hurt at that moment or if he had not learned to differentiate himself from his own pain.

In spite of the conceptualization of empathy from the behavioral-contextual perspective, no specific and basic experimental designs have yet been designed to analyze these components so that clear rules for promoting empathic behavior can be experimentally established. Having said this, we think that the conceptualization is ready to be used to design protocols for teaching empathy, which can then be tested empirically.

Summing up, different researchers have noted the variability in the definitions, conceptualization, and measures used to study empathy, or in the applied protocols promoted to improve empathy. However, despite the confusion, it seems clear that PT skills are at the core of empathy. Expressed more technically, deictic framing establishes the main conditions for experiencing one's own feelings as if sharing emotions in the presence of another's emotion. However, empathetically responding to such emotional feelings is another context, which requires more functions to be brought into play. The point here is that responding to one's own emotions as *sharing* another's emotion might have different functions depending on the history of the person empathizing. Feeling in the sense of sharing emotions might have avoidance and limiting functions, or it might have avoidance or approximate functions oriented to, or in the context of, more relevant and meaningful functions. For some, it might be the case that one's own history brings functions to manipulate or cheat others in such contexts.

To conclude, clarification of which behaviors are defined under the rubric of empathy is needed. Beyond this, it is clear that the development of empathy should run in tandem with the verbal sophistication connected to PT in order to develop an effective repertoire of responding to one's own emotions in relation to others. The implications of not developing empathic actions are substantial. In our view, the most important implication is that the development of a unitary self in responding to others will be highly compromised. In other words, interpersonal problem solving and, more generally, prosocial interactions may not be established. The relational literature on deictic and hierarchical responding might open the door to designing experiments to isolate the conditions for adequate coordination between one's own and others' behavior, as well as the conditions to frame one's own feelings and thoughts in such a way that the relevant functions for effective action are in place.

Compassion

The word "compassion" has its origin in "com" (with/together) and "pati" (to suffer), meaning *to suffer together with*. Most definitions of compassion share the idea that it is a feeling of understanding someone else's suffering, accompanied by the urge to help or the desire to alleviate the other's pain, meaning *to suffer and love with*. Broadly speaking, the identification with others through compassion seems to lead to increased motivation to do something in an effort to relieve their suffering. That is, it induces feelings of kindness and forgiveness, which might allow one to get in touch with such feelings, integrate them, and shift attention to acting toward valued goals. Although lacking unanimity about the core concept or agreement on its nature, the current literature on compassion is massive (e.g., see Goetz, Keltner, & Simon-Thomas, 2010, for a review). On the one hand, compassion has been considered a synonym for "empathic distress" (Ekman, 2003). From this perspective, compassion would be a vicarious experience of distress in response to another's suffering. On the other hand, compassion has been related to emotional responses that normally arise in the context of witnessing another person's suffering and embracing them in a benevolent action toward another in need. These responses have been gathered under several different names, like "pity," "sympathy", "empathy," "kindness," "caring," "warmth," and many more (see Wispé, 1986, for a review).

The relevance of compassion has grown significantly, as will be indicated later. From a broad social perspective, compassion has been claimed as one of the greatest virtues of the human condition, and it has frequently been advocated in all the major religious traditions. It has also appeared on the scene of political and business organizations, in evolution studies, and as a primary component in human social interactions. That is, it has been the core of psychological treatments and is actually one of the relevant cornerstones of the therapist-client interaction in the contextual therapies previously discussed in this chapter.

Traditional Approach and Empirical Status

A brief view of the vast research conducted on compassion shows that most of it is linked to empathy. Beginning with the level of analysis of neuropsychology, several brain activities have been related to strong feelings of compassion in the context of observing pain in others (Immordino-Yang, McColl, Damasio, & Damasio, 2009). Perhaps more informative than the studies correlating brain activation with the observation of others' pain are the studies correlating the reward of neuro-activation when subjects are performing compassionate acts (Rilling et al., 2002). However, although these studies reflect an advancement in detecting brain activation while persons are behaving in a certain way, it is unclear what the participants are doing. Moreover, *the processes by which* compassionate acts occur and activate the brain are unclear.

The evolutionary perspective is another domain where compassion has been found to play a relevant role. For instance, compassion seems to be more likely to occur when one is related to another person in need and/or when the benefits of being compassionate exceed the potential costs (Henrich, 2004). In political domains, compassion has been identified as a characteristic of democratic societies, in that they value the recognition of and identification with others' suffering, as well as knowledge of the sources of suffering and a commitment to reduce it. In the opposite context, the absence of compassion has been found to be a key element of social atrocities (e.g., genocides) by aggressors whose behavior is under the control of exclusion rules such that some persons are nonhuman or are people who do not belong to "good" races (e.g., Hoffman, 1981). This is why *the value of connecting with others* is at the core of compassion and self-compassion (Gilbert, 2010; Ricard, 2015). Consistent with this view, McHugh, Barnes-Holmes, Barnes-Holmes, Stewart, and Dymond (2006) found that the identification with another codevelops with the ability to adopt the other's perspective.

More concrete studies on compassion spread from medicine to psychology. For instance, compassion displayed by physicians plays a mediating role in the effects of sickness and suffering on human behavior. In the same vein, compassion and empathy between patients and their caregivers seems to be a primary motivation to relieve the physical, mental, or emotional suffering of each other (Pedersen, 2009). In spite of the positive correlations between compassion and different social improvements, a dark side has been identified and labeled "compassion fatigue." This has been found in professionals interacting mostly with suffering (e.g., oncology patients), who become entangled in the understanding of others' feelings (Figley, 1995). However, to overcome this, researchers and medical experts have promoted training among practitioners to improve the ability to tolerate one's own pain (e.g., Kraemer, Luberto, O'Bryan, Mysinger, & Cotton, 2016).

Distinguishing Empathy and Compassion

Still, it is difficult to differentiate empathy from compassion. As Sinclair, Hack, McClement, and Raffin-Bouchal (2016) concluded, while the key feature of empathy is an affective state that is isomorphic with the affective state of another, the defining feature of compassion is a *prosocial motivation or behavior that is not necessarily linked with such an isomorphic affect.* At the same time, for effective prosocial actions to take place, people must somehow feel something related to what others are feeling, either by understanding the sources of suffering or, perhaps more effective, by having the ability to picture themselves in similar experiences.

The Functional Contextual Approach

The role of compassion is perhaps more explicit now than before, and it is becoming a key clinical element in psychological therapy, especially in contextual therapies. In this arena, the term "compassion" opens the way to self-compassion, and it has emerged strongly with a myriad of interactions focused on promoting a context of compassion and self-compassion. FAP (Kohlenberg & Tsai, 1991) and ACT (Hayes, Strosahl, & Wilson, 1999, 2012) involve frequent intimate, empathic, or compassionate interactions with the client so that the therapist learns the repertoire of being open to feeling whatever might emerge in a genuine interaction with *oneself* (Gilbert, 2010), and so that client and therapist can feel that they *are in the same boat to do the job of building a flexible or effective repertoire.*

For this to happen, protocols inherently link openness to empathy and compassion toward others and oneself (Hayes, Strosahl, & Wilson, 1999, 2012; Strosahl et al., 2015; Villatte et al., 2016; Wilson et al., 2012). According to this approach, a repertoire of self-compassion is needed, as defined by the integration of one's own whole ongoing experience—the thoughts and emotions that emerge in coordination with the client's experience—and responding under the control of higher or valued significant functions oriented to alleviating the suffering of others. As a collateral effect, these kinds of interactions with one's painful and/or appetitive emotions and thoughts in the context of personal valued actions repeatedly lead to a feeling of personal satisfaction and fulfillment. Ultimately, compassionate acts are equivalent to valued actions, and these actions show a great variability. For instance, Sinclair et al. (2016) point to the variability of actions that are categorized as compassionate ability, and they conceptualize compassion as being as unique and particular as the individuals who enter a profession or engage in research or political activities.

Considering compassion as a pattern or series of different actions under the control of significant or valued functions, it can be categorized as a functional class of behavior built across personal historical interactions. Analyzing behavior in this way emphasizes the function of the actions instead of their topographies or formal aspects. This is useful because it establishes a bridge to understand the variability of actions that can be displayed to connect with another human being, and to understand the key point in compassion as the different actions under the influence of a *motivating, valued, significant, and personal function*. This ability is at the heart of psychological flexibility, of psychological well-being, and it opens the door to somehow connecting different terms and behaviors—in this case, compassion and psychological flexibility—as a functional class of valued or significant personal actions.

Implications and Future Directions

As we have suggested throughout the chapter, perspective taking, empathy, and compassion are topics with important implications for understanding human behavior, future research, and the provision of therapeutic support. In a nutshell, deictic framing is involved in all the applications where we need to identify our own and others' mental and emotional states to act effectively. This extends to building an empathic, compassionate, and self-compassionate response, but it also extends to many areas where we detect problems and do something to resolve them, either personally or otherwise. This is so because, like any other framing, deictic framing can be used to relate any kind of events, either between oneself and others or between oneself and one's own behavior. That is why it is at the core of psychological flexibility. Consequently, without these skills, the development of a unitary and effective self in responding to others becomes highly compromised. In other words, interpersonal problem solving, and, more generally, prosocial interactions, may not be established. This rationale actualizes Skinner's approach to self-knowledge, as we indicated at the beginning of this chapter, by elaborating on his analysis and extending it to relational frames that can be taught and tested. It is our contention that the research and application of deictic and hierarchical framing of one's own behavior might be a never-ending story, not only for analyzing the behaviors addressed in this chapter but for creative functional analytic research that might shed some light on the many obscure areas in the human condition.

Conclusion

"Empathy" and "compassion" are ordinary terms rooted in natural language. Interest in comprehending these concepts has caused the number of publications in the last twenty years to increase, as these concepts appear to be relevant to functioning in almost any human domain. No consensus has been reached concerning the definitions and meanings of these terms, nor about their application. However, the behaviors that constitute PT seem to be involved in all of them.

We have argued that PT is the foundation of empathy and compassion. Empathy involves PT because it focuses on the occurrence of an equivalent or coordinated emotion brought into contact with another's signs of emotions, as an affective resonance with someone else. Compassion involves PT because it focuses on connecting with the other's suffering, and on responding according to an overreaching significant value of helping others.

In view of the relevant role of PT, we have conducted a conceptual analysis beyond the classical context of ToM, in an attempt to identify and analyze the likely behaviors involved, particularly deictic relational framing. The research conducted on deictic framing has shown how to build the skill through multiple exemplar training in order to establish the perspective of I-Here-Now and You-There-Then, and many other combinations that enable us to switch from one perspective to another—without losing the unique and transcendent experience of I-Here-Now in which I integrate the ongoing behavior as a hierarchical perspective.

In conclusion, this chapter provided an overview, conceptual analysis, and review of research, especially that informed by relational frame theory, related to the topics of perspective taking, empathy, and compassion. These topics are central to understanding complex human behavior and many clinically important issues encountered in the lives of humans.

Study Questions

1. Describe traditional concepts of perspective taking (PT) from outside behavior analysis.

2. Describe Skinner's concept of the self and self-knowledge.

3. What are the three key deictic relational frames involved in PT?

4. Distinguish between simple, reversed, and double-reversed deictic relations involved in PT.

5. Describe traditional concepts of empathy from outside behavior analysis.

6. Describe the three stages of the development of empathy, according to an RFT perspective.

7. Interpret how you might extrapolate the three stages of empathy development into a protocol you could use to strengthen the behaviors involved in empathy in the clients you work with.

8. Describe traditional concepts of compassion outside of behavior analysis.

9. Describe the RFT analysis of compassion explained in this chapter.

10. Distinguish between empathy and compassion, as conceptualized through RFT in this chapter.

Glossary of Acronyms

abolishing operation (AO): An antecedent with two functions: (1) decrease the effectiveness of a future consequence as a reinforcer, and (2) temporarily decrease the probability of responses that have been reinforced by that reinforcer in the past.

acceptance and commitment therapy (ACT): A contemporary behavior analytic approach to psychotherapy, based on weakening rigid control by rules involving short-term escape/avoidance contingencies and strengthening repertoires of behaving flexibly with respect to long-term positive reinforcers. When implemented by behavior analysts outside of psychotherapeutic settings, ACT is often referred to as acceptance and commitment *training.*

applied behavior analysis (ABA): The application of behavioral principles of learning and motivation to solving problems of human behavior that are of significance to society.

arbitrarily applicable relational responding (AARR): The term "relational" refers to the fact that AARR is behavior that occurs in response to the relation between two or more antecedent stimuli, rather than in response to a single stimulus. The term "arbitrarily applicable" refers to the fact that AARR does not need to be controlled by the physical characteristics of stimuli, but rather by the arbitrary relational properties. For example, a child learns to say that a dime is bigger than a nickel because it corresponds to a larger amount of money, even though it is physically smaller.

autism spectrum disorder (ASD): A neurodevelopmental disorder characterized by challenges with daily functioning that arise from excessive repetitive behavior and interests, as well as deficits in social communication skills.

behavioral skills training (BST): A highly researched training procedure that involves three components: (1) verbal explanation, (2) modeling, and (3) role-play rehearsal with feedback.

bidirectional naming (BiN): An operant repertoire that involves responding as both speaker and listener to the same environmental stimuli and the ability to switch back and forth between listener and speaker behavior. BiN is characterized by the observation that, when taught one repertoire (i.e., either speaker or listener), the learner can then exhibit the other repertoire, despite not having been taught that repertoire. For example, upon learning to label an apple as "apple," the learner can then point to an apple when asked to "point to apple."

brief and immediate relational responses (BIRRs): Relational responses that occur under time pressure and therefore tend to be relatively brief and unelaborated; that is, the person behaving has not had the opportunity to self-edit the responses. BIRRs are often different from relational responses that the same person would emit if they had a longer duration of time in which to self-edit the response.

complex-to-simple (CTS) protocol: A stimulus equivalence training procedure that involves consecutive training phases followed by testing for the emergence of derived relations individually, starting with the most complex relations.

conditioned stimulus (CS): A stimulus that has respondent functions due to past pairing with another stimulus, for example, a tone that elicits salivation because that tone was paired with food in the past.

conditioned response (CR): A response that occurs in the presence of a stimulus due to past pairing of that stimulus with another stimulus, for example, salivation that occurs in response to a tone because that tone was paired with food in the past.

contextual behavioral science (CBS): CBS is a scientific tradition that is based on functional contextualism and therefore adopts pragmatism as its truth criterion and the ongoing act-in-context as its root metaphor for scientific analysis. CBS contains a reticulated research approach where theoretical, practical, and multifaceted (i.e., basic, analogue, and applied) empirical efforts are mutually influential in fostering CBS's overall progress. The larger purpose of CBS is to produce information that can be applied to successfully reduce human suffering.

derived relational responding (DRR): Behavior that occurs in response to the relation between two or more stimuli, rather than in response to a single stimulus, and that was not directly trained and cannot be accounted for by the physical properties of the stimuli (i.e., is not stimulus generalization). For example, if one is directly taught that Sam is older than Jill and that Jill is older than Mario, one can derive that Mario is younger than Sam, even though one has never been directly taught anything about the relation between Mario and Sam.

dialectical behavior therapy (DBT): A behavioral approach to psychotherapy that integrates the explicit focus on behavior change that characterized first-wave behavior therapies with the shaping of awareness and acceptance of one's immediate experience (Linehan, 1987).

differential arbitrarily applicable relational responding effects (DAARRE): An analytic model that considers how variables affect responding in the implicit relational assessment procedure. The model identifies three key sources of behavioral influence: (1) the relationship between the label and target stimuli (relational cues), (2) the orienting functions of the label and target stimuli (functional cues), and (3) the coherence functions of the two relational coherence indicator response options (e.g., "True" and "False").

differential observing response (DOR): A procedure in which the learner is required to indicate in some way they have observed a stimulus before the procedure continues. For example, a learner may be required to touch a visual stimulus or repeat an auditory stimulus before the next stimulus is presented.

differential reinforcement of low rate (DRL): A reinforcement schedule in which reinforcement is delivered if responding occurs at or below a particular rate.

differential reinforcement of other behavior (DRO): A reinforcement schedule in which a reinforcer is delivered contingent on the absence of a behavior for a specified interval.

discriminative stimulus (SD or S+): An antecedent stimulus that occasions a response because in the past that response was reinforced in the presence of that stimulus more often than in the absence of that stimulus.

early intensive behavioral intervention (EIBI): A highly researched treatment approach for children with autism that contains at least the following elements: (1) starts before the age of three and a half years old, (2) contains thirty or more hours per week of one-to-one intervention, (3) continues for two years or more, (4) is based on the principles of behavior analysis, and (5) is individualized to clients' needs. EIBI is sometimes used with populations other than autism, but the vast majority of published research has been done with children with autism.

English language learner (ELL): An individual whose first language is not English.

equivalence-based instruction (EBI): Teaching procedures based on stimulus equivalence research. Such procedures generally involve directly training relations between some stimuli, usually utilizing match-to-sample procedures, and testing for untrained relations.

establishing operations (EOs): An antecedent with two functions: (1) increase the effectiveness of a future consequence as a reinforcer, and (2) temporarily increase the probability of responses that have been reinforced by that reinforcer in the past.

extended and elaborated relational responses (EERRs): Behaviors that occur under relatively lower time constraints, such that the person responding had adequate time to self-edit their response. Such responses are relatively more likely to be influenced by their social consequences; for example, someone is less likely to emit a response that would be judged as racist by others when engaging in EERRs.

Extrinsic Affective Simon Task (EAST): A task used in mainstream psychology to assess implicit cognitions.

fixed ratio (FR): A reinforcement schedule in which reinforcement is delivered contingent upon a specified number of behaviors occurring.

functional analytic psychotherapy (FAP): A behavioral approach to psychotherapy, based in contextual behavioral science, that focuses on improving interpersonal relationships to help individuals lead more fulfilling lives.

functional contextualism (FC): A philosophy of science that adopts pragmatism as a truth criterion and the ongoing act-in-context as its root metaphor for scientific analysis. Functional contextual science strives to produce increasingly organized statements about nature, with precision, scope, and depth.

Implicit Association Test (IAT): A test developed in mainstream cognitive psychology that tests implicit cognitions.

implicit relational assessment procedure (IRAP): An assessment procedure that requires rapid responding to true or false relations between stimuli. Evaluating the difference in various response latencies provides a procedure for assessing implicit relations, that is, relations that the participant may self-edit if given sufficient opportunity. For example, a person is highly unlikely to report that they are racist, but their latency to respond negatively to a statement that a particular ethnic group is bad may be shorter than their latency to respond saying that same ethnic group is good.

instructive feedback (IF): A procedure that involves adding additional nontarget stimuli to the antecedent or consequence events of direct instructional trials.

inter-stimulus interval (ISI): The time that elapses from the presentation of one stimulus to the presentation of the next.

linear series: A sequence for training relations in a stimulus equivalence experiment. For example, one might train that A = B and then B = C.

many-to-one (MTO): A format for training stimulus relations in an experiment in derived relational responding. One stimulus set is used as the comparison stimuli, whereas two or more other stimulus sets are used as the sample stimuli. For example, one might train A = B, C = B, and D = B.

match-to-sample (MTS): A teaching procedure that involves presenting a single sample stimulus, then an instruction, and then multiple comparison stimuli. For example, a teacher might give a learner a picture of a car, then ask the learner to find the one that is the same, and then provide the opportunity for the learner to scan comparison stimuli consisting of car, truck, and airplane.

motivating operation (MO): The umbrella term that encompasses both abolishing operation and establishing operation.

multiple exemplar instruction (MEI): A teaching procedure that involves teaching more than one example at the same time. MEI can be conducted across multiple different verbal operants for the same target, for example, learning to respond as both speaker and listener to blue objects. MEI can also be conducted within a single operant repertoire but across multiple exemplars of stimuli, for example, by learning to label the color blue by being taught to label ten different blue objects as "blue." Occasionally, MEI is used to distinguish procedures where multiple exemplars are trained *across* operant classes of behavior, as opposed to *within*.

multiple exemplar training (MET): Another term for MEI (see above definition). Occasionally, MET is used to refer to procedures where multiple exemplars are trained *within* operant classes of behavior, as opposed to *across*.

observational learning (OL): A form of learning that involves behavior change as a function of observing happenings in one's environment.

one-to-many (OTM): A stimulus equivalence training procedure, wherein one stimulus set is used as the sample stimuli and relations are trained between that set as sample stimuli and two or more other sets as comparison stimuli. For example, one might train A = B, A = C, and A = D.

peer-mediated interventions (PMIs): Interventions in which peers are actively involved in delivering relevant antecedents, consequences, or both.

Picture Exchange Communication System (PECS): A communication system commonly used by learners who have difficulty producing vocal speech. PECS involves selecting and giving pictures to others as an alternative form of communication. PECS also actively encourages learners to attempt to produce vocal speech while communicating with pictures.

Promoting the Emergence of Advanced Knowledge (PEAK): A recently developed assessment and curriculum, based on relational frame theory, that is intended to be used by practitioners to teach verbal repertoires, including derived relational responding.

random interval (RI): A reinforcement schedule in which reinforcement is delivered contingent upon the first response that occurs after a specified interval of time has elapsed since the last reinforcer was delivered, and where the duration of that interval varies randomly, within specified parameters, after each reinforcer is delivered.

random ratio (RR): A reinforcement schedule in which reinforcement is delivered contingent on the occurrence of a specific number of responses, and where that number varies randomly, within specified parameters, after each reinforcer is delivered.

randomized controlled trial (RCT): An experimental design in which participants are randomly assigned to two or more groups and where those responsible for measuring the dependent variable are generally blind to group assignment. This design is considered the strongest experimental design by most researchers in mainstream psychology and medicine.

relational coherence indicator (RCI): Response options, such as "True" and "False," that are often used to indicate the coherence or incoherence between labels and target stimuli that are presented within an implicit relational assessment procedure.

relational elaboration and coherence (REC) model: An initial relational frame theory approach to implicit cognition, based on the idea that the implicit relational assessment procedure forces participants to emit rapid relational responses that are less likely to be influenced by social variables than the slower, more elaborated relational responses emitted on traditional assessments of bias. The strength of the rapid relational responses emitted toward experimental stimuli was thought to be functionally similar to that of responses toward these stimuli in the participant's preexperimental history, when one does not have the opportunity to edit one's own responses in anticipation of social contingencies.

relational fame theory (RFT): A behavior analytic theory of language and cognition that addresses verbal behavior that occurs in response to relations between stimuli, rather than to single stimuli as antecedents. Such behavior is said to comprise generalized relational operants, learned through a history of multiple exemplar training. These operants are referred to as "relational frames" and demonstrate the properties of being arbitrarily applicable (i.e., they do not depend on the physical properties of antecedent controlling stimuli), displaying mutual entailment (i.e., they are bidirectional), displaying combinatorial entailment (i.e., relations propagate across three or more stimuli in a network), and involving transformation of stimulus functions (i.e., operant and respondent functions transform in accordance with the mutually entailed and combinatorially entailed functions).

rule-governed behavior (RGB): Behavior that occurs due to contact with an antecedent rule and not due to prior contact with the contingencies the rule describes.

S-delta (SΔ or S-): A stimulus that does not occasion a response because the response has not been reinforced in the presence of that stimulus in the past.

self-determined learning model of instruction (SDLMI): A program for teaching problem solving that involves scripted problem-solving instruction delivered by a teacher who follows a sequence predetermined by the investigator.

simple-to-complex (STC) protocol: A stimulus equivalence training protocol that intersperses training phases and derived relations probes. Across the whole program, derived relations are tested individually and tests are arranged from the simplest type of derived relations (i.e., symmetry) to the most difficult (i.e., equivalence).

simultaneous (SIM) protocol: A stimulus equivalence training protocol in which all training phases are grouped and all testing phases are grouped, with no overlap between.

social listener reinforcement (SLR): A procedure designed to build reinforcement for speaking and listening to peers and to increase the learner's conversational units with others. Such procedures often involve a sequence of increasingly complex games, ending with an empathy phase, that use a yoked contingency game board to establish social listener reinforcement.

stimulus-pairing observation (SPO): A procedure for teaching discriminations in which an experimenter briefly presents a stimulus in isolation to the learner, followed by an inter-stimulus interval (ISI) and then presentation of a second stimulus. Thus, the procedure involves pairing of stimuli with no overt response requirement from the participant other than attending to the stimuli presented by the experimenter.

stimulus-stimulus pairing (SSP): A procedure in which an experimenter pairs auditory stimuli (e.g., word sounds) with already established reinforcers in an attempt to condition those word sounds as sources of automatic reinforcement. This procedure often results in temporary increase in the probability of the learner's making those same word sounds.

talk aloud problem solving (TAPS): A problem-solving training procedure that teaches students to perform both as problem solvers and as active listeners.

theory of mind (ToM): An evolutionary-developmental theory that explains perspective-taking behavior in terms of inferred brain mechanisms.

think aloud pair problem solving (TAPPS): A problem-solving training procedure that teaches students to dialogue with themselves to analytically talk themselves through solving problems. The procedure is often used to teach academic skills.

transfer of stimulus control (ToSC): A procedure in which stimulus control is transferred from one stimulus to another, often through gradually changing the topographical properties of the first stimulus until it resembles the second stimulus.

transitive conditioned establishing operations (CMO-T): Previously neutral conditions whose occurrences alter the effectiveness of another stimulus and evoke responses that produce or suppress that stimulus.

unconditioned response (UR): A respondent behavior that occurs in response to unconditioned stimuli and that does not depend on a history of conditioning to occur.

unconditioned stimulus (US): An eliciting stimulus that does not depend on a history of conditioning to be effective at eliciting an unconditioned response.

unidirectional naming (UiN): In the context of rudimentary verbal behavior, UiN refers to the demonstration of the listener component, which involves hearing a speech sound and then responding in a nonvocal way to a nonverbal stimulus (e.g., hearing the word "car" and then pointing to a car).

verbal behavior developmental theory (VBDT): A theoretical approach that combines Skinnerian verbal behavior, stimulus equivalence, naming theory, and relational frame theory to analyze the development of verbal repertoires over the lifetime of the child, emphasizing the transition from unidirectional verbal operants to complex bidirectional operants.

verbal conditional discrimination (VCD): Behavior that is under the control of two antecedent stimuli, where the control that one exerts is conditional upon the presence of the other. For example, when hearing the stimuli "vegetable" and "purple," one might reply "eggplant."

References

Adams, B. J., Fields, L., & Verhave, T. (1993). Effects of the test order on intersubject variability during equivalence class formation. *Psychological Record, 43*, 133–152.

Adkins, T., & Axelrod, S. (2001). Topography-versus selection-based responding: Comparison of mand acquisitions in each modality. *The Behavior Analyst Today, 2*(3), 259–266. doi:10.1037/h0099941

Agran, M., Blanchard, C., Wehmeyer, M., & Hughes, C. (2002). Increasing the problem-solving skills of students with developmental disabilities participating in general education. *Remedial and Special Education, 23*, 279–288.

Aguilar, J. M., Chan, J. M., White, P. J., & Fragale, C. (2017). Assessment of the language preferences of five children with autism from Spanish-speaking homes. *Journal of Behavioral Education*, published online first, 1–14. doi:10.1007/s10864-017-9280-9

Aguirre, A. A., & Rehfeldt, R. A. (2015). An evaluation of instruction in visual imagining on the written spelling performance of adolescents with learning disabilities. *The Analysis of Verbal Behavior, 31*(1), 118–125. doi:10.1007/s40616-015-0028-0

Aguirre, A. A., Valentino, A. L., & LeBlanc, L. A. (2016). Empirical investigations of the intraverbal: 2005–2015. *The Analysis of Verbal Behavior, 32*, 139–153. doi:10.1007/s40616-016-0064-4

Albright, L., Reeve, K. F., Reeve, S. A., & Kisamore, A. N. (2015). Teaching statistical variability with equivalence-based instruction. *Journal of Applied Behavior Analysis, 48*, 883–894.

Albright, L., Schnell, L., Reeve, K. F., & Sidener, T. M. (2016). Using stimulus equivalence-based instruction to teach graduate students in applied behavior analysis to interpret operant functions of behavior. *Journal of Behavioral Education, 25*, 290–309.

Alessi, G. (1987). Generative strategies and teaching for generalization. *The Analysis of Verbal Behavior, 5*, 15–27.

Allan, A. C., Vladescu, J. C., Kisamore, A. N., Reeve, S. A., & Sidener, T. M. (2015). Evaluating the emergence of reverse intraverbals in children with autism. *Analysis of Verbal Behavior, 31*(1), 59–75. doi:10.1007/s40616-014-0025-8

Anderson, C. M., Hawkins, R. P., & Scotti, J. R. (1998). Private events in behavior analysis: Conceptual basis and clinical relevance. *Behavior Therapy, 28*(1), 157–179.

Andronis, P. T., Layng, T. V. J., & Goldiamond, I. (1997). Contingency adduction of "symbolic aggression" by pigeons. *The Analysis of Verbal Behavior, 14*, 5–17.

Archer, A., Gleason, M., & Isaacson, S. (2008). *REWARDS Writing: Sentence Refinement [Curriculum Program].* Longmont, CO: Sopris West.

Arntzen, E. (2006). Delayed matching-to-sample: Probability of stimulus equivalence as a function of delays between sample and comparison stimuli during training. *The Psychological Record, 56*, 5–167.

Arntzen, E., & Almås, I. K. (2002). Effects of mand-tact versus tact-only training on the acquisition of tacts. *Journal of Applied Behavior Analysis, 35*(4), 419–422. doi:10.190/jaba.2002.35-419

Arntzen, E., Grondahl, T., & Eilifsen, C. (2010). The effects of different training structures in the establishment of conditional discriminations and subsequent performance on tests for stimulus equivalence. *The Psychological Record, 60*, 437–462.

Arntzen, E., Halstadtro, L.-B., & Halstradtro, M. (2009). The "silent dog" method: Analyzing the impact of self-generated rules when teaching different computer chains to boys with autism. *The Analysis of Verbal Behavior, 25,* 51–65.

Arntzen, E., Halstadtro, L.-B., Bjerke, E., & Halstadtro, M. (2010). Training and testing music skills in a boy with autism using a matching-to-sample format. *Behavioral Interventions, 25,* 129–143. doi:10.1002/bin.301

Arntzen, E., & Holth, P. (1997). Probability of stimulus equivalence as a function of training design. *Psychological Record, 47,* 309–320.

Arntzen, E., & Holth, P. (2000). Equivalence outcome in single subjects as a function of training structure. *The Psychological Record, 50,* 603–628.

Asaro-Saddler, K. (2016). Using evidence-based practices to teach writing to children with autism spectrum disorders. *Preventing School Failure: Alternative Education for Children and Youth, 60*(1), 79–85. doi:10.1080/1045988x.2014.981793

Austin, J. L. (1962). *How to do things with words.* Oxford, England: Oxford University Press. (Original work published 1955)

Axe, J. B. (2008). Conditional discrimination in the intraverbal relation: A review and recommendations for future research. *The Analysis of Verbal Behavior, 24*(1), 159–174. doi:10.1007/BF03393064

Ayllon, T., & Azrin, N. H. (1966). Punishment as a discriminative stimulus and conditioned reinforcer with humans. *Journal of the Experimental Analysis of Behavior, 9,* 411–419. doi:10.1901/jeab.1966.9-411

Ayllon, T., & Azrin, N. H. (1968). *The token economy: A motivational system for therapy and rehabilitation.* New York, NY: Appleton Century Crofts.

Azrin, N. H., & Foxx, R. M. (1971). A rapid method of toilet training the institutionalized retarded. *Journal of Applied Behavior Analysis, 4,* 89–99.

Azrin, N. H., & Holz, W. C. (1966). Punishment. In W. K. Honig (Ed.), *Operant behavior: Areas of research and application* (pp. 380–447). New York, NY: Appleton-Century-Crofts.

Baer, D. M., Wolf, M. M., & Risley, T. R. (1968). Some current dimensions of applied behavior analysis. *Journal of Applied Behavior Analysis, 1*(1), 91–97. doi:10.1901/jaba.1968.1-91

Baker, K. A. (2014). *The effects of social listener reinforcement and video modeling on the emergence of social verbal operants in preschoolers diagnosed with autism and language delays* (Doctoral dissertation, Order No. 3621578). Available from ProQuest Dissertations & Theses Global. (1552714267). doi:10.7916/D85T3HNQ

Bandura, A. (1961). Psychotherapy as a learning process. *Psychological Bulletin, 58*(2), 143–159.

Bandura, A. (1965). Influence of models' reinforcement contingencies on the acquisition of imitative responses. *Journal of Personality and Social Psychology, 1,* 589–595. doi:10.1037/h0022070

Bandura, A. (1969). *Principles of behavior modification.* New York, NY: Holt, Rinehart, & Winston.

Bandura, A. (1974). Behavior theory and the models of man. *American Psychologist, 29*(12), 859–869.

Bandura, A., Grusec, J. E., & Menlove, F. L. (1966). Observational learning as a function of symbolization and incentive set. *Child Development, 37,* 499–506.

Bandura, A., & Jeffrey, R. W. (1973). Role of symbolic coding and rehearsal processes in observational learning. *Journal of Personality and Social Psychology, 26,* 122–130.

Barbera, M. L., & Kubina, R. M. (2005). Using transfer procedures to teach tacts to a child with autism. *The Analysis of Verbal Behavior, 21*(1), 155–161. doi:10.1007/BF03393017

Barbero-Rubio, A., López-López, J. C., Luciano, C., & Eisenbeck, N. (2016). Perspective-taking measured by implicit relational assessment procedure (IRAP). *The Psychological Record, 66*(2), 243–252.

Barlow, D. H. (1988). *Anxiety and its disorders: The nature and treatment of anxiety and panic.* New York, NY: Guilford Press.

Barlow, D. H., Craske, M. G., Cerny, J. A., & Klosko, J. S. (1989). Behavioral treatment of panic disorder. *Behavior Therapy, 20*, 261–282.

Barlow, K. E., Tiger, J. H., Slocum, S. K., & Miller, S. J. (2013). Comparing acquisition of exchange-based and signed mands with children with autism. *The Analysis of Verbal Behavior, 29(1)*, 59–69. doi:10.1007/BF03393124

Barnes, D., Hegarty, N., & Smeets, P. M. (1997). Relating equivalence relations to equivalence relations: A relational framing model of complex human functioning. *The Analysis of Verbal Behavior, 14*, 57–83.

Barnes, D., Lawlor, H., Smeets, P. M., & Roche, B. (1996). Stimulus equivalence and academic self-concept among mildly mentally handicapped and nonhandicapped children. *The Psychological Record, 46*, 87–107.

Barnes-Holmes, D., & Barnes-Holmes, Y. (2000). Explaining complex behavior: Two perspectives on the concept of generalized operant classes. *The Psychological Record, 50*, 251–265. doi:10.1007/bf03395355

Barnes-Holmes, D., Barnes-Holmes, Y., & Cullinan, V. (2000). Relational frame theory and Skinner's Verbal Behavior: A possible synthesis. *The Behavior Analyst, 23(1)*, 69–84. doi:10.1007/BF03392000

Barnes-Holmes, D., Barnes-Holmes, Y., Stewart, I., & Boles, S. (2010). A sketch of the Implicit Relational Assessment Procedure (IRAP) and the Relational Elaboration and Coherence (REC) model. *The Psychological Record, 60*, 527–542.

Barnes-Holmes, D., Finn, M., McEnteggart, C., Barnes-Holmes, Y. (2017). Derived stimulus relations and their role in a behavior-analytic account of human language and cognition. *Perspectives on Behavior Science, 41*, 155–173. doi:10.1007/s40614-017-0124-7

Barnes-Holmes, D., Murphy, A., Barnes-Holmes, Y., & Stewart, I. (2010). The Implicit Relational Assessment Procedure: Exploring the impact of private versus public contexts and the response latency criterion on pro-white and anti-black stereotyping among white Irish individuals. *The Psychological Record, 60*, 57–66.

Barnes-Holmes, D., O'Hora, D., Roche, B., Hayes, S. C., Bissett, R. T., & Lyddy, F. (2001). Understanding and verbal regulation. In S. Hayes, D. Barnes-Holmes, & B. Roche (Eds.), *Relational frame theory: A post-Skinnerian account of human language and cognition* (pp. 103–117). New York, NY: Springer.

Barnes-Holmes, D., Regan, D., Barnes-Holmes, Y., Commins, S., Walsh, D., Stewart, I., . . . Dymond, S. (2005). Relating derived relations as a model of analogical reasoning: Reaction times and event-related potentials. *Journal of the Experimental Analysis of Behavior, 84(3)*, 435–451.

Barnes-Holmes, Y., Barnes-Holmes, D., & McHugh, L. (2004). Teaching derived relational responding to young children. *Journal of Early and Intensive Behavior Intervention, 1*, 3–12.

Barnes-Holmes, Y., Barnes-Holmes, D., Roche, B., & Smeets, P. M. (2001a). Exemplar training and a derived transformation of function in accordance with symmetry: II. *The Psychological Record, 51*, 589–603.

Barnes-Holmes, Y., Barnes-Holmes, D., Roche, B., & Smeets, P. M. (2001b) The development of self and perspective-taking: A relational frame analysis. *Behavioral Development Bulletin, 10*, 42–45.

Barnes Holmes, Y., Barnes Holmes, D., & Smeets, P. M. (2004). Establishing relational responding in accordance with opposite as generalized operant behavior in young children. *International Journal of Psychology and Psychological Therapy, 4.* 559–586.

Barnes-Holmes, Y., Barnes-Holmes, D., Smeets, P. M., Strand, P., & Friman, P. (2004). Establishing relational responding in accordance with more-than and less-than as generalized operant behavior in young children. *International Journal of Psychology and Psychological Therapy, 4.* 531–558.

Barnes-Holmes, Y., Boorman, J., Oliver, J. E. Thompson, M., McEnteggart, C., & Coulter, C. (2018). Using conceptual developments in RFT to direct case formulation and clinical intervention: Two case summaries. *Journal of Contextual Behavioral Science, 7*, 89–96. doi:10.1016/j.jcbs.2017.11.005

Baron, A., & Galizio, M. (1983). Instructional control of human operant behavior. *The Psychological Record, 33,* 495–520.

Baron-Cohen, S., Leslie, A. M., & Frith, U. (1985). Does the autistic child have a "theory of mind"? *Cognition, 21*(1), 37–46.

Barrera, R. D., Lobato-Barrera, D., & Sulzer-Azaroff, B. (1980). A simultaneous treatment comparison of three expressive language training programs with a mute autistic child. *Journal of Autism and Developmental Disorders, 10*(1), 21–37. doi:10.1007/BF02408430

Barrera, R. D., & Sulzer-Azaroff, B. (1983). An alternating treatment comparison of oral and total communication training programs with echolalic autistic children. *Journal of Applied Behavior Analysis, 16*(4), 379–394. doi:10.1901/jaba.1983.16-379

Barrish, H. H., Saunders, M. S., & Wolf, M. M. (1969). Good behavior game: Effects of individual contingencies for group consequences on disruptive behavior in a classroom. *Journal of Applied Behavior Analysis, 2,* 119–124. doi:10.1901/jaba.1969.2-119

Bast, D. F., & Barnes-Holmes, D. (2015). Priming thoughts of failing versus succeeding and performance on the Implicit Relational Assessment Procedure (IRAP) as a measure of self-forgiveness. *The Psychological Record, 65*(4), 667–678. doi:10.1007/s40732-015-0137-0

Bast, D. F., Linares, I. M. P., Gomes, C., Kovac, R., & Barnes-Holmes, D. (2016). The Implicit Relational Assessment Procedure (IRAP) as a measure of self-forgiveness: The impact of a training history in clinical behavior analysis. *The Psychological Record, 66*(1), 177–190. doi:10.1007/s40732-016-0162-7

Batson, C. D. (2009). These things called empathy: Eight related but distinct phenomena. In J. Decety & W. Ickes (Eds), *Social neuroscience. The social neuroscience of empathy* (pp. 3–15). Cambridge, MA: MIT Press.

Baum, W. M. (2011a). Behaviorism, private events, and the molar view of behavior. *The Behavior Analyst, 34*(2), 185–200.

Baum, W. M. (2011b). No need for private events in a science of behavior: Response to commentaries. *The Behavior Analyst, 34*(2), 237–244.

Baum, W. M. (2012). Rethinking reinforcement: allocation, induction, and contingency. *Journal of the Experimental Analysis of Behavior, 97*(1), 101–124. doi:10.1901/jeab.2012.97-101

Beaulieu, L., Hanley, G. P., & Santiago, J. L. (2014). Improving the conversational skills of a college student with peer-mediated behavioral skills training. *The Analysis of Verbal Behavior, 30*(1), 48–53. doi:10.1007/s40616-013-0001-8

Beck, A. T. (1976). *Cognitive therapy and the emotional disorders.* New York, NY: Meridian.

Beck, A. T. (2005). The current state of cognitive therapy: a 40-year retrospective. *Archives of General Psychiatry, 62*(9), 953–959.

Beck, I. L., McKeown, M. G., Hamilton, R. L., & Kucan, L. (1997). *Questioning the author: An approach for enhancing student engagement with text.* Newark, DE: International Reading Association.

Beidel, D. C., & Turner, S. M. (1986). A critique of the theoretical bases of cognitive-behavioral theories and therapy. *Clinical Psychology Review, 6*(2), 177–197. doi:10.1016/0272-7358(86)90011-5

Belanich, J., & Fields, L. (1999). Tactual equivalence class formation and tactual-to-visual cross-modal transfer. *The Psychological Record, 49,* 75–91.

Belisle, J., Dixon, M. R., Stanley, C. R., Munoz, B., & Daar, J. H. (2016). Teaching foundational perspective-taking skills to children with autism using the PEAK-T curriculum: single-reversal "I–You" deictic frames. *Journal of Applied Behavior Analysis, 49,* 965–969.

Belloso-Díaz, C., & Pérez-González, L. A. (2015). Effect of learning tacts or tacts and intraverbals on the emergence of intraverbals about verbal categorization. *The Psychological Record, 65*(4), 749–760. doi:10.1007/s40732-015-0145-0

Bentall, R. P., Lowe, C. F., & Beasty, A. (1985). The role of verbal behavior in human learning: II Developmental differences. *Journal of the Experimental Analysis of Behavior, 43,* 165–181. doi:10.1901/jeab.1985.43-165

Berens, N. M., & Hayes, S. C. (2007). Arbitrarily applicable comparative relations: Experimental evidence for a relational operant. *Journal of Applied Behavior Analysis*, 40, 45–71. doi:10.1901/jaba.2007.7-06

Bernard-Opitz, V., Sriram, N., & Nakhoda-Sapuan, S. (2001). Enhancing social problem solving in children with autism and normal children through computer-assisted instruction. *Journal of Autism and Developmental Disorders*, 31, 377–384.

Bevill-Davis, A., Clees, T. J., & Gast, D. L. (2004). Correspondence training: A review of the literature. *Journal of Early and Intensive Behavior Intervention*, 1, 13–26. doi:10.1037/h0100276

Biglan, A. (2015) *The nurture effect. How the science of behaviour can improve our lives and our world.* Oakland, CA: New Harbinger.

Bijou, S. W. (1983). The initial development of linguistic behavior. In N. W. Smith, P. T. Mountjoy, & D. H. Ruben (Eds.), *Reassessment in psychology: The interbehavioral alternative* (pp. 213–232). Lanham, MD: University Press of America.

Bijou, S. W. (1989). Psychological linguistics: Implications for a theory of initial development and a method for research. *Advances in child behavior and development*, 21, 221–241.

Bijou, S. W. (1996). Setting factors in the behavior analysis of child development. In S. W. Bijou & E. Ribes (Eds.), *New directions in behavior development* (pp. 147–154). Reno, NV: Context Press.

Bijou, S. W., & Baer, D. M. (1978). *Behavior analysis of child development.* Englewood Cliffs, NJ: Prentice Hall.

Bijou, S. W., Chao, C. C., & Ghezzi, P. M. (1988). Manual of instructions for identifying and analyzing referential interactions II. *The Psychological Record*, 38, 401–414.

Bijou, S. W., Umbreit, J., Ghezzi, P. M., & Chao, C. C. (1986). Manual of instructions for identifying and analyzing referential interactions. *The Psychological Record*, 36, 491–518.

Binder, C. (1996). Behavioral fluency: Evolution of a new paradigm. *The Behavior Analyst*, 19, 163–187.

Binder, C., & Bloom, C. (1989, February). Fluent product knowledge: Application in the financial services industry. *Performance and Instruction*, 28, 17–21.

Binder, C. & Sweeney, L. (2002). Building fluent performance in a customer call center. *Performance Improvement*, 41(2), 29–37.

Binet, A., & Simon, T. (1973). *The development of intelligence in children: The Binet-Simon Scale.* New York, NY: Arno Press. (Original work published 1916)

Bishop, C. D., Erezyilmaz, D. F., Flatt, T., Georgiou, C. D., Hadfield, M. G., Heyland, A., . . . Youson, J. H. (2006). What is metamorphosis? *Integrative and Comparative Biology*, 46, 655–661. doi:10.1093/icb/icl004

Blackburn, I. M., Bishop, S., Glen, A. I., Whalley, L. J., & Christie, J. E. (1981). The efficacy of cognitive therapy in depression: A treatment trial using cognitive therapy and pharmacotherapy, each alone and in combination. *The British Journal of Psychiatry*, 139(3), 181–189.

Blackledge, J. T. (2007). Disrupting verbal processes: Cognitive defusion in acceptance and commitment therapy and other mindfulness-based psychotherapies. *The Psychological Record*, 57(4), 555–576.

Blackledge, J. T., & Drake, C. E. (2013). Acceptance and commitment therapy: Empirical and theoretical considerations. In S. Dymond & B. Roche (Eds.), *Advances in relational frame theory: Research and application* (pp. 219–252). Oakland, CA: New Harbinger.

Blewitt, P. (1994). Understanding categorical hierarchies: The earliest levels of skill. *Child Development*, 65. 1279–1298. doi:10.1111/j.1467-8624.1994.tb00817.x

Bloom, L. (1993). Transcription and coding for child language research: The parts are more than the whole. In J. A. Edwards & M. D. Lampert (Eds.), *Taking data: Transcription and coding in discourse research* (pp. 149–166). Hillsdale, NJ: Lawrence Erlbaum.

Bod, R. (2009). From exemplar to grammar: A probabilistic analogy-based model of language learning. *Cognitive Science*, 33, 752–793.

Boë, L-J., Berthommier, F., Legou, T., Captier, G., Kemp, C., Sawallis, T. R., . . . Fagot, J. (2017). Evidence of a vocalic proto-system in the baboon (Papio papio) suggests pre-hominin speech precursors. *PlosOne*, January 11, 2017. doi:10.1371/journal.pone.0169321

Boone, M. S., & Cannici, J. (2013). Acceptance and commitment therapy (ACT) in groups. In J. Pistorello (Ed.). *Acceptance and mindfulness for counseling college students: Theory and practical applications for intervention, prevention, and outreach.* Oakland, CA: New Harbinger.

Bornstein, M. H., & Mash, C. (2010). Experience-based and on-line categorization of objects in early infancy. *Child Development, 81*, 3, 884–897. doi:10.1111/j.1467-8624.2010.01440.x

Bourret, J., Vollmer T., & Rapp, J.T. (2004). Evaluation of a vocal mand assessment and vocal mand training procedures. *Journal of Applied Behavior Analysis, 37*(2), 129–144. doi:10.1901/jaba.2004.37-129

Bouton, M. E., & Trask, S. (2016). Role of the discriminative properties of the reinforcer in resurgence. *Learning & Behavior, 44*, 137–150. doi:10.3758/s13420-015-0197-7

Bouton, M. E., Winterbauer, N. E., & Todd, T. P. (2012). Relapse processes after the extinction of instrumental learning: renewal, resurgence, and reacquisition. *Behavioural Processes, 90*(1), 130–141. doi:10.1016/j.beproc.2012.03.004

Bower, G.H., & Hilgard, E.R. (1981). *Theories of learning.* Englewood Cliffs, NJ: Prentice Hall.

Brady, D. O., & Smouse, A. D. (1978). A simultaneous comparison of three methods for language training with an autistic child: An experimental single case analysis. *Journal of Autism and Developmental Disorders, 8*(3), 271–279. doi:10.1007/BF01539630

Branch, M. N., & Malagodi, E. F. (1980). Where have all the behaviorists gone? *The Behavior Analyst, 3*(1), 31–38.

Breger, L., & McGaugh, J. L. (1965). Critique and reformulation of "learning-theory" approaches to psychotherapy and neurosis. *Psychological Bulletin, 63*(5), 338–358. doi:10.1037/h0021788

Briscoe, R. V., Hoffman, D. B., & Bailey, J. S. (1975). Behavioral community psychology: Training a community board to problem solve. *Journal of Applied Behavior Analysis, 8*, 157–168.

Brodhead, M. T., Higbee, T. S., Gerencser, K. R., & Akers, J. A. (2016). The use of discrimination-training procedure to teach mand variability to children with autism. *Journal of Applied Behavior Analysis, 49*(1), 34–48. doi:10.1002/jaba.280

Brodsky, J., & Fienup, D. M. (2018). Sidman goes to college: A meta-analysis of equivalence-based instruction. *Perspectives on Behavior Science, 41*, 95–119. doi:10.1007/s40614-018-0150-0

Brown, A. L. (1989). Analogical learning and transfer: What develops? In S. Vosniadou & Ortony (Eds.), *Similarity and Analogical Reasoning* (pp. 369–412). Cambridge, UK: Cambridge University Press.

Brunero, S., Lamont, S., & Coates, M. (2010). A review of empathy education in nursing. *Nursing Inquiry, 17*(1), 65–74.

Burchard, J. D., & Barrera, F. (1972). An analysis of timeout and response cost in a programmed environment. *Journal of Applied Behavior Analysis, 5*, 271–282. doi:10.1901/jaba.1972.5-271

Burns, D. D., & Spangler, D. L. (2001). Do changes in dysfunctional attitudes mediate changes in depression and anxiety in cognitive behavioral therapy? *Behavior Therapy, 32*(2), 337–369.

Byrne, B. L., Rehfeldt, R. A., & Aguirre, A. A. (2014). Evaluating the effectiveness of the stimulus pairing observation procedure and multiple exemplar instruction on tact and listener responses in children with autism. *The Analysis of Verbal Behavior, 30*(2), 160–169. doi:10.1007/s40616-014-0020-0

Cagney, S., Harte, C., Barnes-Holmes, D., Barnes-Holmes, Y., & McEnteggart, C. (2017). Response biases on the IRAP for adults and adolescents with respect to smokers and nonsmokers: The impact of parental smoking status. *The Psychological Record, 67*(4), 473–483. doi:10.1007/s40732-017-0249-9

Cahill, C. S., & Greer, R. D. (2014). Actions vs. words: How we can learn both. *Acta Investigacion Psicologia, 4*, 1716–1745. doi:10.1016/S2007-4719(14)70976-7

Cameron, G., Roche, B., Schlund, M. W., & Dymond, S. (2016). Learned, instructed and observed pathways to fear and avoidance. *Journal of Behavior Therapy and Experimental Psychiatry, 50,* 106–112. doi:10.1016/j.jbtep.2015.06.003

Cameron, G., Schlund, M. W., & Dymond, S. (2015). Generalization of socially transmitted and instructed avoidance. *Frontiers in Behavioral Neuroscience, 9,* 159. doi:10.3389/fnbeh.2015.00159

Carbone, V. J., Lewis, L., Sweeney-Kerwin, E. J., Dixon, J., Louden, R., & Quinn, S. (2006). A comparison of two approaches for teaching VB functions: Total communication vs. vocal-alone. *The Journal of Speech and Language Pathology–Applied Behavior Analysis, 1*(3), 181–192. doi:10.1037/h0100199

Carbone, V. J., Sweeney-Kerwin, E. J., Attanasio, V., & Kasper, T. (2010). Increasing the vocal responses of children with autism and developmental disabilities using manual sign mand training and prompt delay. *Journal of Applied Behavior Analysis, 43*(4), 705–709. doi:10.1901/jaba.2010.43–705

Cariveau, T., Kodak, T., & Campbell, V. (2016). The effects of intertrial interval and instructional format on skill acquisition and maintenance for children with autism spectrum disorders. *Journal of Applied Behavior Analysis, 49*(4), 809–825. doi:10.1002/jaba.322

Carpentier, F., Smeets, P. M., & Barnes-Holmes, D. (2002). Matching functionally same relations: Implications for equivalence-equivalence as a model of analogical reasoning. *The Psychological Record, 52,* 351–370.

Carpentier, F., Smeets, P. M., & Barnes-Holmes, D. (2003). Equivalence-equivalence as a model of analogy: Further analysis. *The Psychological Record, 53,* 349–371.

Carpentier, F., Smeets, P., Barnes-Holmes, D., & Stewart, I. (2004). Matching derived functionally-same stimulus relations. Equivalence-equivalence and classical analogies. *The Psychological Record, 54,* 255–273.

Carr, J. E., & Miguel, C. F. (2012). The analysis of verbal behavior and its therapeutic applications. In G. J. Madden (Ed.), *APA handbook of behavior analysis* (Vol. 2, pp. 329–352). Washington, DC: American Psychological Association.

Carroll, R. A., & Kodak, T. (2015). Using instructive feedback to increase response variability during intraverbal training for children with autism spectrum disorder. *The Analysis of Verbal Behavior, 31*(2), 183–199. doi:10.1007/s40616-015-0039-x

Carter, M., & Grunsell, J. (2001). The behavior chain interruption strategy: A review of research and discussion of future directions. *Journal of the Association for Persons with Severe Handicaps, 26*(1), 37–49. doi:10.2511/rpsd.26.1.37

Cartwright, A., Hussey, I., Roche, B., Dunne, J., & Murphy, C. (2016). An investigation into the relationship between gender binary and occupational discrimination using the Implicit Relational Assessment Procedure. *The Psychological Record, 67,* 121–130. doi:10.1007/s40732-016-0212-1

Cartwright, A., Roche, B., Gogarty, M., O'Reilly, A., & Stewart, I. (2016). Using a modified Function Acquisition Speed Test (FAST) for assessing implicit gender stereotypes. *The Psychological Record, 66*(2), 223–233. doi:10.1007/s40732-016-0164-5

Castro, M., & Rehfeldt, R. A. (2016). Comparing the efficacy of peers versus staff models on observational learning in adults with developmental disorders. *Journal of Developmental and Physical Disabilities, 28,* 609–622. doi:10.1007/s10882-016-9498-9

Catania, A. C. (1997). *Learning.* Upper Saddle River, NJ: Prentice Hall.

Catania, A. C., Shimoff, E., & Matthews, B. A. (1989). An experimental analysis of rule-governed behavior. In S. Hayes (Ed.), *Rule-governed behavior: Cognition, contingencies, and instructional control* (pp. 119–150). Reno, NV: Context Press.

Chambers, M., & Rehfeldt, R. A. (2003). Assessing the acquisition and generalization of two mand forms with adults with severe developmental disabilities. *Research in Developmental Disabilities, 24*(4), 265–280. doi:10.1016/S0891-4222(03)00042-8

Chang, Y. C., & Locke, J. (2016). A systematic review of peer-mediated interventions for children with autism spectrum disorder. *Research in Autism Spectrum Disorders, 27*, 1–10. doi:10.1016/j.rasd.2016.03.010

Charlop, M. H., & Milstein, J. P. (1989). Teaching autistic children conversational speech using video modeling. *Journal of Applied Behavior Analysis, 22*(3), 275–285. doi:10.1901/jaba.1989.22-275

Chase, P. N., & Danforth, J. S. (1991). The role of rules in concept learning. In L. J. Hayes & P. N. Chase (Eds.), *Dialogues on verbal behavior* (pp. 205–236). Reno, NV: Context Press.

Chiasson, C. C., & Hayes, L. J. (1993). The effects of subtle differences between listeners and speakers on the referential speech of college freshman. *The Psychological Record, 43*, 13–24.

Chomsky, N. (1959). A review of B. F. Skinner's *Verbal Behavior. Language, 35*(1), 26–58.

Chomsky, N. (1966). *Topics in the theory of generative grammar.* The Hague, Paris: Mouton & Co. N.V., Publishers.

Chomsky, N., & Place, U. T. (2000). The Chomsky—Place correspondence 1993–1994. *The Analysis of Verbal Behavior, 17*, 7–38.

Christie, S., & Gentner, D. (2014). Language helps children success on a classic analogy task. *Cognitive Science, 38*, 383–397.

Cihon, T. M., White, R., Zimmerman, V. L., Gesick, J., Stordahl, S., & Eshleman, J., (2017). The effects of precision teaching with textual or tact relations on intraverbal relations. *Behavioral Development Bulletin, 22*(1), 129–146. doi:10.1037/bdb0000056

Clayton, M. C., & Hayes, L. J. (2004). A comparison of match-to-sample and respondent type training of equivalence classes. *The Psychological Record, 54*, 579–602.

Clayton, M. C., Hayes, L. J., & Swain, M. A. (2005). The nature and value of scientific system building: The case of interbehaviorism. *The Psychological Record, 55*(3), 335–359. doi:10.1007/BF03395515

Cohen, H. L. (1972). Programming alternatives to punishment: The design of competence through consequences. In Bijou, S. W. & Ribes-Inesta, E. (Eds.), *Behavior modification: Issues and extensions* (pp. 63–84). New York, NY: Academic Press.

Cohen, N. J., Sullivan, J., Minde, K., Novak, C., & Helwig, C. (1981). Evaluation of the relative effectiveness of methylphenidate and cognitive behavior modification in the treatment of kindergarten-aged hyperactive children. *Journal of Abnormal Child Psychology, 9*(1), 43–54.

Connell, J. E., & Witt, J. C. (2004). Applications of computer-based instruction: Using specialized software to aid letter-name and letter-sound recognition. *Journal of Applied Behavior Analysis, 37*, 67–71.

Contreras, B. P., & Betz, A. M. (2016). Using lag schedules to strengthen the intraverbal repertoires of children with autism. *Journal of Applied Behavior Analysis, 49*(1), 3–16. doi:10.1002/jaba.271

Cook, C., & Adams, H. E. (1966). Modification of verbal behavior in speech deficient children. *Behaviour Research and Therapy, 4*, 265–271. doi:10.1016/0005-7967(66)90082-9

Coon, J. T., & Miguel, C. F. (2012). The role of increased exposure to transfer-of-stimulus-control procedures on the acquisition of intraverbal behavior. *Journal of Applied Behavior Analysis, 45*(4), 657–666. doi:10.1901/jaba.2012.45-657

Corcoran, R., Mercer, G. and Frith, C. D. (1995) Schizophrenia, symptomatology and social inference: Investigating theory of mind in people with schizophrenia. *Schizophrenia Research, 17*, 5–13.

Corral, D., & Jones, M. (2014). The effects of relational structure on analogical learning. *Cognition, 132*, 280–300.

Corwin, A., & Greer, R. D. (2017). *Effect of the establishment of Naming on learning from teacher-demonstrations.* Manuscript submitted for publication.

Cossairt, A., Hall, R. V., & Hopkins, B. L. (1973). The effects of experimenter's instructions, feedback, and praise on teacher praise and student attending behavior. *Journal of Applied Behavior Analysis, 6*, 89–100. doi:10.1901/jaba.1973.6-89

Costa, A., & Pelaez, M. (2014). Implementing intensive tact instruction to increase frequency of spontaneous mands and tacts in typically developing children. *Behavioral Development Bulletin, 19*(1), 19–24. doi:10.1037/h0100569

Cote, D. L., Jones, V. L., Barnett, C., Pavelek, K., Nguyen, H., & Sparks, S. L. (2014). Teaching problem solving skills to elementary age students with autism. *Education and Training in Autism and Developmental Disabilities, 49*, 189–199.

Cowley, B. J., Green, G., & Braunling-McMorrow, D. (1992). Using stimulus equivalence procedures to teach name-face matching to adults with brain injuries. *Journal of Applied Behavior Analysis, 25*, 461–475.

Creel, R. (1980). Radical epiphenomenalism: BF Skinner's account of private events. *Behaviorism, 8*(1), 31–53.

Critchfield, T. S. (2014). Online equivalence-based instruction about statistical inference using written explanation instead of match-to-sample training. *Journal of Applied Behavior Analysis, 47*, 606–611.

Critchfield, T. S., & Fienup, D. M. (2010). Using stimulus equivalence technology to teach statistical inference in a group setting. *Journal of Applied Behavior Analysis, 43*, 763–768. doi:10.1901/jaba.2010.43-763

Cullen, C., & Barnes-Holmes, D. (2008). *Implicit pride and prejudice: A heterosexual phenomenon?* In M.A. Morrison & T.G. Morrison (Eds.), *Modern Prejudice* (pp. 195–223). New York, NY: Nova Science.

Cullen, C., Barnes-Holmes, D., Barnes-Holmes, Y., & Stewart, I. (2009). The Implicit Relational Assessment Procedure (IRAP) and the malleability of ageist attitudes. *The Psychological Record, 59*, 591–620.

Cunningham-Williams, R. M., Grucza, R. A., Cottler, L. B., Womack, S. B., Books, S. J., Przybeck, T. R., . . . Cloninger, C. R. (2005). Prevalence and predictors of pathological gambling: Results from the St. Louis personality, health and lifestyle (SLPHL) study. *Journal of Psychiatric Research, 39*, 377–390. doi:10.1016/j.jpsychires.2004.09.002

Daar, J. H., Negrelli, S., & Dixon, M. R. (2015). Derived emergence of wh-question–answers in children with autism. *Research in Autism Spectrum Disorders, 19*, 59–71. doi:10.1016/j.rasd.2015.06.004

D'Amato, M. R., & Colombo, M. (1985). Auditory matching-to-sample in monkeys (Cebus apella). *Animal Learning and Behavior, 13*, 375–382.

Darwin, C. R. (1871). *The descent of man, and selection in relation to sex. Volume 2.* London, UK: John Murray.

Darwin, C. R. (1877). A biographical sketch of an infant. *Mind. A Quarterly Review of Psychology and Philosophy, 2*, 285–294. http://www.jstor.org/stable/2246907

Darwin, C. R. (1974). *Metaphysics, materialism, and the evolution of mind: Early writings of Charles Darwin.* Transcribed and annotated by Paul H. Barrett with a commentary by Howard E. Gruber. Chicago, IL: University of Chicago Press.

Darwin, C. R. (2013). *On the origin of species.* New York, NY: Sheba Blake Publishing. (Original work published 1859)

de Rose, J. C., de Souza, E. G., & Hanna, E. S. (1996). Teaching reading and spelling: Exclusion and stimulus equivalence. *Journal of Applied Behavior Analysis, 29*, 451–469.

de Souza, A. A., Akers, J. S., & Fisher, W. W. (2017). Empirical application of Skinner's *Verbal Behavior* to interventions for children with autism: A review. *The Analysis of Verbal Behavior, 33*(2), 229–259. doi:10.1007/s40616-017-0093-7

de Souza, D. G., de Rose, J. C., & Domeniconi, C. (2009). Applying relational operants to reading and spelling. In R. A. Rehfeldt & Y. Barnes-Holmes (Eds.), *Derived relational responding: Applications for learners with autism and other developmental disabilities* (pp. 173–207). Oakland, CA: New Harbinger.

de Souza, A. A., & Rehfeldt, R. A. (2013). Effects of dictation-taking and match-to-sample training on listing and spelling responses in adults with intellectual disabilities. *Journal of Applied Behavior Analysis, 46*(4), 792–804. doi:10.1002/jaba.75

Deguchi, H. (1984). Observational learning from a radical-behavioristic viewpoint. *The Behavior Analyst, 7,* 83–95.

Delgado, D., & Hayes, L. J. (2013). The integration of learning paradigms by way of a non-causal analysis of behavioral events. *Conductual, 1*(2), 39–54.

Delgado, D., & Hayes, L. J. (2014). An integrative approach to learning processes: Revisiting substitution of functions. *The Psychological Record, 64*(3), 625–637. doi:10.1007/s40732-014-0071-6

Delgado, J. P., & Oblak, M. (2007). The effects of daily tact instruction on the emission of pure mands and tacts in non-instructional settings by three preschool children with developmental delays. *Journal of Early Intensive Behavioral Interventions, 4*(2), 392–41. doi:10.1037/h0100381

Delgado, M., Erickson, N., & Johnson, K. (2015). *Best practices in vocabulary acquisition with both corrective decoding students and middle school students performing independent research.* A paper read at the 41st convention of the Association for Behavior Analysis International, San Antonio, TX.

Delgado, M., & Johnson, K. (2010) *Vocabulary instruction: Teacher-generated definitions vs. student-generated definitions.* A paper read at the 36th convention of the Association for Behavior Analysis International, San Antonio, TX.

Delprato, D. J., & Midgley, B. D. (1992). Some fundamentals of B. F. Skinner's behaviorism. *American Psychologist, 47*(11), 1507–1520. doi:10.1037/0003-066X.47.11.1507

Deneault, J., & Ricard, M. (2006). The assessment of children's understanding of inclusion relations: Transitivity, asymmetry, and quantification. *Journal of Cognition and Development, 7.* 551–570. doi:10.1207/s15327647jcd0704_6

Devany, J. M., Hayes, S. C., & Nelson, R. O. (1986). Equivalence class formation in language-able and language-disabled children. *Journal of the experimental analysis of behavior, 46,* 243–257.

Devine, B., Carp, C. L., Hiett, K. A., & Petursdottir, A. I. (2016). Emergence of intraverbal responding following tact instruction with compound stimuli. *The Analysis of Verbal Behavior, 32*(2), 154–170. doi:10.1007/s40616-016-0062-6

Dewey, J. (1933). How we think. In J. Dewey (1986), *The later works of John Dewey, 1925–1953* (Vol. 8). Carbondale, IL: Southern Illinois University Press.

Dickes, N. R., & Kodak, T. (2015). Evaluating the emergence of reverse intraverbals following intraverbal training in young children with autism spectrum disorder. *Behavioral Interventions, 30*(3), 169–190. doi:10.1002/bin.1412

Dinsmoor, J. A. (1995a). Stimulus control: Part I. *The Behavior Analyst, 18,* 51–68. doi:10.1007/BF03392691

Dinsmoor, J. A. (1995b). Stimulus control: Part II. *The Behavior Analyst, 18,* 253–269. doi:10.1007/BF03392712

Dixon, M. R. (2000). Manipulating the illusion of control: Variations in gambling as a function of perceived control over chance outcomes. *The Psychological Record, 50,* 705–719. doi:10.1007/bf03395379

Dixon, M. R. (2014a). *The PEAK Relational Training System: Direct Training Module.* Carbondale, IL: Shawnee Scientific Press.

Dixon, M. R. (2014b). *The PEAK Relational Training System: Generalization Module.* Carbondale, IL: Shawnee Scientific Press.

Dixon, M. R. (2015). *The PEAK Relational Training System: Equivalence Module.* Carbondale, IL: Shawnee Scientific Press.

Dixon, M. R. (2016). *PEAK Relational Training System: Transformation module.* Carbondale, IL: Shawnee Scientific Press.

Dixon, M. R., Belisle, J., Munoz, B. E., Stanley, C. R., & Rowsey, K. E. (2017). Teaching metaphorical extensions of private events through rival-model observation to children with autism. *Journal of Applied Behavior Analysis, 50*(4), 744–749. doi:10.1002/jaba.418

Dixon, M. R., Belisle, J., Stanley, C. R., Munoz, B. E., & Speelman, R. C. (2017). Establishing derived coordinated symmetrical and transitive gustatory-visual-auditory relations in children with autism and related intellectual disabilities using the PEAK-E curriculum. *Journal of Contextual Behavioral Science, 6*, 91–95. doi:10.1016/j.jcbs.2016.11.001

Dixon, M. R., Belisle, J., Stanley, C. R., Speelman, R. C., Rowsey, K. E., Kime, D., & Daar, J. H. (2017). Establishing derived categorical responding in children with disabilities using the PEAK-E curriculum. *Journal of Applied Behavior Analysis, 50*, 134–145. doi:10.1002/jaba.355

Dixon, M. R., Buono, F. D., & Belisle, J (2016). Contrived motivating operations alter delay-discounting values of disordered gamblers. *Journal of Applied Behavior Analysis, 49*, 986–990. doi:10.1002/jaba.335

Dixon, M. R., & Holton, B. (2009). Altering the magnitude of delay discounting by pathological gamblers. *Journal of Applied Behavior Analysis, 42*, 269–275. doi:10.1901/jaba.2009.42-269

Dixon, M., Rehfeldt, R. A., Zlomke, K.M., & Robinson, A. (2006). Exploring the development and dismantling of equivalence classes involving terrorist stimuli. *The Psychological Record, 56*, 83–103.

Dixon, M. R., Small, S. L., & Rosales, R. (2007). Extended analysis of empirical citations with Skinner's *Verbal Behavior*: 1984–2004. *The Behavior Analyst, 30*(2), 197–209. doi:10.1007/bf03392155

Dixon, M. R., & Zlomke, K. M. (2005). Using the precursor to the relational evaluation procedure (PREP) to establish the relational frames of sameness, opposition, and distinction. *Revista Latinoamericana de Psicologia, 37*, 305–316.

Dollard, J., & Miller, N. E. (1950). *Personality and psychotherapy; an analysis in terms of learning, thinking, and culture.* New York, NY: McGraw-Hill.

Domjan, M. (1983). Biological constraints on instrumental and classical conditioning: Implications for general process theory. *The Psychology of Learning and Motivation, 17*, 215–277. doi:10.1016/S0079-7421(08)60100-0

Domjan, M. (2005). Pavlovian conditioning: A functional perspective. *Annual Review of Psychology, 56*, 179–206. doi:10.1146/annurev.psych.55.090902.141409

Domjan, M. (2016). Elicited versus emitted behavior: Time to abandon the distinction. *Journal of the Experimental Analysis of Behavior, 105*(2), 231–245. doi:10.1002/jeab.197

Donadeli, J. M., & Strapasson, B. A. (2015). Effects of monitoring and social reprimands on instruction-following in undergraduate students. *The Psychological Record, 65*, 177–188. doi:10.1007/s40732-014-0099-7

Donahoe, J. W. (1996). On the relation between behavior analysis and biology. *The Behavior Analyst, 19*(1), 71–73. doi:10.1007/BF03392740

Donahoe, J. W. (2012). Reflections on behavior analysis and evolutionary biology: A selective review of *Evolution Since Darwin—The First 150 Years*. Edited by M. A. Bell, D. J. Futuyama, W. F. Eanes, & J. S. Levinton. *Journal of the Experimental Analysis of Behavior, 97*(2), 249–260. doi:10.1901/jeab.2012.97-249

Donley, C. R., & Greer, R. D. (1993). Setting events controlling social verbal exchanges between students with developmental delays. *Journal of Behavioral Education, 3*(4), 387–401. doi:10.1007/BF00961542

Dougher, M. J. (2013). Behaviorisms and private events. *The Behavior Analyst, 36*(2), 223–227.

Dougher, M. J., Hamilton, D. A., Fink, B. C., & Harrington, J. (2007). Transformation of the discriminative and eliciting functions of generalized relational stimuli. *Journal of the Experimental Analysis of Behavior, 88*, 179–197.

Dougher, M., Perkins, D. R., Greenway, D., Koons, A., & Chiasson, C. (2002). Contextual control of equivalence-based transformation of functions. *Journal of the Experimental Analysis of Behavior, 78*, 63–93.

Drake, C. E., Kellum, K. K., Wilson, K. G., Luoma, J. B., Weinstein, J. H., & Adams, C. H. (2010). Examining the Implicit Relational Assessment Procedure: Four preliminary studies. *The Psychological Record, 60*, 81–86.

Drake, C. E., Kramer, S., Sain, T., Swiatek, R., Kohn, K., & Murphy, M. (2015). Exploring the reliability and convergent validity of implicit racial evaluations. *Behavior and Social Issues, 24*, 68–87. doi:10.5210/bsi.v.24i0.5496

Duker, P., Kraaykamp, M., & Visser, E. (1994). A stimulus control procedure to increase requesting with individuals who are severely/profoundly intellectually disabled. *Journal of Intellectual Disability Research, 38*(2), 177–186. doi:10.1111/j.1365-2788.1994.tb00372.x

Dunne, S., Foody, M., Barnes-Holmes, Y., Barnes-Holmes, D., & Murphy, C. (2014). Facilitating repertoires of coordination, opposition distinction, and comparison in young children with autism. *Behavioral Development Bulletin, 19*, 37–47. doi:10.1037/h0100576

Dymond, S., May, R. J., Munnelly, A., & Hoon, A. E. (2010). Evaluating the evidence base for relational frame theory: A citation analysis. *The Behavior Analyst, 33*, 97–117.

Dymond, S., O'Hora, D., Whelan, R., & O'Donovan, A. (2006). Citation analysis of Skinner's *Verbal Behavior*: 1984–2004. *The Behavior Analyst, 29*(1), 75–88. doi:10.1007/bf03392118

Dymond, S., & Rehfeldt, R. A. (2000). Understanding complex behavior: The transformation of stimulus functions. *The Behavior Analyst, 23*, 239–254.

Dymond, S., & Roche, B. (2009). A contemporary behavior analysis of anxiety and avoidance. *The Behavior Analyst, 32*(1), 7–27.

Dymond, S., & Roche, B. (2013). *Advances in relational frame theory: Research and application*. Oakland, CA: Context Press.

Dymond, S., Roche, B., Forsyth, J. P., Whelan, R., & Rhoden, J. (2007). Transformation of avoidance response functions in accordance with same and opposite relational frames. *Journal of the Experimental Analysis of Behavior, 88*, 249–262.

Eby, C. M., & Greer, R. D. (2017). Effects of social reinforcement on the emission of tacts by preschoolers. *Behavioral Development Bulletin, 22*(1), 23–43. doi:10.1037/bdb0000043

Edrisinha, C., O'Reilly, M., Sigafoos, J., Lancioni, G., & Choi, H. Y. (2011). Influence of motivating operations and discriminative stimuli on challenging behavior maintained by positive reinforcement. *Research in Developmental Disabilities, 32*, 836–845. doi:10.1016/j.ridd.2010.10.006

Egan, C. E., & Barnes-Holmes, D. (2010). Establishing mand emergence: The effects of three training procedures and modified antecedent conditions. *The Psychological Record, 60*(3), 473–488.

Eid, A. M., Alhaqbani, O. A., Asfahani, S. M., Alaql, M., AlSaud, A. N., Mohtasib, R. S., . . . Fryling, M. J. (2017). Learning by doing and learning by observing: Training parents in Saudi Arabia to implement the Natural Language Paradigm. *Journal of Developmental and Physical Disabilities, 29*, 557–565. doi:10.1007/s10882-017-9544-2

Eikeseth, S., & Smith, D. P. (2013). An analysis of verbal stimulus control in intraverbal behavior: Implications for practice and applied research. *The Analysis of Verbal Behavior, 29*(1), 125–135. doi:10.1007/bf03393130

Eisenberg, N. (2000). Emotion, regulation, and moral development. *Annual review of psychology, 51*(1), 665–697.

Ekman, P. (2003) *Emotions revealed: Recognizing faces and feelings to improve communication and emotional life*. New York, NY: Henry Holt.

Endo, K., Ando, S., Shimodera, S., Yamasaki, S., Usami, S., Okazaki, Y., . . . Nishida, A. (2017). Preference for solitude, social isolation, suicidal ideation, and self-harm in adolescents. *Journal of Adolescent Health, 61*, 189–191.

Engelmann, S., & Carnine, D. W. (1982). *Theory of instruction: Principles and applications.* Eugene, OR: ADI Press.

Epstein, R. (1985). The spontaneous interconnection of three repertoires. *The Psychological Record, 35* (2), 131–141.

Epstein, R. (1993). Generativity theory and education. *Educational Technology, 33(10)* 40–45.

Epstein, R. (1999). Generativity theory. In M. A. Runco and S. R. Pritzker (Eds.), *Encyclopedia of creativity* (Vol. 1, pp. 759–766), Cambridge, MA: Academic Press.

Epstein, R., Kirshnit, R., Lanza, R., & Rubin, R. (1984). "Insight" in the pigeon: Antecedents and determinants of an intelligent performance. *Nature, 308,* 61–62.

Estes, W. K., & Skinner, B. F. (1941). Some quantitative properties of anxiety. *Journal of Experimental Psychology, 29*(5), 390–400.

Evans, S. S., & Evans, W. H. (1985). Frequencies that ensure skill competency. *Journal of Precision Teaching, 6* (2), 25–30.

Exposito, P. M., Lopez, M. H., & Valverde, M. R. (2015). Assessment of implicit anti-fat and pro-slim attitudes in young women using the Implicit Relational Assessment Procedure. *International Journal of Psychology and Psychological Therapy, 15,* 17–32.

Eysenck, H. J. (Ed.). (1960). *Behaviour therapy and the neuroses: Readings in modern methods of treatment derived from learning theory.* New York, NY: Pergamon.

Eysenck, H. J. (1964). *Experiments in behaviour therapy.* New York, NY: Macmillan.

Fabrizio, M. A., & Pahl, S. (2007). An experimental analysis of two error correction procedures used to improve the textual behavior of a student with autism. *The Behavior Analyst Today, 8*(3), 260–272. doi:10.1037/h0100618

Farrell, C. (2017). *An investigation into the speaker-as-own-listener repertoire and reverse intraverbal responding* (Doctoral dissertation, Order No. 10278214). Available from ProQuest Dissertations & Theses Global. (1899486948). doi:10.7916/D8P279JG

Farrell, L., Cochrane, A., & McHugh, L. (2015). Exploring attitudes towards gender and science: The advantages of an IRAP approach versus the IAT. *Journal of Contextual Behavioral Science, 4*(2), 121–128. doi:10.1016/j.jcbs.2015.04.002

Fawcett, S. B., Mathews, R. M., & Fletcher, R. K. (1980). Some promising dimensions for behavioral community technology. *Journal of Applied Behavior Analysis, 13,* 505–518.

Feliciano, G. M. (2006). *Multiple exemplar instruction and the listener half of naming in children with limited speaker abilities* (Doctoral dissertation, Order No. 3213505). Available from ProQuest Dissertations & Theses Global. (305360301). Retrieved from http://eduproxy.tc-library.org/?url=/docview/305360301?accountid=14258

Feng, H., Chou, W. C., & Lee, G. T. (2017). Effects of tact prompts on acquisition and maintenance of divergent intraverbal responses by a child with autism. *Focus on Autism and Other Developmental Disabilities, 32*(2), 133–141. doi:10.1177/1088357615610540

Fenske, E. C., Krantz, P. J., & McClannahan, L. E. (2001). Incidental teaching: A not-discrete-trial teaching procedure. In C. Maurice, G. Green, & R. M. Foxx (Eds.), *Making a Difference: Behavioral intervention for autism.* Austin, TX: PRO-ED.

Ferster, C. B., Culbertson, S., & Boren, M. C. P. (1975). *Behavior principles* (2nd ed.). Englewood Cliffs, NJ: Prentice Hall.

Ferster, C. B., & Skinner, B. F. (1957). *Schedules of reinforcement.* New York, NY: Appleton-Century-Crofts.

Fields, L., Garruto, M., & Watanabe, M. (2010). Varieties of stimulus control in a matching-to-sample: A kernel analysis. *The Psychological Record, 60,* 3–26.

Fields, L., Reeve, K. F., Adams, B. J., Brown, J. L., & Verhave, T. (1997). Predicting the extension of equivalence classes from primary generalization gradients: The merger of equivalence classes and perceptual classes. *Journal of the Experimental Analysis of Behavior, 68,* 67–91.

Fields, L., Reeve, K. F., Varelas, A., Rosen, D., & Belanich, J. (1997). Equivalence class formation using stimulus-pairing and yes-no responding. *The Psychological Record, 47*, 661–686.

Fields, L., Travis, R., Roy, D., Yadlovker, E., Aguiar-Rocha, L, & Sturmey, P. (2009). Equivalence class formation: A method for teaching statistical interactions. *Journal of Applied Behavior Analysis, 42*, 575–593.

Fienup, D. M., & Brodsky, J. (2017). Effects of mastery criterion on the emergence of derived equivalence relations. Advance online copy. *Journal of Applied Behavior Analysis.* doi:10.1002/jaba.416

Fienup, D. M., Covey, D. P., & Critchfield, T. S. (2010). Teaching brain-behavior relations economically with stimulus equivalence technology. *Journal of Applied Behavior Analysis, 43*, 19–33. doi:10.1901/jaba.2010.43-19

Fienup, D. M., & Critchfield, T. S. (2011). Transportability of equivalence-based programmed instruction: Efficacy and efficiency in a college classroom. *Journal of Applied Behavior Analysis, 44*, 435–450.

Fienup, D. M., Hamelin, J., Reyes-Giordano, K., & Falcomata, T. S. (2011). College-level instruction: Derived relations and programmed instruction. *Journal of Applied Behavior Analysis, 44*, 413–416.

Fienup, D. M., Mylan, S. E., Brodsky, J., & Pytte, C. (2016). From the laboratory to the classroom: The effects of equivalence-based instruction on neuroanatomy competencies. *Journal of Behavioral Education, 25*, 143–165.

Fienup, D. M., Wright, N. A., & Fields, L. (2015). Optimizing equivalence-based instruction: Effects of training protocols on equivalence class formation. *Journal of Applied Behavior Analysis, 48*, 613–631.

Figley, C. (1995). *Compassion fatigue: Coping with secondary traumatic stress disorder in those who treat the traumatized.* London, UK: Brunner-Routledge

Finkel, A. S., & Williams, R. L. (2001). A comparison of textual and echoic prompts on the acquisition of intraverbal behavior in a six-year-old boy with autism. *The Analysis of Verbal Behavior, 18*(1), 61–70. doi:10.1007/bf03392971

Finn, H. E., Miguel, C. F., & Ahearn, W. H. (2012). The emergence of untrained mands and tacts in children with autism. *Journal of Applied Behavior Analysis, 45*(2), 265–280. doi:10.1901/jaba.2012.45-265

Finn, M., Barnes-Holmes, D., Hussey, I., & Graddy, J. (2016). Exploring the behavioral dynamics of the implicit relational assessment procedure: The impact of three types of introductory rules. *The Psychological Record, 66*(2), 309–321. doi:10.1007/s40732-016-0173-4

Finn, M., Barnes-Holmes, D., & McEnteggart, C. (2018). Exploring the single-trial-type-dominance-effect on the IRAP: Developing a differential arbitrarily applicable relational responding effects (DAARRE) model. *The Psychological Record, 68*, 11–25. doi:10.1007/s40732-017-0262-z

Fiorile, C. A., & Greer, R. D. (2007). The induction of naming in children with no prior tact responses as a function of multiple exemplar histories of instruction. *The Analysis of Verbal Behavior, 23*(1), 71–87. doi:10.1007/BF03393048

Floody, M., Barnes-Holmes, Y., Barnes-Holmes, D., & Luciano, C. (2013). An empirical investigation of hierarchical versus distinction relations in a self-based ACT exercise. *International Journal of Psychology and Psychological Therapy, 13*, 373–385.

Franks, G. J., & Lattal, K. A. (1976). Antecedent reinforcement schedule training and operant response reinstatement in rats. *Animal Learning & Behavior, 4*, 374–378. doi:10.3758/BF03214424

Frias, F. A. (2017). *How stimulus relations accrue for the names of things in preschoolers* (Doctoral dissertation, Order No. 10274980). Available from ProQuest Dissertations & Theses Global. (1896618774). doi:10.7916/D8PZ5N6B

Frost, L., & Bondy, A. (2002). *The Picture Exchange Communication System (PECS) training manual* (2nd ed.). Newark, DE: Pyramid Publications.

Fryling, M. J. (2017). The functional independence of Skinner's verbal operants: Conceptual and applied implications. *Behavioral Interventions, 32*(1), 70–78. doi:10.1002/bin.1462

Fryling, M. J., & Hayes, L. J. (2015). Similarities and differences among alternatives to Skinner's analysis of private events. *The Psychological Record, 65*(3), 579–587. doi:10.1007/s40732-015-0130-7

Fryling, M. J., Johnston, C., & Hayes, L. J. (2011) Understanding observational learning: An interbehavioral approach. *The Analysis of Verbal Behavior, 27*, 191–203.

Furrer, S.D., & Younger, B.A. (2008). The impact of specific prior experiences on infants' extension of animal properties. *Developmental Science, 11*, 5, 712–21. doi:10.1111/j.1467-7687.2008.00721.x

Galizio, M. (1979). Contingency-shaped and rule-governed behavior: Instructional control of human loss avoidance. *Journal of the Experimental Analysis of Behavior, 31*(1), 53–70.

Galton, F. (1889). *Natural inheritance.* London, England: Macmillan.

Gamba, J., Goyos, C., & Petursdottir, A. I. (2015). The functional independence of mands and tacts: Has it been demonstrated empirically? *The Analysis of verbal behavior, 31*(1), 10–38. doi:10.1007/s40616-014-0026-7

Garaigordobil, M., & Maganto, C. (2011). Empathy and conflict resolution during infancy and adolescence. *Revista Latinoamericana de Psicología, 43*(2), 255-266.

Geissmann, T. (2002). Duet-splitting and the evolution of gibbon songs. *Biological Reviews, 77*, 57–76. doi:10.1017/S1464793101005826

Gelman, S. A. (1988). The development of induction within natural kind and artefact properties. *Cognitive Psychology, 20*, 65–95.

Gentner, D. (1983). Structure mapping: A theoretical framework for analogy. *Cognitive Science, 7*, 155–170.

Gentner, D., Holyoak, K. J., & Kokinov, B. N. (2001). *The analogical mind: Perspectives from cognitive science.* Cambridge, MA: MIT Press.

Gerdes, K. E., Segal, E. A., & Lietz, C. A. (2010). Conceptualising and measuring empathy. *British Journal of Social Work, 40*(7), 2326–2343.

Ghezzi, P. M. (1999). Toward a definition of social behavior. In P. M. Ghezzi, W. L. Williams, & J. E. Carr (Eds.), *Autism: Behavior analytic perspectives* (pp. 212–220). Reno, NV: Context Press.

Ghezzi, P. M., & Bijou, S. W. (1994). El entrenamiento de habilidades sociales en ninos solitarios medianamente retardados (Social skills training for withdrawn mildly retarded children). In L. J. Hayes, E. Ribes, & F. Lopez-Valadez (Eds), *Psicologia interconductual: Contribuciones en honor J.R. Kantor* (pp. 91–110). Guadalajara, Mexico: Universidad de Guadalajara.

Ghezzi, P. M., Bijou, S. W., & Chao, C. C. (1987, May). *A comparison of two intervention strategies for improving mildly retarded children's conversation with nonretarded schoolmates.* Presented at the meeting of the Association for Behavior Analysis, Nashville, TN.

Ghezzi, P. M., Bijou, S. W., & Chao, C. C. (1991). A manual for training raters to identify and analyze referential interactions. *The Psychological Record, 41*, 473–486.

Ghezzi, P. M., Bijou, S. W., Umbreit, J., & Chao, C. C. (1987). Influence of age of listener on preadolescents' linguistic behavior. *The Psychological Record, 37*, 109–126.

Ghezzi, P. M., & Lyons, C. A. (1997). Specializations in the language sciences. In L.J . Hayes & P. M. Ghezzi (Eds), *Investigations in behavioral epistemology* (pp. 203–214). Reno, NV: Context Press.

Ghezzi, P. M., Robles, E., & Bijou, S. W. (1992). Relaciones sociometricas en platicar y jugar en ninos primaria (Sociometric relationships between talk and play among elementary school children). *Revista Sonorense de Psicologia, 6*, 15–22.

Gil, E., Luciano, C., Ruiz, F. J., & Valdivia-Salas, S. (2012). A preliminary demonstration of transformation of functions through hierarchical relations. *International Journal of Psychology & Psychological Therapy, 12*, 1–19.

Gil, E., Luciano, C., Ruiz, F. J., & Valdivia-Salas, S. (2014). A further experimental step in the analysis of hierarchical responding. *International Journal of Psychology & Psychological Therapy, 14,* 137–153.

Gil-Luciano B., Ruiz F. J., Valdivia-Salas S., & Suarez-Falcon, J. C. (2016). Promoting psychological flexibility on tolerance tasks: framing behavior through deictic/hierarchical relations and specifying augmental functions. *The Psychological Record, 67*(1), 1–9.

Gilbert, P. (2010). *Compassion focused therapy.* New York, NY: Routledge Press

Gilbert, T, (1962a). Mathetics: The technology of education. *Journal of Mathetics, 1*(1), 7–74.

Gilbert, T. (1962b). Mathetics II: The design of teaching exercises. *Journal of Mathetics, 1*(2), 7–56.

Gilic, L., & Greer, R. D. (2009). Establishing Naming in typically developing two-year-old children as a function of multiple exemplar speaker and listener experiences. *The Analysis of Verbal Behavior, 27*(1), 157–177.

Gilliam, A., Weil, T. M., & Miltenberger, R. G. (2013). Effects of preference on the emergence of untrained verbal operants. *Journal of Applied Behavior Analysis, 46*(2), 523–527. doi:10.1002/jaba.34

Gladstone, B. W., & Cooley, J. (1975). Behavioral similarity as a reinforcer for preschool children. *Journal of the Experimental Analysis of Behavior, 23* (3), 357–368.

Glynn, E. L., Thomas, J. D., & Shee, S. M. (1973). Behavioral self-control of on-task behavior in an elementary classroom. *Journal of Applied Behavior Analysis, 6,* 105–113. doi:10.1901/jaba.1973.6-105

Goetz, J. L., Keltner, D., & Simon-Thomas, E. (2010). Compassion: An evolutionary analysis and empirical review. *Psychological Bulletin, 136*(3), 351–374.

Golan, O., & Baron-Cohen, S. (2006). Systemizing empathy: Teaching adults with Asperger syndrome or high-functioning autism to recognize complex emotions using interactive multimedia. *Development and psychopathology, 18*(2), 591–617.

Golden, J. (2009). The etiology and treatment of significant societal problems: Behaviorists diving into murky waters with strangers. *International Journal of Behavioral Consultation & Therapy, 5*(1), 1–11.

Goldsmith, T. R., LeBlanc, L. A., & Sautter, R. A. (2007). Teaching intraverbal behavior to children with autism. *Research in Autism Spectrum Disorders, 1*(1), 1–13. doi:10.1016/j.rasd.2006.07.001

Goleman, D. (1998). *Working with emotional intelligence.* New York, NY: Bantam Books.

Gore, N. J., Barnes-Holmes, Y., & Murphy, G. (2010). The relationship between intellectual functioning and relational perspective-taking. *International Journal of Psychology and Psychological Therapy, 10.*

Gortner, E. T., Gollan, J. K., Dobson, K. S., & Jacobson, N. S. (1998). Cognitive-behavioral treatment for depression: Relapse prevention. *Journal of Consulting and Clinical Psychology, 66,* 377–384.

Goswami, U., & Brown, A. (1989). Melting chocolate and melting snowmen: Analogical reasoning and causal relations. *Cognition, 35,* 69-95.

Goswami, U., & Brown, A. (1990). Higher-order structure and relational reasoning: Contrasting analogical and thematic relations. *Cognition, 36,* 207–226.

Gould, E., Dixon, D. R., Najdowski, A. C., Smith, M. N., & Tarbox, J. (2011). A review of assessments for determining the content of early intensive behavioral intervention programs for autism spectrum disorders. *Research in Autism Spectrum Disorders, 5*(3), 990–1002. doi:10.1016/j.rasd.2011.01.012

Gould, E., Tarbox, J., & Coyne, L. (2017). Evaluating the effects of Acceptance and Commitment Training on the overt behavior of parents of children with autism. *Journal of Contextual Behavioral Science, 7,* 81–88. doi:10.1016/j.jcbs.2017.06.003

Grannan, L., & Rehfeldt, R. A. (2012). Emergent intraverbal responses via tact and match-to-sample instruction. *Journal of Applied Behavior Analysis, 45*(3), 601–605. doi:10.1901/jaba.2012.45-601

Green, G. (2001). Behavior analytic instruction for learners with autism: Advances in stimulus control technology. *Focus on Autism and Other Developmental Disabilities, 16*, 72–85. doi:10.1177/108835760101600203

Green, D., Charman, T., Pickles, A., Chandler, S., Loucas, T., Simonoff, E., & Baird, G., (2009). Impairment in movement skills of children with autistic spectrum disorders. *Developmental Medicine and Child Neurology, 51*, 311–316. doi:10.1111/j.1469-8749.2008.03242.x

Greenberg, M. S., & Beck, A. T. (1989). Depression versus anxiety: A test of the content-specificity hypothesis. *Journal of Abnormal Psychology, 98*(1), 9–13.

Greene, T. R. (1994). What kindergartners know about class containment hierarchies. *Journal of Experimental Child Psychology, 57*, 72–88. doi:10.1006/jecp.1994.1004

Greer, R. D. (2008). The ontogenetic selection of verbal capabilities: Contributions of Skinner's verbal behavior theory to a more comprehensive understanding of language. *International Journal of Psychology and Psychological Therapy, 8*, 363–386. http://oai.redalyc.org/articulo.oa?id=56080310

Greer, R. D., Corwin, A., & Buttigieg (2011). The effects of the verbal developmental capability of Naming on how children can be taught. *Acta de Investigacion Psicologia, 1*(1), 23–54. Retrieved from http://scielo.unam.mx/pdf/aip/v1n1/v1n1a5.pdf

Greer, R. D., & Du, L. (2010). Generic instruction versus intensive tact instruction and the emission of spontaneous speech. *The Journal of Speech-Language Pathology and Applied Behavior Analysis, 5*(1), 1–19. doi:10.1037/h0100261 IN 1932-4731

Greer, R. D., & Du, L. (2015a). Experience and the onset of the capability to learn names incidentally by exclusion. *The Psychological Record, 65*, 355–373. doi:10.1007/s40732-014-0111-2

Greer, R. D., & Du, L. (2015b). Identification and establishment of reinforcers that make the development of complex social language possible. *International Journal of Behavior Analysis and Autism Spectrum Disorders, 1*(1), 13–34.

Greer, R. D., Pohl, P., Du, L., & Moschella, J. L. (2017). The separate development of children's listener and speaker behavior and the intercept as behavioral metamorphosis. *Journal of Behavioral and Brain Science, 7*, 674–704. doi:10.4236/jbbs.2017.713045

Greer, R. D., & Ross, D. E. (2008). *Verbal behavior analysis: Inducing and expanding complex communication in children with severe language delays.* Boston, MA: Allyn & Bacon.

Greer, R. D., & Singer-Dudek, J. (2008). The emergence of conditioned reinforcement from observation. *Journal of the Experimental Analysis of Behavior, 89*, 15–29. doi:10.1901/jeab.2008.89-15

Greer, R. D., Singer-Dudek, J., & Gautreaux, G. (2006). Observational learning. *International Journal of Psychology, 41*, 486–499. doi:10.1080/00207590500492435

Greer, R. D., Singer-Dudek, J., Longano, J., & Zrinzo, M. (2008). The emergence of praise as conditioned reinforcement as a function of observation in preschool and school age children. *Revista Mexicana de Psicologia, 25*(1), 5–26. Retrieved from http://www.redalyc.org/articulo.oa?id=243016300001

Greer, R. D., & Speckman, J. (2009). The integration of speaker and listener responses: A theory of verbal development. *The Psychological Record, 59*(3), 449. doi:10.1007/bf03395674

Greer, R. D., Stolfi, L., Chavez-Brown, M., & Rivera-Valdez, C. (2005). The emergence of the listener to speaker component of Naming in children as a function of multiple exemplar instruction. *The Analysis of Verbal Behavior, 21*, 123–134. doi:10.1007/BF03393014

Greer, R. D., Yaun, L., & Gautreaux, G. (2005). Novel dictation and intraverbal responses as a function of a multiple exemplar instructional history. *The Analysis of Verbal Behavior, 21*(1), 99–116. doi:10.1007/bf03393012

Gregory, M. K., DeLeon, I. G., & Richman, D. M. (2009). The influence of matching and motor-imitation abilities on rapid acquisition of manual signg and exhange-based communicative responses. *Journal of Applied Behavior Analysis, 42*(2), 399–404. doi:10.1901/jaba.2009.42-399

Greville, W. J., Dymond, S., & Newton, P. M. (2016). The student experience of applied equivalence-based instruction for neuroanatomy teaching. *Journal of Educational Evaluation for Health Professions, 13*, 1–8.

Griffee, K., & Dougher, M. J. (2002). Contextual control of stimulus generalisation and stimulus equivalence in hierarchical categorization. *Journal of Experimental Analysis of Behavior, 78*, 3, 433–447. doi:10.1901/jeab.2002.78-433.

Grossberg, J. M. (1964). Behavior therapy: A review. *Psychological Bulletin, 62*(2), 73–88.

Groves, P. M., & Thompson, R. F. (1970). Habituation: A dual-process theory. *Psychological Review, 77*, 419–450. doi:10.1037/h0029810

Grow, L. L., & Kodak, T. (2010). Recent research on emergent verbal behavior: Clinical applications and future directions. *Journal of Applied Behavior Analysis, 43*(4), 775–778. doi:10.1901/jaba.2010.43-775

Guercio, J. M., Podolska-Schroeder, H., & Rehfeldt, R. A. (2004). Using stimulus equivalence technology to teach emotion recognition to adults with acquired brain injury. *Brain Injury, 18*, 593–601.

Guerrero, M., Alós, F. J., & Moriana, J. A. (2015). Emergent relations with compound stimuli in conditional and simple discriminations: An experimental application in children. *The Psychological Record, 65*(3), 475–486. doi:10.1007/s40732-015-0123-6

Guralnick, M., J. (2001). Social competence with peers and early childhood inclusion. In M. J. Guralnick (Ed.), *Early childhood inclusion: Focus on change* (pp. 481–502). Baltimore, MD: Brookes.

Haaga, D. A., Dyck, M. J., & Ernst, D. (1991). Empirical status of cognitive theory of depression. *Psychological Bulletin, 110*(2), 215–236.

Haegele, K. M., McComas, J. J., Dixon, M., & Burns, M. K. (2011). Using a stimulus equivalence paradigm to teach numerals, English words, and Native American words to preschool-age children. *Journal of Behavioral Education, 20*, 283–296. doi:10.1007/s10864-011-9134-9

Haggar, J., Ingvarsson, E. T., & Braun, E. C. (2018). Further evaluation of blocked trials to teach intraverbal responses under complex stimulus control: Effects of criterion-level probes. *Learning and Motivation, 62*, 29–40. doi:10.1016/j.lmot.2017.02.006

Halford, G. S., Andrews, G., & Jensen, I. (2002). Integration of category induction and hierarchical classification: One paradigm at two levels of complexity. *Journal of Cognition and Development, 3*, 2, 143–177. doi:10.1207/S15327647JCD0302_2.

Hall, G. & Sundberg, M. L. (1987). Teaching mands by manipulating conditioned establishing operations. *The Analysis of Verbal Behavior, 5*(1), 41–53. doi:10.1007/BF03392819

Hall, S. S., DeBernardis, G. M., & Reiss, A. L. (2006). The acquisition of stimulus equivalence in individuals with fragile X syndrome. *Journal of Intellectual Disability Research, 50*, 643–651.

Hanna, E. S., de Souza, D. G., Rose, J. C., & Fonseca, M. (2004). Effects of delayed constructed-response identity matching on spelling of dictated words. *Journal of Applied Behavior Analysis, 37*(2), 223–227. doi:10.1901/jaba.2004.37-223

Hanson, N. R. (1958). *Patterns of discovery: An inquiry into the conceptual foundations of science.* Cambridge, England: Cambridge University Press.

Haq, S. S., & Kodak, T. (2015). Evaluating the effects of massed and distributed practice on acquisition and maintenance of tacts and textual behavior with typically developing children. *Journal of Applied Behavior Analysis, 48*(1), 85–95. doi:10.1002/jaba.178

Haq, S. S., Zemantic, P. K., Kodak, T., LeBlanc, B., & Ruppert, T. E. (2017). Examination of variables that affect the efficacy of instructive feedback. *Behavioral Interventions, 32*(3), 206–216. doi:10.1002/bin.1470

Harmon, K., Strong, R., & Pasnak, R. (1982). Relational responses in tests of transposition with rhesus monkeys. *Learning And Motivation, 13*, 495–504. doi:10.1016/0023-9690(82)90006-6

Harris, S. L. (1975). Teaching language to nonverbal children with emphasis on problems of generalization. *Psychological Bulletin, 82*, 565–580. doi:10.1037/h0076903.

Haughton, E. (1972). Aims: Growing and sharing. In J. B. Jordon and L.S. Robbins (Eds.), *Let's try doing something different kind of thing.* (pp. 20–39). Arlington, VA: Council for Exceptional Children.

Haughton, E. (1980). Practicing practices: Learning by activity. *Journal of Precision Teaching, 1,* 3–20.

Hausman, N. L., Borrero, J. C., Fisher, A., & Kahng, S. (2014). Improving accuracy of portion-size estimations through a stimulus equivalence paradigm. *Journal of Applied Behavior Analysis, 47,* 485–499.

Hausman, N. L., Borrero, J. C., Fisher, A., & Kahng, S. (2017). Teaching young children to make accurate portion size estimations using a stimulus equivalence paradigm. *Behavioral Interventions, 32,* 121–132. doi:10.1002/bin.1466

Hayes, L. J. (1991). Substitution and reference. In L. J. Hayes & P. N. Chase (Eds.), *Dialogues on verbal behavior: The first international institute on verbal relations* (pp. 3–14). Reno, NV: Context Press.

Hayes, L. J. (1992). Equivalence as process. In S. C. Hayes & L. J. Hayes (Eds.), *Understanding verbal relations* (pp. 97–108). Reno, NV: Context Press.

Hayes, L. J., & Chase, P. N. (1991). *Dialogues on verbal behavior: The First International Institute on Verbal Relations.* Reno, NV: Context Press.

Hayes, L. J., & Fryling, M. J. (2009). Overcoming the pseudo-problem of private events in the analysis of behavior. *Behavior and Philosophy,* 39–57.

Hayes, L. J., & Fryling, M. J. (2014). Motivation in behavior analysis: A critique. *The Psychological Record, 64*(2), 339–347. doi:10.1007/s40732-014-0025-z

Hayes, L. J., & Fryling, M. J. (2015). A historical perspective on the future of behavior science. *The Behavior Analyst, 38*(2), 149–161. doi:10.1007/s40614-015-0030-9

Hayes, S. C. (1984). Making sense of spirituality. *Behaviorism, 12,* 99–110.

Hayes, S. C. (1989). Nonhumans have not yet shown stimulus equivalence. *Journal of the Experimental Analysis of Behavior, 51*(3), 385–392.

Hayes, S. C. (1996). Developing a theory of derived stimulus relations. *Journal of the Experimental Analysis of Behavior, 65,* 309–311.

Hayes, S. C. (2004). Acceptance and commitment therapy, relational frame theory, and the third wave of behavioral and cognitive therapies. *Behavior Therapy, 35*(4), 639–665.

Hayes, S. C., Barnes-Holmes, D., & Roche, B. (Eds.). (2001). *Relational frame theory: A post-Skinnerian account of human language and cognition.* New York, NY: Plenum Press.

Hayes, S. C., Barnes-Holmes, D., & Wilson, K. G. (2012). Contextual behavioral science: Creating a science more adequate to the challenge of the human condition. *Journal of Contextual Behavioral Science, 1*(1), 1–16. doi:10.1016/j.jcbs.2012.09.004

Hayes, S. C., Brownstein, A. J., Haas, J. R., & Greenway, D. E. (1986). Instructions, multiple schedules, and extinction: Distinguishing rule-governed from schedule-controlled behavior. *Journal of the Experimental Analysis of Behavior, 46,* 137–147. doi:10.1901/jeab.1986.46-137

Hayes, S. C., Brownstein, A. J., Zettle, R. D., Rosenfarb, I., & Korn, Z. (1986). Rule-governed behavior and sensitivity to changing consequences of responding. *Journal of the Experimental Analysis of Behavior, 45,* 237–256. doi:10.1901/jeab.1986.45-237

Hayes, S. C., Gifford, E. V., Townsend, R. C., & Barnes-Holmes, D. (2001). Thinking, problem-solving, and pragmatic verbal analysis. In S. C. Hayes, D. Barnes-Holmes, & B. Roche (Eds.), *Relational frame theory: A post-Skinnerian account of human language and cognition* (pp. 87–101). New York, NY: Kluwer Academic/Plenum Publishers.

Hayes, S. C, & Hayes, L. J. (1989). The verbal action of the listener as a basis for rule-governance. In S. C. Hayes (Ed.), *Rule-governed behavior: Cognition, contingencies, and instructional control* (pp. 171–173). New York, NY: Plenum Press.

Hayes, S. C., Hayes, L. J., & Reese, H. W. (1988). Finding the philosophical core: A review of Stephen C. Pepper's world hypotheses: A study in evidence. *Journal of the Experimental Analysis of Behavior, 50*(1), 97–111. doi:10.1901/jeab.1988.50-97

Hayes, S. C., Kohlenberg, B., & Hayes, L. J. (1991). The transfer of specific and general consequential functions through simple and conditional equivalence relations. *Journal of the Experimental Analysis of Behavior, 56*, 119–137.

Hayes, S. C., Levin, M. E., Plumb-Vilardaga, J., Villatte, J. L., & Pistorello, J. (2013). Acceptance and commitment therapy and contextual behavioral science: Examining the progress of a distinctive model of behavioral and cognitive therapy. *Behavior Therapy, 44*(2), 180–198. doi:10.1016/j.beth.2009.08.002

Hayes, S. C., Luoma, J., Bond, F., Masuda, A., & Lillis, J. (2006). Acceptance and commitment therapy: Model, processes, and outcomes. *Behavior Research and Therapy, 44*, 1–25.

Hayes, S. C., Pistorello, J., & Levin, M. E. (2012). Acceptance and commitment therapy as a unified model of behavior change. *The Counseling Psychologist, 40*, 976–1002. doi:10.1177/0011000012460836

Hayes, S. C., & Sanford, B. T. (2014). Cooperation came first: Evolution and human cognition. *Journal of Experimental Analysis of Behavior, 101*, 112–129. doi:10.1002/jeab.64

Hayes, S. C., & Sanford, B. T. (2015). Modern psychotherapy as a multidimensional multilevel evolutionary process. *Current Opinion in Psychology, 2*, 16–20. doi:10.1016/j.copsyc.2015.01.009

Hayes, S. C., Sanford, B. T., & Chin, F. T. (2017). Carrying the baton: Evolution science and a contextual behavioral analysis of language and cognition. *Journal of Contextual Behavioral Science*. doi:10.1016/j.jcbs.2017.01.002

Hayes, S. C., Strosahl K. D., Bunting K., Twohig M. P., & Wilson K. G. (2004). What is acceptance and commitment therapy? In Hayes S. C., Strosahl K. D. (Eds.), *A practical guide to acceptance and commitment therapy* (pp. 1–30). New York, NY: Guilford Press.

Hayes, S. C., Strosahl, K. D., & Wilson, K. G. (1999). *Acceptance and commitment therapy: An experiential approach to behavior change.* New York, NY: Guilford Press.

Hayes, S. C., Strosahl, K. D., & Wilson, K. G. (2012). *Acceptance and commitment therapy: The process and practice of mindful change* (2nd ed.). New York, NY: Guilford Press.

Hayes, S. C., Strosahl, K., Wilson, K. G., Bissett, R. T., Pistorello, J., Toarmino, D., . . . Stewart, S. H. (2004). Measuring experiential avoidance: A preliminary test of a working model. *The Psychological Record, 54*(4), 553–578.

Hayes, S. C., & Wilson, K. G. (1994). Acceptance and commitment therapy: Altering the verbal support for experiential avoidance. *The Behavior Analyst, 17*(2), 289–303.

Hayes, S. C., Zettle, R. D., & Rosenfarb, I. (1989). Rule-following. In S. Hayes (Ed.), *Rule-governed behavior: Cognition, contingencies, and instructional control* (pp. 191–220). Reno, NV: Context Press.

Heagle, A. I., & Rehfeldt, R. A. (2006) Teaching perspective-taking skills to typically developing children through derived relational responding. *Journal of Early and Intensive Behavior Intervention, 3*, 1–34.

Healy, O., Barnes, D., & Smeets, P. M. (1998). Derived relational responding as an operant: The effects of between-session feedback. *The Psychological Record, 48*, 511–536.

Healy, O., Barnes-Holmes, D., & Smeets, P. M. (2000). Derived relational responding as generalized operant behavior. *Journal of the Experimental Analysis of Behavior, 74*, 207–227. doi:10.1901/jeab.2000.74-207

Heffner, H. E., & Heffner, R. S. (2007). Hearing ranges of laboratory animals. *Journal of the American Association for Laboratory Animal Science, 46*, 11–13.

Heider, N., Spruyt, A., & De Houwer, J. (2015). Implicit beliefs about ideal body image predict body image dissatisfaction. *Frontiers in Psychology, 6*, 1402. doi:10.3389/fpsyg.2015.01402

Henrich, J. (2004). Cultural group selection, coevolutionary processes and large-scale cooperation. *Journal of Economic Behavior & Organization, 53*, 5–35.

Hermann, J. A., Montes, A. I. D., Domínguez, B., Montes, F., & Hopkins, B. L. (1973). Effects of bonuses for punctuality on the tardiness of industrial workers. *Journal of Applied Behavior Analysis, 6*, 563–570. doi:10.1901/jaba.1973.6-563

Herrnstein, R. J. (1990). Levels of stimulus control: A functional approach. *Cognition, 37*(1), 133–166.

Herrnstein, R. J., Loveland, D. H., & Cable, C. (1979). Natural concepts in pigeons. *Journal of Experimental Psychology: Animal Behavior Processes, 2*, 285–302. doi:10.1037/0097-7403.2.4.285

Hinton, E. C., Dymond, S., Von Hecker, U., & Evans, C. J. (2010). Neural correlates of relational reasoning and the symbolic distance effect: Involvement of parietal cortex. *Neuroscience, 168*, 138–148.

Hobbs, T. R., & Holt, M. (1976). The effects of token reinforcement on the behavior of delinquents in cottage settings. *Journal of Applied Behavior Analysis, 9*, 189–198. doi:10.1901/jaba.1976.9-189

Hoffman, M. L. (1981). Is altruism part of human nature? *Journal of Personality and Social Psychology, 40*, 121–137.

Holt, G. L. (1971). Effect of reinforcement contingencies in increasing programmed reading and mathematics behaviors in first-grade children. *Journal of Experimental Child Psychology, 12*, 362–369. doi:10.1016/0022-0965(71)90031-2

Holyoak, K. J., & Thagard, P. R. (1989). Analogical mapping by constraint satisfaction. *Cognitive Science, 13*, 295–355.

Holz, W. C., & Azrin, N. H. (1961). Discriminative properties of punishment. *Journal of the Experimental Analysis of Behavior, 4*, 225–232. doi:10.1901/jeab.1961.4-225

Honig, W. K., & Urcuioli, P. J. (1981). The legacy of Guttman and Kalish (1956): 25 years of research on stimulus generalization. *Journal of the Experimental Analysis of Behavior, 36*, 405–445. doi:10.1901/jeab.1981.36-405

Hood, S. A., Luczynski, K. C., & Mitteer, D. R. (2017). Toward meaningful outcomes in teaching conversation and greeting skills to with individuals with autism spectrum disorder. *Journal of Applied Behavior Analysis, 50*, 459–486.

Horne, P. J., & Lowe, C. F. (1996). On the origins of naming and other symbolic behavior. *Journal of the Experimental Analysis of Behavior, 65*, 185–241. doi:10.1901/jeab.1996.65-185

Horner, R. H., & Day, H. M. (1991). The effects of response efficiency on functionally equivalent competing behaviors. *Journal of Applied Behavior Analysis, 24*(4), 719–732. doi:10.1901/jaba.1991.24-719

Horowitz, F. D. (1987). *Exploring developmental theories: Toward a structural/behavioral model of development.* Hillsdale, NJ: Lawrence Erlbaum.

Howlin, P., Baron-Cohen, S., & Hadwin, J. (1999). *Teaching children with autism to mind-read: A practical guide for teachers and parents.* Chichester, UK: Wiley.

Hübner, M. M. C., Austin, J., & Miguel, C. F. (2008). The effects of praising qualifying autoclitics on the frequency of reading. *The Analysis of Verbal Behavior, 24*(1), 55–62. doi:10.1007/BF03393056

Hughes, C. (1992). Teaching self-instruction utilizing multiple exemplars to produce generalized problem-solving among individuals with severe mental retardation. *American Journal on Mental Retardation, 97*, 302–314.

Hughes, S., Barnes-Holmes, D., & Smyth, S. (2017). Implicit cross-community biases revisited: Evidence for ingroup favoritism in the absence of outgroup derogation in Northern Ireland. *The Psychological Record, 67*, 97–107. doi:10.1007/s40732-016-0210-3

Hughes, S., Barnes-Holmes, D., & Vahey, N. (2012). Holding on to our functional roots when exploring new intellectual islands: A voyage through implicit cognition research. *Journal of Contextual Behavioral Science, 1*(1), 17–38. doi:10.1016/j.jcbs.2012.09.003

Hussey, I., & Barnes-Holmes, D. (2012). The implicit relational assessment procedure as a measure of implicit depression and the role of psychological flexibility. *Cognitive and Behavioral Practice, 19*(4), 573–582. doi:10.1016/j.cbpra.2012.03.002

Ilardi, S. S., & Craighead, W. E. (1994). The role of nonspecific factors in cognitive-behavior therapy for depression. *Clinical Psychology: Science and Practice, 1*(2), 138–155.

Imada, T., Zhang, Y., Cheour, M., Taulu, S., Ahonen, A., & Kuhl, P. K. (2006). Infant speech perception activates Broca's area: A developmental magnetoencephalography study. *Neuroreport, 17*(10),
957–962. doi:10.1097/01.wnr.0000223387.51704.89

Imam, A. A., & Warner, T. A. (2014). Test order effects in simultaneous protocols. *Learning & Behavior,
42*, 93–103.

Immordino-Yang, M. H., McColl, A., Damasio, H., Damasio, A. (May 2009). Neural correlates of
admiration and compassion. *Proceedings of the National Academy of Sciences, 106*, 19,
8021–8026.

Ingvarsson, E. T., & Hollobaugh, T. (2011). A comparison of prompting tactics to establish intraverbals
in children with autism. *Journal of Applied Behavior Analysis, 44*(3), 659–664. doi:10.1901/
jaba.2011.44-659

Ingvarsson, E. T., Kramer, R. L., Carp, C. L., Pétursdóttir, A. I., & Macias, H. (2016). Evaluation of a
blocked-trials procedure to establish complex stimulus control over intraverbal responses in children with autism. *The Analysis of Verbal Behavior, 32*(2), 205–224. doi:10.1007/
s40616-016-0071-5

Inhelder, B., & Piaget, J. (1964). *The early growth of logic in the child.* London: Routledge & Kegan Paul.

Jackson, M. L., Mendoza, D. R., & Adams, A. N. (2014). Teaching a deictic relational repertoire to
children with autism. *The Psychological Record, 64*, 791–802.

Jacobs, K. W., Morford, Z. H., King, J. E., & Hayes, L. J. (2017). Predicting the effects of interventions:
A tutorial on the disequilibrium model. *Behavior Analysis in Practice.* doi:10.1007/
s40617-017-0176-x

Jacobson, N. S., Dobson, K. S., Truax, R. A., Addis, M. E., Koerner, K., Gollan, J. K., . . . Prince, S. E.
(1996). A component analysis of cognitive-behavioral treatment for depression. *Journal of
Consulting and Clinical Psychology, 64*, 295–304.

Johnson, K. (2015). Behavioral education in the 21st century. *Journal of Organizational Behavior
Management, 35*, 135–150. doi:10.1080/01608061.2015.1036152

Johnson, K., & Layng, T. V. J. (1992). Breaking the structuralist barrier: Literacy and numeracy with
fluency. *American Psychologist, 47*, 1475–1498.

Johnson, K., & Layng, T. V. J. (1994). The Morningside Model of Generative Instruction. In R.
Gardner, D. Sainato, J. Cooper, T. Heron, W. Heward, J. Eshleman, & T. Grossi (Eds.), *Behavior
analysis in education: Focus on measurably superior instruction* (pp. 173–197). Belmont, CA:
Brooks-Cole.

Johnson, K., & Street, E. M. (2004). *The Morningside model of generative instruction: What it means to
leave no child behind.* Concord, MA: Cambridge Center for Behavioral Studies.

Johnson, K. J., & Street, E. M. (2012). From the laboratory to the field and back again: Morningside
Academy's 32 years of improving students' academic performance. *The Behavior Analyst Today,
13*, 20–40.

Johnson, K., & Street, E. M. (2013). *Response to intervention and precision teaching: Creating synergy in
the classroom.* New York, NY: Guilford Publications

Johnston, J. (1996). Distinguishing between applied research and practice. *The Behavior Analyst, 19*,
35–47.

Jonah, B. A., & Grant, B. A. (1985). Long-term effectiveness of selective traffic enforcement programs
for increasing seat belt use. *Journal of Applied Psychology, 70*, 257–263.
doi:10.1037/0021-9010.70.2.257

Joyce, B. G., Joyce, J. H., & Wellington, B. (1993). Using stimulus equivalence procedures to teach
relationships between English and Spanish words. *Education & Treatment of Children, 16*, 48–65.

Juarascio, A. S., Forman, E. M., Timko, C. A., & Herbert, J. D. (2011). Implicit internalization of the
thin ideal as a predictor of increases in weight, body dissatisfaction, and disordered eating. *Eating
Behaviors, 12*, 207–213. doi:10.1016/j.eatbeh.2011.04.004

Kalish, C. W., & Gelman, S. A. (1992). On wooden pillows: Multiple classification and children's category-based inductions. *Child Development, 63*, 6, 1536–1557.

Kamin, L. J. (1969). Predictability, surprise, attention, and conditioning. In B. A. Campbell & R. M. Church (Eds.), *Punishment and aversive behavior* (pp. 279–296). New York, NY: Appleton-Century-Crofts.

Kanfer, F. H. (1959). Verbal rate, content, and adjustment ratings in experimentally structured interviews. *Journal of Abnormal Psychology, 58*(3), 305–311.

Kanfer, F. H. (1961). Comments on learning in psychotherapy. *Psychological Reports, 9*(3), 681–699.

Kanfer, F. H., & McBrearty, J. F. (1962). Minimal social reinforcement and interview content. *Journal of Clinical Psychology, 18*, 210–215.

Kanfer, F. H., Phillips, J. S., Matarazzo, J. D., & Saslow, G. (1960). Experimental modification of interviewer content in standardized interviews. *Journal of Consulting Psychology, 24*, 528–536.

Kantor, J. R. (1921). An objective interpretation of meanings. *American Journal of Psychology, 32*, 231–248.

Kantor, J. R. (1922). An analysis of language data. *Psychological Review, 29*, 267–309.

Kantor, J. R. (1924). *Principles of psychology* (vol. 1). New York, NY: Alfred Knopf.

Kantor, J. R. (1926). *Principles of psychology.* (vol. II). New York, NY: Alfred Knoph.

Kantor, J. R. (1928). Can psychology contribute to the study of linguistics? *Monist, 26*, 630–648.

Kantor, J. R. (1929). Language as behavior and as symbolism. *Journal of Philosophy, 26*, 150–159.

Kantor, J. R. (1933). *A survey of the science of psychology.* Chicago, IL: Principia Press.

Kantor, J. R. (1936). *An objective psychology of grammar.* Chicago, IL: The Principia Press.

Kantor, J. R. (1938). The role of language in logic and science. *Journal of Philosophy, 35*, 449–463.

Kantor, J. R. (1953). *The logic of modern science.* Chicago, IL: Principia Press.

Kantor, J. R. (1958). *Interbehavioral psychology.* Chicago, IL: Principia Press.

Kantor, J. R. (1963), Behaviorism: Whose image? *The Psychological Record, 13*, 499–512.

Kantor, J. R. (1975). Psychological linguistics. *Mexican Journal of Behavior Analysis, 1*, 249–268.

Kantor, J. R. (1977). *Psychological linguistics.* Chicago, IL: Principia Press.

Kantor, J. R. (1981). Reflections on speech and language. *Mexican Journal of Behavior Analysis, 7*, 91 106.

Kantor, J. R. (1982). *Cultural psychology.* Chicago, IL: The Principia Press.

Kantor, J. R., & Smith, N. W. (1975). *The science of psychology: An interbehavioral survey.* Chicago, IL: Principia Press.

Karmali, I., Greer, R. D., Nuzzolo-Gomez, R., Ross, D. E., & Rivera-Valdes, C. (2005). Reducing palilalia by presenting tact corrections to young children with autism. *The Analysis of Verbal Behavior, 21*(1), 145–153. doi:10.1007/BF03393016

Kato, O. M., de Rose, J. C., & Faleiros, P. B. (2008). Topography of responses in conditional discrimination influences formation of equivalence classes. *The Psychological Record, 58*, 245–267.

Kaufman, A., Baron, A., & Kopp, R. E. (1966). Some effects of instructions on human operant behavior. *Psychonomic Monograph Supplements, 1*, 243–250.

Kazdin, A. E. (1979). Fictions, factions, and functions of behavior therapy. *Behavior Therapy, 10*(5), 629–654. doi:10.1016/S0005-7894(79)80066-0

Keane, M. T. (1997). What makes an analogy difficult? The effects of order and causal structure on analogical mapping. *Journal of Experimental Psychology: Learning, Memory, and Cognition, 23*, 4, 946–967.

Keintz, K. S., Miguel, C. F., Kao, B., & Finn, H. E. (2011). Using conditional discrimination training to produce emergent relations between coins and their values in children with autism. *Journal of Applied Behavior Analysis, 44*, 909–913. doi:10.1901/jaba.2011.44-909

Keller, F. S. (1968). "Good-bye, teacher…" *Journal of Applied Behavior Analysis*, 1, 79–89. doi:10.1901/jaba.1968.1-79

Keohane, D. D., Pereira Delgado, J. A., & Greer, R. D. (2009). Observing responses: Foundations of higher-order verbal operants. In R. A. Rehfeldt & Y. Barnes-Holmes (Eds.), *Derived relational responding: Applications for learners with autism and other developmental disabilities* (pp. 41–62). Oakland, CA: New Harbinger Publications.

Keuleers, E., Diependaele, K., & Brysbaert, M. (2010). Practice effects in large-scale visualword recognition studies: A lexical decision study on 14,000 Dutch mono-and disyllabic words and nonwords. *Frontiers in Psychology*, 1, 174.

Killeen, P. R., & Fetterman, J. G. (1988). A behavioral theory of timing. *Psychological Review*, 95, 274–295. doi:10.1037/0033-295X.95.2.274

Killeen, P. R., & Jacobs, K. W. (2017a). Coal is not black, snow is not white, food is not a reinforcer: the roles of affordances and dispositions in the analysis of behavior. *The Behavior Analyst*, 40(1), 17–38. doi:10.1007/s40614-016-0080-7

Killeen, P. R., & Jacobs, K. W. (2017b). The modulated contingency. *The Behavior Analyst*, online first. doi:10.1007/s40614-017-0101-1

King, C. M., & Quigley, S. P. (1985). *Reading and deafness*. San Diego, CA: College Hill Press.

Kinloch, J. M., McEwan, J. S. A., & Foster, T. M. (2013). Matching-to-sample and stimulus-pairing-observation procedures in stimulus equivalence: The effects of number of trials and stimulus arrangement. *The Psychological Record*, 63, 157–174.

Kisamore, A. N., Carr, J. E., & LeBlanc, L. A. (2011). Training preschool children to use visual imagining as a problem-solving strategy for complex categorization tasks. *Journal of Applied Behavior Analysis*, 44(2), 255–278. doi:10.1901/jaba.2011.44-255

Kisamore, A. N., Karsten, A. M., & Mann, C. C. (2016). Teaching multiply controlled intraverbals to children and adolescents with autism spectrum disorders. *Journal of Applied Behavior Analysis*, 49(4), 826–847. doi:10.1002/jaba.344

Kitchener, R. F. (1977). Behavior and behaviorism. *Behaviorism*, 5, 11–71.

Kleinert, K. (2018). *A comparison of bidirectional naming for familiar and non-familiar stimuli and the effects of a repeated probe procedure for first grade students* (Order No. 10784944). Available from ProQuest Dissertations & Theses Global. (2031071957). Retrieved from https://tc.idm.oclc.org/login?url=https://search-proquest-com.tc.idm.oclc.org/docview/2031071957?accountid=14258

Klintwall, L., & Eikeseth, S. (2014). Early and intensive behavioral intervention (EIBI) in autism. In Patel, V. B., Preedy, V., R., & Mortin, C. R. (Eds.), *Comprehensive Guide to Autism* (pp. 117–137). New York, NY: Springer.

Kodak, T., Campbell, V., Bergmann, S., LeBlanc, B., Kurtz-Nelson, E., Cariveau, T., . . . Mahon, J. (2016). Examination of efficacious, efficient, and socially valid error-correction procedures to teach sight words and prepositions to children with autism spectrum disorder. *Journal of Applied Behavior Analysis*, 49(3), 532–547. doi:10.1002/jaba.310

Kodak, T., Clements, A., & Ninness, C. (2009). Acquisition of mands and tacts with concurrent echoic training. *Journal of Applied Behavior Analysis*, 42(4), 839–843. doi:10.1901/jaba.2009.42-839

Kodak, T., Fuchtman, R., & Paden, A. R. (2012). A comparison of intraverbal training procedures for children with autism. *Journal of Applied Behavior Analysis*, 45(1), 155–160. doi:10.1901/jaba.2012.45-155

Kohlenberg, R. J., Bolling, M. Y., Kanter, J. W., & Parker, C. R. (2002). Clinical behavior analysis: Where it went wrong, how it was made good again, and why its future is so bright. *The Behavior Analyst Today*, 3(3), 248–253.

Kohlenberg, R. J., & Tsai, M. (1991). *Functional analytic psychotherapy. Creating intense and curative therapeutic relationships*. New York, NY: Springer.

Kohlenberg, R., & Tsai, M. (1995). *Functional analytic psychotherapy: A behavioral approach to intensive treatment.* Washington, DC: American Psychological Association.

Kohlenberg, R. J., Tsai, M., & Dougher, M. J. (1993). The dimensions of clinical behavior analysis. *The Behavior Analyst, 16*(2), 271–282.

Kooistra, E. T., Buchmeier, A. L., & Klatt, K. P. (2012). The effect of motivating operations on the transfer from tacts to mands for children diagnosed with autism. *Research in Autism Spectrum Disorders, 6*(1), 109–114. doi:10.1016/j.rasd.2011.03.010

Kraemer, K. M., Luberto, C. M., O'Bryan, E. M., Mysinger, E., & Cotton, S. (2016). Mind-body skills training to improve distress tolerance in Medical students: A pilot study. *Teaching Learning Medicine, 28*(2), 219–28.

Krantz, P. J., Land, S. E., & McClannahan, L. E. (1989). Conversational skills for autistic adolescents: An autistic peer as prompter. *Behavioral Interventions, 4*(3), 171–189. doi:10.1002/bin.2360040303

Krantz, P. J., & McClannahan, L. E. (1993). Teaching children with autism to initiate to peers: Effects of a script-fading procedure. *Journal of Applied Behavior Analysis, 26*(1), 121–132. doi:10.1901/jaba.1993.26-121

Krasner, L. (1963). Reinforcement, verbal behavior and psychotherapy. *The American Journal of Orthopsychiatry, 33*, 601–613.

Kubina, R. M., & Yurich, K. K. L. (2012). *The precision teaching book.* Lemont, PA: Greatness Achieved.

Kuhl, P. (2003). Human speech and birdsong: Communication and the social brain. *Proceedings of the National Academy of Sciences, 100*, 9645–9646. http://www.pnas.org/content/100/17/9645.short

Kuhl, P. (2004). Early language acquisition: Cracking the speech code. *Nature Reviews Neuroscience, 5*, 831–843. doi:10.1038/nrn1533

Kuo, Z. Y. (1967). *The dynamics of behavior development: An epigenetic view.* New York, NY: Random House.

Lamarre, J., & Holland, J. G. (1985). The functional independence of mands and tacts. *Journal of the Experimental Analysis of Behavior, 43*(1), 5–19. doi:10.1901/jeab.1985.43-5

Landa, R. K., Hansen, B., & Shillingsburg, A. (2017). Teaching mands for information using 'when' to children with autism. *Journal of Applied Behavior Analysis, 50*(3), 538–551. doi:10.1002/jaba.387

Lane, S., & Critchfield, T. S. (1998). Classification of vowels and consonants by individuals with moderate mental retardation: Development of arbitrary relations via match-to-sample training with compound stimuli. *Journal of Applied Behavior Analysis, 31*, 21–41.

Lang, R., Rispoli, M., Sigafoos, J., Lancioni, G., Andrews, A., & Ortega, L. (2011). Effects of language of instruction on response accuracy and challenging behavior in a child with autism. *Journal of Behavioral Education, 20*, 252–259. doi:10.1007/s10864-011-9130-0

Lanzoni, S. (2015). A short history of empathy. *The Atlantic.* Retrieved from https://www.theatlantic.com/health/archive/2015/10/a-short-history-of-empathy/409912

Laraway, S., Snycerski, S., Michael, J., & Poling, A. (2003). Motivating operations and terms to describe them: Some further refinements. *Journal of Applied Behavior Analysis, 36*(3), 407–414. doi:10.1901/jaba.2003.36-407

LaRue, R. H., Pepa, L., Delmolino, L., Sloman, K. N., Fiske, K., Hansford, A., . . . Weiss, M. J. (2016). A brief assessment for selecting communication modalities for individuals with autism spectrum disorders. *Evidence-Based Communication Assessment and Intervention, 10*(1), 32–43. doi:10.1080/17489539.2016.1204767

Lattal, K. A., Cançado, C. R., Cook, J. E., Kincaid, S. L., Nighbor, T. D., & Oliver, A. C. (2017). On defining resurgence. *Behavioural Processes, 141*, 85–91. doi:10.1016/j.beproc.2017.04.018

Lawson, T. R., & Walsh, D. (2007). The effects of observational training on the acquisition of reinforcement for listening. *The Journal of Early and Intensive Behavioral Intervention, 4*(2), 430. doi:10.1037/h0100383

Layng, T. V. J., Twyman, J. S., & Stikeleather, G. (2004a). Engineering discovery learning: The contingency adduction of some precursors of textual responding in a beginning reading program. *Analysis of Verbal Behavior, 20,* 99–109.

Layng, T. V. J., Twyman, J. S., & Stikeleather, G. (2004b) Selected for success: How Headsprout Reading Basics teaches beginning reading. In D. J. Moran and R. Malott (Eds.), *Evidence based educational methods* (pp. 171–197). St. Louis, MO: Elsevier Science/Academic Press.

Leader, G., & Barnes-Holmes, D. (2001a). Establishing fraction-decimal equivalence using a respondent-type training procedure. *The Psychological Record, 51,* 151–165.

Leader, G., & Barnes-Holmes, D. (2001b). Matching to sample and respondent-type training as methods for producing equivalence relations: Isolating the critical variable. *The Psychological Record, 51,* 429–444.

Leaf, J. B., Oppenheim-Leaf, M. L., Leaf, R., Courtemanche, A. B., Taubman, M., McEachin, J., . . . Sherman, J. A. (2012). Observational effects on the preferences of children with autism. *Journal of Applied Behavior Analysis, 45,* 473-483. doi:10.1901/jaba.2012.45-473

Leaf, J. B., Oppenheim-Leaf, M. L., Townley-Cochran, D., Leaf, J. A., Alcalay, A., Milne, C., . . . McEachin, J. (2016). Changing preference from tangible to social activities through an observation procedure. *Journal of Applied Behavior Analysis, 49,* 49-57. doi:10.1002/jaba.276

LeBlanc, L. A., Coates, A. M., Daneshvar, S., Charlop-Christy, M. H., Morris, C., & Lancaster, B. M. (2003). Using video modeling and reinforcement to teach perspective-taking skills to children with autism. *Journal of Applied Behavior Analysis, 36,* 253–257.

LeBlanc, L. A., Miguel, C. F., Cummings, A. R., Goldsmith, T. R., & Carr, J. E. (2003). The effects of three stimulus-equivalence testing conditions on emergent US geography relations of children diagnosed with autism. *Behavioral Interventions, 18,* 279–289.

Lechago, S. A., Carr, J. E., Kisamore, A. N., & Grow, L. L. (2015). The effects of multiple exemplar instruction on the relation between listener and intraverbal categorization repertoires. *The Analysis of Verbal Behavior, 31*(1), 76–95. doi:10.1007/s40616-015-0027-1

Lechago, S. A., & Low, A. (2015). A review of the mand-for-information training research literature. *International Journal of Behavior Analysis & Autism Spectrum Disorders, 1*(1), 35–54.

Lee, G. T., Chou, W. C., & Feng, H. (2017). Using intraverbal prompts to increase divergent intraverbal responses by a child with autism. *Behavioral Interventions, 32*(4), 334–344. doi:10.1002/bin.1496

Lee, R., & Sturmey, P. (2006). The effects of lag schedules and preferred materials on variable responding in students with autism. *Journal of Autism and Developmental Disorders, 36*(3), 421–428. doi:10.1007/s10803-006-0080-7

Lee, R., & Sturmey, P. (2014). The effects of script-fading and a Lag-1 schedule on varied social responding in children with autism. *Research in Autism Spectrum Disorders, 8,* 440–448. doi:10.1016/j.rasd.2014.01.003

Leech, A., Barnes-Holmes, D., & McEnteggart, C. (2017). Spider fear and avoidance: A preliminary study of the impact of two verbal rehearsal tasks on a behavior–behavior relation and its implications for an experimental analysis of defusion. *The Psychological Record, 67*(3), 387–398. doi:10.1007/s40732-017-0230-7

Leon, A. L., & Rosales, R. (2017). Effects of bilingual instruction for a child with communication disorder. *Journal of Behavioral Edcuation,* printed online first. doi:10.1007/s10864-017-9272-9

Lerman, D. C., Parten, M., Addison, L. R., Vorndran, C. M., Volkert, V. M., & Kodak, T. (2005). A methodology for assessing the functions of emerging speech in children with developmental disabilities. *Journal of Applied Behavior Analysis, 38*(3), 303–316. doi:10.1901/jaba.2005.106-04

Leslie, J. C., Tierney, K.J., Robinson, C.P., Keenan, M., Watt, A., & Barnes, D. (1993). Differences between clinically anxious and non-anxious subjects in a stimulus equivalence training task involving threat words. *The Psychological Record, 43,* 153–161.

Levin, M. E., Hayes, S. C., & Vilardaga, R. (2012). Acceptance and commitment therapy: Applying an iterative translational research strategy in behavior analysis. *APA Handbook of Behavior Analysis*, *2*, 455–480.

Lewon, A. B. (2019). *Referential behavior and interactions of young children with ASD and their mothers in an EIBI program: A longitudinal study*. Manuscript in preparation.

Lewon, M., & Hayes, L. J. (2014). Toward an analysis of emotions as products of motivating operations. *The Psychological Record*, *64*, 813–825. doi:10.1007/s40732-014-0046-7

Lin, E. L., & Murphy, G. L. (2001). Thematic relations in adults' concepts. *Journal of Experimental Psychology*, *130*, 1, 3–28.

Linden, M., & Whimbey, A. (1990). *Why Johnny can't write*. Hillsdale, NJ: Erlbaum.

Lindsley, O. R. (1960). Characteristics of the behavior of chronic psychotics as revealed by free-operant conditioning methods. *Diseases of the Nervous System*, *21*, monograph supplement, 66–78.

Lindsley, O. R. (1992). Precision teaching: Discoveries and effects. *Journal of Applied Behavior Analysis*, *25*, 51–57. doi:10.1901/jaba.1992.25-51

Linehan, M. M. (1987). Dialectical behavior therapy for borderline personality disorder: Theory and method. *Bulletin of the Menninger Clinic*, *51*(3), 261–276.

Lipkens, R., & Hayes, S. C. (2009). Producing and recognising analogical relations. *Journal of Experimental Analysis of Behaviour*, *91*, 105–126.

Lipkens, R., Hayes, S. C., & Hayes, L. J. (1993). Longitudinal study of the development of derived relations in an infant. *Journal of Experimental Child Psychology*, *56*, 201–239. doi:10.1006/jecp.1993.1032

Lo, C. (2016). *How the listener half of Naming leads to multiple stimulus control* (Doctoral dissertation, Order No. 10100022). Available from ProQuest Dissertations & Theses Global. (1784011549). doi:10.7916/D8C82988

Lodhi, S., & Greer, R. D. (1989). The speaker as listener. *Journal of the Experimental Analysis of Behavior*, *51*, 353–559. doi:10.1901/jeab.1989.51-353

Longano, J. M., & Greer, R. D. (2014). Is the source of Naming multiple conditioned reinforcers for observing responses? *The Analysis of Verbal Behavior*, *31*, 96–117. doi:10.1007/s40616-014-0022-y

López, J. C., & Luciano, C. (2017). An experimental analysis of defusion interactions based on deictic and hierarchical framings and their impact on cognitive performance. *The Psychological Record*, *67*, 485–497.

Lorah, E. R., Parnell, A., Whitby, P. S., & Hantula, D. (2015). A systematic review of tablet computers and portable media players as speech generating devices for individuals with autism spectrum disorder. *Journal of Autism and Developmental Disorders*, *45*(12), 3792–3804. doi:10.1007/s10803-014-2314-4

Lorenz, K. (1965). *Evolution and modification of behavior*. London, England: Methuen.

Lotfizadeh, A. D., Edwards, T. L., Redner, R., & Poling, A. (2012). Motivating operations affect stimulus control: A largely overlooked phenomenon in discrimination learning. *The Behavior Analyst*, *35*, 89-100. doi:10.1007/BF03392268

Lovett, S., Rehfeldt, R. A., Garcia, Y., & Dunning, J. (2011). Comparison of a stimulus equivalence protocol and traditional lecture for teaching single-subject designs. *Journal of Applied Behavior Analysis*, *44*, 819–833.

Lowenkron, B. (1989). Instructional control of generalized relational matching to sample in children. *Journal of the Experimental Analysis of Behavior*, *52*, 293–309.

Lu, H., Chen, D., & Holyoak, K. J. (2012). Bayesian analogy with relational transformations. *Psychological Review*, *119*, 3, 617–648.

Lubinski, D., & Thompson, T. (1987). An animal model of the interpersonal communication of interoceptive (private) states. *Journal of the Experimental Analysis of Behavior*, *48*, 1–15. doi:10.1901/jeab.1987.48-1

Luciano, C., Ruiz, F. J., Vizcaíno-Torres, R., Sánchez, V., Gutiérrez-Martínez, O., & López-López, J. C. (2011). A relational frame analysis of defusion interactions in ACT. A preliminary and quasi-experimental study with at-risk adolescents. *International Journal of Psychology and Psychological Therapy, 11*, 165–182.

Luciano, C., Valdivia-Salas, S., Cabello, F., & Hernández, M. (2009). Developing self-directed rules. In R. A. Rehfeldt & Y. Barnes-Holmes (Eds.), *Derived relational responding: Applications for learners with autism and other developmental disabilities* (pp. 335–352). Oakland, CA: New Harbinger.

Luciano, C., Valdivia, S., & Ruiz, F. J. (2012). The self as the context for rule-governed behavior. In L. McHugh & I. Stewart (Eds.), *The self and perspective taking: Research and applications* (pp. 143–160). Oakland, CA: Context Press.

Luciano, M. C., Herruzo, J., & Barnes-Holmes, D. (2001). Generalization of say-do correspondence. *The Psychological Record, 51*, 111–130. doi:10.1007/bf03395389

Luo, Q., Perry, C., Peng, D., Jin, Z., Xu, D., Ding, G., & Xu, S. (2003). The neural substrate of analogical reasoning: An fMRI study. *Cognitive Brain Research, 17*, 527–534.

Lynch, D. C., & Cuvo, A. J. (1995). Stimulus equivalence instruction of fraction-decimal relations. *Journal of Applied Behavior Analysis, 28*, 115–126.

Lyons, C. A., & Williamson, P. N. (1988). Contributions of Kantor's "Psychological Linguistics" to understanding psychotic speech. *Behavior Analysis, 23*(3), 110–113.

MacDonald, J., & Ahearn, W. H. (2015). Teaching observational learning to children with autism. *Journal of Applied Behavior Analysis, 48*, 800–816. doi:10.1002/jaba.257

MacDonald, R. P. F., Dixon, L. S., & LeBlanc, J. M. (1986). Stimulus class formation following observational learning. *Analysis and Intervention in Developmental Disabilities, 6*, 73–87.

Mackintosh, N. J. (1976). Overshadowing and stimulus intensity. *Animal Learning & Behavior, 4*, 186–192. doi

Mackintosh, N. J. (1977). Stimulus control: Attentional factors. In W. K. Honig & J. E. R. Staddon (Eds.), *Handbook of operant behavior* (pp. 481–513). Englewood Cliffs, NJ: Prentice-Hall.

Mahoney, M. J. (1974). *Cognition and behavior modification*. Cambridge, MA: Ballinger.

Malcolm, N. (1963). *Knowledge and certainty*. Englewood Cliffs, NJ: Prentice-Hall.

Maloney, E., & Barnes-Holmes, D. (2016). Exploring the behavioral dynamics of the Implicit Relational Assessment Procedure: The role of relational contextual cues versus relational coherence indicators as response options. *The Psychological Record, 66*(3), 395–403. doi:10.1007/s40732-016-0180-5

Maloney, M., Desjardins, A., & Broad, P. (1990). Teach your children well. *Journal of Precision Teaching, 7*(2), 36–58.

Marchand-Martella, N. E., Slocum, T. A., & Martella, R. C. (Eds.). (2004). *Introduction to direct instruction*. Boston, MA: Pearson.

Marchese, N. V., Carr, J. E., LeBlanc, L. A., Rosati, T. C., & Conroy, S. A. (2012). The effects of the question "What is it?" on tact training outcomes of children with autism. *Journal of Applied Behavior Analysis, 45*(3), 539–547. doi:10.1901/jaba.2012.45-539

Marcus, A., & Wilder, D. A. (2009). A comparison of peer video modeling and self-video modeling to teach textual responses in children with autism. *Journal of Applied Behavior Analysis, 42*(2), 335–341. doi:10.1901/jaba.2009.42-335

Markman, E. M. (1989). *Categorization and naming in children: Problems of induction*. Cambridge, MA: The MIT Press.

Markman, E. M., & Seibert, J. (1976). Classes and collections: Internal organization and resulting holistic properties. *Cognitive Psychology, 8*, 516–577.

Marler, P. (1970a). Birdsong and speech development: Could there be parallels? *American Scientist, 58*, 669–673. Retrieved from http://www.jstor.org/stable/27829317

Marler, P. (1970b). A comparative approach to vocal learning: Song development in white-crowned sparrows. *Journal of Comparative and Physiological Psychology, 71*, 1-25. Retrieved from http://psycnet.apa.org/doi/10.1037/h0029144

Marschark, M. (1993). *Psychological development of deaf children.* New York, NY: Oxford University Press.

Marschark, M., Mourandian, V., & Halas, M. (1994). Discourse rules in the language productions of deaf and hearing children. *Journal of Experimental Child Psychology, 57*, 89–107.

Masia, C. L., & Chase, P. N. (1997). Vicarious learning revisited: A contemporary behavior analytic interpretation. *Journal of Behavior Therapy & Experimental Psychiatry, 28*, 41–51.

Mathews, R. M., & Dix, M. (1992). Behavior change in the funny papers: Feedback to cartoonists on safety belt use. *Journal of Applied Behavior Analysis, 25*, 769–775. doi:10.1901/jaba.1992.25-769

Matter, A. L., & Zarcone, J. R. (2017). A comparison of existing and novel communication responses used during functional communication training. *Behavioral Interventions, 32*(3), 217–224. doi:10.1002/bin.1481

Matthews, B. A., Catania, A. C., & Shimoff, E. (1985). Effects of uninstructed verbal behavior on nonverbal responding: Contingency descriptions versus performance descriptions. *Journal of the Experimental Analysis of Behavior, 43*, 155–164. doi:10.1901/jeab.1985.43-155

May, R. J., Hawkins, E., & Dymond, S. (2013). Brief report: Effects of tact training on emergent intra-verbal vocal responses in adolescents with autism. *Journal of Autism and Developmental Disorders, 43*(4), 996–1004. doi:10.1007/s10803-012-1632-7

McAuliffe, D., Hughes, S., & Barnes-Holmes, D. (2014). The dark-side of rule governed behavior: An experimental analysis of problematic rule-following in an adolescent population with depressive symptomatology. *Behavior Modification, 38*, 587–613. doi:10.1177/0145445514521630

McClay, L., Schafer, M. C. M., van der Meer, L., Couper, L., McKenzie, E., O'Reilly, M. F., . . . Sutherland, D. (2016). Acquisition, preference, and follow-up comparison across two modalities taught to two children with autism spectrum disorder. *International Journal of Disability, Development and Education, 64*(2), 117–130. doi:10.1080/1034912X.2016.1188892

McDowell, E. E. (1968). A programed method of reading instruction for use with kindergarten children. *The Psychological Record, 18*, 233–239. doi:10.1007/BF03393766

McHugh, L., Barnes-Holmes, Y., & Barnes-Holmes, D. (2004). A relational frame account of the development of complex cognitive phenomena: Perspective-taking, false belief understanding, and deception. *International Journal of Psychology and Psychological Therapy, 4*(2), 303–324.

McHugh, L., Barnes-Holmes, Y., Barnes-Holmes, D., Stewart, I., & Dymond, S. (2006). False belief as generalized operant behavior. *The Psychological Record, 56*, 341–364.

McHugh, L., Stewart, I., & Hooper, N. (2012). A contemporary functional analytic account of perspective taking. In L. McHugh & I. Stewart (Eds.), *The self and perspective taking* (pp. 55–72). Oakland, CA: Context Press.

McLay, L. K., Sutherland, D., Church, J., & Tyler-Merrick, G. (2013). The formation of equivalence classes in individuals with autism spectrum disorder: A review of literature. *Research in Autism Spectrum Disorders, 7*, 418–431.

McMorrow, M. J., Foxx, R. M., Faw, G. D., & Bittle, R. G. (1987). Cues-pause-point language training: Teaching echolalics functional use of their verbal labeling repertoires. *Journal of Applied Behavior Analysis, 20*(1), 11–22. doi:10.1901/jaba.1987.20-11

McSweeney, F. K., & Murphy, E. S. (2009). Sensitization and habituation regulate reinforcer efficacy. *Neurobiology of Learning and Memory, 92*, 189–198. doi:10.1016/j.nlm.2008.07.002

Meichenbaum, D. (1977). *Cognitive-behaviour modification: An integrative approach.* New York, NY: Plenum.

Mellor, J. R., Barnes, C. S., & Rehfeldt, R. A. (2015). The effects of auditory tact and auditory imagining instructions on the emergence of novel intraverbals. *The Analysis of Verbal Behavior, 31*(2), 236–254. doi:10.1007/s40616-015-0036-0

Mercer, C. D., Mercer, A. R., & Evans, S. (1982). The use of frequency in establishing instructional aims. *Journal of Precision Teaching, 3,* 57–59.

Merwin, I. M., & Wilson, K. G. (2005). Preliminary findings on the effects of self-referring and evaluative stimuli on stimulus equivalence class formation. *The Psychological Record, 55,* 561–575.

Metzner, R. (1963). *Learning theory and the therapy of neurosis.* Cambridge University Press.

Michael, J. (1982). Distinguishing between discriminative and motivational functions of stimuli. *Journal of Experimental Analysis of Behavior, 37,* 149–155. doi:10.1901/jeab.1982.37-149

Michael, J. (1985). Two kinds of verbal behavior plus a possible third. *The Analysis of Verbal Behavior, 3*(1), 1–4. doi:10.1007/BF03392802

Michael, J. (1988). Establising operations and the mand. *The Analysis of Verbal Behavior, 6*(1), 3–9. doi:10.1007/BF03392824

Michael, J. (1993). Establishing operations. *The Behavior Analyst, 16,* 191–206. doi:10.1007/BF03392623

Michael, J., Palmer, D. C., & Sundberg, M. L. (2011). The multiple control of verbal behavior. *The Analysis of Verbal Behavior, 27*(1), 3–22. doi:10.1007/bf03393089

Miguel, C. (2016). Common and intraverbal bidirectional Naming. *The Analysis of Verbal Behavior, 32,* 125–138. doi:10.1007/s40616-016-0066-2

Miguel, C. F., Yang, H. G., Finn, H. E., & Ahearn, W. H. (2009). Establishing derived textual control in activity schedules with children with autism. *Journal of Applied Behavior Analysis, 42*(3), 703–709. doi:10.1002/bin.1365

Ming, S., Mulhern, T., Stewart, I., Moran, L., & Bynum, K. (2018). Testing and training class inclusion in typically developing young children and individuals with autism. *Journal of Applied Behavior Analysis, 51,* 1, 53–60.

Mizael, T. M., de Almeida, J. H., Silveira, C. C., & de Rose, J. C. (2016). Changing racial bias by transfer of functions in equivalence classes. *The Psychological Record, 66*(3), 451–462. doi:10.1007/s40732-016-0185-0

Monclus, B., Uribio, G., & Szabo, T. G. (2016). *Deriving rules from context: An RFT approach to teaching problem-solving skills to children with autism.* Paper presented at the Annual Convention of the Association for Behavior Analysis International, Chicago, IL.

Montoya, M. M., Molina-Cobos, F.J., & McHugh, L. (2017). A review of relational frame theory research into deictic relational responding. *The Psychological Record, 67,* 569–579.

Moore, J. (1980). On behaviorism and private events. *The Psychological Record, 30*(4), 459–475.

Moore, J. (2009). Why the radical behaviorist conception of private events is interesting, relevant, and important. *Behavior and Philosophy, 37,* 21–37.

Mori, A., & Cigala, A. (2016). Perspective taking: Training procedures in developmentally typical preschoolers. Different intervention methods and their effectiveness. *Educational Psychology Review, 28,* 267–294.

Morris, E. K. (1982). Some relationships between interbehavioral psychology and radical behaviorism. *Behaviorism, 10,* 187–216.

Morris, E. K. (1984). Interbehavioral psychology and radical behaviorism: Some similarities and differences. *The Behavior Analyst, 7,* 197–204. doi:10.1007/BF03391903

Mueller, M. M., Palkovic, C. M., & Maynard, C. S. (2007). Errorless learning: Review and practical application for teaching children with pervasive developmental disorders. *Psychology in the Schools, 44*(7), 691–700. doi:10.1002/pits.20258

Mulhern, T., Stewart, I., & Elwee, J. M. (2017). Investigating relational framing of categorization in young children. *The Psychological Record, 67*(4), 519–536. doi:10.1007/s40732-017-0255-y

Mulhern, T., Stewart, I., & McElwee, J. (2018). Facilitating relational framing of classification in young children. *Journal of Contextual Behavioral Science, 8,* 55–68.

Murayama, T., & Tobayama, T. (1997). Preliminary study on stimulus equivalence in beluga (Delphinapterus leucas). *Japanese Journal of Animal Psychology, 47,* 79–89. doi:10.2502/janip.47.79

Murphy, C., & Barnes-Holmes, D. (2009a). Derived more–less relational mands in children diagnosed with autism. *Journal of Applied Behavior Analysis, 42*(2), 253–268. doi:10.1901/jaba.2009.42-253

Murphy, C., & Barnes-Holmes, D. (2009b). Establishing derived manding for specific amounts with three children: An attempt at synthesizing Skinner's *Verbal Behavior* with relational frame theory. *The Psychological Record, 59*(1), 75–92.

Murphy, C., & Barnes-Holmes, D. (2010). Establishing five dervied mands in three adolescent boys with autism. *Journal of Applied Behavior Analysis, 43*(3), 537–541. doi:10.1901/jaba.2010.43-537

Murphy, C., Barnes-Holmes, D., & Barnes-Holmes, Y. (2005). Derived manding with seven children diagnosed with autism: Synthesizing Skinner's *Verbal Behavior* with relational frame theory. *Journal of Applied Behavior Analysis, 38*(4), 445–462. doi:10.1901/jaba.2005.97-04

Murphy, C., Hussey, T., Barnes-Holmes, D., & Kelly, M. (2015). The Implicit Relational Assessment Procedure (IRAP) and attractiveness bias. *Journal of Contextual Behavioral Science, 4*(4), 292–299. doi:10.1016/j.jcbs.2015.08.001

Murphy, C., MacCarthaigh, S., & Barnes-Holmes, D. (2014). Implicit Relational Assessment Procedure and attractiveness bias: Directionality of bias and influence of gender of participants. *International Journal of Psychology and Psychological Therapy, 14*(3), 333–351.

Najdowski, A. C. (2017). *Flexible and focused: Teaching executive function skills to individuals with autism and attention disorders.* New York, NY: Elsevier.

National Governors Association Center for Best Practices, & Council of Chief State School Officers. (2010). Common Core State Standards. Retrieved from http://www.corestandards.org

Ninness, C., Barnes-Holmes, D., Rumph, R., McCuller, G., Ford, Payne, R., . . . Elliot, M. P. (2006). Transformations of mathematical and stimulus functions. *Journal of Applied Behavior Analysis, 39,* 299–321.

Ninness, C., Dixon, M., Barnes-Holmes, D., Rehfeldt, R. A., Rumph, R., McCuller, G., & McGinty, J. (2009). Constructing and deriving reciprocal trigonometric relations: A functional analytic approach. *Journal of Applied Behavior Analysis, 42,* 191–208.

Nolan, J., Murphy, C., & Barnes-Holmes, D. (2013). Implicit Relational Assessment Procedure and body-weight bias: Influence of gender of participants and targets. *The Psychological Record, 63,* 467–488. doi:10.11133/j.tpr.2013.63.3.005

NoRo, F. (2005). Using stimulus equivalence procedures to teach receptive emotional labeling to a child with autistic disorder. *The Japanese Journal of Special Education, 42,* 483–496.

Nuzzolo-Gomez, R., & Greer, R. D. (2004). Emergence of untaught mands or tacts of novel adjective-object pairs as a fucntion of instructional history. *The Analysis of Verbal Behavior, 20*(1), 63–76. doi:10.1007/BF03392995

O'Connor, M., Farrell, L., Munnelly, A., & McHugh, L. (2017). Citation analysis of relational frame theory: 2009–2016. *Journal of Contextual Behavioral Science, 6,* 152–158. http://dx.doi.org/10.1016/j.jcbs.2017.04.009

O'Hare, F. (1973). *Sentence combining: Improving student writing without formal grammar instruction.* Urbana, IL: National Council of Teachers of English.

O'Hora, D., Roche, B., Barnes-Holmes, D., & Smeets, P. M. (2002). Response latencies to multiple derived stimulus relations: Testing two predictions of relational frame theory. *The Psychological Record, 52,* 51–75.

O'Neill, J., & Rehfeldt, R. A. (2017). Computerized behavioral skills training with selection-based instruction and lag reinforcement schedules for responses to interview questions. *Behavior Analysis: Research and Practice, 17*(1), 42–54. doi:10.1037/bar0000043

O'Neill, J., Rehfeldt, R. A., Ninness, C., Munoz, B. E., & Mellor, J. (2015). Learning Skinner's verbal operants: Comparing an online stimulus equivalence procedure to an assigned reading. *Analysis of Verbal Behavior, 31,* 255–266.

O'Neill, J., & Weil, T. M. (2014). Training deictic relational responding in people diagnosed with schizophrenia. *The Psychological Record, 64,* 301–310.

O'Reilly, A., Roche, B., Ruiz, M., Tyndall, I., & Gavin, A. (2012). The Function Speed Acquisition Test (FAST): A behavior analytic implicit test for assessing stimulus relations. *The Psychological Record, 62,* 507–528. doi:10.1007/BF03395817

O'Reilly, M. F. (1997). Functional analysis of episodic self-injury correlated with recurrent otitis media. *Journal of Applied Behavior Analysis, 30,* 165–167. doi:10.1901/jaba.1997.30-165

O'Reilly, M., Aguilar, J., Fragale, C., Lang, R., Edrisinha, C., Sigafoos, J., . . . Didden, R. (2012). Effects of a motivating operation manipulation on the maintenance of mands. *Journal of Applied Behavior Analysis, 45*(2), 443–447.

O'Reilly, M. F., Lacey, C., & Lancioni, G. E. (2000). Assessment of the influence of background noise on escape-maintained problem behavior and pain behavior in a child with Williams Syndrome. *Journal of Applied Behavior Analysis, 33,* 511–514. doi:10.1901/jaba.2000.33-511

Observer. (1970). Wanted: A better direction for linguistic psychology. *The Psychological Record, 20,* 263–265.

Observer. (1971a). Comments and queries: Words, words, words. *The Psychological Record, 21,* 269–271.

Observer. (1971b). Comments and queries: Toward an improved linguistic model for science. *The Psychological Record, 21,* 429–434.

Observer. (1976). Comments and queries: What meaning means in linguistics. *The Psychological Record, 26,* 441–445.

Observer. (1983a). Comments and queries: Meanings as events and as constructions in psychology and linguistics. *The Psychological Record, 33,* 433–440.

Observer. (1983b). Comments and queries: The role of tabula metaphors in psychology and in language study. *The Psychological Record, 33,* 279–284.

Oden, D. L., Thompson, R. K. R., & Premack, D. (1988). Spontaneous transfer of matching by infant chimpanzees. Journal of Experimental Psychology: *Animal Behavior Processes, 14,* 140–145.

Ogawa, A., Yamazaki, Y., Ueno, K., Cheng, K., & Iriki, A. (2010). Neural correlates of species-typical illogical cognitive bias in human inference. *Journal of Cognitive Neuroscience, 22,* 2120–2130. doi:10.1162/jocn.2009.21330

Oppenheim, R. W. (1980). Metamorphosis and adaptation in the behavior of developing organisms. *Developmental Psychobiology, 13*(4), 353–356. doi:10.1002/dev.420130402

Overton, D. A. (1984). State dependent learning and drug discriminations. In L. L. Iversen et al. (Eds.), *Drugs, neurotransmitters, and behavior* (pp. 59–127). New York, NY: Springer.

Pack, A. A., Herman, L.M., & Roitblat, H. L. (1991). Generalization of visual matching and delayed matching by a California sea lion (Zalophus califomianus). *Animal Learning and Behavior, 19,* 37–48.

Padilla Dalmau, Y. C., Wacker, D., Harding, J., Berg, W., Schieltz, K., Lee, J., . . . Kramer, A. R. (2011). A preliminary evaluation of functional communication training effectiveness and language preference when Spanish and English are manipulated. *Journal of Behavioral Education,20*(4), 233–251. doi:10.1007/s10864-011-9131-z.

Palmer, D. C. (1991). A behavioral interpretation of memory. In L. J. Hayes & P. N. Chase (Eds.), *Dialogues on verbal behavior* (pp. 261–279). Reno, NV: Context Press.

Palmer, D. C. (2009). The role of private events in the interpretation of complex behavior. *Behavior and Philosophy, 37,* 3–19.

Palmer, D. C. (2011). Consideration of private events is required in a comprehensive science of behavior. *The Behavior Analyst, 34*(2), 201–207.

Palmer, D. C. (2012). The role of atomic repertoires in complex behavior. *The Behavior Analyst, 35,* 59–73.

Palmer, D. C. (2016). On intraverbal control and the definition of the intraverbal. *The Analysis of Verbal Behavior, 32*(2), 96–106. doi:10.1007/s40616-016-0061-7

Paniagua, F.A. (1990). A procedural analysis of correspondence training techniques. *The Behavior Analyst, 13*, 107–119.

Paniagua, F. A., & Baer, D. M. (1982). The analysis of correspondence training as a chain reinforceable at any point. *Child Development, 53*, 786–798. doi:10.2307/1129393

Parker, L. H., Cataldo, M. F., Bourland, G., Emurian, C. S., Corbin, R. J., & Page, J. M. (1984). Operant treatment of orofacial dysfunction in neuromuscular disorders. *Journal of Applied Behavior Analysis, 17*, 413–427. doi:10.1901/jaba.1984.17-413

Parrott, L. J. (1983). Systemic foundations for the concept of "private events." In N. W. Smith, P. T. Mountjoy, & D. H. Ruben (Eds.), *Reassessment in psychology: The Interbehavioral alternative* (pp. 251–268). Lanham, MD: University Press of America.

Parrott, L. J. (1984a). J. R. Kantor's contributions to psychology and philosophy: A guide to further study. *The Behaviour Analyst, 7*, 169–181.

Parrott, L. J. (1984b). Listening and understanding. *The Behavior Analyst, 7*, 29. doi:10.1007/bf03391883

Parrott, L. J. (1986). On the role of postulation in the analysis of inapparent events. In H. W. Reese & L. J. Parrott (Eds.), *Behavior science: Philosophical, methodological, and empirical advances* (pp. 35–60). Hillsdale, NJ: Erlbaum.

Parrott, L. J. (1987). Rule-governed behavior: An implicit analysis of reference. In S. Modgil & C. Modgil (Eds.), *B. F. Skinner: Consensus and controversy* (pp. 265–276). New York, NY: Falmer Press.

Partington, J. W. (2008). *The assessment of basics language and learning skills-revised: Scoring instructions and IEP development guide* (2nd ed). Pleasant Hill, CA: Behavior Analysts.

Partington, J. W., Sundberg, M. L., Newhouse, L., & Spengler, S. M. (1994). Overcoming an autistic child's failure to acquire a tact repertoire. *Journal of Applied Behavior Analysis, 27*(4), 733–734. doi:10.1901/jaba.1994.27-733

Pavlov, I. P. (1927). *Conditioned reflexes: an investigation of the physiological activity of the cerebral cortex.* Oxford, England: Oxford Univ. Press.

Pedersen, R. (2009). Empirical research on empathy in medicine—A critical review. *Patient Education and Counseling, 76*(3), 307–322.

Peláez, M. (2013). Dimensions of rules and their correspondence to rule-governed behavior. *European Journal of Behavior Analysis, 14*, 259–270.

Pennington, R. C. (2016). Write on! Using assistive technology and systematic instruction to teach sentence writing to students with moderate to severe disability. *Journal of Special Education Technology, 31*(1), 50–57. doi:10.1177/0162643416633336

Pennington, R. C., & Delano, M. E. (2012). Writing instruction for students with autism spectrum disorders: A review of literature. *Focus on Autism and Other Developmental Disabilities, 27*(3), 158–167. doi:10.1177/1088357612451318

Pennington, R. C., Foreman, L. H., & Gurney, B. N. (2018). An evaluation of procedures for teaching students with moderate to severe disabilities to write sentences. *Remedial and Special Education, 39*(1), 27–38. doi:10.1177/0741932517708428

Pereira Delgado, J. A., & Greer, R. D. (2009). The effects of peer monitoring training on the emergence of the capability to learn from observing instruction received by peers. *The Psychological Record, 59*, 407–434.

Pérez-González, L. A., & Alonso-Álvarez, B. (2008). Common control by compound samples in conditional discriminations. *Journal of the Experimental Analysis of Behavior, 90*(1), 81–101. doi:10.1901/jeab.2008.90-81

Pérez-González, L. A., & Carnerero, J. J. (2014). Emerging tacts and selections from previous learned skills: A comparison between two types of naming. *The Analysis of Verbal Behavior, 30*, 184–192. doi:10.1007/s40616-014-0011-1

Pérez-González, L. A., Garcia-Asenjo, L., Williams, G., & Carnerero, J. J. (2007). Emergence of intra-verbal antonyms in children with pervasive development disorder. *Journal of Applied Behavior Analysis, 40*, 697–701. doi:10.1901/jaba.2007.697-701

Perkins, D. D., & Zimmerman, M. A. (1995). Empowerment theory, research, and application. *American Journal of Community Psychology, 23*, 569–579.

Perkins, F. T. (1931). A further study of configurational learning in the goldfish. *Journal of Experimental Psychology, 14*, 508–538.

Persicke, A., Tarbox, J., Ranick, J., & St. Clair, M. (2012). Establishing metaphorical reasoning in children with autism. *Research in Autism Spectrum Disorders, 6*, 913–920. doi:10.1016/j.rasd.2011.12.007

Peters, L. C., & Thompson, R. H. (2015). Teaching children with autism to respond to conversational partners' interests. *Journal of Applied Behavior Analysis, 48*, 544–562.

Petursdottir, A. I., Carp, C. L., Matthies, D. W., & Esch, B. E. (2011). Analyzing stimulus-stimulus pairing effects on preferences for speech sounds. *The Analysis of Verbal Behavior, 27*(1), 45–60. doi:10.1007/BF03393091

Petursdottir, A., & Devine, B. (2017). The impact of verbal behavior on the scholarly literature from 2005 to 2016. *The Analysis of Verbal Behavior, 33*(2), 212–228. doi:10.1007/s40616-017-0089-3

Petursdottir, A., Carr, J. E., Lechago, S. A., & Almason, S. M. (2008). An evaluation of intraverbal training for teaching categorization skills. *Journal of Applied Behavior Analysis, 41*(1), 53–68. doi:10.1901/jaba.2008.41-53

Phillips, J. S., Matarazzo, R. G., Matarazzo, J. D., Saslow, G., & Kanfer, F. H. (1961). Relationships between descriptive content and interaction behavior in interviews. *Journal of Consulting Psychology, 25*, 260–266.

Piaget, J. (1970). Piaget's theory. In P. H. Mussen (Ed.), *Carmichael's manual of child psychology* (pp. 703–732). New York, NY: Wiley.

Piaget, J., Montangero, J., & Billeter, J. (1977). Les correlates [Correlations]. In J. Piaget (Ed.), *L'abstraction refléchissante* (pp.115–129). Paris: Presses Universitaires de France.

Pierce, W. D., & Cheney, C. D. (2013). *Behavior analysis and learning* (4th ed.). New York, NY: Psychology Press.

Pistoljevic, N., & Greer, R. D. (2006). The effects of daily intensive tact instruction on preschool students' emission of pure tacts and mands in non-instructional setting. *Journal of Early and Intensive Behavioral Interventions, 3*, 103–120. Retrieved from http://psycnet.apa.org/doi/10.1037/h0100325

Pituch, K. A., Green, V. A., Didden, R., Lang, R., O'Reiley, M. F., Lancioni, G. E., & Sigafoos, J. (2011). Parent reported treatment priorities for children with autism spectrum disorders. *Research in Autism Spectrum Disorders, 5*, 135–143.

Pohl, P. (1983). Central auditory processing. V. Ear advantages for acoustic stimuli in baboons. *Brain and Language, 20*, 44–53. doi:10.1016/0093-934X(83)90031-7

Pohl, P. (1984). Ear advantages for temporal resolution in baboons. *Brain and Cognition, 3*, 438–444. doi:10.1016/0278-2626(84)90033-2

Pohl, P., Greer, R. D., Du, L., & Moschella, J. L. (2018). Verbal development, behavioral metamorphosis, and the evolution of language. *Perspectives on Behavior Science*, 1–18. doi:10.1007/s40614-018-00180-0

Pohl, P., Grubmüller, H. G., & Grubmüller, R. (1984). Developmental changes in dichotic right ear advantage (REA). *Neuropediatrics, 15*, 139–144. doi:10.1055/s-2008-1052357

Polya, G. (1954). *Mathematics and Plausible Reasoning: Volume 1. Induction and Analogy in Mathematics.* Princeton, NJ: Princeton University Press.

Power, P. M., Harte, C., Barnes-Holmes, D., Barnes-Holmes, Y. (2017a). Exploring racial bias in a country with a recent history of immigration of black Africans. *The Psychological Record, 67*(3), 365–375 doi.org/10.1007/s40732-017-0223-6

Power, P. M., Harte, C., Barnes-Holmes, D., Barnes-Holmes, Y. (2017b). Combining the Implicit Relational Assessment Procedure and the recording of event related potentials in the analysis of racial bias: A preliminary study. *The Psychological Record, 67*(4), 499–506. doi:10.1007/s40732-017-0252-1

Power, P., Barnes-Holmes, D., Barnes-Holmes, Y., & Stewart, I. (2009). The Implicit Relational Assessment Procedure (IRAP) as a measure of implicit relative preferences: A first study. *The Psychological Record, 59*, 621–640. doi:10.1007/BF03395684

Powers, M. B., Vörding, M. B. Z. V. S., & Emmelkamp, P. M. (2009). Acceptance and commitment therapy: A meta-analytic review. *Psychotherapy and Psychosomatics, 78*(2), 73–80.

Premack, D. (1959). Toward empirical behavior laws: I. Positive reinforcement. *Psychological Review, 66*(4), 219–233. doi:10.1037/ h0040891

Premack, D. G., & Woodruff, G. (1978). Does the chimpanzee have a "theory of mind"? *Behavioral and Brain Sciences, 1*, 515–526.

Proffitt, J. B., Coley, J. D., & Medin, D. L. (2000). Expertise and category-based induction. *Journal of Experimental Psychology: Learning, Memory & Cognition, 26*, 4, 811–828. doi:10.10371/0278-7393.26.4.811

Pytte, C. L., & Fienup, D. M. (2012). Using equivalence-based instruction to increase efficiency in teaching neuroanatomy. *The Journal of Undergraduate Neuroscience Education, 10*, A125–A131.

Rabelo, L. Z., Bortoloti, R., & Souza, D. H. (2014). Dolls are for girls and not for boys: Evaluating the appropriateness of the Implicit Relational Assessment Procedure for school-age children. *The Psychological Record, 64*, 71–77. doi:10.1007/s40732-014-0006-2

Rachlin, H. (1984). Mental, yes. Private, no. *Behavioral and Brain Sciences, 7*(4), 566–567.

Rachlin, H. (2011). Baum's private thoughts. *The Behavior Analyst, 34*(2), 209–212.

Rachman, S. (1967). Systematic desensitization. *Psychological Bulletin, 67*(2), 93–103. doi:10.1037/ h0024212

Ramirez, J., & Rehfeldt, R. A. (2009). Observational learning and the emergence of symmetry relations in teaching Spanish vocabulary words to typically developing children. *Journal of Applied Behavior Analysis, 42*, 801–805. doi:10.1901/jaba.2009.42-801

Reese, H. W. (1994). Cognitive and behavioral approaches to problem solving. In S. C. Hayes, L. J. Hayes, M. Sato, & K. Ono (Eds.), *Behavior analysis of language and cognition* (197–258). Reno, NV: Context Press.

Rehfeldt, R. A. (2011). Toward a technology of derived stimulus relations: An analysis of articles published in the *Journal of Applied Behavior Analysis, 1992–2009. Journal of Applied Behavior Analysis, 44*, 109–119. doi:10.1901/jaba.2011.44-109

Rehfeldt, R. A., & Barnes-Holmes, Y. (Eds.). (2009). *Derived relational responding: Applications for learners with autism and other developmental disabilities: A progressive guide to change.* Oakland, CA: New Harbinger Publications.

Rehfeldt, R. A., Dillen, J. E., Ziomek, M. M., & Kowalchuk, R. K. (2007). Assessing relational learning deficits in perspective-taking in children with high-functioning autism spectrum disorder. *The Psychological Record, 57*, 23.

Rehfeldt, R. A., & Hayes, L. J. (1998). The operant-respondent distinction revisited: Toward an understanding of stimulus equivalence. *The Psychological Record, 48*, 187–210. doi:10.1007/BF03395266

Rehfeldt, R. A., Latimore, D., & Stromer, R. (2003). Observational learning and the formation of classes of reading skills by individuals with autism and other developmental disabilities. *Research in Developmental Disabilities, 24*, 333–358. doi:10.1016/S0891-4222(03)00059-3

Rehfeldt, R. A., & Root, S. L. (2005). Establishing derived requesting skills in adults with severe developmental disabilities. *Journal of Applied Behavior Analysis, 38*(1), 101–105. doi:10.1901/jaba.2005.106-03

Rescorla, R. A. (1967). Pavlovian conditioning and its proper control procedures. *Psychological Review, 74*, 71–80. doi:10.1037/h0024109

Rescorla, R. A. (1988). Pavlovian conditioning: It's not what you think it is. *American Psychologist, 43*, 151–160. doi

Rescorla, R. A., & Wagner, A. R. (1972). A theory of Pavlovian conditioning: Variations in the effectiveness of reinforcement and nonreinforcement. In A. H. Black & W. F. Prokasy (Eds.), *Classical conditioning II: Current research and theory* (pp. 64–99). East Norwalk, CT: Appleton-Century-Crofts.

Reyes-Giordano, K., & Fienup, D. M. (2015). Emergence of topographical responding following equivalence-based neuroanatomy instruction. *The Psychological Record, 65*, 495–507.

Reynolds, G. S. (1961). Attention in the pigeon. *Journal of the Experimental Analysis of Behavior, 4*, 203–208. doi:10.1901/jeab.1961.4-203

Ribeiro, D. M., Elias, N. C., Goyos, C., & Miguel, C. F. (2010). The effects of listener training on the emergence of tact and mand signs by individuals with intellectual disabilities. *The Analysis of Verbal Behavior, 26*(1), 65–72. doi:10.1007/BF03393084

Ribeiro, D. M., Miguel, C. F., & Goyos, C. (2015). The effects of listener training on discriminative control by elements of compound stimuli in children with disabilities. *Journal of the Experimental Analysis of Behavior, 104*(1), 48–62. doi:10.1002/jeab.161

Ribeiro, T. A., Gallano, T. P., Souza, D. de H., & de Souza, D. das G. (2017). Responding and learning by exclusion in 2-year-olds: The case of adjectives. *Psychological Record, 67*, 293–314.

Ribes, E. (1977). Relationship between behavior theory, experimental research and behavior modification techniques. *The Psychological Record, 2*, 417–424.

Ribes, E. (1981). Reflexiones sobre el concepto de inteligencia y su desarrollo. *Revista Mexicana de Análisis de la Conducta, 7*, 107–116.

Ribes, E. (1989). La inteligencia como comportamiento un análisis conceptual. *Revista Mexicana de Análisis de la Conducta, 15*, 51–67.

Ribes, E. (1993). Behavior as the functional content of language. In S. C. Hayes, L. J. Hayes, T. R. Sarbin, & H. W. Reese (Eds.), *Varieties of contextualism* (pp. 283–297). Reno, NV: Context Press.

Ribes, E. (1997). Causality and contingency: Some conceptual considerations. *The Psychological Record, 47*, 619–639.

Ribes, E. (1999). *Teoría del condicionamiento y lenguaje. Un análisis histórico-Conceptual*. México: Taurus.

Ribes, E. (2001). Functional dimensions of social behavior: Theoretical considerations and some preliminary data. *Mexican Journal of Behavior Analysis, 27* (2), 285–306.

Ribes, E. (2003). Concepts and theories: Relation to scientific categories. In K. A. Lattal & P. Chase (Eds.), *Behavior theory and philosophy* (pp. 147–164). New York, NY: Kluver-Plenum.

Ribes, E. (2004a). Behavior is abstraction, not ostension: Conceptual and historical remarks on the nature of psychology. *Behavior & Philosophy, 32*, 55–68.

Ribes, E. (2004b). Theory, scientific research, and technical applications: How related in operant psychology? In J. E. Burgos & E. Ribes (Eds.), *Theory, basic and applied research, and technological applications in behavior science: Conceptual and methodological issues* (pp. 19–44). Guadalajara, México: Universidad de Guadalajara.

Ribes, E. (2006a). Human Behavior as language: Some thoughts on Wittgenstein. *Behavior & Philosophy, 34*, 109–121.

Ribes, E. (2006b). Which should be the contribution of psychology to education? In Q. Jing, M. Rosenzweig, G. D'Ydewalle, H. Zhang, H. Chih, & K. Zhang (Eds), *Progress in science around the world* (pp. 23–34). Hove, UK: Psychology Press.

Ribes, E. (2007). On two functional meanings of "knowing." In J. E. Burgos & E. Ribes (Eds.), *Knowledge, cognition, and behavior* (pp. 139–150). Guadalajara, México: Universidad de Guadalajara.

Ribes, E. (2008). Educación básica, desarrollo psicológico y planeación de competencias. *Revista Mexicana de Psicología, 25*, 193–207.

Ribes, E. (2011). El concepto de competencia: Su pertinencia en el desarrollo psicológico y la educación. *Bordón: Revista de Pedagogía, 63*, 33–45.

Ribes, E. (2018). *El estudio científico de la conducta individual: introducción a la teoríade la psicología.* Ciudad de México: El Manual Moderno.

Ribes, E., Pulido, L., Rangel, N., & Sánchez-Gatell, E. (2016). *Sociopsicología: instituciones yrelaciones interindividuales.* Madrid: La Catarata.

Ricard, M. (2015). *Altruism: The power of compassion to change yourself and the world.* London, UK: Atlantic Books Ltd.

Richards, M., Mossey, J., & Robins, D. L. (2016). Parents' concerns as they relate to their child's development and later diagnosis of autism spectrum disorder. *Journal of Developmental and Behavioral Pediatrics, 37*(7), 532–540.

Rilling, J. K., Gutman, D. A., Zeh, T. R., Pagnoni, G., Berns, G. S., & Kilts, C. D. (2002). A neural basis for social cooperation. *Neuron, 35*(2), 395–405.

Rilling, M. (1977). Stimulus control and inhibitory processes. In W. K. Honig & J. E. R. Staddon (Eds.), *Handbook of operant behavior* (pp. 432–480). Englewood Cliffs, NJ: Prentice-Hall.

Ringdahl, J. E., Falcomata, T. S., Christensen, T. J., Bass-Ringdahl, S. M., Lentz, A., Dutt, A., & Schuh-Claus, J. (2009). Evaluation of a pre-treatment assessment to select mand topographies for functional communication training. *Research in Developmental Disabilities, 30*(2), 330–341. doi:10.1016/j.ridd.2008.06.002

Risley, T. R., & Hart, B. (1968). Developing correspondence between the non-verbal and verbal behavior of preschool children. *Journal of Applied Behavior Analysis, 1*, 267–281. doi:10.1901/jaba.1968.1-267

Ritzert, T. R., Forsyth, J. P., Berghoff, C. R., Barnes-Holmes, D., & Nicholson, E. (2015). The impact of a cognitive defusion intervention on behavioral and psychological flexibility: An experimental evaluation in a spider fearful non-clinical sample. *Journal of Contextual Behavioral Science, 4*(2), 112–120. doi:10.1016/j.jcbs.2015.04.001

Robbins, J. K. (2011). Problem solving and analytical thinking in a classroom environment. *The Behavior Analyst Today, 12*, 40–47.

Robbins, J. K. (2014). *Learn to Reason with TAPS: A Problem Solving Approach* [Curriculum program]. Available at http://www.talkaloudproblemsolving.com.

Robbins, J. K., Layng, T. V. J., & Jackson, P. J. (1995). *Fluent thinking skills.* Seattle, WA: Robbins/Layng & Associates.

Robertson, D. L., & Peláez, M. (2016). Behavior analytic concepts and change in a large metropolitan research university: The Graduation Success Initiative. *Journal of Organizational Behavior Management, 36*, 123–153. doi:10.1080/01608061.2016.1200513

Robinson, G. E., & Barron, A. B. (2017). Epigenetics and the evolution of instincts: Instincts evolve from learning and share the same cellular and molecular mechanisms. *Science, 365*(6333), 26–27. doi:10.1126/science.aam6142

Roche, B., & Barnes, D. (1997). A transformation of respondently conditioned stimulus function in accordance with arbitrarily applicable relations. *Journal of the Experimental Analysis of Behavior, 67*, 275–301.

Roche, B., Linehan, C., Ward, T. E., Dymond, S., & Rehfeldt, R. A. (2004). The unfolding of the relational operant: A real-time analysis using electroencephalography and reaction time measures. *International Journal of Psychology and Psychological Therapy, 4*, 587–603.

Roddy, S., Stewart, I., & Barnes-Holmes, D. (2010). Anti-fat, pro-slim, or both? Using two reaction-time based measures to assess implicit attitudes to the slim and overweight. *Journal of Health Psychology, 15*, 416–425. doi:10.1177/1359105309350232

Roddy, S., Stewart, I., & Barnes-Holmes, D. (2011). Facial reactions reveal that slim is good but fat is not bad: Implicit and explicit measures of body-size bias. *European Journal of Social Psychology, 41*, 688–694. doi:10.1002/ejsp.839

Rogers-Warren, A., & Baer, D. M. (1976). Correspondence between saying and doing: Teaching children to share and praise. *Journal of Applied Behavior Analysis, 9,* 335–354. doi:10.1901/jaba.1976.9-335

Romanes, G. J. (1888). *Mental evolution in man: Origins of human faculty.* London, England: Keegan Paul.

Ronspies, J., Schmidt, A. F., Melnikova, A., Krumova, R., Zolfagari, A., & Banse, R. (2015). Indirect measurement of sexual orientation: Comparison of the Implicit Relational Assessment Procedure, viewing time, and choice reaction time. *Archives of Sexual Behavior, 44*(5), 1483–1492. doi:10.1007/s10508-014-0473-1

Rosales-Ruiz, J., & Baer, D. M. (1997). Behavioral cusps: A developmental and pragmatic concept for behavior analysis. *Journal of Applied Behavior Analysis, 30,* 533–544. doi:10.1901/jaba.1997.30-533

Rosales, R., & Rehfeldt, R. A. (2007). Contriving transitive conditioned establishing operations to establish derived manding skills in adults with severe developmental disabilities. *Journal of Applied Behavior Analysis, 40*(1), 105–121. doi:10.1901/jaba.2007.117-05

Rosales, R., Rehfeldt, R. A., & Huffman, N. (2012). Examining the utility of the stimulus pairing observation procedure with preschool children learning a second language. *Journal of Applied Behavior Analysis, 45,* 173–177. doi:10.1901/jaba.2012.45-173

Rosales, R., Rehfeldt, R. A., & Lovett, S. (2011). Effects of multiple exemplar training on the emergence of derived relations in preschool children learning a second language. *The Analysis of Verbal Behavior, 27,* 61–74.

Ross, S. M., & Proctor, S. (1973). Frequency and duration of hierarchy item exposure in a systematic desensitization analogue. *Behaviour Research and Therapy, 11*(3), 303–312.

Ruiz, F. J. (2010). A review of acceptance and commitment therapy (ACT) empirical evidence: Correlational, experimental psychopathology, component and outcome studies. *International Journal of Psychology and Psychological Therapy, 10,* 125–162.

Ruiz, F. J. (2012). Acceptance and commitment therapy versus traditional cognitive behavioral therapy: A systematic review and meta-analysis of current empirical evidence. *International Journal of Psychology and Psychological Therapy, 12*(3), 333–357.

Ruiz, F. J., & Luciano, C. (2011). Cross-domain analogies as relating derived relations among two separate relational networks. *Journal of the Experimental Analysis of Behaviour, 95*(3), 369–385.

Ruiz, F. J., & Luciano, C. (2015). Common physical properties among relational networks improve analogy aptness. *Journal of the Experimental Analysis of Behaviour, 103,* 3, 498–510.

Ruiz, F. J., Riaóo, D., Suárez, J., & Luciano, C. (2016). Effect of a one-session ACT protocol in disrupting repetitive negative thinking: A randomized multiple-baseline design. *International Journal of Psychology and Psychological Therapy, 16*(3), 213–233.

Ryle, G. (1949). *The concept of mind.* New York, NY: Barnes & Noble.

Ryle, G. (1962). *Dilemmas.* Cambridge, England: Cambridge University Press.

Salkovskis, P. M., Wroe, A. L., Gledhill, A., Morrison, N., Forrester, E., Richards, C., . . . Thorpe, S. (2000). Responsibility attitudes and interpretations are characteristic of obsessive compulsive disorder. *Behaviour Research and Therapy, 38*(4), 347–372.

Sandoz, E. K., & Anderson, R. S. (2015). Building awareness, openness, and action: Values work in behavior therapy. *The Behavior Therapist, 38,* 60–69.

Sandoz, E. K., & Hebert, E. R. (2016). Using derived relational responding to model statistics learning across participants with varying degrees of statistics anxiety. *European Journal of Behavior Analysis,* 1–19.

Saunders, R. R., Drake, K. M., & Spradlin, J. E. (1999). Equivalence class establishment, expansion, and modification in preschool children. *Journal of the Experimental Analysis of Behavior, 71,* 195–214.

Saunders, R. R., Wachter, J. A., & Spradlin, J. E. (1988). Establishing auditory stimulus control over an eight-member equivalence class via conditional discrimination procedures. *Journal of the Experimental Analysis of Behavior, 49*, 95–115.

Sautter, R. A., & LeBlanc, L. A. (2006). Empirical applications of Skinner's analysis of *Verbal Behavior* with humans. *The Analysis of Verbal Behavior, 22*(1), 35–48. doi:10.1007/BF03393025

Sautter, R. A., LeBlanc, L. A., Jay, A. A., Goldsmith, T. R., & Carr, J. E. (2011). The role of problem solving in complex intraverbal repertoires. *Journal of Applied Behavior Analysis, 44*(2), 227–244. doi:10.1901/jaba.2011.44-227

Schauffler, G., & Greer, R. D. (2006). The effects of intensive tact instruction on audience-accurate tacts and conversational units. *Journal of Early and Intensive Behavioral Interventions, 3*, 120–132. doi:10.1037/h0100326

Scheel, M. H., Fischer, L. A., McMahon, A. J., Wolf, J. E. (2011). The Implicit Relational Assessment Procedure (IRAP) as a measure of women's stereotype about gay men. *Current Research in Social Psychology, 18*(2), 11–23.

Scheel, M. H., Roscoe, B. H., Scaewe, V. G., & Yarbrough, C. S. (2014). Attitudes towards Muslims are more favorable on a survey than on an Implicit Relational Assessment Procedure (IRAP). *Current Research in Social Psychology, 22*(3), 22–32.

Schlinger, H. D. (2008). Consciousness is nothing but a word. *Skeptic, 13*(4), 58–63.

Schlinger, H. D. (2017). Reflections on *Verbal Behavior* at 60. *The Analysis of Verbal Behavior, 33*(2), 179–190. doi:10.1007/s40616-017-0087-5

Schlund, M. W., Cataldo, M. F., & Hoehn-Saric, R. (2008). Neural correlates of derived relational responding on tests of stimulus equivalence. *Behavioral and Brain Functions, 4*, 6.

Schlund, M. W., Hoehn-Saric, R., & Cataldo, M. F. (2007). New knowledge derived from learned knowledge: Functional-anatomic correlates of stimulus equivalence. *Journal of the Experimental Analysis of Behavior, 87*, 287–307.

Schmelzkopf, J., Greer, R. D., Singer-Dudek, J., & Du, L. (2017). Experiences that establish preschoolers' interest in speaking and listening to others. *Behavioral Development Bulletin, 22*, 44. doi:10.1037/bdb0000026

Schutte, R. C., & Hopkins, B. L. (1970). The effects of teacher attention on following instructions in a kindergarten class. *Journal of Applied Behavior Analysis, 3*, 117–122. doi:10.1901/jaba.1970.3-117

Scott, J. P., & Nagy, Z. M. (1980) Behavioral metamorphosis in mammalian development. In E. C. Simmel (Ed.), *Early experiences and early behavior: Implications for social development* (pp. 15–37). New York, NY: Academic Press.

Seaver, J. L., & Bourret, J. C. (2014). An evaluation of response prompts for teaching behavior chains. *Journal of Applied Behavior Analysis, 47*(4), 777–792. doi:10.1002/jaba.159

Sella, A. C., Ribeiro, D. M., & White, G. W. (2014). Effects of an online stimulus equivalence teaching procedure on research design open-ended questions performance of international undergraduate students. *The Psychological Record, 64*, 89–103. doi:10.1007/s40732-014-0007-1

Sellers, T. P., Kelley, K., Higbee, T. S., & Wolfe, K. (2016). Effects of simultaneous script training on use of varied mand frames by preschoolers with autism. *The Analysis of Verbal Behavior, 32*(1), 15–26. doi:10.1007/s40616-015-0049-8

Sevdalis, V., & Raab, M. (2014). Empathy in sports, exercise, and the performing arts. *Psychology of sport and Exercise, 15*(2), 173–179.

Shafer, E. (1993). Teaching topography-based and selection-based verbal behavior to developmentally disabled individuals: Some considerations. *The Analysis of Verbal Behavior, 11*(1), 117–133. doi:10.1007/BF03392892

Shatz, M., & Gelman, R. (1973). The development of communication skills: Modifications in the speech of young children as a function of listener. *Monographs of the Society for Research in Child Development, 30*, 1–38.

Shevrin, H., & Dickman, S. (1980). The psychological unconscious: A necessary assumption for all psychological theory? *American Psychologist, 35*(5), 421–434.

Shillingsburg, M. A., Frampton, S. E., Cleveland, S. A., & Cariveau, T. (2018). A clinical application of procedures to promote the emergence of untrained intraverbal relations with children with autism. *Learning and Motivation, 62,* 51–66. doi:10.1016/j.lmot.2017.02.003

Shillingsburg, M. A., Hollander, D. L., Yosick, R. N., Bowen, C., & Muskat, L. R. (2015). Stimulus-stimulus pairing to increase vocalizations in children with language delays: A review. *Analysis of Verbal Behavior, 31*(2), 215–235. doi:10.1007/s40616-015-0042-2

Shimoff, E., Catania, A. C., & Matthews, B. A. (1981). Uninstructed human responding: Sensitivity of low-rate performance to schedule contingencies. *Journal of the Experimental Analysis of Behavior, 36,* 207–220. doi:10.1901/jeab.1981.36-207

Shoenfeld, W. N. (1969). J. R. Kantor's *Objective Psychology of Grammar* and *Psychology and Logic*: A retrospective appreciation. *Journal of the Experimental Analysis of Behavior, 12,* 329–347.

Sidman, M. (1971). Reading and auditory-visual equivalences. *Journal of Speech & Hearing Research, 14,* 5–13. doi:10.1044/jshr.1401.05

Sidman, M. (1994). *Equivalence relations and behavior: A research story.* Boston, MA: Authors Cooperative.

Sidman, M., & Cresson, O. (1973). Reading and crossmodal transfer of stimulus equivalences in severe retardation. *American Journal of Mental Deficiency, 77,* 515–523.

Sidman, M., & Tailby, W. (1982). Conditional discrimination vs. matching to sample: An expansion of the testing paradigm. *Journal of the Experimental Analysis of Behavior, 37,* 5–22. doi:10.1901/jeab.1982.37-5

Siegler, R. S. (1983). Information processing approaches to development. In P. H. Mussen (Ed.), *Handbook of child psychology: Volume I. History, theory, and methods* (pp. 129–211). New York, NY: Wiley.

Sigafoos, J., Kerr, M., Roberts, D., & Couzens, D. (1994). Increasing opportunities for requesting in classrooms serving children with developmental disabilities. *Journal of Autism and Developmental Disorders, 24*(5), 631–645. doi:10.1007/BF02172143

Silver, M., & Oakes, P. (2001). Evaluation of a new computer intervention to teach people with autism or Asperger syndrome to recognize and predict emotions in others. *Autism, 5*(3), 299–316.

Simic, J., & Bucher, B. (1980). Development of spontaneous manding in language deficient children. *Journal of Applied Behavior Analysis, 13*(3), 523–528. doi:10.1901/jaba.1980.13-523

Sinclair, S., Hack, T. F., McClement, S., & Raffin-Bouchal, S. (2016). Peeling the onion: Patients' perspectives and experiences of the similarities and differences of sympathy, empathy and compassion. *Journal of Pain and Symptom Management, 52,* 147–148.

Singer-Dudek, J., & Oblak, M. (2013). Peer presence and the emergence of conditioned reinforcement from observation. *Journal of Applied Behavior Analysis, 46,* 592–602. doi:10.1002/jaba.72

Singer-Dudek, J., Oblak, M., & Greer, R. D. (2011). Establishing books as conditioned reinforcers for preschool children as a function of an observational intervention. *Journal of Applied Behavior Analysis, 44,* 421–434.

Skinner, B. F. (1938). *The behavior of organisms: An experimental analysis.* New York, NY: Appleton-Century Crofts.

Skinner, B. F. (1945). The operational analysis of psychological terms. *Psychological Review, 52*(5), 270–277. doi:10.1037/h0062535

Skinner, B. F. (1953). *Science and human behavior.* New York, NY: The Free Press.

Skinner, B. F. (1956). A case history in scientific method. *American Psychologist, 11*(5), 221–233. doi:10.1037/h0047662

Skinner, B. F. (1957). *Verbal behavior.* New York, NY: Appleton-Century-Crofts.

Skinner, B. F. (1963). Operant behavior. *American Psychologist, 18*(8), 503–515. doi

Skinner, B. F. (1966a). The phylogeny and ontogeny of behavior. *Science, 153* (3741), 1205–1213. doi:10.1126/science.153.3741.1205

Skinner, B. F. (1966b). What is the experimental analysis of behavior? *Journal of the Experimental Analysis of Behavior, 9*, 213–218. doi:10.1901/jeab.1966.9-213

Skinner, B. F. (1969) *Contingencies of reinforcement: A theoretical analysis.* New York, NY: Appleton-Century-Crofts.

Skinner, B. F. (1974a). *About behaviorism.* New York, NY: Alfred A. Knopf.

Skinner, B. F. (1974b). *Walden two.* New York, NY: Macmillan.

Skinner, B. F. (1981). Selection by consequences. *Science, 213*(4507), 501–504. doi:10.1126/science.7244649

Skinner, B. F. (1989). The behavior of the listener. In S. Hayes (Ed.), *Rule-governed behavior: Cognition, contingencies, and instructional control* (pp. 85–96). Reno, NV: Context Press.

Slattery, B., & Stewart, I. (2014). Hierarchical classification as relational framing. *Journal of the Experimental Analysis of Behavior, 101*, 1, 61–75. doi:10.1002/jeab.63.

Slattery, B., Stewart, I., & O'Hora, D. (2011). Testing for transitive class containment as a feature of hierarchical classification. *Journal of the Experimental Analysis of Behavior, 96*, 2, 243–260. doi:10.1901/jeab.2011.96-243.

Smeets, P. M., Leader, G., & Barnes, D. (1997). Establishing stimulus classes in adults and children using a respondent-type training procedure: A follow-up study. *The Psychological Record, 47*, 285–308.

Smith, D. P., Eikeseth, S., Fletcher, S. E., Montebelli, L., Smith, H. R., & Taylor, J. C. (2016). Emergent intraverbal forms may occur as a result of listener training for children with autism. *The Analysis of Verbal Behavior, 32*(1), 27–37. doi:10.1007/s40616-016-0057-3

Smith, N. W. (2016). *The myth of mind: A challenge to mainstream psychology and its imposed constructs.* St. Petersburg, FL: BookLocker.com, Inc.

Smyth, S., Barnes-Holmes, D., & Forsyth, J. P. (2006). A derived transfer of simple discrimination and self-reported arousal functions in spider fearful and non-fearful participants. *Journal of the Experimental Analysis of Behavior, 85*, 223–246. doi:10.1901/jeab.2006.02-05

Soha, J. A., & Peters, S. (2015). Vocal learning in songbirds and humans: A retrospective in honor of Peter Marler. *Ethology, 121*, 933–945. doi:10.1111/eth.12415

Spradlin, J. E., & Brady, N. (2008). A behavior analytic interpretation of theory of mind. *International Journal of Psychology and Psychological Therapy, 8*(3), 335–350.

Sprinkle, E. C., & Miguel, C. F. (2013). Establishing derived textual activity schedules in children with autism. *Behavioral Interventions, 28*(3), 185–202. doi:10.1002/bin.1365

Stanley, C. R., Belisle, J., & Dixon, M. R. (2018). Equivalence-based instruction of academic skills: Application to adolescents with autism. *Journal of Applied Behavior Analysis, 51*, 352–359. doi:10.1002/jaba.446

Stauch, T., LaLonde, K., Plavnick, J. B., Bak, M. S., & Gatewood, K. (2017). Intraverbal training for individuals with autism: The current status of multiple control. *The Analysis of Verbal Behavior, 33*(1), 98–116. doi:10.1007/s40616-017-0079-5

Steele, D., & Hayes, S. C. (1991). Stimulus equivalence and arbitrarily applicable relational responding. *Journal of the Experimental Analysis of Behavior, 56*, 519–555. doi:10.1901/jeab.1991.56-519

Sterkin, V. L. (2012). *The effects of the social listener reinforcement protocol on the audience control of stereotypy and social operants for students with developmental delays.* (Doctoral dissertation, Columbia University). doi:10.7916/D8DF6Z94

Sternberg, R. J. (1977). Component processes in analogical reasoning. *Psychological Review, 84*, 353–378.

Stevens, M. J., & Pfost, K. S. (1983). The role of cognition in cognitive behavior therapy. *Psychology: A Journal of Human Behavior, 20*(3–4), 20–24.

Stewart, I., Barnes-Holmes, D., & Roche, B. (2004). A functional-analytic model of analogy using the relational evaluation procedure. *Psychological Record, 54,* 531–552.

Stewart, I., Barnes-Holmes, D., Roche, B., & Smeets, P. (2001). Generating derived relational networks via the abstraction of common physical properties: A possible model of analogical reasoning. *The Psychological Record, 51,* 381–408.

Stewart, I., Barnes-Holmes, D., Roche, B., & Smeets, P. (2002). A functional-analytic model of analogy: A relational frame analysis. *Journal of the Experimental Analysis of Behavior, 78*(3), 375–396.

Stewart, I., McElwee, J., & Ming, S. (2013a). Erratum to: Language generativity, response generalization, and derived relational responding. *The Analysis of Verbal Behavior, 29*(1), 137–155. doi:10.1007/s40616-016-0060-8

Stewart, I., McElwee, J., & Ming, S. (2013b). Language generativiy, response generalization, and derived relational responding. *The Analysis of Verbal Behavior, 29*(1), 137–155. doi:10.1007/BF03393131

Stewart, I., Slattery, B., Chambers, M., & Dymond, S. (2018). An empirical investigation of part-whole hierarchical relations. *European Journal of Behaviour Analysis, 19,* 1, 105–124. doi:10.1080/150211 49.2017.1416525

Still, K., Rehfeldt, R. A., Whelan, R., May, R., & Dymond, S. (2014). Facilitating requesting skills using high-tech augmentative and alternative communication devices with individuals with autism spectrum disorders: A systematic review. *Research in Autism Spectrum Disorders, 8*(9), 1184–1199. doi:10.1016/j.rasd.2014.06.003

Stockwell, F. M. J., Hopkins, L. S., & Walker, D. J. (2017). Implicit and explicit attitudes toward mainstream and BDSM sexual practices and their relation to interviewer behavior: An analogue study. *The Psychological Record, 67,* 435-446. doi:10.1007/s40732-017-0225-4

Stockwell, F. M. J., Walker, D. J., & Eshleman, J. W. (2010). Measures of implicit and explicit attitudes toward mainstream and BDSM sexual terms using the IRAP and questionnaire with BDSM/ fetish and student participants. *The Psychological Record, 60,* 307–324. doi:10.1007/BF03395709

Stokes, T. F., & Baer, D. M. (1977). An implicit technology of generalization. *Journal of Applied Behavior Analysis, 10,* 349–367. doi:10.1901/jaba.1977.10-349

Stolfi, L. (2005). *The induction of observational learning repertoires in preschool children with developmental disabilities as a function of peer-yoked contingencies* (Doctoral dissertation, Order No. 3174899). Available from ProQuest Dissertations & Theses Global. (305016342). Retrieved from http:// eduproxy.tc-library.org/?url=/docview/305016342?accountid=14258

Storlie, J. L., Rehfeldt, R. A., & Aguirre, A. A. (2015). Observational learning across three verbal operants in a child with autism. *International Journal of Behavior Analysis & Autism Spectrum Disorders, 1,* 113–121.

Street, E. M., & Johnson, K. (2014). The sciences of learning, instruction, and assessment as underpinnings of the Morningside Model of Generative Instruction. *Acta de Investigación Psicológica, 4,* 1773–1793.

Stromer, R., & Mackay, H. A. (1992). Spelling and emergent picture-printed word relations established with delayed identity matching to complex samples. *Journal of Applied Behavior Analysis, 25,* 893–904.

Strosahl, K. D., Robinson, P. J., & Gustavsson, T. (2015). *Inside this moment.* Oakland, CA. Context Press.

Sullivan, J., & Barner, D. (2014). The development of structural analogy in number-line estimation. *Journal of Experimental Child Psychology, 128,* 171–189.

Sundberg, M. L. (2008). *VB-MAPP: Verbal Behavior Milestones Assessment and Placement Program: A language and social skills assessment program for children with autism or other developmental disabilities.* Concord, CA: AVB Press.

Sundberg, M. L. (2013). Thirty points about motivation from Skinner's book *Verbal Behavior. The Analysis of Verbal Behavior, 29,* 13–40. doi:10.1007/BF03393120

Sundberg, M. L. (2016). Verbal stimulus control and the intraverbal relation. *The Analysis of Verbal Behavior, 32*(2), 107–124. doi:10.1007/s40616-016-0065-3

Sundberg, M. L., Endicott, K., & Eigenheer, P. (2000). Using intraverbal prompts to establish tacts for children with autism. *The Analysis of Verbal Behavior, 17*(1), 89–104. doi:10.1007/BF03392958

Sundberg, M. L., & Michael, J. (2001). The benefits of Skinner's analysis of verbal behavior for children with autism. *Behavior Modification, 25*(5), 698–724. doi:10.1177/0145445501255003

Sundberg, M. L., Michael, J., Partington, J. W., & Sundberg, C. A. (1996). The role of automatic reinforcement in early language acquisition. *The Analysis of Verbal Behavior, 13*(1), 21–37. doi:10.1007/BF03392904

Sundberg, M. L., & Partington, J. W. (2013). *Teaching language to children with autism and other developmental disabilities* (2nd ed.) Pleasant Hill, CA: Behavior Analysts, Inc.

Sundberg, M. L., & Sundberg, C. A. (2011). Intraverbal behavior and verbal conditional discriminations in typically developing children and children with autism. *The Analysis of Verbal Behavior, 27*(1), 23–44. doi:10.1007/bf03393090

Tajfel, H. (1981). *Human groups and social categories: Studies in Social Psychology.* Cambridge, UK: Cambridge University Press.

Takahashi, K., Yamamoto, J., & Noro, F. (2011). Stimulus pairing training in children with autism spectrum disorder. *Research in Autism Spectrum Disorders, 5,* 547–553. doi:10.1016/j.rasd.2010.06.021

Tarbox, J., Tarbox, R., & O'Hora, D. (2009). Nonrelational and relational instructional control. In R. A. Rehfeldt & Y. Barnes-Holmes (Eds.), *Derived relational responding: Applications for learners with autism and other developmental disabilities: A progressive guide to change* (pp. 111–128). Oakland, CA: New Harbinger Publications.

Tarbox, J., Zuckerman, C. K., Bishop, M. R., Olive, M. L., & O'Hora, D. P. (2011). Rule-governed behavior: Teaching a preliminary repertoire of rule-following to children with autism. *The Analysis of Verbal Behavior, 27,* 125–139. doi:10.1007/bf03393096

Taylor, B. A., & DeQuinzio, J. A. (2012). Observational learning and children with autism. *Behavior Modification, 36,* 341–360. doi:10.1177/0145445512443981

Taylor, B. A., DeQuinzio, J. A., & Stine, J. (2012). Increasing observational learning of children with autism: A preliminary analysis. *Journal of Applied Behavior Analysis, 45,* 815–820. doi:10.1901/jaba.2012.45-815

Taylor, B. A., Levin, L., & Jasper, S. (1999). Increasing play-related statements in children with autism toward their siblings: Effects of video modeling. *Journal of Developmental and Physical Disabilities, 11,* 253–264. doi:10.1023/A:1021800716392

Taylor, I., & O'Reilly, M. F. (1997). Toward a functional analysis of private verbal self-regulation. *Journal of Applied Behavior Analysis, 30,* 43-58.

Taylor, I., & O'Reilly, M. F. (2000). Generalization of supermarket shopping skills for individuals with mild intellectual disabilities using stimulus equivalence training. *The Psychological Record, 50,* 49–62.

Terrace, H. S. (1966). Stimulus control. In W. K. Honig (Ed.), *Operant behavior: Areas of research and application* (pp. 271–344). New York, NY: Appleton-Century-Crofts.

Thomas, B. R., Lafasakis, M., & Sturmey, P. (2010). The effects of prompting, fading, and differential reinforcement on vocal mands in non-verbal preschool children with autism spectrum disorders. *Behavioral Interventions, 25*(2), 157–168. doi:10.1002/bin.300

Thorndike, E. L. (1911). *Animal intelligence.* New York, NY: The MacMillan Co.

Tiemann, P., & Markle, S. (1990). *Analyzing instructional content: A guide to instruction and evaluation.* (4th Ed.) Champaign, IL: Stipes.

Timberlake, W. (1988). The behavior of organisms: Purposive behavior as a type of reflex. *Journal of the Experimental Analysis of Behavior, 50*(2), 305–317. doi:10.1901/jeab.1988.50-305

Timberlake, W. (2004). Is the operant contingency enough for a science of purposive behavior? *Behavior and Philosophy, 32*(1), 197–229.

Timberlake, W., & Allison, J. (1974). Response deprivation: An empirical approach to instrumental performance. *Psychological Review, 81*(2), 146–164. doi:10.1037/h0036101

Timberlake, W., & Farmer-Dougan, V. A. (1991). Reinforcement in applied settings: Figuring out ahead of time what will work. *Psychological Bulletin, 110*(3), 379–391. doi:10.1037/0033-2909.110.3.379

Timmins, L., Barnes-Holmes, D., & Cullen, C. (2016). Measuring implicit sexual response biases to nude male and female pictures in androphilc and gynephilic men. *Archives of Sexual Behavior, 45*, 829–841. doi:10.1007/s10508-016-0725-3

Tincani, M. (2004). Comparing the picture exchange communication system and sign language training for children with autism. *Focus on Autism and Other Developmental Disabilities, 19*(3), 152–163. doi:10.1177/10883576040190030301

Tincani, M., & Devis, K. (2011). Quantitative synthesis and component analysis of single-participant studies on the picture exchange communication system. *Remedial and Special Education, 32*(6), 458–470. doi:10.1177/0741932510362494

Tomasello, M. (2008). *Origins of human communication.* Cambridge, MA: MIT Press.

Tomonaga, M., Matzusawa, T., Fujita, K., & Yamamoto, J. (1991). Emergence of symmetry in a visual conditional discrimination by chimpanzees (Pan troglodytes). *Psychological Reports, 68*, 51–60.

Torelli, J. N., Lambert, J. M., Da Fonte, M. A., Denham, K. N., Jedrzynski, T. M., & Houchins-Juarez, N. J. (2016). Assessing acquisition of and preference for mand topographies during functional communication training. *Behavior Analysis in Practice, 9*(2), 165–168. doi:10.1007/s40617-015-0083-y

Törneke, N. (2010). *Learning RFT: An introduction to relational frame theory and its clinical application.* Oakland, CA: New Harbinger.

Törneke, N., Luciano, C., Barnes-Holmes, Y., & Bond, F. (2016). RFT for clinical practice: Three core strategies in understanding and treating human suffering. In R. D. Zettle, S. C. Hayes, D. Barnes-Holmes, & T. Biglan (Eds.), *Handbook of Contextual Behavioral Science* (pp. 254–272). Chichester, UK: Wiley Blackwell.

Toussaint, K. A., & Tiger, J. H. (2010). Teaching early braille literacy skills within a stimulus equivalence paradigm to children with degenerative visual impairments. *Journal of Applied Behavior Analysis, 43*, 181–194. doi:10.1901/jaba.2010.43-181

Towe, A. L. (1954). A study of figural equivalence in the pigeon. *Journal of Comparative and Physiological Psychology, 47*, 283–287.

Townley-Cochran, D., Leaf, J. B., Taubman, M., Leaf, R., & McEachin, J. (2015). Observational learning for students diagnosed with autism: A review paper. *Review Journal of Autism and Developmental Disorders, 2*, 262–272. doi:10.1007/s40489-015-0050-0

Trucil, L. M., Vladescu, J. C., Reeve, K. F., DeBar, R. M., & Schnell, L. K. (2015). Improving portion-size estimation using equivalence-based instruction. *The Psychological Record, 65*, 761–770

Tullis, C. A., Frampton, S. E., Delfs, C. H., & Shillingsburg, M. A. (2017). Teaching problem explanations using instructive feedback. *The Analysis of Verbal Behavior, 33*(1), 64–79. doi:10.1007/s40616-016-0075-1

Twyman, J. S. (1996). The functional independence of impure mands and tacts of abstract stimulus properties. *The Analysis of Verbal Behavior, 13*(1), 1–19. doi:10.1007/BF03392903

U.S. Department of Education, National Center for Education Statistics. (2017). *The Condition of Education 2017* (NCES 2017–144).

Vahey, N., Boles, S., & Barnes-Holmes, D. (2010). Measuring adolescents' smoking-related social identity preferences with the Implicit Relational Assessment Procedure (IRAP) for the first time: A starting point that explains later IRAP evolutions. *International Journal of Psychology and Psychological Therapy, 10*(3), 453–474.

Valdivia-Salas, S., Luciano, C., Gutiérrez, O., & Visdómine, C. (2009). Establishing empathy. In R. A. Rehfeldt & Y. Barnes-Holmes (Eds.), *Derived relational responding applications for learners with autism and other developmental disabilities: A progressive guide to change* (pp. 301–312). Oakland, CA: New Harbinger.

Valdovinos, M. G., & Kennedy, C. H. (2004). A behavior-analytic conceptualization of the side effects of psychotropic medication. *The Behavior Analyst, 27,* 231–238. doi:10.1007/BF03393182

Valentino, A. L., Conine, D. E., Delfs, C. H., & Furlow, C. M. (2015). Use of a modified chaining procedure with textual prompts to establish intraverbal storytelling. *The Analysis of Verbal Behavior, 31*(1), 39–58. doi:10.1007/s40616-014-0023-x

Vallinger-Brown, M., & Rosales, R. (2014). An investigation of stimulus pairing and listener training to establish emergent intraverbals in children with autism. *The Analysis of Verbal Behavior, 30*(2), 148–159. doi:10.1007/s40616-014-0014-y

Valverde, M. R., Luciano, C., & Barnes-Holmes, D. (2009). Transfer of aversive respondent elicitation in accordance with equivalence relations. *Journal of the Experimental Analysis of Behavior, 92,* 85–111.

van der Meer, L., Sutherland, D., O'Reilly, M. F., Lancioni, G. E., & Sigafoos, J. (2012). A further comparison of manual sign, picture exchange, and speech generating devices as communication modes for children with autism spectrum disorder. *Research in Autism Spectrum Disorders, 6,* 1247–1257. doi:10.1016/j.rasd.2012.04.005

Van Houten, R. (1980). *Learning through feedback: A systematic approach for improving academic performance.* New York, NY: Human Sciences Press.

Varelas, A., & Fields, L. (2017). Equivalence based instruction by group based clicker training and sorting tests. *The Psychological Record,* 1–10.

Vaughan, M. E., & Michael, J. L. (1982). Automatic reinforcement: An important but ignored concept. *Behaviorism, 10*(2), 217–227.

Vedora, J., & Conant, E. (2015). A comparison of prompting tactics for teaching intraverbals to young adults with autism. *The Analysis of Verbal Behavior, 31*(2), 267–276. doi:10.1007/s40616-015-0030-6

Vilardaga, R. (2009). A relational frame theory account of empathy. *International Journal of Behavioral Consultation and Therapy, 5, 2,* 178–184.

Vilardaga, R., Estévez, A., Levin, M. E., & Hayes, S. C. (2012). Deictic relational responding, empathy, and experiential avoidance as predictors of social anhedonia: Further contributions from relational frame theory. *The Psychological Record, 62,* 409–432.

Villatte, J. L, Villatte, M., & Hayes, S. C. (2012). A naturalistic approach to transcendence: Deictic framing, spirituality, and prosociality. In L. McHugh & I. Stewart (Eds.), *The self and perspective-taking* (pp. 199-216). Oakland, CA: New Harbinger.

Villatte, M., Monestès, J. L., McHugh, L., Freixa i Baqué, E., & Loas, G. (2008) Assessing deictic relational responding in social anhedonia: A functional approach to the development of theory of mind impairments. *International Journal Behavioral Consultation and Therapy, 4* (4), 360–373.

Villatte, M., Monestès, J. L., McHugh, L., Freixa i Baqué, E., & Loas, G. (2010). Assessing perspective taking in schizophrenia using relational frame theory. *The Psychological Record, 60,* 413.

Villatte, M., Vilardaga, R., & Monestès, J. L. (2012). How the self relates to others when perspective-taking is impaired. In L. McHugh & I. Stewart (Eds.), *The self and perspective-taking* (pp. 109–124). Oakland, CA: New Harbinger.

Villatte, M., Villatte, J. L., & Hayes, S. C. (2016). *Mastering the clinical conversation. Language as intervention.* New York, NY: The Guilford Press.

Vitale, A., Barnes-Holmes, Y., Barnes-Holmes, D., & Campbell, C. (2008). Facilitating responding in accordance with the relational frame of comparison: Systematic empirical analyses. *The Psychological Record, 58,* 365.

Vosniadou, S., & Ortony, A. (1989). Similarity and analogical reasoning: A synthesis. In S. Vosniadou & A. Ortony (Eds.), *Similarity and Analogical Reasoning* (pp. 1–18). Cambridge, UK: Cambridge University Press.

Vygotsky, L. S. (1967). Play and its role in the mental development of the child. *Soviet Psychology, 5*(3), 6–18.

Walker, B. D., & Rehfeldt, R. A. (2012). An evaluation of the stimulus equivalence paradigm to teach single-subject design to distance education students via Blackboard. *Journal of Applied Behavior Analysis, 45*, 329–344.

Walker, B. D., Rehfeldt, R. A., & Ninness, C. (2010). Using the stimulus equivalence paradigm to teach course material in an undergraduate rehabilitation course. *Journal of Applied Behavior Analysis, 43*, 615–633. doi:10.1901/jaba.2010.43-615

Wallace, M. D., Iwata, B. A., & Hanley, G. P. (2006). Establishment of mands following tact training as a function of reinforcer strength. *Journal of Applied Behavior Analysis, 39*(1), 17–24. doi:10.1901/jaba.2006.119-04

Wang, J. M. (2015). Preference-for-solitude and depressive symptoms in Chinese adolescents. *Personality and Individual Differences, 100*, 151–156.

Ward, W. D., & Stare, S. W. (1990). The role of subject verbalization in generalized correspondence. *Journal of Applied Behavior Analysis, 23*, 129–136. doi:10.1901/jaba.1990.23-129

Watkins, C. L., Pack-Teixeira, L., & Howard, J. S. (1989). Teaching intraverbal behavior to severely retarded children. *The Analysis of Verbal Behavior, 7*(1), 69–81. doi:10.1007/bf03392838

Watson, J. B. (1913). Psychology as the behaviorist views it. *Psychological Review, 20*(2), 158–177. doi:10.1037/h0074428

Watt, A. W., Keenan, M., Barnes, D., & Cairns, E. (1991). Social categorization and stimulus equivalence. *The Psychological Record, 41*, 371–388.

Watts, A. C., Wilder, D. A., Gregory, M. K., Leon, Y., & Ditzian, K. (2013). The effect of rules on differential reinforcement of other behavior. *Journal of Applied Behavior Analysis, 46*, 680–684. doi:10.1002/jaba.53

Wehmeyer, M. L., Palmer, S. B., Agran, M., Mithaug, D. E., & Martin, J. (2000). Teaching students to become causal agents in their lives: The self-determining learning model of instruction. *Exceptional Children, 66*, 439–453.

Weil, T. M., Hayes, S. C., & Capurro, P. (2011) Establishing a deictic relational repertoire in young children. *The Psychological Record, 61*, 371–390.

Wells, A. (2000). *Emotional disorders and metacognition: Innovative cognitive therapy.* Chichester, UK: Wiley.

Wells, A., & Matthews, G. (1994). *Attention and emotion: A clinical perspective.* Hove, UK: Erlbaum.

West-Eberhard, M. J. (2003). *Developmental plasticity and evolution.* Oxford, UK: Oxford University Press.

Whelan, R., & Barnes-Holmes, D. (2004). The transformation of consequential functions in accordance with the relational frames of same and opposite. *Journal of the Experimental Analysis of Behavior, 82*, 177–195.

Whelan, R., Barnes-Holmes, D., & Dymond, S. (2006). The transformation of consequential functions in accordance with the relational frames of more-than and less-than. *Journal of the Experimental Analysis of Behavior, 86*, 317–335. doi:10.1901/jeab.2006.113-04

Whimbey, A. (1990). *Analytical reading and reasoning.* (2nd ed.). Cary, NC: Innovative Sciences.

Whimbey, A. (1995). *Mastering reading through reasoning.* Cary, NC: Innovative Sciences.

Whimbey, A., & Jenkins, E. L. (1987). *Analyze. Organize. Write.* (rev. ed.). Hillsdale, NJ: Erlbaum.

Whimbey, A., Johnson, M. H., Williams, E., Sr., & Linden, M. (2017). *Blueprint for educational change: Improving reasoning, literacies, and science achievement with cooperative learning.* Seattle, WA: Morningside. (Original work published in 1993 in Washington, DC: Right Combination, Inc.).

Whimbey, A., & Lochhead, J. (1999). *Problem solving and comprehension.* (6th ed.). Mahwah, NJ: Erlbaum.

Williams, B. A. (1987). The other psychology of animal learning: A review of Mackintosh's *Conditioning and Associative Learning. Journal of the Experimental Analysis, 48,* 175–186. doi:10.1901/jeab.1987.48-175

Williams, B. A. (1994). Conditioned reinforcement: Experimental and theoretical issues. *The Behavior Analyst, 17,* 261–285. doi:10.1007/BF03392675

Willmoth, V., Lewon, A. B., Taylor, E., & Ghezzi, P. M. (May, 2017). *Teaching conversational interactions to a young child with autism.* Presented at the annual meeting of the Association for Behavior Analysis International, Denver, CO.

Wilson, D. S., Hayes, S. C., Biglan, A., & Embry, D. D. (2014). Evolving the future: Toward a science of intentional change. *Behavioral and Brain Sciences, 37*(4), 395–416. doi:10.1017/S0140525X13001593

Wilson, G. T., & Davison, G. C. (1971). Processes of fear reduction in systematic desensitization: Animal studies. *Psychological Bulletin, 76*(1), 1–14.

Wilson, K. G., Bordieri, M., & Whiteman, K. (2012). The self and mindfulness. In L. McHugh & I. Stewart (Eds.), *The self and perspective-taking* (pp. 181–198). Oakland, CA: New Harbinger.

Wilson, K. G., & Sandoz, E. K. (2008). Mindfulness, values, and the therapeutic relationship in Acceptance and Commitment Therapy. In S. F. Hick & T. Bein (Eds.), *Mindfulness and the therapeutic relationship* (pp. 89–106). New York, NY, Guilford Press.

Wilson, K. G., Sandoz, E. K., Kitchens, J., & Roberts, M. (2010). The Valued Living Questionnaire: Defining and measuring valued action within a behavioral framework. *The Psychological Record, 60*(2), 249–272.

Winborn-Kemmerer, L., Ringdahl, J. E., Wacker, D. P., & Kitsukawa, K. (2009). A demonstration of individual preference for novel mands during functional communication training. *Journal of Applied Behavior Analysis, 42*(1), 185–189. doi:10.1901/jaba.2009.42-185

Wiskow, K. M., Matter, A. L., & Donaldson, J. M. (2018). An evaluation of lag schedules and prompting methods to increase variability of naming category items in children with autism spectrum disorder. *The Analysis of Verbal Behavior, 34*(1–2), 100–123. doi:10.1007/s40616-018-0102-5

Wispé L. (1986) The distinction between sympathy and empathy: To call forth a concept, a word is needed. *Journal of Personality and Social Psychology, 50,* 314–321.

Wittgenstein, L. (1953). *Philosophical investigations.* Oxford, England: Basil & Blackwell.

Wittgenstein, L. (1969). *On certainty.* Oxford, England: Basil & Blackwell.

Wittgenstein, L. (1980). *Remarks on the philosophy of psychology* (Vol. 2). Oxford, England: Basil & Blackwell.

Wolf, M. M. (1978). Social validity: The case for subjective measurement or how behavior analysis is finding its heart. *Journal of Applied Behavior Analysis, 11,* 203–214.

Wolf, M. M., Phillips, E. L., Fixsen, D. L., Braukmann, C. J., Kirigin, K. A., Willner, A. G., & Schumaker, J. (1976). Achievement place: The teaching-family model. *Child Care Quarterly, 5*(2), 92–103.

Wolpe, J. (1958). *Psychotherapy by reciprocal inhibition.* Palo Alto, CA: Stanford University Press.

Wolpe, J. (1961). The systematic desensitization treatment of neuroses. *The Journal of Nervous and Mental Disease, 132*(3), 189–203.

Wolpe, J. (1976a). Behavior therapy and its malcontents—I. Denial of its bases and psychodynamic fusionism. *Journal of Behavior Therapy and Experimental Psychiatry, 7*(1), 1–5. doi:10.1016/0005-7916(76)90032-X

Wolpe, J. (1976b). Behavior therapy and its malcontents—II. Multimodal eclecticism, cognitive exclusivism and "exposure" empiricism. *Journal of Behavior Therapy and Experimental Psychiatry, 7*(2), 109–116. doi:10.1016/0005-7916(76)90066-5

Wolpe, J. (1978). Cognition and causation in human behavior and its therapy. *American Psychologist*, *33*(5), 437–446. doi:10.1037/0003-066X.33.5.437

World Health Organization. (2016). Health statistics and information systems. Estimates for 2000–2012. *World Health Organization*.

Wulfert, E. (2002). Can contextual therapies save clinical behavior analysis? *The Behavior Analyst Today*, *3*(3), 254–258. doi:10.1037/h0099984

Wulfert, E., Greenway, D. E., Farkas, P., Hayes, S. C., & Dougher, M. J. (1994). Correlation between self-reported rigidity and rule-governed insensitivity to operant contingencies. *Journal of Applied Behavior Analysis*, *27*, 659–671. doi:10.1901/jaba.1994.27-659

Wymer, S. C., Tarbox, J., Beavers, G. A., & Tullis, C. A. (2016). Teaching children with autism to follow rules specifying a behavior and consequence. *The Analysis of Verbal Behavior*, *32*, 265–274. doi:10.1007/s40616-016-0059-1

Wynne, L. (2004). The missing theory: Why behavior analysis has little impact on voluntary adult outpatient services. *Ethical Human Psychology And Psychiatry: An International Journal of Critical Inquiry*, *6*(2), 135–146.

Yamamoto, J., & Asano, T. (1995). Stimulus equivalence in a chimpanzee (Pan troglodytes). *The Psychological Record*, *45*, 3–21.

Yoon, S. Y., & Bennett, G. M. (2000). Effects of a stimulus-pairing procedure on conditioning vocal sounds as reinforcers. *The Analysis of Verbal Behvior*, *17*(1), 75–88. doi:10.1007/BF03392957

Yorio, A., Tabullo, Á., Wainselboim, A., Barttfeld, P., & Segura, E. (2008). Event-related potential correlates of perceptual and functional categories: Comparison between stimuli matching by identity and equivalence. *Neuroscience Letters*, *443*, 113–118.

Zaki, J., & Ochsner, K. N. (2012). The neuroscience of empathy: Progress, pitfalls and promise. *Nature Neuroscience*, *15*(5), 675.

Zax, M., & Klein, A. (1960). Measurement of personality and behavior changes following psychotherapy. *Psychological Bulletin*, *57*(5), 435–448.

Zentall, T. R., Galizio, M., & Critchfield, T. S. (2002). Categorization, concept learning, and behavior analysis: An introduction. *Journal of the Experimental Analysis of Behavior*, *78*, 237–248. doi:10.1901/jeab.2002.78-237

Zettle, R. D., & Hayes, S. C. (1982). Rule-governed behavior: A potential theoretical framework for cognitive-behavior therapy. *Advances in cognitive-behavioral research and therapy*, *1*, 73–118.

Zettle, R. D., & Hayes, S. C. (1986). Dysfunctional control by client verbal behavior: The context of reason-giving. *The Analysis of Verbal Behavior*, *4*, 30–38. doi:10.1007/bf03392813

Zettle, R.D., Hayes, S. C., Barnes-Holmes, D., & Biglan, A. (Eds.) (2016). *The Wiley handbook of contextual behavioral science*. UK: Wiley, Blackwell.

Ziomek, M. M., & Rehfeldt, R.A. (2008). Investigating the acquisition, generalization, and emergence of untrained verbal operants for mands acquired using the Picture Exchange Communication System in adults with severe developmental disabilities. *The Analysis of Verbal Behavior*, *24*(10), 15–30. doi:10.1007/BF03393054

Zuriff, G. E. (1979). Ten inner causes. *Behaviorism*, *7*, 1–8.

Editor **Mitch Fryling, PhD, BCBA-D**, is associate professor and chair of the division of special education and counseling at California State University, Los Angeles. He has authored and coauthored many scholarly publications, primarily in the area of behavioral theory and philosophy, especially as it pertains to complex human behavior and system development in behavior analysis. He is current editor of *The Psychological Record*.

Editor **Ruth Anne Rehfeldt, PhD, BCBA**, is professor of behavior analysis and therapy at Southern Illinois University in Carbondale, IL. She holds doctoral and master's degrees in psychology from the University of Nevada, Reno; and a bachelor's degree in psychology from the University of Puget Sound. She is also a board-certified behavior analyst. Ruth Anne is a fellow of the Association for Behavior Analysis International, and previous editor of *The Psychological Record*. She has published numerous articles in the area of verbal behavior and derived relational responding for individuals with autism spectrum disorder (ASD) and other developmental disabilities.

Editor **Jonathan Tarbox, PhD, BCBA-D**, is director of the master of science in applied behavior analysis program at the University of Southern California, as well as director of research at FirstSteps for Kids. He is editor in chief of the journal, *Behavior Analysis in Practice*, and serves on the editorial boards of several scientific journals related to autism and behavior analysis. He has published four books on autism treatment; is series editor of the Elsevier book series, *Critical Specialties in Treating Autism and Other Behavioral Challenges*; and author of well over seventy peer-reviewed journal articles and chapters in scientific texts. His research focuses on behavioral interventions for teaching complex skills to individuals with autism, applications of acceptance and commitment therapy (ACT) training inside of applied behavior analysis, and applications of applied behavior analysis to issues of diversity and social justice.

Editor **Linda J. Hayes, PhD**, is professor of psychology, and founder and director of the behavior analysis program at the University of Nevada, Reno.

Index

emotions: contingency adduction and, 151–152; empathy development and, 293

empathy, 291–294; definition and description of, 291; distinguishing compassion from, 296; functional contextual approach to, 296–297; perspective taking related to, 282–283, 291, 298; relational framing account of, 292–294; research studies on, 291–292. *See also* compassion

English language learner (ELL), 35, 303

Epstein, Robert, 133

equivalence class formation, 161, 164, 167, 169

equivalence procedure, 138

equivalence relations, 137, 141–143, 159, 200, 218

equivalence-based instruction (EBI), 157–172, 303; applications for, 166–169; explanatory overview of, 158; future directions for, 169–172; instructional design choices in, 160–166; match-to-sample procedures in, 161–162; research study typifying, 159–160; response generalization in, 165–166; training protocols for, 163–165; training structures for, 162–163

equivalence-equivalence responding, 201–202

Erickson, Nicole, 145

errorless learning, 16, 44

establishing operations (EOs), 17, 18, 25, 303

event-related potentials (ERPs), 202

evolutionary perspective, 295–296

exclusion procedure, 138, 140

experiential acceptance, 258–259

explicitness of rules, 219

extended and elaborated relational responses (EERRs), 272, 273, 303

extension contacts, 103

extinction, 12–13

extinction burst, 12–13

Extrinsic Affective Simon Task (EAST), 267, 303

F

fading process, 16

Ferster, Charles, 153

Fienup, Daniel M., 157

first-wave behavior therapies, 252–253

fixed ratio (FR) reinforcement schedule, 227, 303

flexible responding, 34

framing: definition of, 285; repertoires of, 242

frequency building, 150–151

Fryling, Mitch, 115

Function Acquisition Speed Test (FAST), 267

functional analysis, 22

functional analytic psychotherapy (FAP), 256, 285, 304

functional aptitude, 110

functional classes, 119

functional competence, 110

functional contextualism (FC), 7, 256–257, 304

functional independence, 30–33

functional MRIs (fMRIs), 195

G

gambling behavior, 223–224

Garcia, Yors A., 20, 38

Garcia-Zambrano, Sebastian, 20, 38

gender bias, 269–270

generalization processes, 119, 165–166

generalized echoic responding, 23

generalized operants, 181–182

generative instruction, 132, 154, 155

generative repertoires, 145–149

generative responding, 132, 155

generativity: contingency adduction and, 133–134; explanation of, 131–132

Ghezzi, Patrick M., 4, 72

Gil-Luciano, Bárbara, 281

Greer, R. Douglas, 55

H

habituation, 7

Harte, Colin, 264

Haughton, Eric, 150

Hayes, Linda J., 1, 6

hierarchical classification, 205

hierarchical part-whole analysis, 205

hierarchical relations, 192–193

hierarchies, 205–211; analytic, 206, 209; child development and, 209–211; classification, 206–207, 208–209; contextual cues for,

MORE BOOKS *from*
NEW HARBINGER PUBLICATIONS

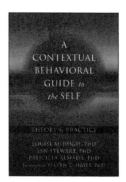
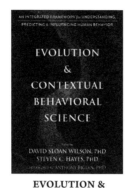

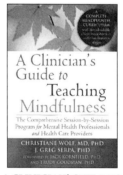